Unreal Engine 4.x Scripting with C++ Cookbook
Second Edition

Develop quality game components and solve scripting
problems with the power of C++ and UE4

John P. Doran
William Sherif
Stephen Whittle

BIRMINGHAM - MUMBAI

Unreal Engine 4.x Scripting with C++ Cookbook
Second Edition

Acquisition Editor: Larissa Pinto
Content Development Editor: Arun Nadar
Technical Editor: Rutuja Vaze
Copy Editor: Safis Editing
Project Coordinator: Kinjal Bari
Proofreader: Safis Editing
Indexer: Rekha Nair
Graphics: Alishon Mendonsa
Production Coordinator: Tom Scaria

First published: October 2016
Second edition: March 2019

Production reference: 1290319

Published by Packt Publishing Ltd.
Livery Place
35 Livery Street
Birmingham
B3 2PB, UK.

ISBN 978-1-78980-950-3

www.packtpub.com

Contributors

About the authors

John P. Doran is a passionate and seasoned technical game designer, software engineer, and author based in Peoria, Illinois.

For over a decade, John has gained extensive hands-on expertise in game development, working in various roles ranging from game designer to lead UI programmer. Additionally, John has worked in game development education teaching in Singapore, South Korea, and the United States. To date, he has authored over 10 books pertaining to game development.

John is currently an instructor in residence at Bradley University. Prior to his present ventures, he was an award-winning videographer.

William Sherif is a C++ programmer with more than eight years' experience in the programming world, ranging from game programming to web programming. He also worked as a university course instructor (sessional) for seven years. Additionally, he released several apps on the iTunes store, including Strum and MARSHALL OF THE ELITE SQUADRON. In the past, he has won acclaim for delivering course material in an easy-to-understand manner.

Stephen Whittle is a game developer and educator with nearly 10 years' development experience, most of which has been done using the Unreal Engine. He is a community contributor to the engine, having features or bug fixes included in almost every major version of the engine since its public release.

About the reviewer

Agne Skripkaite is a UE4 software engineer with a particular interest in **Virtual Reality (VR)** applications. They have a BSc physics degree with honors from the University of Edinburgh and became a full-time engineer partway through a physics PhD program at Caltech. Over the last few years, Agne has developed for room-scale and seated VR games as part of two-engineer team, along with working in large development teams. They have also served as a user comfort and motion sickness mitigation expert for seated VR applications.

Packt is searching for authors like you

If you're interested in becoming an author for Packt, please visit authors.packtpub.com and apply today. We have worked with thousands of developers and tech professionals, just like you, to help them share their insight with the global tech community. You can make a general application, apply for a specific hot topic that we are recruiting an author for, or submit your own idea.

`mapt.io`

Mapt is an online digital library that gives you full access to over 5,000 books and videos, as well as industry leading tools to help you plan your personal development and advance your career. For more information, please visit our website.

Why subscribe?

- Spend less time learning and more time coding with practical eBooks and Videos from over 4,000 industry professionals

- Improve your learning with Skill Plans built especially for you

- Get a free eBook or video every month

- Mapt is fully searchable

- Copy and paste, print, and bookmark content

Packt.com

Did you know that Packt offers eBook versions of every book published, with PDF and ePub files available? You can upgrade to the eBook version at `www.packt.com` and as a print book customer, you are entitled to a discount on the eBook copy. Get in touch with us at `customercare@packtpub.com` for more details.

At `www.packt.com`, you can also read a collection of free technical articles, sign up for a range of free newsletters, and receive exclusive discounts and offers on Packt books and eBooks.

Table of Contents

Preface

Unreal Engine 4 (UE4) is a complete suite of game development tools made by game developers, for game developers. With more than 100 practical recipes, this book is a guide showcasing techniques to unlock the power of C++ scripting while developing games with UE 4.21. This book starts off by showing how to add and edit C++ classes from within the Unreal Editor. It will delve into one of Unreal's primary strengths: the ability for designers to customize programmer-developed actors and components. It will help you understand the benefits of using C++ in conjunction with the many tools included with this powerful game engine. With a blend of task-oriented recipes, this book will provide actionable information about writing code for games with UE4 and manipulating the game and the development environment using C++. Toward the end of the book, you will be empowered to become a top-notch developer with Unreal Engine 4 using C++ as the scripting language!

Who this book is for

This book is intended for game developers who understand the fundamentals of game design and C++ and would like to incorporate native code into the games they make with Unreal.

The readers will likely be programmers who want to extend the engine or implement systems and actors that provide designers with control and flexibility when building levels.

What this book covers

Chapter 1, *UE4 Development Tools*, outlines basic recipes to get you started with UE4 game development and the basic tools used to create the code that makes your game.

Chapter 2, *Creating Classes*, focuses on how to create C++ classes and structs that integrate well with the UE4 Blueprints Editor. These classes will be graduated versions of regular C++ classes, called UCLASSES.

Chapter 3, *Memory Management, Smart Pointers, and Debugging,* takes the reader through using all three types of pointer, and mentions some common pitfalls regarding automatic garbage collection. This chapter also shows readers how to use Visual Studio or Xcode to interpret crashes or confirm that the functionality is implemented correctly.

Chapter 4, *Actors and Components,* deals with creating custom actors and components, what purpose each of these serves, and how they work together.

Chapter 5, *Handling Events and Delegates,* describes delegates, events, and event handlers, and guides you through creating your own implementations.

Chapter 6, *Input and Collision,* shows how to connect user input to C++ functions and how to handle collisions in C++ from UE4. It will also provide default handling of game events such as user input and collision, allowing designers to override when necessary using Blueprint.

Chapter 7, *Communication Between Classes and Interfaces: Part I,* shows you how to write your own UInterfaces, and demonstrates how to take advantage of them within C++ to minimize class coupling and help keep your code clean.

Chapter 8, *Communication Between Classes and Interfaces: Part II,* continues the content covered in Chapter 7, discussing in more detail how to get UInterfaces to work in collaboration with Blueprints.

Chapter 9, *Integrating C++ and the Unreal Editor: Part I,* shows you how to customize the editor by creating custom Blueprint and animation nodes from scratch.

Chapter 10, *Integrating C++ and the Unreal Editor: Part II,* shows you how to implement custom editor windows and custom detail panels to inspect types created by users.

Chapter 11, *User Interfaces – UI and UMG,* demonstrates that displaying feedback to the player is one of the most important elements within game design, and this will usually involve some sort of HUD, or at least menus, within your game.

Chapter 12, *AI for Controlling NPCs,* covers recipes to control your NPC characters with a bit of **Artificial Intelligence (AI)**.

Chapter 13, *Working with UE4 APIs,* explains that the API is the way in which you, as the programmer, can instruct the engine (and thus the PC) what to do. Each module has an API for it. To use an API, there is a very important linkage step, where you must list all APIs that you will use in your build in the `ProjectName.Build.cs` file.

Chapter 14, *Multiplayer Networking in UE4*, discusses how to replicate properties and functions over the network, while also testing your game as a client and server simultaneously.

To get the most out of this book

- This book assumes familiarity with the C++ programming language, an understanding of what different programming operators mean, and basic knowledge of the concepts of object-oriented programming
- Basic familiarity with using the Unreal Engine editor is beneficial, but not required

Download the example code files

You can download the example code files for this book from your account at www.packt.com. If you purchased this book elsewhere, you can visit www.packt.com/support and register to have the files emailed directly to you.

You can download the code files by following these steps:

1. Log in or register at www.packt.com.
2. Select the **SUPPORT** tab.
3. Click on **Code Downloads & Errata**.
4. Enter the name of the book in the **Search** box and follow the onscreen instructions.

Once the file is downloaded, please make sure that you unzip or extract the folder using the latest version of:

- WinRAR/7-Zip for Windows
- Zipeg/iZip/UnRarX for Mac
- 7-Zip/PeaZip for Linux

The code bundle for the book is also hosted on GitHub at https://github.com/PacktPublishing/Unreal-Engine-4.x-Scripting-with-C-Cookbook---Second-edition. In case there's an update to the code, it will be updated on the existing GitHub repository.

We also have other code bundles from our rich catalog of books and videos available at https://github.com/PacktPublishing/. Check them out!

Download the color images

We also provide a PDF file that has color images of the screenshots/diagrams used in this book. You can download it here: `https://www.packtpub.com/sites/default/files/downloads/9781789809503_ColorImages.pdf`.

Conventions used

There are a number of text conventions used throughout this book.

`CodeInText`: Indicates code words in text, database table names, folder names, filenames, file extensions, pathnames, dummy URLs, user input, and Twitter handles. Here is an example: "Start typing `Theme Editor` into the search box at the right."

A block of code is set as follows:

```
FString name = "Tim";
int32 mana = 450;
FString string = FString::Printf( TEXT( "Name = %s Mana =
  %d" ), *name, mana );
```

When we wish to draw your attention to a particular part of a code block, the relevant lines or items are set in bold:

```
// Fill out your copyright notice in the Description page of Project
Settings.

#include "Chapter_01GameModeBase.h"

void AChapter_01GameModeBase::BeginPlay()
{
 Super::BeginPlay();
}
```

Bold: Indicates a new term, an important word, or words that you see onscreen. For example, words in menus or dialog boxes appear in the text like this. Here is an example: "Play around with the font and font size of **Text Editor/Plain Text**."

Warnings or important notes appear like this.

 Tips and tricks appear like this.

Sections

In this book, you will find several headings that appear frequently (*Getting ready, How to do it..., How it works..., There's more...,* and *See also*).

To give clear instructions on how to complete a recipe, use these sections as follows:

Getting ready

This section tells you what to expect in the recipe and describes how to set up any software or any preliminary settings required for the recipe.

How to do it...

This section contains the steps required to follow the recipe.

How it works...

This section usually consists of a detailed explanation of what happened in the previous section.

There's more...

This section consists of additional information about the recipe in order to make you more knowledgeable about the recipe.

See also

This section provides helpful links to other useful information for the recipe.

Get in touch

Feedback from our readers is always welcome.

General feedback: If you have questions about any aspect of this book, mention the book title in the subject of your message and email us at `customercare@packtpub.com`.

Errata: Although we have taken every care to ensure the accuracy of our content, mistakes do happen. If you have found a mistake in this book, we would be grateful if you would report this to us. Please visit `www.packt.com/submit-errata`, selecting your book, clicking on the Errata Submission Form link, and entering the details.

Piracy: If you come across any illegal copies of our works in any form on the Internet, we would be grateful if you would provide us with the location address or website name. Please contact us at `copyright@packt.com` with a link to the material.

If you are interested in becoming an author: If there is a topic that you have expertise in and you are interested in either writing or contributing to a book, please visit `authors.packtpub.com`.

Reviews

Please leave a review. Once you have read and used this book, why not leave a review on the site that you purchased it from? Potential readers can then see and use your unbiased opinion to make purchase decisions, we at Packt can understand what you think about our products, and our authors can see your feedback on their book. Thank you!

For more information about Packt, please visit `packt.com`.

UE4 Development Tools 1

In this chapter, we will outline some basic recipes for getting started in **Unreal Engine 4 (UE4)** game development, and the basic tools that we will use for creating the code that makes our game. This will include the following recipes:

- Installing Visual Studio
- Creating and building your first C++ project in Visual Studio
- Changing the code font and color in Visual Studio
- Extension – changing the color theme in Visual Studio
- Formatting your code (Autocomplete settings) in Visual Studio
- Shortcut keys in Visual Studio
- Extended mouse usage in Visual Studio
- UE4 – installation
- UE4 – first project
- UE4 – creating your first level
- UE4 – hot reloading
- UE4 – logging with UE_LOG
- UE4 – making an FString from FStrings and other variables

Introduction

Creating a game is an elaborate task that will require a combination of **assets** and **code**. To create assets and code, we'll need some pretty advanced tools, including **art tools**, **sound tools**, **level-editing tools**, and **code-editing tools**. In this chapter, we'll discuss finding suitable tools for asset creation and coding. Assets include any visual artwork (2D sprites, 3D models), audio (music and sound effects), and game levels. Code is the text (usually C++) that instructs the computer on how to tie these assets together to make a game world and level, and how to make that game world *play*. There are dozens of very good tools for each task; we will explore a couple of each, and make some recommendations. Game editing tools, especially, are hefty programs that require a powerful CPU and lots of memory, and very good, ideal GPUs for good performance. Protecting your assets and work is also a necessary practice. We'll explore and describe source control, which is how you back up your work on a remote server. An introduction to UE4 programming is also included, and we will also explore basic logging functions and library use. Significant planning is also required to get these tasks done, so we'll use a task planner software package to do so.

Technical requirements

As listed on UE4's FAQs page, it is recommend to have a a desktop PC with Windows 7 64-bit or a Mac with macOS X 10.9.2 or later, 8 GB of RAM, a quad-core Intel or AMD processor, and a DX11-compatible video card. UE4 will run on desktops and laptops below these recommendations, but performance may be limited.

For those using a Mac computer, Visual Studio for Mac currently does not support C++. You'll need to use a different IDE, such as Visual Studio Code or Xcode, instead.

Installing Visual Studio

Visual Studio is an essential package for code editing when editing the C++ code for your UE4 game.

Getting ready

We're going to set up a C++ coding environment to build our UE4 applications. We'll download Visual Studio 2017, install it, and set it up for UE4 C++ coding.

How to do it...

1. Begin by visiting `https://www.visualstudio.com/en-us/products/visual-studio-community-vs.aspx`. Click on **Download VS Community 2017**. This downloads the ~1,250 KB loader/installer:

You can compare editions of Visual Studio at `https://visualstudio.microsoft.com/vs/compare/`. The Community Edition of Visual Studio is fully adequate for UE4 development purposes in this book, that is, as long as you're an individual developer, doing academic research, or have fewer than six people on your team.

2. Launch the installer, and continue through the installer until you get to the window where you select the components of Visual Studio 2017 that you want to add to your PC. Keep in mind that the more features you select, the larger your installation will be.

3. Support for C++ is now an optional part of Visual Studio and isn't installed by default, so we have to select that we want it installed. Under the **Workloads** section, scroll down to the **Mobile and Gaming** heading and check the **Game development with C++** option:

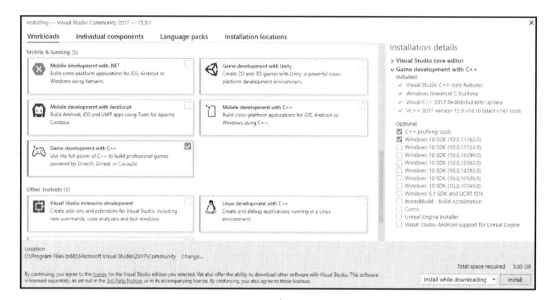

It is possible to download the Unreal Engine installer at this point as well by selecting it under the **Optional** section in the **Installation details** menu, but we will be getting the latest version of the Epic Games launcher and Unreal Engine directly from Epic Games in a separate recipe later on in this chapter.

4. After you have selected the tools you'd like to add on to Visual Studio, click the **Install** button. The installer tool will download the required components and continue setup. After finishing installation, the installer may ask you to restart your computer. Go ahead and do so.

5. After you download and install Visual Studio 2017, launch it. You will be presented with a **Sign in** dialog box:

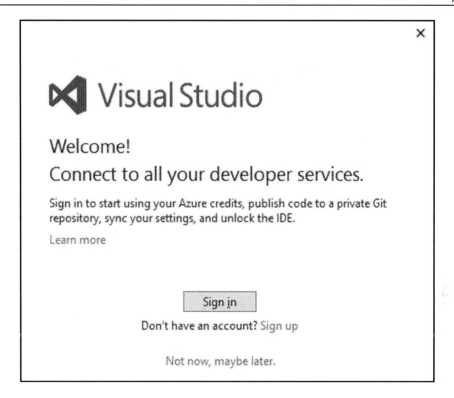

You can **Sign in** with your Microsoft account (the one you use to sign into Windows 10) or **Sign up** for a new account. After you've signed in or signed up, you will be able to sign into Visual Studio itself. It may seem odd to sign into a desktop code editing program, but your sign-in will be used for source control commits to your repositories. On first signing into Visual Studio, you can select (one time only) a unique URL for your source code repositories, as hosted on Visualstudio.com (https://visualstudio.microsoft.com/).

How it works...

Visual Studio is an excellent editor, and you will have a fantastic time coding within it. In the next recipe, we'll discuss how to create and compile our own code.

 For more information on the Visual Studio setup process for C++ and UE4, check out https://docs.unrealengine.com/en-us/ Programming/Development/VisualStudioSetup

Creating and building your first C++ project in Visual Studio

In order to compile and run code from Visual Studio, it must be done from within a project.

Getting ready

In this recipe, we will identify how to create an actual executable running program from Visual Studio. We will do so by creating a project in Visual Studio to host, organize, and compile the code.

How to do it...

In Visual Studio, each group of code is contained within something called a **Project**. A project is a buildable conglomerate of code and assets that produce either an executable (.exe runnable) or a library (.lib or .dll). A group of projects can be collected into something called a **Solution**. Let's start by constructing a Visual Studio solution and a project for a console application, followed by constructing a UE4 sample project and solution:

1. Open Visual Studio and go to **File** | **New** | **Project...**.
2. You will see a dialog, as follows:

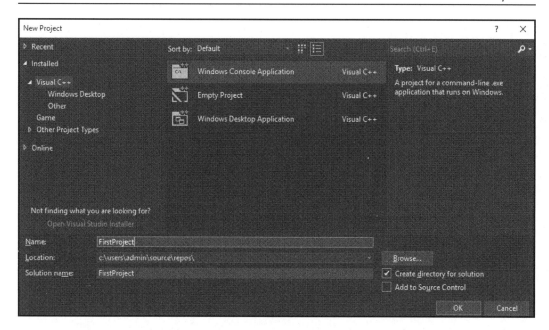

3. Select **Visual C++** in the pane on the left-hand side. In the middle pane, hit **Windows Console Application**. Name your project in the lower box, and then hit **OK**:

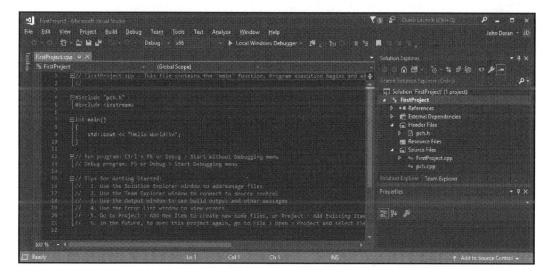

Once the application wizard completes, you will have created your first project. Both a solution and a project will be created.

4. To see these, you need **Solution Explorer**. To ensure that **Solution Explorer** is showing, go to **View** | **Solution Explorer** (or press *Ctrl + Alt + L*). **Solution Explorer** is a window that usually appears docked on the right-hand side of the main editor window, as shown in the following screenshot:

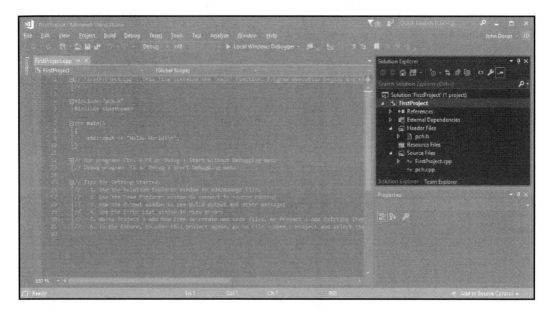

Solution Explorer location

 It is possible to arrange your layout however you like inside Visual Studio. If you ever want to go back to the default layout, you can go to **Window** | **Reset Window Layout**.

The **Solution Explorer** also displays all the files that are part of the project. This default solution already contains a few files, and we can add and remove new files in this section from here. As your project grows, more and more files are going to be added to your project. In the Source Files folder, you'll also notice a file created called FirstProject.cpp, which will look as follows:

```
// FirstProject.cpp : This file contains the 'main' function.
Program execution begins and ends there.
//

#include "pch.h"
```

```cpp
#include <iostream>

int main()
{
    std::cout << "Hello World!\n";
}


// Run program: Ctrl + F5 or Debug > Start Without Debugging
menu
// Debug program: F5 or Debug > Start Debugging menu

// Tips for Getting Started:
// 1. Use the Solution Explorer window to add/manage files
// 2. Use the Team Explorer window to connect to source
control
// 3. Use the Output window to see build output and other
messages
// 4. Use the Error List window to view errors
// 5. Go to Project > Add New Item to create new code files,
or Project > Add Existing Item to add existing code files to
the project
// 6. In the future, to open this project again, go to File >
Open > Project and select the .sln file
```

5. Press *Ctrl + Shift + B* to build the project, then *Ctrl + F5* to run the project.

6. Your executable will be created, and you will see a small black window with the results of your program's run:

How it works...

Building an executable involves translating your C++ code from text language into a binary file. Running the file runs your game program, which is just the code text that occurs in the `main()` function between { and }.

There's more...

Build configurations are **styles** of build that we will discuss here. There are at least two important build configurations you should know about: **Debug** and **Release**. The **Build** configuration that's currently selected is at the top of the editor, just below the toolbar in the default position:

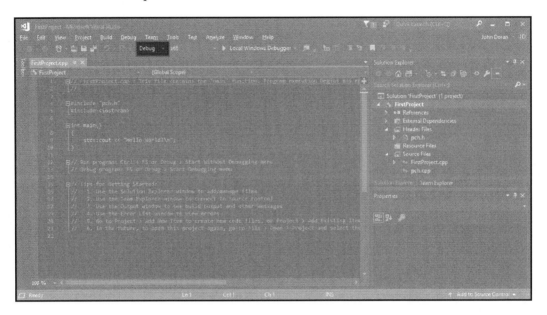

Location of the currently selected Build Configuration

Depending on which configuration you select, different compiler options are used. A **Debug** configuration typically includes extensive debug information in the build, as well as the ability to turn off optimizations to speed up compilation. **Release** builds are often optimized (either for size or for speed) and take a bit longer to build; they result in smaller or faster executables. Stepping through a file's behavior by moving through with the debugger line by line is often better in the **Debug** mode than the **Release** mode.

Changing the code font and color in Visual Studio

Customizing the font and color in Visual Studio is not just about flexibility. Due to monitor resolutions being too high or low, it may become a necessity!

Getting ready

Visual Studio is a highly customizable code editing tool. You might find the default fonts too small for your screen. This is easily adjustable by holding down the *Ctrl* key and using the mouse wheel to increase or decrease the size, but you may want to change the default value. Or, perhaps you may want to have more control, as you may want to change your code's font size and color. You may also want to completely customize the coloration of keywords and the text background colors. The **Fonts and Colors** dialog box, which we'll show you how to use in this section, allows you to completely customize every aspect of the code editor's font and color:

How to do it...

1. From within Visual Studio, go to **Tools | Options...**:

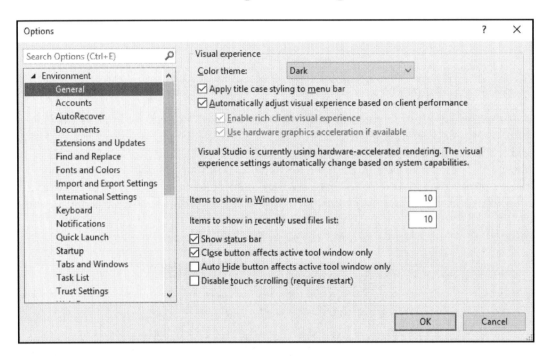

2. Select **Environment | Fonts and Colors** from the dialog that appears. It will look like what's shown in the following screenshot:

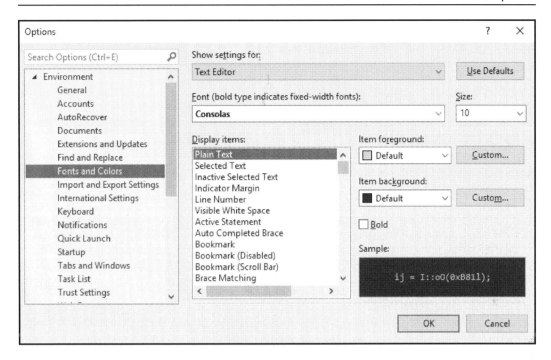

3. Play around with the font and font size of **Text Editor/Plain Text**. Click **OK** on the dialog, and see the results in the code-text editor:

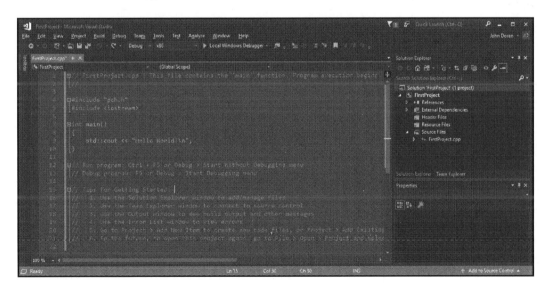

Modified font and colors

Text Editor/Plain Text describes the font and size that's used for all code text within the regular code editor. If you change the size of the font, the size changes for any text that's entered into the coding window (for all languages, including C, C++, C#, and others).

To return to what the menu has by default based on your theme, click on the **Use Defaults** button to the right of the **Show Settings for:** option.

The color (foreground and background) is completely customizable for each item. Try this for the **Text Editor/Keyword** setting (affects all languages), or for items specific to C++, such as **Text Editor/C++ Functions**. Click **OK**, and you will see the changed color of the item reflected in the code editor.

You may also want to configure the font size of the **Output Window**, under the **Show settings for:** option, so click on the drop-down and select **Output Window**, as shown in the following screenshot:

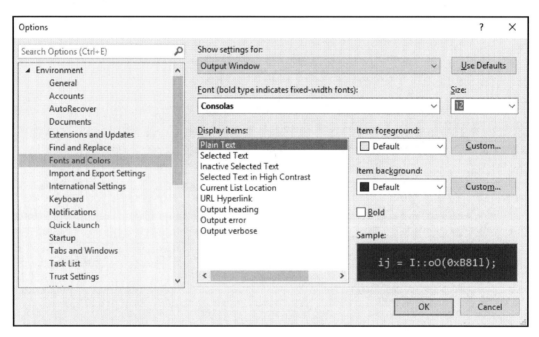

The **Output Window** is the little window at the bottom of the editor that displays build results and compiler errors.

You can't save-out (export) or bring in (import) your changes to the **Fonts and Colors** dialog. But you can use something called the **Visual Studio Theme Editor Extension**. To learn more, refer to the *Extension – changing the color theme in Visual Studio* recipe of this chapter, to learn how to export and import customized color themes.

For this reason, you may want to avoid changing font colors from this dialog. You must use this dialog to change the font and font size, however, for any setting (at the time of writing).

How it works...

The **Fonts and Colors** dialog simply changes the appearance of code in the text editor as well as for other windows, such as the output window. It is very useful for making your coding environment more comfortable.

There's more...

Once you have customized your settings, you'll find that you may want to save your customized **Fonts and Colors** settings for others to use, or to put into another installation of Visual Studio, which you have on another machine. Unfortunately, by default, you won't be able to save-out your customized **Fonts and Colors** settings. You will need something called the Visual Studio Theme Editor extension to do so. We will explore this in the next recipe.

See also

- The *Extension – changing the color theme in Visual Studio* recipe describes how to import and export color themes

Extension – changing the color theme in Visual Studio

By default, you cannot save the changes you make to the font colors and background settings that you make in the **Fonts and Colors** dialog. To fix this issue, Visual Studio has a feature called **Themes**. If you go to **Tools** I **Options** I **Environment** I **General**, you can change the theme to one of the three pre-installed stock themes (**Light**, **Blue**, and **Dark**):

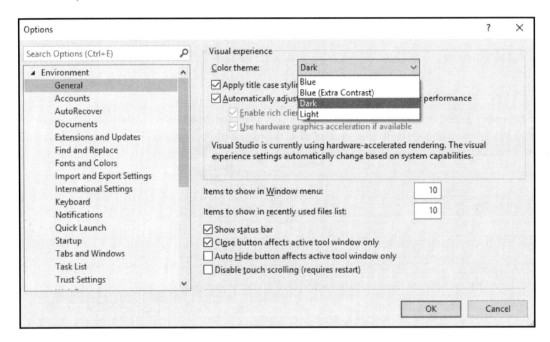

A different theme completely changes the look of Visual Studio, from the colors of the title bars to the background color of the text editor window.

You can also customize the theme of Visual Studio completely, but you'll need an extension to do so. Extensions are little programs that can be installed into Visual Studio to modify its behavior.

By default, your customized color settings cannot be saved or reloaded into another Visual Studio installation without the extension. With the extension, you will also be able to save your own color theme to share with others. You can also load the color settings made by another person or by yourself into a fresh copy of Visual Studio.

How to do it...

1. Go to **Tools | Extensions and Updates...**.
2. From the dialog that appears, choose **Online** in the panel on the left-hand side. Start typing `Theme Editor` into the search box on the right. The **Color Theme Editor for Visual Studio** option will pop up in your search results:

3. Click the small **Download** button in the top right-hand corner of the entry. Click through the installation dialog prompts, allowing the plugin to install. You'll then notice on the bottom of the window that it is scheduled for installation but will wait until Visual Studio is closed.

4. Close the window and Visual Studio, saving our project. After our program has closed, the VSIX Installer window will come up to confirm that you want to install the software. Click on the **Modify** button and it should start:

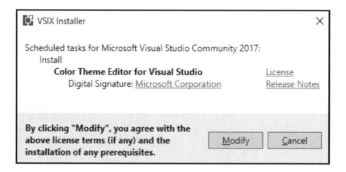

Alternatively, visit `https://marketplace.visualstudio.com/items?itemName=VisualStudioPlatformTeam.VisualStudio2017ColorThemeEditor` and download/install the extension by double-clicking the `.vsix` file that comes from your browser.

5. Once it has finished installing, open up Visual Studio again and open our project. One of the quickest ways to do so is from the **Recent** section on the **Start Page**:

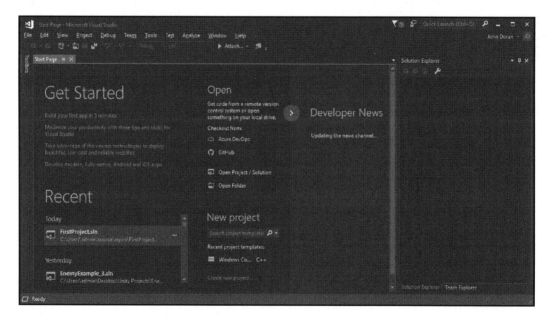

6. After restarting, go to **Tools | Customize Colors** to open the **Color Themes** editor page:

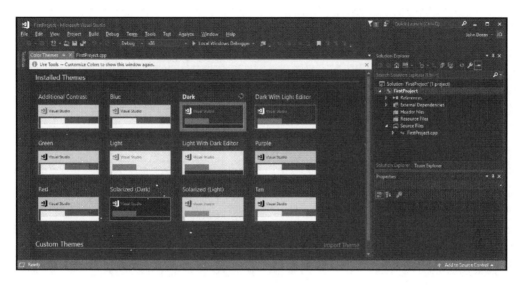

The Color Themes editor page

7. From the **Color Themes** dialog that appears, click on the little palette-shaped icon on the upper-right corner of the theme that you want to use as your base or starting theme (I've clicked on the palette for the **Light** theme here, as you can see in the following screenshot):

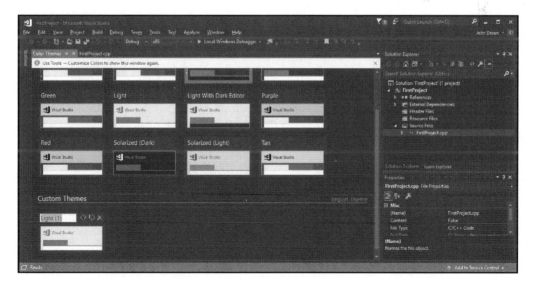

8. A copy of the theme will appear in the **Custom Themes** section in the lower part of the **Color Themes** window. Click on **Edit Theme** to modify the theme that is the middle button that appears when you hover over the custom theme. When you are editing the theme, you can change everything from the font text color to the C++ keyword color.

9. The main area you are interested in is the C++ Text Editor section. To gain access to all the C++ Text Editor options, be sure to select the Show All Elements option at the top of the Theme Editor window, as shown in the following screenshot:

Be sure to select the Show All Elements option in the Theme Editor window to show text editor settings specific to C++. Otherwise, you'll be left with only Chrome/GUI-type modifications being possible.

10. Note that, while most of the settings you are interested in will be under **Text Editor | C/C++**, some will not have the **C++** subheading. For example, the setting for the main/plain text inside the editor window (for all languages) is under **Text Editor | Plain Text** (without the **C++** subheading).

11. Select the theme to use from **Tools | Options | Environment | General**. Any new themes you have created will appear automatically in the dropdown menu.

How it works...

Once we load the plugin, it integrates into Visual Studio quite nicely. Exporting and uploading your themes to share with others is quite easy too.

Adding a theme to your Visual Studio installs it as an extension in **Tools | Extensions and Updates...**. To remove a theme, simply **Uninstall** its extension:

Formatting your code (Autocomplete settings) in Visual Studio

Code-writing formatting with Visual Studio is a pleasure. In this recipe, we'll discuss how to control the way Visual Studio lays out the text of your code.

Getting ready

Code has to be formatted correctly. You and your co-programmers will be able to better understand, grok, and keep your code bug-free if it is consistently formatted. This is why Visual Studio includes a number of auto-formatting tools inside the editor.

How to do it...

1. Go to **Tools** | **Options.** Once there, go to the **Text Editor** | **C/C++** section and select it. This dialog displays a window that allows you to toggle **Automatic brace completion**:

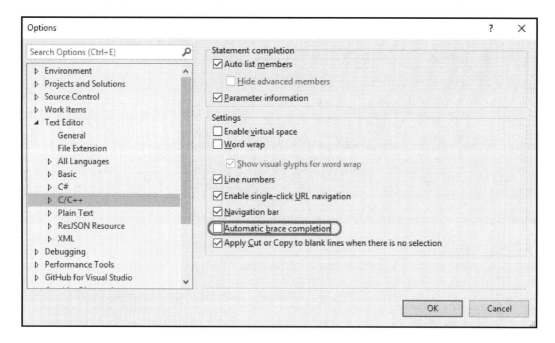

Automatic brace completion is a feature where, when you type {, a corresponding } is automatically typed for you. This feature may irk you if you don't like the text editor inserting characters for you unexpectedly.

You generally want **Auto list members** on, as that displays a nice dialog with the complete names of data members listed for you as soon as you start typing. This makes it easy to remember variable names, so you don't have to memorize them:

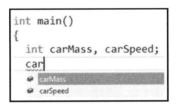

If you press *Ctrl* + spacebar inside the code editor at any time, the auto list pops up.

2. Some more autocomplete behavior options are located under **Text Editor | C/C++ | Formatting**:

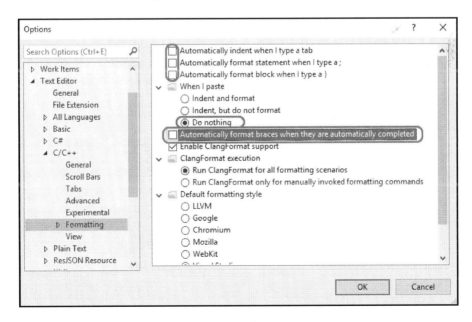

I recommend using all of the options at first and then disabling them only if they interrupt your workflow.

 You can also autoformat a section of text by highlighting a section of text and selecting **Edit | Advanced | Format Selection** (*Ctrl + K, Ctrl + F*).

How it works...

The default autocomplete and autoformat behaviors may irk you. You need to converse with your team on how you want your code to be formatted (spaces or tab indents, size of indent, and so on), and then configure your Visual Studio settings accordingly.

Shortcut keys in Visual Studio

There are a number of shortcut keys that will make coding and project navigation much faster and more efficient for you. In this recipe, we will describe how to use some of the common shortcut keys that will really enhance your coding speed.

Getting ready

To get started, you will need to have Visual Studio installed and a project opened to look at the features.

How to do it...

The following are some very useful keyboard shortcuts for you to try:

1. Click on one part of the code, then click somewhere else, at least 10 lines of code away. Now, press *Ctrl + -* [navigate backwards]. Navigation through different pages of source code (the last place you were at, and the place you are at now) is done by pressing *Ctrl + -* and *Ctrl + Shift + -*, respectively:

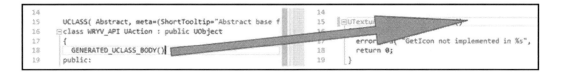

Note that the being mentioned is the one near the 0 key on your keyboard and will not work with the on the numpad.

Warping around in the text editor using *Ctrl + -*. The cursor will jump back to the last location it was in that is more than 10 lines of code away, even if the last location was in a separate file.

Say, for example, you're editing code in one place, and you want to go back to the place you've just been (or go back to the section in the code you came from). Simply press *Ctrl + -*, and that will warp you back to the location in the code you were at last. To warp forward to the location you were at before, press *Ctrl + -*, press *Ctrl + Shift + -*. To warp back, the previous location should be more than 10 lines away, or in a different file. These correspond to the forward and back menu buttons in the toolbar:

The back and forward navigation buttons in the toolbar correspond to the *Ctrl + -* and *Ctrl + Shift + -* shortcuts, respectively.

2. Press *Ctrl + W* to highlight a single word.
3. Press and hold *Ctrl + Shift + right arrow* (or *left arrow*) (not *Shift + right arrow*) just to move to the right and left of the cursor, selecting entire words.
4. Press *Ctrl + C* to copy text, *Ctrl + X* to cut text, and *Ctrl + V* to paste text.

5. **Clipboard ring**: The clipboard ring is a kind of a reference to the fact that Visual Studio maintains a stack of the last copy operations. By pressing *Ctrl + C*, you push the text that you are copying into an effective stack. Pressing *Ctrl + C* a second time on different text pushes that text into the **Clipboard Stack**. For example, in the following diagram, we pressed *Ctrl + C* on the word *cyclic* first, then *Ctrl + C* on the word *paste* afterward.

As you know, pressing *Ctrl + V* pastes the top item in the stack. Pressing *Ctrl + Shift + **Insert*** accesses a very long history of all the items ever copied in that session, that is, items underneath the top item in the stack. After you exhaust the list of items, the list wraps back to the top item in the stack. This is an odd feature, but you may find it useful occasionally.

6. *Ctrl + M* collapses a code section:

```
UTexture* UBuildAction::GetIcon()                UTexture* UBuildAction::GetIcon() { ... }
{
    return Game->GetData( BuildingType ).Portrait;
}
```

How it works...

Keyboard shortcuts allow you to speed up work in the code editor by reducing the number of mouse- reaches that you have to perform in a coding session.

Extended mouse usage in Visual Studio

The mouse is a pretty handy tool for selecting text. In this section, we'll highlight how to use the mouse in an advanced way so that you can make quick edits to your code's text.

How to do it...

1. Hold down the *Ctrl* key while clicking to select an entire word:

```
FString::Printf( TEXT(
```

2. Hold down the *Alt* key to select a box of text (*Alt* + left-click + drag):

```
// initialize a bunch of cooldow
FString name = FString::Printf(
Clock* clock = new Clock( name,
```

You can then either cut, copy, or overwrite the box-shaped text area; in the latter case, the characters you type will be repeated in all selected rows.

How it works...

Mouse-clicking alone can be tedious, but with the help of *Ctrl* + *Alt*, it becomes quite cool.

Installing Unreal Engine 4 (UE4)

There are a number of steps to follow to install and configure UE4 properly. In this recipe, we'll walk through the correct installation and setup of the engine.

Getting ready

UE4 takes up quite a few GB of space, so you should have at least 20 GB or so free for the installation on the target drive. Note that every project is also at least 1 GB as well, so you will need more space on your computer (or an additional hard drive) for more projects you wish to create.

How to do it...

1. Visit `unrealengine.com` in your web browser of choice:

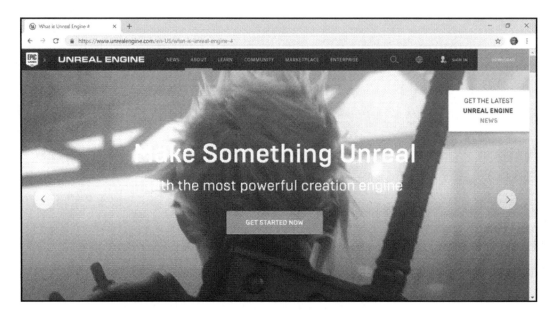

2. On the top-right corner of the screen, click on the **Download** button. You'll then be asked to create an Epic Games account. If you already have one, you can scroll down to the bottom of the screen and click the **Sign in** option.
3. Run the installer for the Epic Games Launcher program by double-clicking the `EpicGamesLauncherInstaller-x.x.x-xxx.msi` installer. Install it in the default location.
4. Once the Epic Games Launcher program is installed, open it by double-clicking its icon, which can be found on your desktop or in the Start menu:

5. You'll need to sign in with the same login information you created or used earlier, and then you'll arrive at the main page of the launcher:

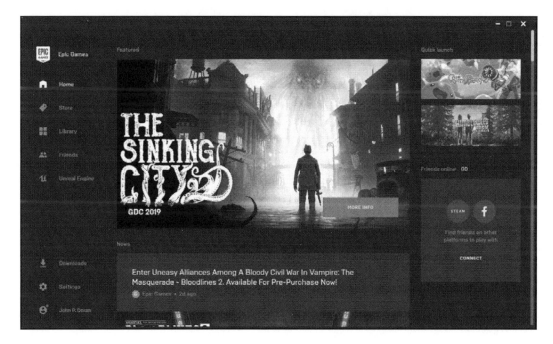

6. There are a lot of available options, but we want to click on the **Unreal Engine** option on the top-left of the screen.

7. Browse the start page and take a look around. Eventually, you will need to install an engine. Click on the large orange **Install Engine** button on the screen, as shown in the following screenshot:

8. A pop-up dialog will ask you to agree to an **End Licence Agreement**. Afterwards, you'll be asked to choose an install location. Then, click the **Install** button:

The launcher will start downloading the engine. It is about 7 GB, so it may take a while. Once finished, your screen should look something like this:

After the engine has installed, the **Install Engine** button will change to a **Launch Engine** button.

How it works...

The Epic Games Launcher is the program that you need to start up the engine itself. It keeps a copy of all your projects and libraries in the **Library** tab.

There's more...

As you learn more about working in UE4, you should check out some of the free library packages in the **Library | Vault** section. For that, click the **Library** item on the left-hand side and scroll down until you see **Vault**, underneath **My Projects**.

Creating your first project in UE4

Setting up a project within UE4 takes a number of steps. It is important to get your options correct so that you can have the setup that you like, so carefully follow this recipe when constructing your first project.

Each project that you create within UE4 takes up at least 1 GB of space or so, so you should decide whether you want your created projects on the same target drive or on an external or separate HDD.

How to do it...

1. From the Epic Games Launcher, click on the **Launch Unreal Engine 4.21.2** button on the left side of the screen. Once you are inside the engine, an option to create a new project or load an existing one will present itself.

 Note that depending on when you are reading this book, the version number could be different, but the steps should be the same, if not incredibly similar.

2. Select the **New Project** tab.
3. Decide whether you will be using C++ to code your project, or blueprints exclusively:

   - If you're using blueprints exclusively, make your selection of a template to use from the **Blueprint** tab.
   - If you're using C++ in addition to blueprints to construct your project, select the project template to construct your project based on the **C++** tab.
   - If you're not sure what template to base your code on, **Basic Code** is an excellent starting point for any C++ project (or **Blank** for a blueprint-exclusive (Unreal's built-in visual scripting language) project):

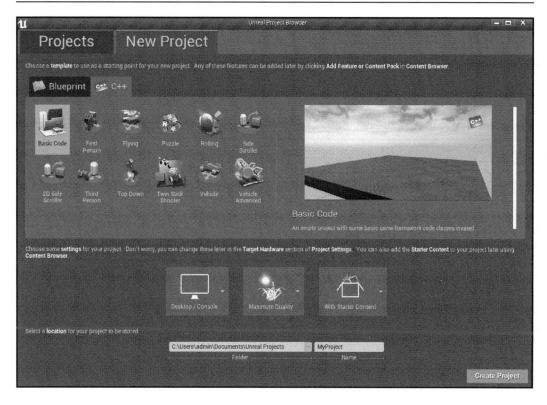

For the purpose of this book, we will always be using a C++ project:

1. Take a look at the three icons that appear beneath the template listing. There are three options here to configure:

    - You can choose to target desktop or mobile applications.
    - You have an option to alter the quality settings (the picture of a plant with the sun above it), but you probably don't need to alter these. The quality settings are reconfigurable under **Engine** | **Engine Scalability Settings** anyway.
    - The last option is whether to include **Starter Content** with the project or not. You can probably use the **Starter Content** package in your project. It has some excellent materials and textures available within it that are invaluable for a beginner, but as you start creating your own advanced projects, you will likely no longer need it.

If you don't like the **Starter Content** package, try the packages in the UE4 Marketplace. There is some excellent free content there, including the **GameTextures Material Pack**.

2. Select the drive and folder in which you will save your project. Keep in mind that each project is roughly 1 GB in size, and you will need at least that much space on the destination drive.
3. Name your project. Preferably, name it something unique and specific to what you are planning on creating.
4. Hit **Create**. Both the UE4 Editor and Visual Studio 2017 windows should pop up, enabling you to edit your project.

 In the future, keep in mind that you can open the Visual Studio 2017 Solution using one of two methods. The first is using your local file explorer. Navigate to the root of where your project is stored and double-click on the `ProjectName.sln` file. The second way is from UE4: click on **File | Open Visual Studio**.

Creating your first level in UE4

Creating levels in UE4 is easy and facilitated by a great all-around UI. In this recipe, we'll outline basic editor usage and describe how to construct your first level once you have your first project launched.

Getting ready

Complete the previous recipe, *Creating your first project in UE4*. Once you have a project constructed, we can proceed with creating a level.

How to do it...

1. The default level that gets set up when you start a new project will contain some default geometry and scenery if the starter content was included when creating the project:

The MinimalDefault level and interface of Unreal Engine 4

You don't need to start with this starter stuff, however. If you don't want to build from it, you can delete it, or create a new level.

2. To create a new level, click **File | New Level...**:

From here, you can select to create a level with a background sky (**Default**), or without a background sky (**Empty Level**).

If you choose to create a level without a background sky, keep in mind that you must add a **light** to it to see the geometry you add to it.

3. If you loaded the **Starter Content** on your project's creation (or some other content), then you can use the **Content Browser** to pull content into your level. Simply drag and drop instances of your content from the **Content Browser** into the level and save it, and then play the game by hitting the **Play** button.

4. Add some geometry to your level using the **Modes** panel (**Window | Modes**). Be sure to click on the left-most button with the picture of a light bulb and cube on it to access the placeable geometry:

By default, the **Basic** option is selected, which contains general geometry and other common features that are needed in Unreal. You can also add lights via the **Modes** tab by clicking on the **Lights** subtab on the left-hand side of the **Modes** tab. These can be added to a level by dragging and dropping as well.

The **Modes** panel contains two useful items for level construction: some sample geometry to add (cubes and spheres and the like), as well as a panel full of lights. Try these out and experiment to begin laying out your level.

If you are interested in learning more about building levels inside Unreal Engine, check out https://docs.unrealengine.com/en-us/Engine/QuickStart

UE4 – hot reloading

When you created a new Unreal Engine 4 C++ project, you saw that both Visual Studio and Unreal Engine 4 opened up. In this recipe, we will go through an example of modifying a script in Visual Studio and then compiling the code to see the changes.

Getting ready

To see the effects of changing one of the classes, we have to actually be using the class. Unreal automatically creates one of these classes for us by default (AChapter01_GameModeBase), so for this simple example, we will make use of it.

Note that everywhere you see `Chapter01` in the recipes in this chapter, I am referring to the project name, and if yours is named differently, you may see different text.

1. From the Unreal Editor, go to **Edit | Project Settings**. Select the **Maps & Modes** option under the **Project** section.
2. Under **Default GameMode**, select **Chapter01_GameMode**:

Note that the class name is `AChapter01_GameModeBase` in code, while in Unreal's menus it doesn't have the `A`. This is because Unreal's naming convention for classes always adds an `A` to classes that inherit from the `Actor` class. We will discuss this in greater detail later on in this book.

A **game mode** is a class that will contain the rules of your game type.

> For more information on game modes, check out `https://docs.`
> `unrealengine.com/en-US/Gameplay/Framework/GameMode`.

How to do it...

1. Inside Visual Studio under the **Solution Explorer**, you will see a number of pre-created files. Open the `Games/Chapter_01/Source/Chapter_01` folder and you should see the `Chapter01GameModeBase.h` and `.cpp` files. Double-click on the `.h` file to open it:

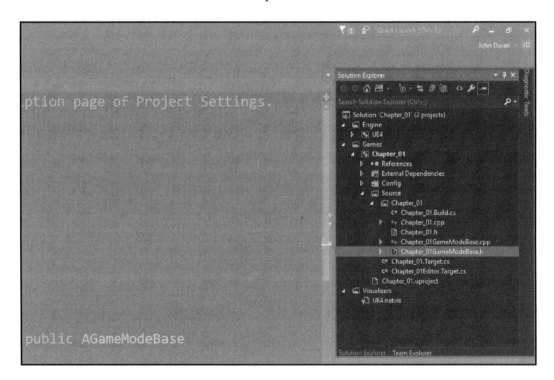

2. Add the following code (in bold) to the file:

```
// Fill out your copyright notice in the Description page of
Project Settings.

#pragma once

#include "CoreMinimal.h"
#include "GameFramework/GameModeBase.h"
#include "Chapter_01GameModeBase.generated.h"

/**
 *
 */
UCLASS()
class CHAPTER_01_API AChapter_01GameModeBase : public
AGameModeBase
{
  GENERATED_BODY()
public:
    void BeginPlay();

};
```

3. Next, open the .cpp file and update it to have the following:

```
// Fill out your copyright notice in the Description page of
Project Settings.

#include "Chapter_01GameModeBase.h"

void AChapter_01GameModeBase::BeginPlay()
{
    Super::BeginPlay();
}
```

This code currently doesn't do anything, but it gives us the ability to add changes to it later on in the future recipes of this chapter.

4. Save both files and return to the Unreal editor. From the editor, click on the **Compile** button:

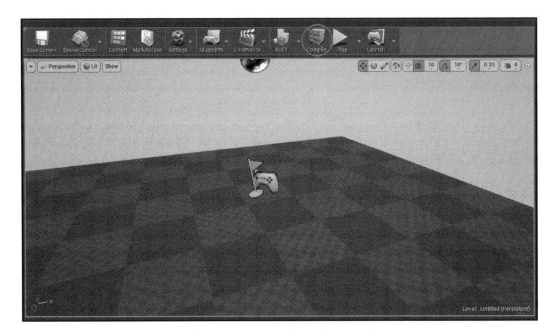

If all goes well, you should see a menu appear on the bottom-right of the screen, and after a period of time, you should see it say **Compile Complete!**:

It is also possible to compile your code in Visual Studio by right-clicking on the project from the **Solution Explorer** and selecting **Build**. Upon completion, when we go back to the Unreal editor, it should automatically load the changes that were made.

It is important for us to remember to compile our code any time we make changes to our code files. Otherwise, we will not be able to see those changes reflected in our project.

 For more information on compiling your own code for Unreal Engine 4, check out `https://docs.unrealengine.com/en-US/Programming/QuickStart`.

UE4 – logging with UE_LOG

Logging is extremely important for outputting internal game data. Using log tools lets you print information into a handy little **Output Log** window in the UE4 editor.

Getting ready

When coding, we may sometimes want to send some debug information out to the UE log window. This is possible using the UE_LOG macro. A **macro** is a fragment of code that has been given a name. Whenever the name is used in code, it is replaced by the contents of the macro at compile time. Log messages are an extremely important and convenient way to keep track of information in your program as you are developing it.

You should have a code file to complete this recipe. If this is your first time coding in Unreal, you should complete the previous recipe before continuing with this one.

How to do it...

1. In your code, enter a line of code using the following form:

```
UE_LOG(LogTemp, Warning, TEXT("Some warning message") );
```

For instance, if you wanted to add this to the script in the previous recipe, it may look like this:

```
#include "Chapter_01GameModeBase.h"

void AChapter_01GameModeBase::BeginPlay()
{
  Super::BeginPlay();

  // Basic UE_LOG message
  UE_LOG(LogTemp, Warning, TEXT("Some warning message") );
}
```

2. Turn on the **Output Log** inside the UE4 editor by going to **Window** |
   Developer Tools | **Output Log** to see your log messages printed in that
   window as your program is running:

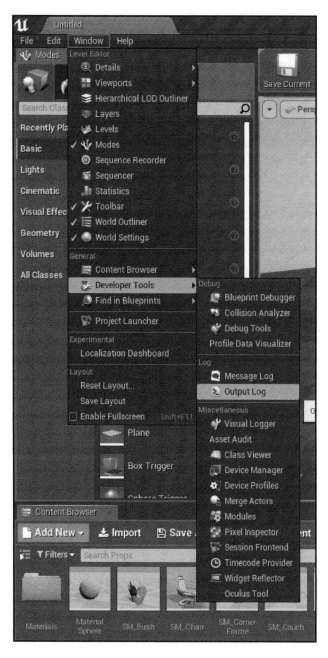

3. If you play your game by clicking on the Play button from the top toolbar, you should notice our text being displayed in yellow on the log:

```
☰ Content Browser    📄 Output Log

▼ Filters ▾  Search Log                                                                    🔍
LogTemp: Repeating last play command: Selected Viewport
LogBlueprintUserMessages: Early PlayInEditor Detection: Level '/Temp/Untitled_1.Untitled_1:Persis
LogPlayLevel: PlayLevel: No blueprints needed recompiling
PIE: New page: PIE session: Untitled_1 (Nov 17, 2018, 3:54:52 PM)
LogPlayLevel: Creating play world package: /Temp/UEDPIE_0_Untitled_1
LogPlayLevel: PIE: StaticDuplicateObject took: (0.002391s)
LogAIModule: Creating AISystem for world Untitled_1
LogPlayLevel: PIE: World Init took: (0.000488s)
LogPlayLevel: PIE: Created PIE world by copying editor world from /Temp/Untitled_1.Untitled_1 to
LogInit: XAudio2 using 'Speakers (Realtek(R) Audio)' : 2 channels at 48 kHz using 32 bits per sam
LogInit: FAudioDevice initialized.
LogLoad: Game class is 'Chapter_01GameModeBase'
LogWorld: Bringing World /Temp/UEDPIE_0_Untitled_1.Untitled_1 up for play (max tick rate 60) at 2
LogWorld: Bringing up level for play took: 0.000423
LogTemp: Warning: Some warning message
PIE: Play in editor start time for /Temp/UEDPIE_0_Untitled_1 -0.232
LogBlueprintUserMessages: Late PlayInEditor Detection: Level '/Temp/Untitled_1.Untitled_1:Persist

Cmd ▾  Enter Console Command
```

To make your output easier to see, you can clear the **Output Log** at any time by right-clicking on it within the window and selecting **Clear Log**.

How it works...

The UE_LOG macro accepts a minimum of three parameters:

- The Log category (we used LogTemp here to denote a log message in a temporary log)
- The Log level (we used a warning here to denote a log message, printed in yellow warning text)
- A string for the actual text of the log message itself

Do not forget the TEXT() macro around your log message text, as it will convert the text into a format that is usable by UE_LOG. For those more familiar with coding, the TEXT() macro promotes the enclosed text to Unicode (it prepends an L) when the compiler is set to run with Unicode on.

UE_LOG also accepts a variable number of arguments, just like printf() from the C programming language:

```
#include "Chapter_01GameModeBase.h"

void AChapter_01GameModeBase::BeginPlay()
{
  Super::BeginPlay();

  // Basic UE_LOG message

  UE_LOG(LogTemp, Warning, TEXT("Some warning message") );

  // UE_LOG message with arguments
  int intVar = 5;
  float floatVar = 3.7f;
  FString fstringVar = "an fstring variable";
  UE_LOG(LogTemp, Warning, TEXT("Text, %d %f %s"), intVar, floatVar,
*fstringVar );
}
```

There will be an asterisk * just before the FString variable when using UE_LOG to dereference the FString to a regular C-style TCHAR pointer. This means that it is converting the pointer into the actual value it is pointing at.

TCHAR is usually defined as a variable type where, if Unicode is being used in the compile, the TCHAR resolves to the built-in data type, wchar_t . If Unicode is off (the _UNICODE compiler switch is not defined), then TCHAR resolves to simply the standard char type.

For more information on TCHAR and working with strings in general with C++, check out https://docs.microsoft.com/en-us/ windows/desktop/learnwin32/working-with-strings#tchars.

Don't forget to clear your log messages after you no longer need them from the source! Otherwise, your console may become bloated with messages and make it difficult to find things you are looking for.

UE4 – making an FString from FStrings and other variables

When coding in UE4, you often want to construct a string from variables. This is pretty easy using the FString::Printf or FString::Format function.

Getting ready

For this, you should have an existing project into which you can enter some UE4 C++ code. Putting variables into a string is possible via **printing**. It may be counter intuitive to print into a string, but you can't just concatenate variables together and hope that they will automatically convert into strings, as in some languages, such as JavaScript.

How to do it...

In this recipe, we will see how to print in two different ways. First, we will be using FString::Printf():

1. Consider the variables you'd like to be printed into your string. Note what each variable type is.
2. Open and take a look at a reference page of the printf format specifiers, such as http://en.cppreference.com/w/cpp/io/c/fprintf. For each variable you want to print, node what the specifier is. For example, %s for a formatted string.
3. Try code such as the following:

```
FString name = "Tim";
int32 mana = 450;
FString string = FString::Printf( TEXT( "Name = %s Mana =
    %d" ), *name, mana );
```

Notice how the preceding code block uses the format specifiers precisely like the traditional printf function does. In the preceding example, we used %s to place a string in the formatted string, and %d to place an integer in the formatted string. Different format specifiers exist for different types of variables, and you should look them up on a site such as cppreference.com.

It is also possible to print a string using `FString::Format()`.

4. Write code in the following form:

```
FString name = "Tim";
int32 mana = 450;
TArray< FStringFormatArg > args;
args.Add( FStringFormatArg( name ) );
args.Add( FStringFormatArg( mana ) );
FString string = FString::Format( TEXT( "Name = {0} Mana =
   {1}" ), args );

UE_LOG( LogTemp, Warning, TEXT( "Your string: %s" ),
        *string );
```

With `FString::Format()`, instead of using correct format specifiers, we use simple integers and a `TArray` of `FStringFormatArg` instead. `FstringFormatArg` helps `FString::Format()` deduce the type of variable to put in the string. Refer to the following screenshot:

No matter which method you use, upon calling `UE_LOG` and you will get the same output.

2
Creating Classes

This chapter will cover the following recipes:

- Making a UCLASS – deriving from UObject
- Creating a blueprint from your custom UCLASS
- Creating a user-editable UPROPERTY
- Accessing a UPROPERTY from blueprints
- Specifying a UCLASS as the type of a UPROPERTY
- Instantiating UObject-derived classes (ConstructObject<> and NewObject <>)
- Destroying UObject-derived classes
- Creating a USTRUCT
- Creating a UENUM()

Introduction

This chapter focuses on how to create C++ classes and structs that integrate well with the UE4 blueprints editor.

The classes we will be creating in this chapter are graduated versions of the regular C++ classes, and are called UCLASS.

A UCLASS is just a C++ class with a whole lot of UE4 macro decoration on top. The macros generate additional C++ header code that enables integration with the UE4 editor itself.

Using UCLASS is a great practice to get into. The UCLASS macro, if configured correctly, can possibly make your UCLASS blueprintable, which can enable your custom C++ objects to be used within Unreal's visual-scripting language blueprints. This can be really useful if you have designers on your team, as they can access and tweak aspects of your project without having to dive into code.

We can have blueprint's visually editable properties (UPROPERTY) with handy UI widgets such as text fields, sliders, and model selection boxes. You can also have functions (such as UFUNCTION) that are callable from within a blueprints diagram. Both of these are shown in the following screenshots:

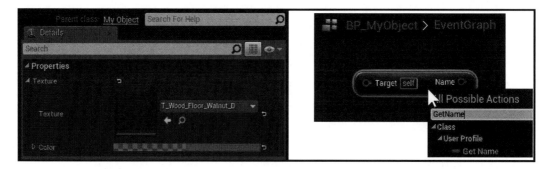

On the left, two UPROPERTY decorated class members (a UTexture reference and an FColor) show up for editing in a C++ class's blueprint. On the right, a C++ GetName function marked as BlueprintCallable UFUNCTION shows up as callable from a blueprints diagram.

 Code generated by the UCLASS macro will be located in a ClassName.generated.h file, which will be the last #include required in your UCLASS header file, ClassName.h.

 You will notice that the sample objects we create in this class, even when blueprintable, will not be placed in levels. That is because in order to be placed in levels, your C++ class must derive from the Actor base class, or a subclass below it. See Chapter 4, *Actors and Components*, for further details.

UE4 code is, typically, very easy to write and manage once you know the patterns. The code we write to derive from another UCLASS, or to create a UPROPERTY or UFUNCTION instance, is very consistent. This chapter provides recipes for common UE4 coding tasks revolving around basic UCLASS derivation, property and reference declaration, construction, destruction, and general functionality.

Technical requirements

This chapter requires the use of Unreal Engine 4 and uses Visual Studio 2017 as the IDE. Instructions on how to install both pieces of software and the requirements for them can be found in Chapter 1, *UE4 Development Tools*.

Making a UCLASS – deriving from UObject

When coding with C++, you can have your own code that compiles and runs as native C++ code, with appropriate calls to the new and delete operators to create and destroy your custom objects. Native C++ code is perfectly acceptable in your UE4 project as long as your new and delete calls are appropriately paired so that no memory leaks are present in your code.

You can, however, also declare custom C++ classes, which behave like UE4 classes, by declaring your custom C++ objects using the UCLASS macro. The UCLASS macro tells the class to make use of UE4's smart pointers and memory management routines for allocation and de-allocation according to their smart pointer rules, which can be loaded and read by the UE4 editor automatically, and can optionally be accessed from blueprints.

Note that when you use the UCLASS macro, your UCLASS object's creation and destruction must be completely managed by UE4: you must use the ConstructObject function to create an instance of your object (not the C++ native keyword new), and call the UObject::ConditionalBeginDestroy() function to destroy the object (not the C++ native keyword delete).

Getting ready

In this recipe, we will outline how to write a C++ class that uses the UCLASS macro to enable managed memory allocation and de-allocation, as well as to permit access from the UE4 editor and blueprints. To complete this recipe, you will need a UE4 project that you can add new code to.

How to do it...

To create your own UObject derivative class, follow these steps:

1. From your running project, select **File** | **New C++ Class** inside the UE4 editor.
2. In the **Add C++ Class** dialog that appears, go to the upper-right-hand side of the window and tick the **Show All Classes** checkbox:

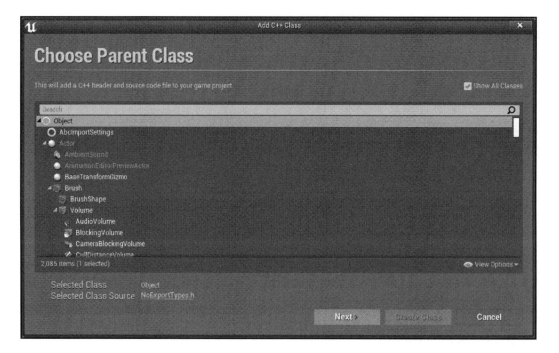

3. Select `Object` (top of the hierarchy) as the parent class to inherit from, and then click on **Next**.

Note that although `Object` will be written in the dialog box, in your C++ code, the C++ class you will be deriving from is actually `UObject` with a leading uppercase `U`. This is the naming convention of UE4.

`UCLASS` deriving from `UObject` (on a branch other than `Actor`) must be named with a leading `U`.

`UCLASS` deriving from `Actor` must be named with a leading `A` (`Chapter 4`, *Actors and Components*).

C++ classes (that are not `UCLASS`) deriving from nothing do not have a naming convention, but can be named with a leading `F` (for example, `FAssetData`), if preferred.

Direct derivatives of `UObject` will not be level-placeable, even if they contain visual representation elements such as `UStaticMeshes`. If you want to place your object inside a UE4 level, you must at least derive from the `Actor` class or beneath it in the inheritance hierarchy. See `Chapter 4`, *Actors and Components*, for more information how to derive from the `Actor` class for a level-placeable object.

This chapter's example code will not be placeable in the level, but you can create and use blueprints based on the C++ classes that we write in this chapter in the UE4 editor.

4. Name your new `Object` derivative something appropriate for the object type that you are creating. I'll call mine `UserProfile`:

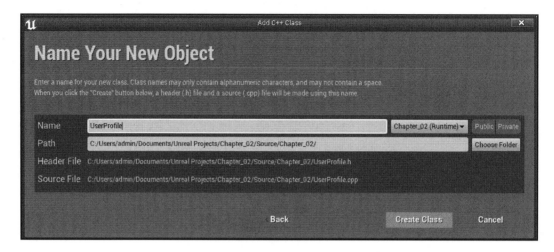

This comes off as `UUserObject` in the naming of the class in the C++ file that UE4 generates to ensure that the UE4 conventions are followed (In C++, class names with a `UCLASS` are preceded with a leading `U`).

5. Click on **Create Class** and the files should be created after file compilation is completed. Afterwards, Visual Studio should open (otherwise, open the solution by going to **File | Open Visual Studio**), and will open up the `.cpp` file of the class we just created (`UserProfile.cpp`). Open the header rule (`UserProfile.h`) for your class and ensure your class file has the following form:

```
#pragma once

#include "CoreMinimal.h"
#include "UObject/NoExportTypes.h"
#include "UserProfile.generated.h"

/**
 *
 */
UCLASS()
class CHAPTER_02_API UUserProfile : public UObject
{
  GENERATED_BODY()
};
```

6. Compile and run your project. You can now use your custom UCLASS object inside Visual Studio, as well as inside the UE4 editor. See the following recipes for more details on what you can do with it.

How to create and destroy your UObject-derived classes is outlined in the *Instantiating UObject-derived classes (ConstructObject ◇ and NewObject ◇)* and *Destroying UObject-derived classes* recipes later in this chapter.

How it works...

UE4 generates and manages a significant amount of code for your custom UCLASS. This code is generated as a result of the use of the UE4 macros such as UPROPERTY, UFUNCTION, and the UCLASS macro itself. The generated code is put into UserProfile.generated.h. You must #include the UCLASSNAME.generated.h file with the UCLASSNAME.h file for compilation to succeed, which is why, by default, the editor includes this automatically. Without including the UCLASSNAME.generated.h file, compilation would fail.

It is also important to note that the UCLASSNAME.generated.h file must be included as the last #include in the list of #include in UCLASSNAME.h.

Here's a correct example:

```
#pragma once

#include "CoreMinimal.h"
#include "UObject/NoExportTypes.h"

#include <list> // Newly added include

// CORRECT: generated file is the last file included
#include "UserProfile.generated.h"
```

And here is an incorrect one:

```
#pragma once

#include "CoreMinimal.h"
#include "UObject/NoExportTypes.h"
#include "UserProfile.generated.h"

// WRONG: NO INCLUDES AFTER .generated.h FILE
#include <list> // Newly added include
```

If the UCLASSNAME.generated.h file is not the last item within the list of #include statements shown in the previous code sample, you will get the following error:

```
>> #include found after .generated.h file - the .generated.h file
   should always be the last #include in a header
```

There's more...

There are a bunch of keywords that we want to discuss here, which modify the way a UCLASS behaves. A UCLASS can be marked as follows:

- Blueprintable: This means that you want to be able to construct a blueprint from the **Class Viewer** inside the UE4 editor (when you right-click it, **Create Blueprint Class...** becomes available). Without the Blueprintable keyword, the **Create Blueprint Class...** option will not be available for your UCLASS, even if you can find it from within the **Class Viewer** and right-click on it:

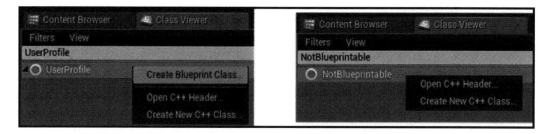

- The **Create Blueprint Class...** option is only available if you specify Blueprintable in your UCLASS macro definition.
- BlueprintType: Using this keyword implies that the UCLASS is usable as a variable from another blueprint. You can create blueprint variables from the **Variables** group in the left-hand panel of any blueprint's **EventGraph**.

- `NotBlueprintType`: Using this keyword specifies that you cannot use this blueprint variable type as a variable in a blueprints diagram. Right-clicking the `UCLASS` name in the **Class Viewer** will not show **Create Blueprint Class...** in its context menu:

You may be unsure whether to declare your C++ class as a `UCLASS` or not. The general rule of thumb is to use `UCLASS` unless you have a good reason not to. Unreal Engine 4's code is very well-written and has been tested thoroughly by this point. If you like smart pointers, you may find that `UCLASS` not only makes for safer code, but also makes the entire code base more coherent and more consistent.

See also

- To add additional programmable `UPROPERTY` to the blueprints diagrams, see the *Creating a user-editable UPROPERTY* recipe
- For details on referring to instances of your `UCLASS` using appropriate smart pointers, refer to `Chapter 3`, *Memory Management, Smart Pointers, and Debugging*
- For more information on `UCLASS`, `UPROPERTY`, and all of the other similar macros and how they are used by UE4, check out `https://www.unrealengine.com/en-US/blog/unreal-property-system-reflection`

Creating a blueprint from your custom UCLASS

Blueprinting is just the process of deriving a blueprint class for your C++ object. Creating blueprint-derived classes from your UE4 objects allows you to edit the custom UPROPERTY visually inside the editor. This avoids hardcoding any resources into your C++ code. In addition, your C++ class to be placeable within the level, it must be blueprinted first. But this is only possible if the C++ class underlying the blueprint is an Actor class-derivative.

 There is a way to load resources (such as textures) using FStringAssetReferences and StaticLoadObject. These pathways to loading resources (by hardcoding path strings into your C++ code) are generally discouraged, however. Providing an editable value in a UPROPERTY() and loading from a proper concretely typed asset reference is a much better practice.

Getting ready

You need to have a constructed UCLASS that you'd like to derive a Blueprint class from (see the *Making a UCLASS – deriving from UObject* recipe earlier in this chapter) to follow this recipe. You must have also marked your UCLASS as Blueprintable in the UCLASS macro for blueprinting to be possible inside the engine.

How to do it...

1. To blueprint your UserProfile class, first ensure that UCLASS has the Blueprintable tag in the UCLASS macro. This should look as follows:

```
UCLASS( Blueprintable )
class CHAPTER2_API UUserProfile : public UObject
```

2. Compile your code.

3. Find the `UserProfile` C++ class in the **Class Viewer** (**Window | Developer Tools | Class Viewer**). Since the previously created `UCLASS` does not derive from `Actor`, to find your custom `UCLASS`, you must turn off **Filters | Actors Only** in the **Class Viewer** (which is checked by default):

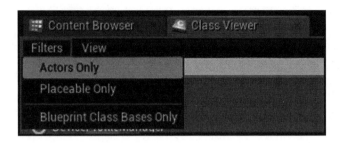

If you don't do this, then your custom C++ class may not show!

Keep in mind that you can use the small search box inside the **Class Viewer** to easily find the `UserProfile` class by starting to type it in:

4. Find your `UserProfile` class in the **Class Viewer**, right-click on it, and create a blueprint from it by selecting **Create Blueprint...**.
5. Name your blueprint. Some prefer to prefix the blueprint class name with `BP_`.
   You may choose to follow this convention; just be sure to be consistent.
6. You will be able to edit any fields that are created for each `UserProfile` blueprint instance you create.

If the blueprint editor does not open automatically, you can open it by double-clicking on the file in the **Content Browser**.

How it works...

Any C++ class you create that has the `Blueprintable` tag in its `UCLASS` macro can be blueprinted within the UE4 editor. A blueprint allows you to customize properties on the C++ class in the visual GUI interface of UE4.

Creating a user-editable UPROPERTY

Each `UCLASS` that you declare can have any number of `UPROPERTY` declared for it within it. Each `UPROPERTY` can be a visually editable field, or a blueprints-accessible data member of the `UCLASS`.

There are a number of qualifiers that we can add to each `UPROPERTY`, which change the way it behaves from within the UE4 Editor, such as `EditAnywhere` (specifying that the `UPROPERTY` can be changed through code or in the editor), and `BlueprintReadWrite` (specifying that blueprints can both read and write the variable at any time, in addition to the C++ code being allowed to do so).

Getting ready

To use this recipe, you should have a C++ project that you can add C++ code to. In addition, you should have completed the preceding recipe, *Making a UCLASS – deriving from UObject*.

How to do it...

1. First, we will need to mark the class as `Blueprintable` and then add the following members to your `UCLASS` declaration, which are shown in bold:

```
/**
 * UCLASS macro options sets this C++ class to be
 * Blueprintable within the UE4 Editor
 */
UCLASS( Blueprintable )
class CHAPTER_02_API UUserProfile : public UObject
{
  GENERATED_BODY()

public:
```

```
UPROPERTY(EditAnywhere, BlueprintReadWrite, Category =
Stats)
   float Armor;

UPROPERTY(EditAnywhere, BlueprintReadWrite, Category =
Stats)
   float HpMax;
};
```

2. Return to Unreal Editor and then hit the **Compile** button to update our code.

3. Once updated, create a blueprint of your `UObject` class derivative, if it hasn't been created already.

   This can be done in the same way that we saw in the previous recipe, but it is also possible to do by hand, which we will do now.

4. To do this, go to the **Content Browser** tab and click on the folder icon to select what section of the project you want to work in. From the window that pops up, select the **Content** section:

Selecting the Content folder in the Content Browser

5. From there, select the **Add New** button and then select **Blueprint Class**:

Creating a Blueprint Class from the Content Browser

6. From the **Pick Parent Class** menu, you'll see some buttons for **Common Classes**. Below that, you'll see the **All Classes** option with an arrow to click on to expand it. From there, type in the name of your class (in our case, UserProfile) and then select it from the list. Afterwards, click on the **Select** button:

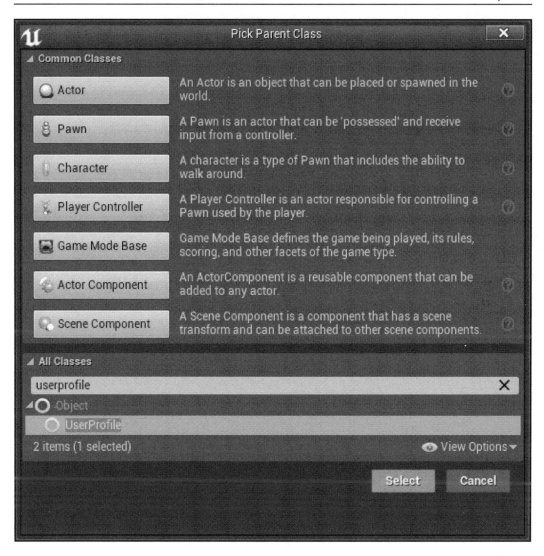

7. From there, you'll see the item appear in the `Content Browser`, where you can rename the instance to whatever you'd like; I named mine `MyProfile`.
8. Once created, we can open the blueprint in the UE4 Editor by double-clicking it.

9. You can now specify values in blueprints for the default values of these new UPROPERTY fields:

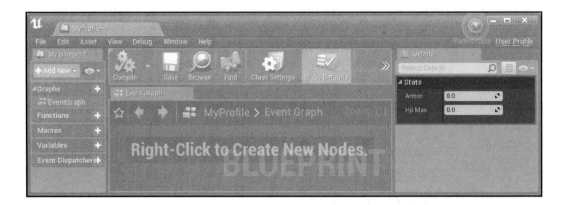

 Since the blueprint is empty, it may open as a data-only blueprint that does not include the middle and left-hand side sections. To see the full blueprint menu, you may need to click **Open Full Blueprint Editor** at the top of the menu to make the screen look like the one in the previous screenshot. However, the variables should still be visible and modifiable, either way.

10. Specify the per-instance values by creating new instances of the blueprint and editing the values on the object that's placed (by double-clicking on them).

How it works...

The parameters that are passed to the UPROPERTY() macro specify a couple of important pieces of information regarding the variable. In the preceding example, we specified the following:

- EditAnywhere: This means that the property can be edited either directly from the Blueprint, or on each instance of the UClass object as placed in the game level. Contrast this with the following:
  - EditDefaultsOnly: The blueprint's value is editable, but it is not editable on a per-instance basis.
  - EditInstanceOnly: This would allow editing of the property in the game-level instances of the UClass object, and not on the base blueprint itself.

- `BlueprintReadWrite`: This indicates that the property is both readable and writable from the blueprints diagrams. `UPROPERTY()` with `BlueprintReadWrite` must be public members; otherwise, compilation will fail. Contrast this with the following:
    - `BlueprintReadOnly`: The property must be set from C++ and cannot be changed from the blueprints.
- `Category`: You should always specify a `Category` for your `UPROPERTY()` as it's a good practice to stay organized. The `Category` determines which submenu the `UPROPERTY()` will appear under in the property editor. All `UPROPERTY()` specified under `Category=Stats` will appear in the same `Stats` area in the blueprints editor. If no category is specified, the `UPROPERTY` will appear under the default category, `UserProfile` (or whatever one called their class).

There's more...

It is important to understand the entire process, which is why we went through everything here, but you can also create a Blueprint class from a script by right-clicking on the class from the **C++ Classes** section of the **Content Browser** and then selecting **Create Blueprint class based on UserProfile**. Refer to the following screenshot:

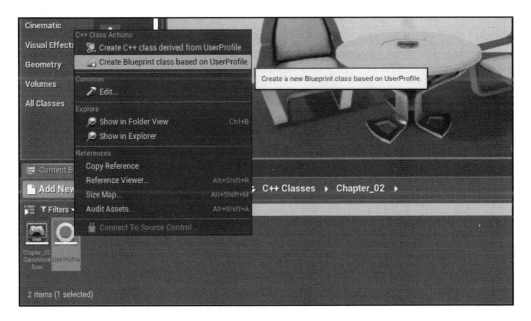

See also

- A complete UPROPERTY listing is located at https://docs.unrealengine. com/latest/INT/Programming/UnrealArchitecture/Reference/ Properties/Specifiers/index.html. Give it a browse.

Accessing a UPROPERTY from blueprints

Accessing a UPROPERTY from blueprints is fairly simple. The member must be exposed as a UPROPERTY on the member variable that you want to access from your blueprints diagram. You must qualify the UPROPERTY in your macro declaration as being either BlueprintReadOnly or BlueprintReadWrite to specify whether you want the variable to be either readable (only) from Blueprints, or even writable from Blueprints.

You can also use the special value BlueprintDefaultsOnly to indicate that you only want the default value (before the game starts) to be editable from the blueprints editor. BlueprintDefaultsOnly indicates that the data member cannot be edited from Blueprints at runtime.

How to do it...

1. Create some UObject-derivative class, specifying both Blueprintable and BlueprintType, such as in the following code, using the same class we created previously:

```
/**
 * UCLASS macro options sets this C++ class to be
 * Blueprintable within the UE4 Editor
 */
UCLASS(Blueprintable, BlueprintType)
class CHAPTER_02_API UUserProfile : public UObject
{
  GENERATED_BODY()

public:
  UPROPERTY(EditAnywhere, BlueprintReadWrite, Category =
Stats)
  float Armor;
```

```
UPROPERTY(EditAnywhere, BlueprintReadWrite, Category =
Stats)
  float HpMax;

UPROPERTY(EditAnywhere, BlueprintReadWrite, Category =
Stats)
  FString Name;
};
```

The BlueprintType declaration in the UCLASS macro is required to use the UCLASS as a type within a blueprints diagram.

2. Save and compile your code.
3. Within the UE4 editor, derive a blueprint class from the C++ class if needed, as shown in the previous recipe or in the *Creating a Blueprint from your custom UCLASS* recipe.
4. Double-click on your instance and change the **Name** variable to have a new value, for instance, Billy. Afterwards, hit the **Compile** button to save all of your changes:

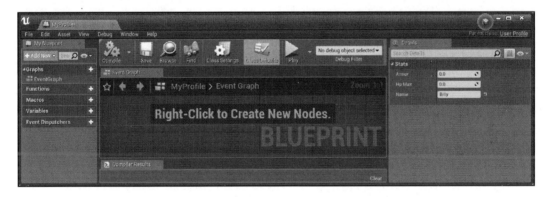

5. In a blueprints diagram that allows function calls (such as the **Level Blueprint**, which is accessible via **Blueprints | Open Level Blueprint**), we can now try to make use of the variable we added. Perhaps we can try printing the **Name** property whenever the game starts.

6. To have something happen at the start of the game, we will need to create a **BeginPlay** event. You can do this by right-clicking in the blueprint graph and selecting **Add Event | Event BeginPlay**:

Now, need to create an instance of the class. Since it's derived from `UObject`, we cannot instantiate it from drag and drop, but we can create something through the **Construct Object from Class Blueprint** node.

7. Right-click to the right of the node that was just created and from the search bar, type in `construct` and select the **Construct Object from Class** node from the list:

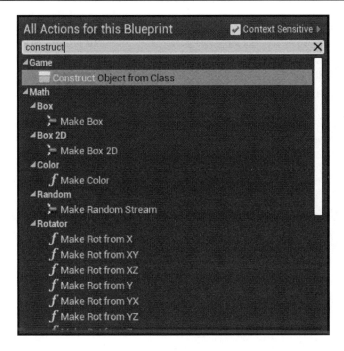

8. Next, connect the line from the right of the **Event BeginPlay** node to the left of the **Construct Node** by dragging the arrow on the bottom-right of the **Event BeginPlay** node to the arrow on the left-hand side of the **Construct Node** and releasing it.

> Navigating blueprints diagrams is easy. Right-click and drag to pan a blueprints diagram, *Alt* + right-click + drag, or use the mouse wheel to zoom. You can left-click and drag any node to position it wherever you want. You can also select multiple nodes at the same time and move them all together. You can find more information on blueprints here: `https://docs.unrealengine.com/en-US/Engine/Blueprints/BestPractices`.

9. Under the **Class** section, click on the dropdown and type in the name of the blueprint you created (**MyProfile**) and select it from the list.

10. You also need to select something for the **Outer** property that will be the owner of the object. Click and drag the blue circle and move the mouse to the left of the node, and then let go of the mouse to create a new node. When the menu pops up, type in the word `self` and then select the **Get a reference to self** option. If all went well, your blueprint should look something like this:

This will create a variable using the information from the **MyProfile** instance we created earlier. However, we have no way to use it yet unless we make it a variable. Drag and drop this to the right of the **Return Value** property and select **Promote to a variable**. This will automatically create a variable called `NewVar_0` and create a **Set** node, but you can rename it to whatever you want using the menu on the left-hand side of the menu.

11. To the right of the **SET** node, drag and drop the white arrow on the top right of the node and create a **Print Text** node.

12. We now need something to print, and the **Name** property will work perfectly for this. To the right of the **SET** node, drag and drop the blue node and select the **Variables | Stats | Get Name** node.

13. Finally, connect the **Name** value to the **In Text** property of the **Print Text** node. It will automatically create a conversion node to change the name string into a **Text** object that it can understand.

In the end, the entire blueprint should look something like this:

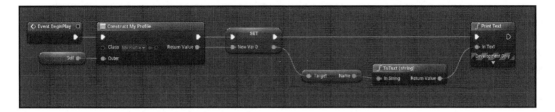

The completed blueprint

If all went well, you should be able to hit the **Compile** button and then play the game by hitting the **Play** button on the top of the menu:

Upon playing, you should see Billy show up on the screen, just as we set previously!

How it works...

UPROPERTYs are automatically written Get/Set methods for UE4 classes and can be used to access and assign values for properties, as we just saw.

Specifying a UCLASS as the type of a UPROPERTY

So, you've constructed some custom UCLASS, intended for use inside UE4. We created one in the editor using blueprints in the previous recipe, but how do you instantiate them in C++? Objects in UE4 are reference-counted and memory-managed objects, so you should not allocate them directly using the C++ keyword new. Instead, you'll have to use a function called ConstructObject so that we can instantiate your UObject derivative.

ConstructObject doesn't just take the C++ class name of the object you are creating; it also requires a blueprint class derivative of the C++ class (a UClass* reference). A UClass* reference is just a pointer to a blueprint.

How do we instantiate an instance of a particular blueprint from the C++ code? C++ code does not, and should not, know concrete UCLASS names, since these names are created and edited in the UE4 editor, which you can only access after compilation. We need a way to somehow hand back the blueprint class name to instantiate with the C++ code.

The way we do this is by having the UE4 programmer select the UClass that the C++ code is to use from a simple drop-down menu listing all the blueprints available (derived from a particular C++ class) inside the UE4 editor. To do this, we simply have to provide a user-editable UPROPERTY with a TSubclassOf<C++ClassName> typed variable. Alternatively, you can use FStringClassReference to achieve the same objective.

 UCLASS should be considered as resources to the C++ code, and their names should never be hardcoded into the code base.

Getting ready

In your UE4 code, you're often going to need to refer to different UCLASS in the project. For example, say you need to know the UCLASS of the player object so that you can use SpawnObject in your code on it. Specifying a UCLASS from C++ code is extremely awkward, because the C++ code is not supposed to know about the concrete instances of the derived UCLASS that were created in the blueprints editor at all. Just as we don't want to bake specific asset names into the C++ code, we don't want to hardcode derived blueprints class names into the C++ code.

So, we use a C++ variable (for example, UClassOfPlayer), and select that from a blueprints dialog in the UE4 editor. You can do so using a TSubclassOf member or an FStringClassReference member.

How to do it...

1. Navigate to the C++ class that you'd like to add the UCLASS reference member to.
2. From inside a UCLASS, use code of the following form to declare a UPROPERTY that allows for the selection of a UClass (blueprint class) that derives from UObject in the hierarchy:

```
UCLASS(Blueprintable, BlueprintType)
class CHAPTER_02_API UUserProfile : public UObject
{
  GENERATED_BODY()

public:
  UPROPERTY(EditAnywhere, BlueprintReadWrite, Category =
Stats)
  float Armor;

  UPROPERTY(EditAnywhere, BlueprintReadWrite, Category =
Stats)
  float HpMax;

  UPROPERTY(EditAnywhere, BlueprintReadWrite, Category =
Stats)
  FString Name;

  // Displays any UClasses deriving from UObject in a dropdown
  // menu in Blueprints
  UPROPERTY(EditAnywhere, BlueprintReadWrite, Category = Unit)
```

```
TSubclassOf<UObject> UClassOfPlayer;

// Displays string names of UCLASSes that derive from
// the GameMode C++ base class
UPROPERTY( EditAnywhere, meta=(MetaClass="GameMode"),
           Category = Unit )
FStringClassReference UClassGameMode;
};
```

Visual Studio may underline the `UClassOfPlayer` variable and say that an incomplete class is not allowed. This is one of those cases when Visual Studio errors aren't right and can be ignored as it will compile fine inside UE4.

3. Blueprint the C++ class, and then open that blueprint:

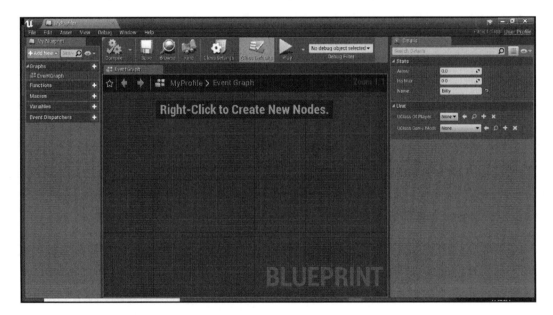

Notice that we now have a second category, **Unit**, and it has the two properties we specified in our script.

4. Click on the drop-down menu beside your `UClassOfPlayer` menu.

5. Select the appropriate `UClassOfPlayer` member from the drop-down menu of the listed `UClass`:

How it works...

Unreal Engine 4 give us a number of ways to specify a UClass or expected class type.

TSubclassOf

The TSubclassOf< > member will allow you to specify a UClass name using a drop-down menu inside the UE4 editor when editing any blueprints that have TSubclassOf< > members.

FStringClassReference

The MetaClass tag refers to the base C++ class from which you expect the UClassName to derive. This limits the drop-down menu's contents to only the blueprints derived from that C++ class. You can leave the MetaClass tag out if you wish to display all the blueprints in the project.

Instantiating UObject-derived classes (ConstructObject< > and NewObject< >)

Creating class instances in C++ is traditionally done using the keyword new. However, UE4 actually creates instances of its classes internally and requires you to call special factory functions to produce copies of any UCLASS that you want to instantiate. You produce instances of the UE4 blueprints classes, not the C++ class alone. When you create UObject-derived classes, you will need to instantiate them using special UE4 Engine functions.

The factory method allows UE4 to exercise some memory management on the object, controlling what happens to the object when it is deleted. This method allows UE4 to track all references to an object so that on object destruction, all references to the object can be easily unlinked. This ensures that no dangling pointers with references to invalidated memory exist in the program. This process is usually called **garbage collection**.

Getting ready

Instantiating UObject-derived classes that are not AActor class derivatives does not use UWorld::SpawnActor< >. Instead, we have to a special global function: ConstructObject< > or NewObject< >. Note that you should not use the bare C++ keyword new to allocate new instances of your UE4 UObject class derivatives.

You will need at least two pieces of information to properly instantiate your UCLASS instance:

- A C++ typed UClass reference to the class type that you would like to instantiate (blueprint class)
- The original C++ base class from which the blueprint class derives

How to do it...

In a globally accessible object (such as your GameMode object), add a TSubclassOf< YourC++ClassName > UPROPERTY() to specify and supply the UCLASS name to your C++ code. To do this with the GameMode, do the following:

1. From Visual Studio, open up the Chapter02_GameModeBase.h file from the **Solution Explorer**. From there, update the script to the following:

```
#pragma once

#include "CoreMinimal.h"
#include "GameFramework/GameModeBase.h"
#include "UserProfile.h"
#include "Chapter_02GameModeBase.generated.h"

/**
 *
 */
```

```
UCLASS()
class CHAPTER_02_API AChapter_02GameModeBase : public
AGameModeBase
{
  GENERATED_BODY()
public:
  UPROPERTY( EditAnywhere, BlueprintReadWrite, Category =
UClassNames )
  TSubclassOf<UUserProfile> UPBlueprintClassName;
};
```

2. Save and compile your code.
3. From the UE4 editor, create a blueprint from this class. Double-click on it to enter the blueprints editor and then select your `UClass` name from the drop-down menu so that you can see what it does. Save and exit the editor:

4. In your C++ code, find the section where you want to instantiate the UCLASS instance.

5. Instantiate the object using `ConstructObject< >` with the following formula:

```
ObjectType* object = ConstructObject< ObjectType >(
    UClassReference );
```

For example, using the `UserProfile` object that we specified in the last recipe, we would get code such as this:

```
// Get the GameMode object, which has a reference to
// the UClass name that we should instantiate:
AChapter2GameMode *gm = Cast<AChapter2GameMode>(
GetWorld()->GetAuthGameMode());
if( gm )
{
   UUserProfile* newobject = NewObject<UUserProfile>(
                               (UObject*)GetTransientPackage(),
                               UUserProfile::StaticClass() );
}
```

You can see an example of this being used in the `Chapter_02GameModeBase.cpp` file in this book's example code.

How it works...

Instantiating a `UObject` class using `NewObject` is simple. `ConstructObject` will instantiate an object of the blueprint-class type, and return a C++ pointer of the correct type.

Unfortunately, `NewObject` has a nasty first parameter that requires you to pass `GetTransientPackage()` with each call.

Do not use the keyword `new` when constructing your UE4 `UObject` derivative! It will not be properly memory-managed.

For more information on `NewObject` and other object creation functions, check out `https://docs.unrealengine.com/en-us/ Programming/UnrealArchitecture/Objects/Creation`.

There's more...

The `NewObject` function is what the OOP world refers to as a factory, and is a common design pattern. You ask the factory to make you the object; you don't go about constructing it by yourself. Using a factory pattern enables the engine to easily track objects as they are created.

For more information on design patterns, including the factory pattern, check out *Design Patterns: Elements of Reusable Object-Oriented Software* by Erich Gamma.

If you are interested in learning more about design patterns for game development, you may wish to check out *Game Development Patterns and Best Practices*, also available from Packt Publishing.

Destroying UObject-derived classes

Removing any `UObject` derivative is simple in UE4. When you are ready to delete your `UObject`-derived class, we will simply call a single function (`ConditionalBeginDestroy()`) on it to begin teardown. We do not use the native C++ `delete` command on `UObject` derivatives. We will show this in the following recipe.

Getting ready

To complete this recipe, you will need to have an object (`objectInstance`, in this case) that you wish to destroy in your project.

How to do it...

1. Call `objectInstance->ConditionalBeginDestroy()` on your object instance.
2. Null all your references to `objectInstance` in your client code, and do not use `objectInstance` again after `ConditionalBeginDestroy()` has been called on it:

```
// Destroy object
if(newobject)
{
  newobject->ConditionalBeginDestroy();
  newobject = nullptr;
}
```

How it works...

The `ConditionalBeginDestroy()` function begins the destruction process by removing all internal engine linkages to it. This marks the object for destruction as far as the engine is concerned. The object is then destroyed some time later by destroying its internal properties, followed by actual destruction of the object.

After `ConditionalBeginDestroy()` has been called on an object, your (client) code must consider the object to be destroyed, and must no longer use it.

Actual memory recovery happens some time later than when `ConditionalBeginDestroy()` has been called on an object. There is a garbage collection routine that finishes clearing the memory of objects that are no longer referenced by the game program at fixed time intervals. The time interval between garbage collector calls is listed in `C:\Program Files (x86)\Epic Games\Launcher\Engine\Config\BaseEngine.ini`, and defaults to one collection every 61.1 seconds:

```
gc.TimeBetweenPurgingPendingKillObjects=61.1
```

TIP

If the memory seems low after several `ConditionalBeginDestroy()` calls, you can trigger memory cleanup by calling `GetWorld()->ForceGarbageCollection(true)` to force an internal memory cleanup.

Usually, you do not need to worry about garbage collection or the interval unless you urgently need memory cleared. Do not call garbage collection routines too often, as this may cause unnecessary lag in the game.

Creating a USTRUCT

You may want to construct a blueprints editable property in UE4 that contains multiple members. The `FColoredTexture` struct that we will create in this recipe will allow you to group together a texture and its color inside the same structure for inclusion and specification in any other `UObject`-derivative, `Blueprintable` class:

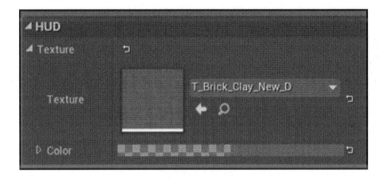

The `FColoredTexture` structure does have the visual within the blueprints appearance, as shown in the preceding screenshot.

This is for good organization and convenience of your other `UCLASS` `UPROPERTIES()`.

You may want to construct a C++ structure in your game using the `struct` keyword.

Getting ready

A `UObject` is the base class of all UE4 class objects, while an `FStruct` is just any plain old C++ style struct. All objects that use the automatic memory management features within the engine must derive from this class.

> If you may recall from the C++ language, the only difference between a C++ `class` and a C++ `struct` is that C++ classes have default `private` members, while structs default to `public` members.
>
> In languages such as C#, this isn't the case. In C#, a struct is value-typed, while a class is reference-typed.

How to do it...

We'll create a structure called `FColoredTexture` in C++ code to contain a texture and a modulating color:

1. From Visual Studio, right-click on the **Games/Chapter_02/Source/Chapter_02** folder and select **Add | New item...**. From the menu, select a **Header file (.h)** and then name the file `ColoredTexture.h` (not `FColoredTexture`).
2. Under **Location**, make sure that you select the same folder as the other script files in the project (in my case, `C:\Users\admin\Documents\Unreal Projects\Chapter_02\Source\Chapter_02`) that is not the default:

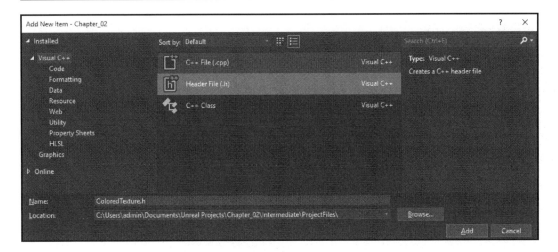

3. Once created, use the following code in `ColoredTexture.h`:

```cpp
#pragma once

#include "ObjectMacros.h"
#include "ColoredTexture.generated.h"

USTRUCT(Blueprintable)
struct CHAPTER_02_API FColoredTexture
{
  GENERATED_USTRUCT_BODY()

public:
  UPROPERTY( EditAnywhere, BlueprintReadWrite, Category = HUD
)
  UTexture* Texture;

  UPROPERTY( EditAnywhere, BlueprintReadWrite, Category = HUD
)
  FLinearColor Color;
};
```

4. Use `ColoredTexture.h` as a UPROPERTY() in a blueprintable UCLASS(), using a UPROPERTY() declaration such as this:

```cpp
#include "CoreMinimal.h"
#include "UObject/NoExportTypes.h"
#include "ColoredTexture.h"
#include "UserProfile.generated.h"
```

```
/**
 * UCLASS macro options sets this C++ class to be
 * Blueprintable within the UE4 Editor
 */
UCLASS(Blueprintable, BlueprintType)
class CHAPTER_02_API UUserProfile : public UObject
{
  GENERATED_BODY()

public:
  UPROPERTY(EditAnywhere, BlueprintReadWrite, Category =
Stats)
    float Armor;

  UPROPERTY(EditAnywhere, BlueprintReadWrite, Category =
Stats)
    float HpMax;

  UPROPERTY(EditAnywhere, BlueprintReadWrite, Category =
Stats)
    FString Name;

  // Displays any UClasses deriving from UObject in a dropdown
  // menu in Blueprints
  UPROPERTY(EditAnywhere, BlueprintReadWrite, Category = Unit)
    TSubclassOf<UObject> UClassOfPlayer;

  // Displays string names of UCLASSes that derive from
  // the GameMode C++ base class
  UPROPERTY(EditAnywhere, meta=(MetaClass="GameMode"),
Category = Unit )
    FStringClassReference UClassGameMode;

  // Custom struct example
  UPROPERTY(EditAnywhere, BlueprintReadWrite, Category = HUD)
    FColoredTexture Texture;
};
```

5. Save your script and compile your changes. Upon entering your object blueprint, you should notice the new properties:

How it works...

The UPROPERTY() specified for the FColoredTexture will show up in the editor as editable fields when included as UPROPERTY() fields inside another class, as shown in step 3.

There's more...

The main reason for making a struct, that is, a USTRUCT() instead of just a plain old C++ struct, is to interface with the UE4 Engine functionality. You can use plain C++ code (without creating USTRUCT() objects) for quick small structures that don't ask the engine to use them directly.

Creating a UENUM( )

C++ enum instances are very useful in typical C++ code. UE4 has a custom type of enumeration called UENUM(), which allows you to create an enum that will show up in a drop-down menu inside a blueprint that you are editing.

How to do it...

1. Go to the header file that will use the UENUM() you are specifying, or create a
   file called EnumName.h.
2. Use the following code:

```
UENUM()
enum Status
{
    Stopped     UMETA(DisplayName = "Stopped"),
    Moving      UMETA(DisplayName = "Moving"),
    Attacking   UMETA(DisplayName = "Attacking"),
};
```

3. Use your UENUM() in a UCLASS(), as follows:

```
UPROPERTY(EditAnywhere, BlueprintReadWrite, Category =
    Status)
TEnumAsByte<Status> status;
```

How it works...

UENUM() shows up nicely in the code editor as a drop-down menu in the blueprints editor, from which you can only select one of a few values:

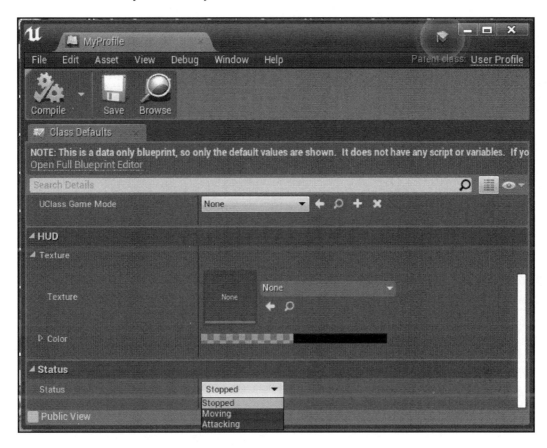

As you can see, the values that were specified are there!

3
Memory Management, Smart Pointers, and Debugging

In this chapter, we are going to cover the following topics:

- Unmanaged memory – using malloc()/free()
- Unmanaged memory – using new/delete
- Managed memory – using NewObject< > and ConstructObject< >
- Managed memory – de-allocating memory
- Managed memory – using smart pointers (TSharedPtr, TWeakPtr, TAutoPtr) to track an object
- Using TScopedPointer to track an object
- Unreal's garbage collection system and UPROPERTY()
- Forcing garbage collection
- Breakpoints and stepping through code
- Finding bugs and using call stacks
- Using the profiler to identify hot spots

Introduction

Memory management is always one of the most important things to get right in your computer program to ensure stability and good, bug-free operation of your code. A dangling pointer (*pointer* referring to something that has been removed from memory) is an example of a bug that is hard to track if it occurs.

In any computer program, memory management is extremely important. UE4's UObject reference-counting system is the default way that memory is managed for actors and classes derived from the UObject class. This is the default way that your memory will be managed within your UE4 program.

If you write custom C++ classes of your own, which do not derive from UObject, you may find the TSharedPtr / TWeakPtr reference-counted classes useful to use. These classes provide reference counting and automatic deletion for objects when they have no more references.

This chapter provides recipes for memory management within UE4. It also provides information on debugging your code through some of the useful features that Visual Studio includes for us, including breakpoints and the profiler.

Technical requirements

This chapter requires the use of Unreal Engine 4 and uses Visual Studio 2017 as the IDE. Instructions on how to install both pieces of software and the requirements for them can be found in Chapter 1, *UE4 Development Tools*, of this book.

Unmanaged memory – using malloc( ) / free( )

The basic way to allocate memory to your computer program in C (which is still possible to use in C++) is by using the malloc() function. This function designates a block of the computer system's memory for your program's use. Once your program is using a segment of memory, no other program can use or access that segment of memory. An attempt to access a segment of memory not allocated to your program will generate a **segmentation fault**, and represents an illegal operation on most systems.

How to do it...

Let's look at some example code that allocates a pointer variable, i, then assigns memory to it using malloc(). We allocate a single integer behind an int* pointer. After allocation, we store a value inside int, using the dereferencing operator *:

```
// CREATING AND ALLOCATING MEMORY FOR AN INT VARIABLE i

// Declare a pointer variable i
int * i;

// Allocates system memory
```

```
i = ( int* )malloc( sizeof( int ) );

// Assign the value 0 into variable i
*i = 0;

// Use the variable i, ensuring to
// use dereferencing operator * during use
printf( "i contains %d", *i );

// RELEASING MEMORY OCCUPIED BY i TO THE SYSTEM

// When we're done using i, we free the memory
// allocated for it back to the system.
free( i );

// Set the pointer's reference to address 0
i = 0;
```

How it works...

The preceding code does what is shown in the diagram that follows:

1. The first line creates an int * pointer variable, i, which starts as a dangling pointer referring to a segment of memory that probably won't be valid for your program to reference.
2. In the second step of the diagram, we use a malloc() call to initialize the variable i to point to a segment of memory precisely the size of an int variable, which will be valid for your program to refer to.
3. We then initialize the contents of that memory segment to the value 0 using the command *i = 0;. Refer to the following diagram:

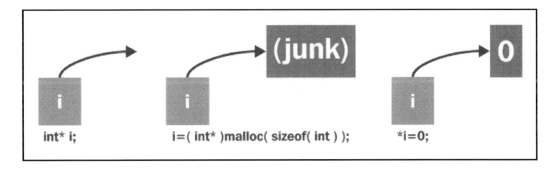

Note the difference between the assignment to a pointer variable (`i =`), which tells the pointer which memory address to refer to, and the assignment to what it is inside the memory address that the pointer variable refers to (`*i =`).

When the memory in the variable `i` needs to be released back to the system, we do so using a `free()` de-allocation call, as shown in the following diagram. `i` is then assigned to point to the memory address, `0`, shown in this diagram by the **electrical grounding** symbol reference, :

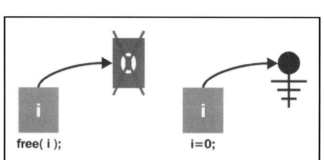

The reason we set the variable `i` to point to the `NULL` reference is to make it clear that the variable `i` does not refer to a valid segment of memory.

Unmanaged memory – using new/delete

The `new` operator is almost the same as a `malloc` call, except that it invokes a constructor call on the object created immediately after the memory is allocated. Objects allocated with the `new` operator should be de-allocated with the `delete` operator (and not `free()`).

Getting ready

In C++, use of `malloc()` was replaced as a best practice by use of the `new` operator. The main difference between the functionality of `malloc()` and the `new` operator is that `new` will call the constructor on object types after memory allocation. Refer to the following table:

malloc	Allocates a zone of contiguous space for use
new	Allocates a zone of contiguous space for use Calls constructor as an object type used as an argument to the new operator.

How to do it...

In the following code, we declare a simple `Object` class, then construct an instance of it using the `new` operator:

```cpp
class Object
{
  Object()
  {
    puts( "Object constructed" );
  }
  ~Object()
  {
    puts( "Object destructed" );
  }
};

// Invokes constructor
Object * object = new Object();

// Invokes deconstrctor
delete object;

// resets object to a null pointer
object = 0;
```

How it works...

The `new` operator works by allocating space just as `malloc()` does. If the type used with the `new` operator is an object type, the constructor is invoked automatically with the use of the `new` keyword, whereas the constructor is never invoked with the use of `malloc()`.

There's more...

You should avoid using naked heap allocations with the `new` keyword (or `malloc` for that matter). Managed memory is preferred within the engine so that all memory use is tracked and clean. If you allocate a `UObject` derivative, you definitely need to use `NewObject< >` or `ConstructObject< >` (outlined in subsequent recipes).

Managed memory – using NewObject< > and ConstructObject< >

Managed memory refers to memory that is <indexentry content="managed memory:allocating, NewObject used">allocated and de-allocated by some programmed subsystem above the `new`, `delete`, `malloc`,, and `free` calls in C++. These subsystems are commonly created so that the programmer does not forget to release memory after allocating it. Unreleased, occupied, but unused memory chunks are called **memory leaks**, as follows:

```
// generates memory leaks galore!
for( int i = 0; i < 100; i++ )
{
  int** leak = new int[500];
}
```

In the preceding example, the memory allocated is not referenceable by any variable! So, you can neither use the allocated memory after the `for` loop, nor free it. If your program allocates all available system memory, then what will happen is that your system will run out of memory entirely, and your OS will flag your program and close it for using up too much memory.

Memory management prevents forgetting to release memory. In memory-managed programs, it is commonly remembered by objects that are dynamically <indexentry content="managed memory:allocating, ConstructObject used">allocated the number of pointers referencing the object. When there are zero pointers referencing the object, it is either automatically deleted immediately, or flagged for deletion on the next run of the garbage collector.

Use of managed memory is automatic within UE4. Any allocation of an object to be used within the engine must be done using the `NewObject< >()` or `SpawnActor< >()` function.

The release of objects is done by removing the reference to the object and then occasionally calling the garbage cleanup routine (listed further in this chapter).

Getting ready

When you need to construct any `UObject` derivative that is not a derivative of the `Actor` class, you should always use the `NewObject< >` function. `SpawnActor< >` should be used only when the object is an `Actor` or its derivative.

How to do it...

Let's say we are trying to construct an object of a `UAction` type that itself derives from `UObject`—for example, the following class:

```
UCLASS(BlueprintType, Blueprintable,
       meta=(ShortTooltip="Base class for any Action type") )
class CHAPTER_03_API UAction : public UObject
{
   GENERATED_BODY()

public:
   UPROPERTY(EditAnywhere, BlueprintReadWrite, Category=Properties)
   FString Text;
   UPROPERTY(EditAnywhere, BlueprintReadWrite, Category=Properties)
   FKey ShortcutKey;

};
```

To construct an instance of the `UAction` class, we'd do the following:

```
// Create an object
UAction * action = NewObject<UAction>(GetTransientPackage(),
                                      UAction::StaticClass()
                                      /* RF_* flags */ );
```

How it works...

Here, `UAction::StaticClass()` gets you a base `UClass *` for the `UAction` object. The first argument to `NewObject< >` is `GetTransientPackage()`, which simply retrieves the transient package for the game. A package (`UPackage`) in UE4 is just a data conglomerate. Here we use the **Transient Package** to store our heap-allocated data. You could also use `UPROPERTY() TSubclassOf<AActor>` from Blueprints to select a `UClass` instance.

The third argument (optional) is a combination of parameters that indicate how `UObject` is treated by the memory management system.

There's more...

There is another function very similar to `NewObject< >` called `ConstructObject< >`. `ConstructObject< >` provides more parameters in construction, and you may find it useful if you need to initialize certain properties. Otherwise, `NewObject` works just fine.

> You can find out more about the ConstructObject function here: https://docs.unrealengine.com/en-us/Programming/ UnrealArchitecture/Objects/Creation#constructobject.

See also

You may also want to see the documentation for the RF_* flags at https://docs. unrealengine.com/latest/INT/Programming/UnrealArchitecture/Objects/ Creation/index.html#objectflags.

Managed memory – de-allocating memory

The UObject instances are reference-counted and garbage-collected when there are no more references to the UObject instance. Memory allocated on a UObject class derivative using ConstructObject<> or NewObject< > can also be de-allocated manually (before the reference count drops to 0) by calling the UObject::ConditionalBeginDestroy() member function.

Getting ready

You'd only do this if you were sure you no longer wanted UObject or the UObject class derivative instance in memory. Use the ConditionalBeginDestroy() function to release memory.

How to do it...

The following code demonstrates the de-allocation of an instance of the UObject class:

```
UObject *o = NewObject< UObject >( ... );
o->ConditionalBeginDestroy();
```

This concept also works with any class derived from the UObject class. So, for instance, if we wanted to do this with the UAction object we created in the previous recipe, we would add the bold text in the following snippet:

```
// Create an object
UAction * action = NewObject<UAction>(GetTransientPackage(),
                    UAction::StaticClass()
                    /* RF_* flags */ );

// Destroy an object
action->ConditionalBeginDestroy();
```

How it works...

The ConditionalBeginDestroy() command begins the de-allocation process, calling the BeginDestroy() and FinishDestroy() overrideable functions.

Be careful not to call `UObject::ConditionalBeginDestroy()` on any object still being referenced in memory by other objects' pointers.

Managed memory – smart pointers (TSharedPtr, TWeakPtr, TAutoPtr) to track an object

When people are afraid that they'll forget the `delete` call for standard C++ objects they create, they often use smart pointers to prevent memory leaks. `TSharedPtr` is a very useful C++ class that will make any custom C++ object reference-counted—with the exception of `UObject` derivatives, which are already reference-counted. An alternate class, `TWeakPtr`, is also provided for pointing to a reference-counted object with the strange property of being unable to prevent deletion (hence, *weak*):

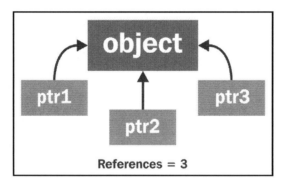

`UObject` and its derivative classes (anything created with `NewObject` or `ConstructObject`) cannot use `TSharedPtr`!

Getting ready

If you don't want to use raw pointers and manually track deletes into your C++ code that do not use UObject derivatives, then that code is a good candidate for using smart pointers such as TSharedPtr, TSharedRef, and the like. When you use a dynamically allocated object (created using the new keyword), you can wrap it up in a reference-counted pointer so that de-allocation happens automatically. The different types of smart pointers determine the smart pointer behavior and deletion call time. They are as follows:

- TSharedPtr: A thread-safe (provided you supplied ESPMode::ThreadSafe as the second argument to the template) reference-counted pointer type that indicates a shared object. The shared object will be de-allocated when there are no more references to it.
- TAutoPtr: A non-thread-safe shared pointer.

How to do it...

We can demonstrate the use of the four types of smart pointers referred to previously using a short code segment. In all of this code, the starting pointer can either be a raw pointer, or a copy of another smart pointer. All you have to do is take the C++ raw pointer and wrap it in a constructor call to any of the following: TSharedPtr, TSharedRef, TWeakPtr,, or TAutoPtr.

For example, take a look at the following code snippet:

```cpp
// C++ Class NOT deriving from UObject
class MyClass { };
TSharedPtr<MyClass>sharedPtr( new MyClass() );
```

How it works...

There are some differences between weak pointers and shared pointers. Weak pointers do not have the capability to keep the object in memory when the reference count drops to 0.

The advantage of using a weak pointer (over a raw pointer) is that, when the object underneath the weak pointer is manually deleted (using `ConditionalBeginDestroy()`), the weak pointer's reference becomes a `NULL` reference. This enables you to check whether the resource underneath the pointer is still allocated properly by checking a statement of the following form:

```
if( ptr.IsValid() ) // Check to see if the pointer is valid
{
}
```

There's more...

Shared pointers are thread-safe. This means that the underlying object can safely be manipulated on separate threads.

Always remember that you cannot use `TSharedRef` with `UObjects` or `UObject` derivatives; you can only use them on your custom C++ classes. Your `FStructures` can use the `TSharedPtr`, `TSharedRef`, and `TWeakPtr` classes to wrap up a raw pointer.

If you want to use smart pointers to point to an object, you must use `TWeakObjectPointer` or `UPROPERTY()`.

You can use `TAutoPtr` if you do not need the thread-safety guarantee of `TSharedPtr`. `TAutoPtr` will automatically delete an object when the number of references to it drops to 0.

 If you are interested in learning more about Unreal's smart pointers, check out `https://docs.unrealengine.com/en-us/Programming/UnrealArchitecture/SmartPointerLibrary`.

Using TScopedPointer to track an object

A **scoped** pointer is a pointer that is auto-deleted at the end of the block in which it was declared. Recall that a scope is just a section of code during which a variable is *alive*. A scope will last until the first closing brace, }, that appears.

For example, in the following block, we have two scopes. The outer scope declares an integer variable x (valid for the entire outer block), while the inner scope declares an integer variable y (valid for the inner block, after the line on which it is declared):

```
{
  int x;
  {
    int y;
  } // scope of y ends
} // scope of x ends
```

Getting ready

Scoped pointers are useful when it is important that a reference-counted object (that is in danger of going out of scope) is retained for the duration of the usage.

How to do it...

To declare a scoped pointer, we simply use the following syntax:

```
TScopedPointer<AWarrior> warrior(this );
```

This declares a scoped pointer referencing an object of the type declared within the angle brackets: < AWarrior >.

How it works...

The TScopedPointer variable type automatically adds a reference count to the variable pointed to. This prevents the de-allocation of the underlying object for at least the life of the scoped pointer.

Unreal's garbage collection system and UPROPERTY( )

When you have an object (such as TArray< >) as a UPROPERTY() member of UCLASS(), you need to declare that member as UPROPERTY() (even if you won't edit it in Blueprints); otherwise, TArray will not stay allocated properly.

How to do it...

Say we have a UCLASS() macro as follows:

```
UCLASS()
class MYPROJECT_API AWarrior : public AActor
{
  //TArray< FSoundEffect > Greets; // Incorrect
  UPROPERTY() TArray< FSoundEffect > Greets; // Correct
};
```

You'd have to list the TArray member as UPROPERTY() for it to be properly reference-counted. If you don't do so, you'll get an unexpected memory error-type bug sitting about in the code.

How it works...

The UPROPERTY() declaration tells UE4 that TArray must be properly memory-managed. Without the UPROPERTY() declaration, your TArray won't work properly.

Forcing garbage collection

When memory fills up, and you want to free some of it, garbage collection can be forced. You seldom need to do this, but you can do it in the case of having a very large texture (or set of textures) that are reference-counted and that you need to clear.

Getting ready

Simply call ConditionalBeginDestroy() on all UObjects that you want de-allocated from memory, or set their reference counts to 0.

How to do it...

Garbage collection is performed by calling the following:

```
GetWorld()->ForceGarbageCollection( true );
```

Breakpoints and stepping through code

Breakpoints are how you pause your C++ program to temporarily stop the code from running, and have a chance to analyze and inspect your program's operation. You can peer at variables, step through code, and change variable values.

Getting ready

Breakpoints are easy to set in Visual Studio. All you have to do is press *F9* on the line of code where you want the operation to pause, or click in the gray margin to the left of the line of code where you want the operation to pause. The code will pause when the operation reaches the line indicated.

How to do it...

1. Press *F9* on the line where you want the execution to pause. This will add a breakpoint to the code, indicated by a red dot, as shown in the following screenshot. Clicking on the red dot toggles it:

```
8       UObject *o = NewObject<UObject>( GetTransientPackage(),
9           UObject::StaticClass() );
```

2. Set the **Build Configuration** to any of the configurations with **Debug** in the title (**DebugGame Editor** or simply **DebugGame** if you launch it without the editor):

3. Launch your code by pressing *F5* (without holding *Ctrl*), or select the **Debug | Start Debugging** menu option.
4. When the code reaches the red dot, the code's execution will pause.

5. The paused view will take you to the code editor in **Debug mode**. In this mode, the windows may appear re arranged, with **Solution Explorer** possibly moved to the right, and new windows appearing at the bottom, including **Locals**, **Watch 1**, and **Call Stack**. If these windows do not appear, find them under the **Debug | Windows** submenu.

6. Check out your variables under the **Locals** window (**Debug | Windows | Locals**).

7. Press *F10* to step over a line of code.

8. Press *F11* to step into a line of code.

How it works...

Debuggers are powerful tools that allow you to see everything about your code as it is running, including variable states.

Stepping over a line of code (*F10*) executes the line of code in its entirety, and then pauses the program again, immediately, at the next line. If the line of code is a function call, then the function is executed without pausing at the first line of code of the function call, as follows:

```
void f()
{
  // F11 pauses here
  UE_LOG( LogTemp, Warning, TEXT( "Log message" ) );
}
int main()
{
  f(); // Breakpoint here: F10 runs and skips to next line
}
```

Stepping into a line of code (*F11*) will pause execution at the very next line of code run.

Finding bugs and using call stacks

When you have a bug in your code that causes a crash, a thrown exception, and so on, Visual Studio will attempt to halt execution of code and will allow you to inspect the code. The place at which Visual Studio halts won't always be the exact location of the bug, but it can be close. It will at least be at a line of code that doesn't execute properly.

Getting ready

In this recipe, we'll describe the **Call Stack,** and how to trace where you think an error may come from. Try adding a bug to your code, or adding a breakpoint somewhere interesting where you'd like to pause for inspection.

How to do it...

1. Run the code to a point where a bug occurs by pressing *F5*, or selecting the **Debug | Start Debugging** menu option. For example, add these lines of code:

```
UObject *o = 0; // Initialize to an illegal null pointer
o->GetName(); // Try and get the name of the object (has
bug)
```

2. The code will pause at the second line (`o->GetName()`).

 Note that this code will only execute (and thus crash) when the game is played in the editor.

3. When the code pauses, navigate to the **Call Stack** window (**Debug | Windows | Call Stack**).

How it works...

The **Call Stack** is a list of function calls that were executed. When a bug occurs, the line on which it occurred is listed at the top of the **Call Stack**. Refer to the following screenshot:

Call Stack
Name
➪ UE4Editor-MyProject.dll!NewObject<UObject>(UObject * Outer, UClass * Class, FName Name, EObjectFlags Flags,
UE4Editor-MyProject.dll!AMyProjectGameMode::AMyProjectGameMode(const FObjectInitializer & PCIP) Line 11

Using the profiler to identify hot spots

The C++ profiler is extremely useful for finding sections of code that require a high amount of processing time. Using the profiler can help you find sections of code to focus on during optimization. If you suspect that a region of code runs slowly, then you can actually confirm that it isn't slow if it doesn't appear highlighted in the profiler.

How to do it...

1. Go to **Debug** | **Performance Profiler...**:

2. In the dialog shown in the preceding screenshot, select the type of analysis you'd like displayed. You can choose to analyze **CPU Usage**, **GPU Usage**, **Memory Usage**, or step through a **Performance Wizard** to assist you in selecting what you want to see.

3. Make sure to run the game without the editor and then click on the **Start** button at the bottom of the dialog.

4. Stop the code after a brief time (less than a minute or two) to halt sample collection.

Do not collect too many samples or the profiler, as then it will take a really long time to start up.

5. Inspect the results that appear in the `.diagsession` file. Be sure to browse all the available tabs that open up. Available tabs will vary depending on the type of analysis performed.

How it works...

The C++ profiler samples and analyzes the running code, and presents you with a series of diagrams and images about how the code is performed.

You can find more information about the performance profiler by going to `https://docs.microsoft.com/en-us/visualstudio/profiling/?view=vs-2017`.

4
Actors and Components

In this chapter, we will cover the following recipes:

- Creating a custom Actor in C++
- Instantiating an Actor using SpawnActor
- Creating a UFUNCTION
- Destroying an Actor using Destroy and a Timer
- Destroying an Actor after a delay using SetLifeSpan
- Implementing the Actor functionality by composition
- Loading assets into components using FObjectFinder
- Implementing the Actor functionality by inheritance
- Attaching components to create a hierarchy
- Creating a custom Actor Component
- Creating a custom Scene Component
- Creating an InventoryComponent for an RPG
- Creating an OrbitingMovement Component
- Creating a building that spawns units

Introduction

Actors are classes that have some presence in the game world. Actors gain their specialized functionality by incorporating Components. This chapter deals with creating custom Actors and Components, the purpose that they serve, and how they work together.

Technical requirements

This chapter requires the use of Unreal Engine 4 and uses Visual Studio 2017 as the IDE. Instructions on how to install both pieces of software and the requirements for them can be found in Chapter 1, *UE4 Development Tools*, of this book.

Creating a custom Actor in C++

While there are different types of Actors that ship with Unreal as part of the default installation, you will find yourself needing to create custom Actors at some point during your project's development. This might happen when you need to add functionality to an existing class, combine Components in a combination that's not present in the default subclasses, or add additional member variables to a class. The following two recipes demonstrate how to use either composition or inheritance to customize Actors.

Getting ready

Make sure that you have installed Visual Studio and Unreal 4 as per the recipe in Chapter 1, *UE4 Development Tools.* You'll also need to have an existing project – if you don't, you can create a new one using the Unreal-provided wizard.

How to do it...

1. Open up your project within the Unreal Editor and click on the **Add New** button in **Content Browser**:

2. Select **New C++ Class...**:

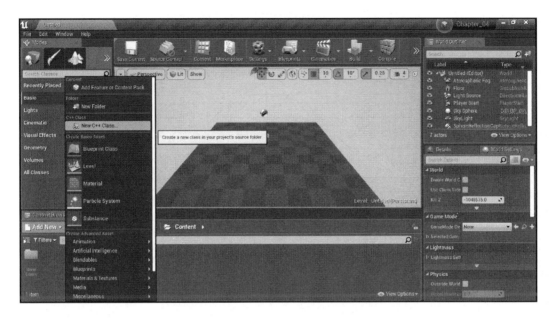

3. In the dialog that opens, select **Actor** from the list:

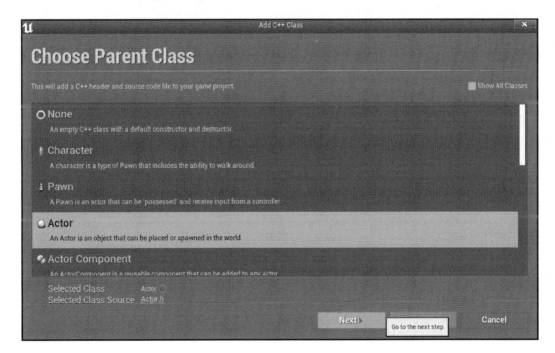

4. Give your **Actor** a name, such as `MyFirstActor`, and then click on **OK** to launch Visual Studio:

By convention, class names for `Actor` subclasses begin with an `A`. When using this class creation wizard, make sure you don't prefix your class with `A`, as the engine automatically adds the prefix for you.

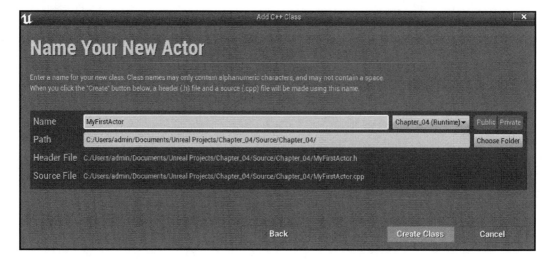

5. When Visual Studio loads, you should see something very similar to the following listing:

```cpp
// MyFirstActor.h

#pragma once

#include "CoreMinimal.h"
#include "GameFramework/Actor.h"
#include "MyFirstActor.generated.h"

UCLASS()
class CHAPTER_04_API AMyFirstActor : public AActor
{
  GENERATED_BODY()
public:
  // Sets default values for this actor's properties
  AMyFirstActor();

protected:
  // Called when the game starts or when spawned
```

```
      virtual void BeginPlay() override;

public:
  // Called every frame
  virtual void Tick(float DeltaTime) override;

};

// MyFirstActor.cpp

#include "MyFirstActor.h"

// Sets default values
AMyFirstActor::AMyFirstActor()
{
   // Set this actor to call Tick() every frame. You can turn
this off to improve performance if you don't need it.
   PrimaryActorTick.bCanEverTick = true;

}

// Called when the game starts or when spawned
void AMyFirstActor::BeginPlay()
{
   Super::BeginPlay();
}

// Called every frame
void AMyFirstActor::Tick(float DeltaTime)
{
   Super::Tick(DeltaTime);

}
```

How it works...

In time, you'll become familiar with the standard code, so you will be able to just create new classes from Visual Studio without using the Unreal wizard.

In MyFirstActor.h, we have the following aspects:

- #pragma once: This preprocessor statement, or pragma, is Unreal's expected method of implementing include guards pieces of code that prevent an include file from causing errors by being referenced multiple times.

- `#include "CoreMinimal.h"`: This file includes a number of definitions of classes that are often used, such as `FString`, `TArray`, `Vector`, and so on, and is included by default in created script files for that reason, though it could still compile at this point without it.

- `#include "GameFramework/Actor.h"`: We're going to create an `Actor` subclass so, naturally, we need to include the `header` file for the class we are inheriting from so that we know about its contents.

- `#include "MyFirstActor.generated.h"`: All Actor classes need to include their `generated.h` file. This file is automatically created by the **Unreal Header Tool** (**UHT**) based on the macros that it detects in your files.

- `UCLASS()`: `UCLASS` is one such macro that allows us to indicate that a class will be exposed to Unreal's reflection system. Reflection allows us to inspect and iterate object properties during runtime, as well as manage references to our objects for garbage collection.

- `class CHAPTER_04_API AMyFirstActor : public AActor`: This is the actual declaration of our class. The `CHAPTER_04_API` macro is created by the UHT, and is necessary to help our project compile properly on Windows by ensuring that our project module's classes are exported correctly in the DLL. You will also notice that both `MyFirstActor` and `Actor` have the prefix `A` – this is the naming convention that Unreal requires for native classes that are inherited from `Actor`.

 Note that, in this case, `Chapter_04` is the name of the project, and your project may have a different name.

- `GENERATED_BODY()`: `GENERATED_BODY` is another UHT macro that has been expanded to include the automatically generated functions that the underlying UE type system requires.

Inside the `MyFirstActor.cpp` file, we have the following aspects to note:

- `PrimaryActorTick.bCanEverTick = true;`: Inside the constructor implementation, this line enables ticking for this `Actor`. All Actors have a function called `Tick`, and this Boolean variable means that the `Actor` will have that function called once per frame, enabling the actor to perform actions in every frame as necessary. As a performance optimization, this is disabled by default.

- `BeginPlay/Tick`: You can also see the implementation of two default methods, `BeginPlay` and `Tick`, which are called once an object is spawned and every frame it is alive, respectively. Currently, these only call the parent's version of the function via `Super::FunctionName`.

Instantiating an Actor using SpawnActor

For this recipe, you'll need to have an `Actor` subclass ready to instantiate. You can use a built-in class such as `StaticMeshActor`, but it would help to practice with the custom `Actor` you made in the previous recipe.

How to do it...

1. Create a new C++ class, like in the previous recipe. This time, select **Game Mode Base** as your base class:

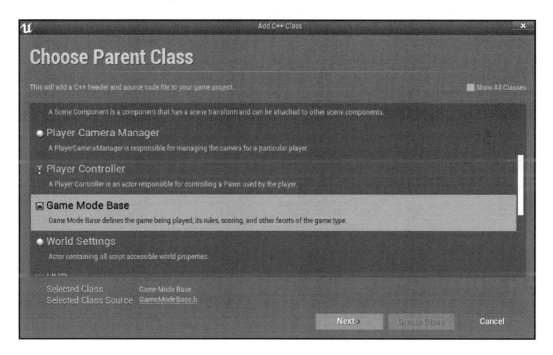

2. Once you have clicked **Next**, give the new class a name, such as `UE4CookbookGameModeBase`.

3. Declare a function override in the .h file of your new GameModeBase class:

```cpp
#pragma once

#include "CoreMinimal.h"
#include "GameFramework/GameModeBase.h"
#include "UECookbookGameModeBase.generated.h"

/**
 *
 */
UCLASS()
class CHAPTER_04_API AUECookbookGameModeBase : public
AGameModeBase
{
  GENERATED_BODY()

public:
  virtual void BeginPlay() override;
};
```

4. Implement the BeginPlay function in the .cpp file:

```cpp
#include "UECookbookGameModeBase.h"
#include "MyFirstActor.h" // AMyFirstActor

void AUECookbookGameModeBase::BeginPlay()
{
  // Call the parent class version of this function
  Super::BeginPlay();

  // Displays a red message on the screen for 10 seconds
  GEngine->AddOnScreenDebugMessage(-1, 10, FColor::Red,
                                   TEXT("Actor Spawning"));

  // Spawn an instance of the AMyFirstActor class at the
  //default location.
  FTransform SpawnLocation;
  GetWorld()->SpawnActor<AMyFirstActor>
                        (AMyFirstActor::StaticClass(),
                         SpawnLocation);
}
```

5. Compile your code, either through Visual Studio or by clicking on the **Compile** button in Unreal Editor:

6. Open the **World Settings** panel for the current level by clicking on the **Settings** toolbar icon, and then pick **World Settings** from the drop-down menu:

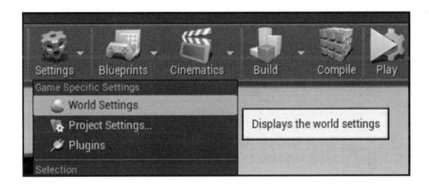

7. In the **GameMode Override** section, change the game mode to the `GameMode` subclass you just created:

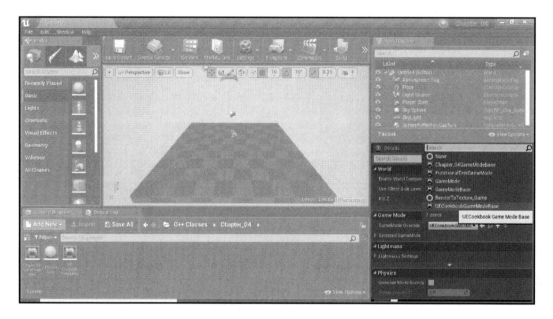

Setting the GameMode Override property

8. Start the level and verify that `GameMode` spawns a copy of your `Actor` in the world by looking at the **World Outliner** panel. You can verify that the `BeginPlay` function is being run by viewing the **Actor Spawning** text being displayed on screen. If it doesn't spawn, make sure that there are no obstructions at the world origin to prevent the `Actor` from being spawned. You can search the list of objects in the world by typing in the search bar at the top of the **World Outliner** panel. This will filter the entities that are shown:

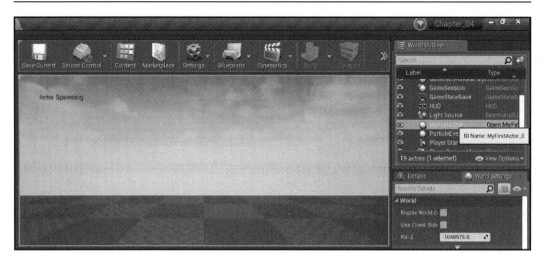

How it works...

GameMode is a special type of actor that is part of the Unreal Game Framework. Your map's GameMode is instantiated by the engine automatically when the game starts.

By placing some code into the BeginPlay method of our custom GameMode, we can run it automatically when the game begins.

Inside BeginPlay, we create an FTransform, which is going to be used by the SpawnActor function. By default, FTransform is constructed to have zero rotation and a location at the origin.

We then get a reference to the current level's UWorld instance using GetWorld, and then we call its SpawnActor function. We pass in FTransform, which we created earlier, to specify that the object should be created at its location, that is, the origin.

Creating a UFUNCTION

UFUNCTION() is useful because it is a C++ function that can be called from both your C++ client code as well as Blueprint diagrams. Any C++ function can be marked as a UFUNCTION().

How to do it...

1. Construct a `UClass` class or a derived class (such as `AActor`) with a member function that you'd like to expose to Blueprints. Decorate that member function with `UFUNCTION( BlueprintCallable, Category=SomeCategory)` to make it callable from Blueprints.

2. For example, let's create an `Actor` class called `Warrior` and use the following scripts for it:

```cpp
//Warrior.h
#pragma once

#include "CoreMinimal.h"
#include "GameFramework/Actor.h"
#include "Warrior.generated.h"

UCLASS()
class CHAPTER_04_API AWarrior : public AActor
{
  GENERATED_BODY()

public:
  // Sets default values for this actor's properties
  AWarrior();

  // Name of the Actor
  UPROPERTY(EditAnywhere, BlueprintReadWrite,
                          Category = Properties)
  FString Name;

  // Returns message containing the Name property
  UFUNCTION(BlueprintCallable, Category = Properties)
  FString ToString();

protected:
  // Called when the game starts or when spawned
  virtual void BeginPlay() override;

public:
  // Called every frame
  virtual void Tick(float DeltaTime) override;

};

// Warrior.cpp
```

```
#include "Warrior.h"

// Sets default values
AWarrior::AWarrior()
{
    // Set this actor to call Tick() every frame. You can turn
this off to improve performance if you don't need it.
    PrimaryActorTick.bCanEverTick = true;

}

// Called when the game starts or when spawned
void AWarrior::BeginPlay()
{
    Super::BeginPlay();
}

// Called every frame
void AWarrior::Tick(float DeltaTime)
{
    Super::Tick(DeltaTime);

}

FString AWarrior::ToString()
{
    return FString::Printf(TEXT("An instance of AWarrior: %s"),
*Name);
}
```

3. Create an instance of your `Warrior` class by going to the **Content Browser** and opening the `C++ Classes\Chapter_04` folder. Once there, drag the `Warrior` icon onto your game world and release the mouse.

4. You should see the item in the **World Outliner** tab. By selecting the newly added object, you should be able to see the **Name** property that we added. Go ahead and put in a value here, such as John:

5. From Blueprints (**Blueprints | Open Level Blueprint**), get a reference to your Warrior object. One way to do this is by dragging and dropping the object from the **World Outliner** into the Level Blueprint's **Event Graph** and letting go.
6. Click and hold the blue circle handle on the right-hand side of the **Warrior1** node and drag it over a little bit to the right. Once you release the mouse, you'll see a number of actions you can pick from.

7. Call the `ToString()` function on that `Warrior` instance by clicking on your `Warrior` instance. Then, in a Blueprint diagram, type in `ToString`. It should look as follows:

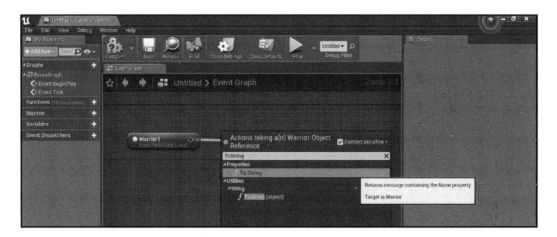

How it works...

`UFUNCTION()` is really a C++ function, but with additional metadata that makes it accessible to Blueprints. This can be incredibly useful in allowing your designers to have access to functions that you've written.

Destroying an Actor using Destroy and a Timer

This recipe will reuse the `GameMode` from the previous recipe, *Instantiating an Actor using SpawnActor*, so you should complete that recipe first.

How to do it...

1. Make the following changes to the `GameMode` declaration:

```
UCLASS()
class CHAPTER_04_API AUECookbookGameModeBase : public
AGameModeBase
```

```
{
  GENERATED_BODY()

public:
  virtual void BeginPlay() override;

  UPROPERTY()
  AMyFirstActor* SpawnedActor;

  UFUNCTION()
  void DestroyActorFunction();
};
```

2. Add `#include "MyFirstActor.h"` to the implementation file's include statements. Remember, we need to place it above the `.generated` file:

```
#pragma once

#include "CoreMinimal.h"
#include "GameFramework/GameModeBase.h"
#include "MyFirstActor.h"
#include "UECookbookGameModeBase.generated.h"
```

3. **Assign the results of `SpawnActor` to the new `SpawnedActor` variable:**

```
#include "UECookbookGameModeBase.h"
#include "MyFirstActor.h" // AMyFirstActor

void AUECookbookGameModeBase::BeginPlay()
{
  // Call the parent class version of this function
  Super::BeginPlay();

  // Displays a red message on the screen for 10 seconds
  GEngine->AddOnScreenDebugMessage(-1, 10, FColor::Red,
                  TEXT("Actor Spawning"));

  // Spawn an instance of the AMyFirstActor class at the
  // default location.
  FTransform SpawnLocation;
  SpawnedActor = GetWorld()->SpawnActor<AMyFirstActor>(
                          AMyFirstActor::StaticClass(),
                          SpawnLocation);
}
```

4. Add the following to the end of the `BeginPlay` function:

```
FTimerHandle Timer;
GetWorldTimerManager().SetTimer(Timer, this,
&AUECookbookGameModeBase::DestroyActorFunction, 10);
```

5. Lastly, implement `DestroyActorFunction`:

```
void AUECookbookGameModeBase::DestroyActorFunction()
{
  if (SpawnedActor != nullptr)
  {
    // Displays a red message on the screen for 10 seconds
    GEngine->AddOnScreenDebugMessage(-1, 10, FColor::Red,
                                     TEXT("Actor Destroyed"));
    SpawnedActor->Destroy();
  }
}
```

6. Load the level you created in the previous recipe, which had the game mode set to your custom class.

7. Play your level and use the **World Outliner** to verify that your `SpawnedActor` is deleted after 10 seconds:

How it works...

We declare a UPROPERTY to store our spawned Actor instance, and a custom function so that we can call Destroy() on a timer:

```
UPROPERTY()
AMyFirstActor* SpawnedActor;
UFUNCTION()
void DestroyActorFunction();
```

In BeginPlay, we assign the spawned Actor to our new UPROPERTY:

```
SpawnedActor = GetWorld()->SpawnActor<AMyFirstActor>
  (AMyFirstActor::StaticClass(), SpawnLocation);
```

We then declare a TimerHandle object and pass it to GetWorldTimerManager::SetTimer. SetTimer calls DestroyActorFunction on the object that was pointed to by this pointer after 10 seconds. SetTimer returns an object – a handle – to allow us to cancel the timer if necessary. The SetTimer function takes the TimerHandle object in as a reference parameter, and so we declare it in advance so that we can pass it into the function properly, even if we aren't going to be using it again:

```
FTimerHandle Timer;
GetWorldTimerManager().SetTimer(Timer, this,
  &AUE4CookbookGameMode::DestroyActorFunction, 10);
```

DestroyActorFunction checks whether we have a valid reference to a spawned Actor:

```
void AUE4CookbookGameMode::DestroyActorFunction()
{
  if (SpawnedActor != nullptr)
  {
    // Then we know that SpawnedActor is valid
  }
}
```

If we do, it calls Destroy on the instance so it will be destroyed and, eventually, garbage-collected:

```
SpawnedActor->Destroy();
```

Destroying an Actor after a delay using SetLifeSpan

Let's look at how we can destroy an `Actor`.

How to do it...

1. If you haven't already, create a new C++ class using the wizard. Select `Actor` as your base class. In our case, I will reuse the `AWarrior` class we created previously in this chapter.

2. In the implementation of `Actor`, add the following code to the `BeginPlay` function:

```
// Called when the game starts or when spawned
void AWarrior::BeginPlay()
{
  Super::BeginPlay();

  // Will destroy this object in 10 seconds
  SetLifeSpan(10);
}
```

3. Drag a copy of your custom `Actor` into the viewport within the Editor.

4. Play your level and look at the Outliner to verify that your `Actor` instance disappears after 10 seconds, having destroyed itself.

How it works...

We insert our code into the `BeginPlay` function so that it executes when the game starts.

The `SetLifeSpan` function allows us to specify a duration in seconds, after which the `Actor` calls its own `Destroy()` method.

Implementing the Actor functionality by composition

Custom Actors without components don't have a location, and can't be attached to other Actors. Without a root Component, an Actor doesn't have a base transform, and so it has no location. Most Actors, therefore, require at least one Component to be useful.

We can create custom Actors through composition by adding a number of components to our `Actor`, where each component provides some of the functionality that's required.

Getting ready

This recipe will use the `Actor` class we created in the *Creating a custom Actor in C++* recipe.

How to do it...

1. Add a new member to your custom class in C++ by making the following changes in the `public` section of the `MyFirstActor.h` file:

```
UPROPERTY()
UStaticMeshComponent* Mesh;
```

2. Add the following lines to the constructor inside the `MyFirstActor.cpp` file:

```
// Sets default values
AMyFirstActor::AMyFirstActor()
{
    // Set this actor to call Tick() every frame. You can turn
    // this off to improve performance if you don't need it.
    PrimaryActorTick.bCanEverTick = true;

    // Creates a StaticMeshComponent on this object and assigns
    // Mesh to it
    Mesh = CreateDefaultSubobject<UStaticMeshComponent>
            ("BaseMeshComponent");
}
```

3. Once finished, save both files and compile them by using the **Compile** button in the editor, or building the project in Visual Studio.

4. Once you've compiled this code, drag an instance of your class from the **Content Browser** out into the game environment. Here, you will be able to verify that it now has a transform and other properties, such as a Static Mesh, which comes from the `StaticMeshComponent` that we added:

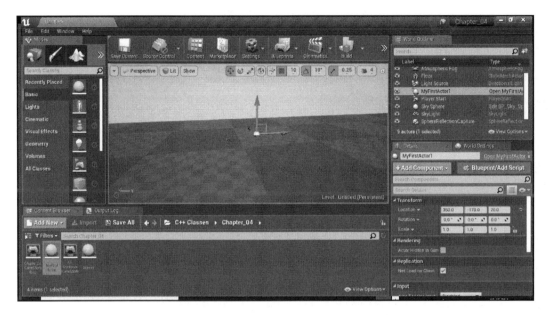

Selecting the instantiated actor

You can use the search bar on the top of the **Details** tab to search for specific components, such as the **Static Mesh** component.

How it works...

The UPROPERTY macro we added to the class declaration is a pointer to hold the component we are using as a subobject of our Actor:

```
UPROPERTY()
UStaticMeshComponent* Mesh;
```

Using the UPROPERTY() macro ensures that the object that was declared in the pointer is considered to be referenced, and won't be garbage-collected (that is, deleted) out from under us, leaving the pointer dangling.

We're using a Static Mesh component, but any of the Actor Component subclasses would work. Note that the asterisk is connected to the variable type in accordance with Epic's style guide.

In the constructor, we initialize the pointer to a known valid value by using a template function, template<class TReturnType> TReturnType* CreateDefaultSubobject(FName SubobjectName, bool bTransient = false).

This function is responsible for calling the engine code to appropriately initialize the component, and return a pointer to the newly constructed object so that we can give our component pointer a default value. This is important because it ensures that the pointer has a valid value at all times, minimizing the risk of dereferencing uninitialized memory.

The function is templated based on the type of object to create, but also takes two parameters – the first one is the name of the subobject, which ideally should be human-readable, and the second is whether the object should be transient (that is, not saved along with the parent object).

See also

- The following recipe shows you how to reference a mesh asset in your Static Mesh Component so that it can be displayed without requiring a user to specify a mesh in the Editor

Loading assets into components using FObjectFinder

In the previous recipe, we created a Static Mesh Component, but we didn't try to load a mesh for the Component to display. While it's possible to do this in the Editor, it is sometimes helpful to specify a default in C++.

Getting ready

Complete the previous recipe so that you have a custom `Actor` subclass with a Static Mesh Component ready.

In your **Content Browser**, click on the **View Options** button and select **Show Engine Content**:

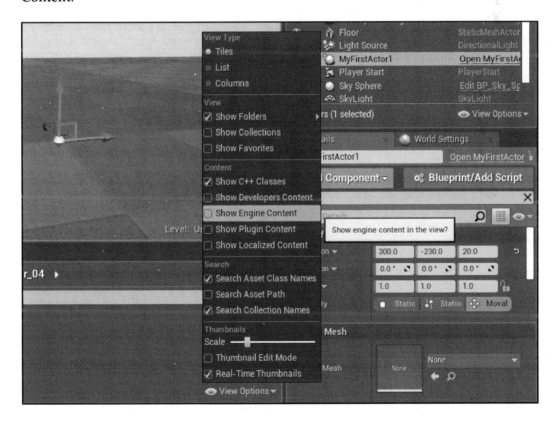

Click on the **Show/Hide Sources** panel button or click on the Folder icon to view the folders in the Content Browser. From there, browse to **Engine Content** and then to **BasicShapes** to see the **Cube** we will be using in this recipe:

How to do it...

1. Add the following code to the constructor of your class:

```cpp
// Sets default values
AMyFirstActor::AMyFirstActor()
{
    // Set this actor to call Tick() every frame. You can turn
this off
    // to improve performance if you don't need it.
    PrimaryActorTick.bCanEverTick = true;

    // Creates a StaticMeshComponent on this object and assigns
Mesh
    // to it
    Mesh = CreateDefaultSubobject<UStaticMeshComponent>
        ("BaseMeshComponent");

    auto MeshAsset =
ConstructorHelpers::FObjectFinder<UStaticMesh>
(TEXT("StaticMesh'/Engine/BasicShapes/Cube.Cube'"));

    // Check if the MeshAsset is valid before setting it
    if (MeshAsset.Object != nullptr)
    {
```

```
Mesh->SetStaticMesh(MeshAsset.Object);
    }


}
```

2. Compile and verify in the Editor that an instance of your class now has a mesh as its visual representation:

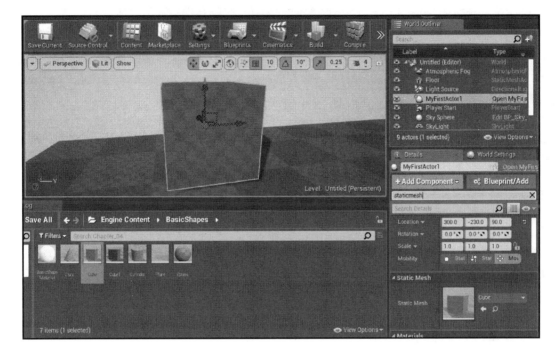

If the actor was placed in the world before these changes, the mesh may only appear after you try moving the actor in the viewport. For whatever reason, it doesn't always update automatically.

How it works...

We create an instance of the FObjectFinder class, passing in the type of asset that we are trying to load as a template parameter.

FObjectFinder is a class template that helps us load assets. When we construct it, we pass in a string that contains a path to the asset that we are trying to load.

The string is of the format `"{ObjectType}'/Path/To/Asset.Asset'"`. Note the use of single quotes in the string.

To get the string for an asset that already exists in the editor, you can right-click on the asset in the **Content Browser** and select **Copy Reference**. This gives you the string so that you can paste it into your code:

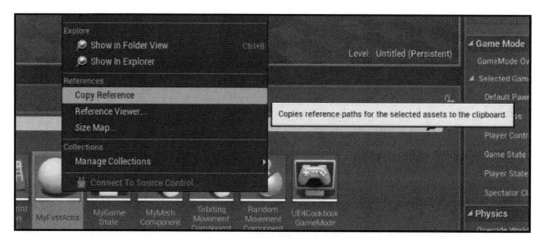

We use the `auto` keyword, from C++11, to avoid typing out our whole object type in its declaration; the compiler deduces it for us. Without `auto`, we would have to use the following code instead:

```
ConstructorHelpers::FObjectFinder<UStaticMesh> MeshAsset =
    ConstructorHelpers::FObjectFinder<UStaticMesh>(TEXT("Static
    Mesh'/Engine/BasicShapes/Cube.Cube'"));
```

The `FObjectFinder` class has a property called `Object` that will either have a pointer to the desired asset, or will be `NULL` if the asset cannot be found.

This means that we can check it against `nullptr`, and if it isn't null, assign it to `Mesh` using `SetStaticMesh`.

Implementing the Actor functionality by inheritance

Inheritance is the second way to implement a custom `Actor`. This is commonly done to make a new subclass, which adds member variables, functions, or a Component to an existing `Actor` class. In this recipe, we are going to add a variable to a custom `GameState` subclass.

How to do it...

1. In the Unreal Editor, click on **Add New** in the **Content Browser**. Then, in **New C++ Class...**, select **Game State Base** as the base class, and give your new class a name (I'll be using the default `MyGameStateBase` by creating the `AMyGameStateBase` class):

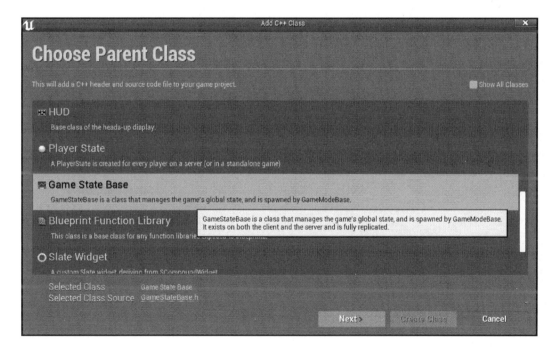

The GameState class is responsible for information that is meant to be shared by all players and is specific to the Game Mode, but is not specific to any individual player. Let's say we are working on a cooperative game and all players are working together for a combined score. It would make sense for this information to be included in this class.

2. Add the following code to the new class header:

```
UCLASS()
class CHAPTER_04_API AMyGameStateBase : public AGameStateBase
{
    GENERATED_BODY()

public:
    // Constructor to initialize CurrentScore
    AMyGameStateBase();

    // Will set the CurrentScore variable
    UFUNCTION()
    void SetScore(int32 NewScore);

    // Getter
    UFUNCTION()
    int32 GetScore();

private:
    UPROPERTY()
    int32 CurrentScore;
};
```

3. Add the following code to the .cpp file:

```
#include "MyGameStateBase.h"

AMyGameStateBase::AMyGameStateBase()
{
  CurrentScore = 0;
}

int32 AMyGameStateBase::GetScore()
{
  return CurrentScore;
}

void AMyGameStateBase::SetScore(int32 NewScore)
{
  CurrentScore = NewScore;
```

}

4. Confirm that your code looks like the following listing, and compile it
using the **Compile** button in the Unreal Editor:

```
//MyGameStateBase.h
#pragma once

#include "CoreMinimal.h"
#include "GameFramework/GameStateBase.h"
#include "MyGameStateBase.generated.h"

/**
 *
 */
UCLASS()
class CHAPTER_04_API AMyGameStateBase : public AGameStateBase
{
    GENERATED_BODY()

public:
    // Constructor to initialize CurrentScore
    AMyGameStateBase();

    // Will set the CurrentScore variable
    UFUNCTION()
    void SetScore(int32 NewScore);

    // Getter
    UFUNCTION()
    int32 GetScore();

private:
    UPROPERTY()
    int32 CurrentScore;
};

//MyGameState.cpp
#include "MyGameStateBase.h"

AMyGameStateBase::AMyGameStateBase()
{
  CurrentScore = 0;
}

int32 AMyGameStateBase::GetScore()
{
    return CurrentScore;
```

```
    }

    void AMyGameStateBase::SetScore(int32 NewScore)
    {
      CurrentScore = NewScore;
    }
```

How it works...

First, we add the declaration of a default constructor:

```
AMyGameState();
```

This allows us to set our new member variable to a safe default value of 0 on object initialization:

```
AMyGameState::AMyGameState()
{
  CurrentScore = 0;
}
```

We use the int32 type when declaring our new variable to ensure portability between the various compilers that Unreal Engine supports. This variable is going to be responsible for storing the current game score while it is running.

 If you want the value to only be positive, you can use the uint32 type instead, which is for unsigned numbers only.

As always, we will be marking our variable with UPROPERTY so that it is garbage-collected appropriately. This variable is marked private so that the only way to change the value is through our functions:

```
UPROPERTY()
int32 CurrentScore;
```

The GetScore function will retrieve the current score and return it to the caller. It is implemented as a simple accessor, which simply returns the underlying member variable.

The second function, SetScore, sets the value of the member variable, allowing external objects to request a change to the score. Placing this request as a function ensures that the GameState can vet such requests, and only allow them when they're valid, to prevent cheating. The specifics of such a check are beyond the scope of this recipe, but the SetScore function is the appropriate place to make them.

 Cedric 'eXi' Neukirchen has created an excellent and very extensive document on this topic here: `http://cedric-neukirchen.net/Downloads/Compendium/UE4_Network_Compendium_by_Cedric_eXi_Neukirchen_BW.pdf`.

Our score functions are declared using the UFUNCTION macro for a number of reasons. First, UFUNCTION, with some additional code, can be called or overridden by Blueprints. Second, UFUNCTION can be marked as exec, which means that they can be run as console commands by a player or developer during a play session, which enables debugging.

See also

- Chapter 9, *Integrating C++ and the Unreal Editor: Part II,* has a recipe called *Creating new console commands,* which you can refer to for more information regarding exec and the console command functionality

Attaching components to create a hierarchy

When creating custom Actors from components, it is important to consider the concept of **attaching**. Attaching components creates a relationship where transformations that are applied to the parent component will also affect the components that are attached to it.

How to do it...

1. Create a new class derived from the `Actor` class using the editor and call it `HierarchyActor`.

2. Add the following properties to your new class in the header file (`HierarchyActor.h`):

```
UCLASS()
class CHAPTER_04_API AHierarchyActor : public AActor
{
    GENERATED_BODY()
public:
    // Sets default values for this actor's properties
    AHierarchyActor();

    UPROPERTY(VisibleAnywhere)
    USceneComponent* Root;

    UPROPERTY(VisibleAnywhere)
    USceneComponent* ChildSceneComponent;

    UPROPERTY(VisibleAnywhere)
    UStaticMeshComponent* BoxOne;
    UPROPERTY(VisibleAnywhere)
    UStaticMeshComponent* BoxTwo;

protected:
    // Called when the game starts or when spawned
    virtual void BeginPlay() override;

public:
    // Called every frame
    virtual void Tick(float DeltaTime) override;

};
```

3. Add the following code to the class constructor:

```
// Sets default values
AHierarchyActor::AHierarchyActor()
{
    // Set this actor to call Tick() every frame. You can turn
this
    // off to improve performance if you don't need it.
    PrimaryActorTick.bCanEverTick = true;

    // Create four subobjects
```

```
    Root = CreateDefaultSubobject<USceneComponent>("Root");

    ChildSceneComponent =
CreateDefaultSubobject<USceneComponent>
                            ("ChildSceneComponent");

    BoxOne =
CreateDefaultSubobject<UStaticMeshComponent>("BoxOne");

    BoxTwo =
CreateDefaultSubobject<UStaticMeshComponent>("BoxTwo");

    // Get a reference to the cube mesh
    auto MeshAsset =
ConstructorHelpers::FObjectFinder<UStaticMesh>
(TEXT("StaticMesh'/Engine/BasicShapes/Cube.Cube'"));
    // Give both boxes a mesh
    if (MeshAsset.Object != nullptr)
    {
        BoxOne->SetStaticMesh(MeshAsset.Object);
        BoxTwo->SetStaticMesh(MeshAsset.Object);
    }

    RootComponent = Root;

    // Set up the object's hierarchy
    BoxOne->AttachTo(Root);
    BoxTwo->AttachTo(ChildSceneComponent);

    ChildSceneComponent->AttachTo(Root);

    // Offset and scale the child from the root
    ChildSceneComponent->SetRelativeTransform(
                            FTransform(FRotator(0, 0, 0),
                                FVector(250, 0, 0),
                                FVector(0.1f))
                                    );


}
```

4. Compile and launch the editor. Drag a copy of `HierarchyActor` into the scene:

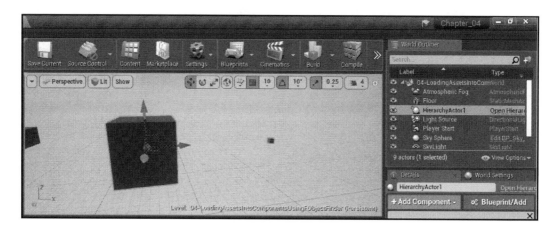

5. Verify that `Actor` has components in a hierarchy, and that the second box is a smaller size:

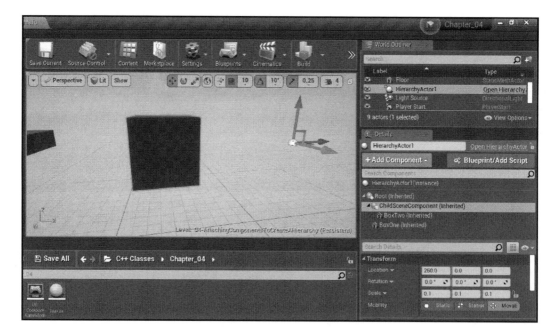

If you do not see the **Root (Inherited)** section under the **Details** tab, it is possible to drag the mouse above the search bar to extend it out.

How it works...

As usual, we create some tagged UPROPERTY Components for our actor. In this case, we added an additional parameter to the tag called VisibleAnywhere, so that we can see our variables within the **Details** tab. We create two Scene Components and two Static Mesh components.

In the constructor, we create default subobjects for each component, as usual.

We then load the static mesh, and if loading is successful, assign it to the two static mesh components so that they have a visual representation.

We then construct a hierarchy within our Actor by attaching components.

We set the first Scene Component as the Actor root. This component will determine the transformations that are applied to all other components in the hierarchy.

We then attach the first box to our new root component and parent the second scene component to the first one.

We attach the second box to our child scene component to demonstrate how changing the transform on that scene component affects its children, but no other components in the object.

Lastly, we set the relative transform of that scene component so that it moves a certain distance away from the origin, and is one-tenth of the scale.

This means that in the Editor, you can see that the BoxTwo component has inherited the translation and scaling of its parent component, ChildSceneComponent.

Creating a custom Actor Component

Actor components are an easy way to implement common functionality that should be shared between Actors. Actor components aren't rendered, but can still perform actions such as subscribing to events, or communicating with other components of the Actor that they are inside.

How to do it...

1. Create an `ActorComponent` named `RandomMovementComponent` using the Editor wizard:

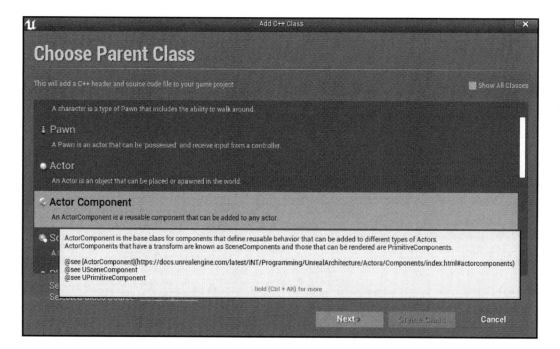

2. Add the following UPROPERTY to the class header in the public section:

```
#pragma once

#include "CoreMinimal.h"
#include "Components/ActorComponent.h"
#include "RandomMovementComponent.generated.h"
```

```
UCLASS( ClassGroup=(Custom),
meta=(BlueprintSpawnableComponent) )
class CHAPTER_04_API URandomMovementComponent : public
UActorComponent
{
    GENERATED_BODY()

public:
    // Sets default values for this component's properties
    URandomMovementComponent();

    UPROPERTY()
    float MovementRadius;

protected:
    // Called when the game starts
    virtual void BeginPlay() override;

public:
    // Called every frame
    virtual void TickComponent(float DeltaTime, ELevelTick
    TickType, FActorComponentTickFunction* ThisTickFunction)
    override;

};
```

3. Add the following code to the constructor's implementation:

```
// Sets default values for this component's properties
URandomMovementComponent::URandomMovementComponent()
{
    // Set this component to be initialized when the game
    // starts, and to be ticked every frame. You can turn
    // these features
    // off to improve performance if you don't need them.
    PrimaryComponentTick.bCanEverTick = true;

    // ...
    MovementRadius = 5;
}
```

4. Lastly, add the following code to the implementation of `TickComponent(` `)`:

```cpp
// Called every frame
void URandomMovementComponent::TickComponent(float DeltaTime,
ELevelTick TickType, FActorComponentTickFunction*
ThisTickFunction)
{
    Super::TickComponent(DeltaTime, TickType,
    ThisTickFunction);

    // ...
    AActor* Parent = GetOwner();

    if (Parent)
    {
        // Find a new position for the object to go to
        auto NewPos = Parent->GetActorLocation() +
                        FVector
                        (
                        FMath::FRandRange(-1, 1) *
                        MovementRadius,
                        FMath::FRandRange(-1, 1) *
                        MovementRadius,
                        FMath::FRandRange(-1, 1) *
                        MovementRadius
                        );
        // Update the object's position
        Parent->SetActorLocation( NewPos );
    }
}
```

5. Compile your project. In the editor, create an empty `Actor` and add your **Random Movement** Component to it. For example, from the **Modes** tab, go to the **Basic** option and drag and drop a Cube into your level.

6. Afterwards, ensure that the **Transform** component's **Mobility** property is set to **Moveable** from the **Details** tab:

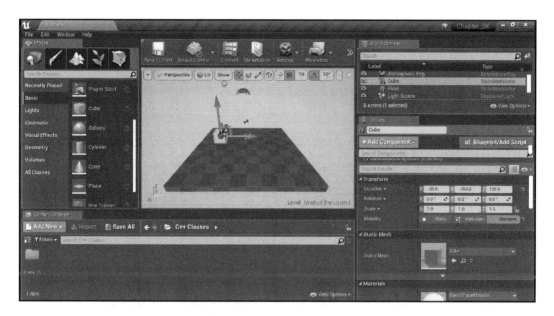

7. Then, with the object selected, click on **Add Component** in the **Details** panel and select **Random Movement**:

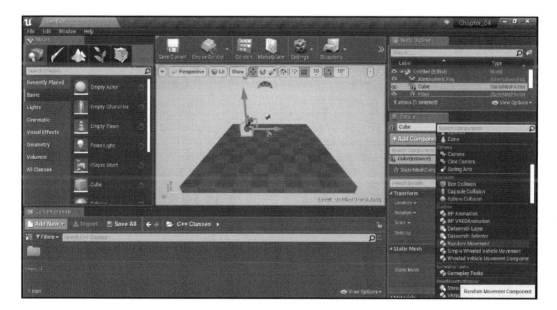

8. Play your level and observe the actor randomly moving around as its location changes every time the `TickComponent` function is called:

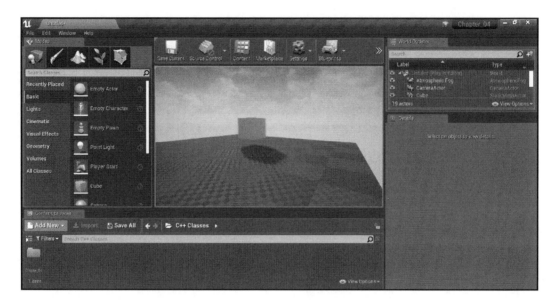

How it works...

First, we add a few specifiers to the `UCLASS` macro that was used in our component's declaration. Adding `BlueprintSpawnableComponent` to the class's meta values means that instances of the component can be added to Blueprint classes in the editor. The `ClassGroup` specifier allows us to indicate what category of class our Component belongs to in the list of classes:

```
UCLASS( ClassGroup=(Custom),
 meta=(BlueprintSpawnableComponent) )
```

Adding `MovementRadius` as a property to the new component allows us to specify how far the component will be allowed to wander in a single frame:

```
UPROPERTY()
float MovementRadius;
```

In the constructor, we initialize this property to a safe default value:

```
MovementRadius = 5;
```

`TickComponent` is a function that is called every frame by the engine, just like `Tick` is for Actors. In its implementation, we retrieve the current location of the component's owner, that is, the `Actor` that contains our component, and we generate an offset in the world space:

```
AActor* Parent = GetOwner();

if (Parent)
{
    // Find a new position for the object to go to
    auto NewPos = Parent->GetActorLocation() +
                FVector
                (
                FMath::FRandRange(-1, 1) * MovementRadius,
                FMath::FRandRange(-1, 1) * MovementRadius,
                FMath::FRandRange(-1, 1) * MovementRadius
                );
    // Update the object's position
    Parent->SetActorLocation( NewPos );
}
```

We add the random offset to the current location to determine a new location and move the owning actor to it. This causes the actor's location to randomly change from frame to frame and dance about.

Creating a custom Scene Component

`Scene` Components are a subclass of `Actor` Components that have a transform, that is, a relative location, rotation, and scale. Just like `Actor` Components, `Scene` Components aren't rendered themselves, but can use their transform for various things, such as spawning other objects at a fixed offset from an `Actor`.

How to do it...

1. Create a custom `SceneComponent` called `ActorSpawnerComponent`:

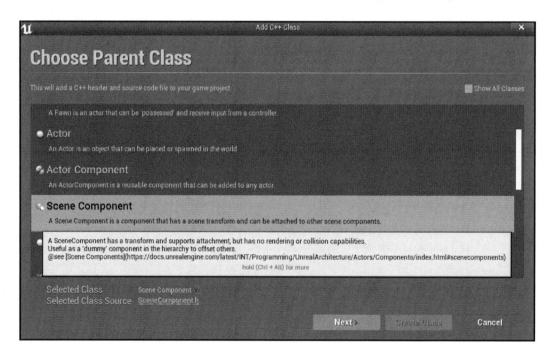

2. Make the following changes to the header:

```
#include "CoreMinimal.h"
#include "Components/SceneComponent.h"
#include "ActorSpawnerComponent.generated.h"


UCLASS( ClassGroup=(Custom),
meta=(BlueprintSpawnableComponent) )
class CHAPTER_04_API UActorSpawnerComponent : public
USceneComponent
{
  GENERATED_BODY()

public:
  // Sets default values for this component's properties
  UActorSpawnerComponent();

  // Will spawn actor when called
```

```
UFUNCTION(BlueprintCallable, Category=Cookbook)
void Spawn();

UPROPERTY(EditAnywhere)
TSubclassOf<AActor> ActorToSpawn;

protected:
  // Called when the game starts
  virtual void BeginPlay() override;

public:
  // Called every frame
  virtual void TickComponent(float DeltaTime, ELevelTick
TickType, FActorComponentTickFunction* ThisTickFunction)
override;

};
```

3. Add the following function implementation to the `.cpp` file:

```
void UActorSpawnerComponent::Spawn()
{
    UWorld* TheWorld = GetWorld();
    if (TheWorld != nullptr)
    {
        FTransform
ComponentTransform(this->GetComponentTransform());
TheWorld->SpawnActor(ActorToSpawn,&ComponentTransform);
    }
}
```

4. Compile and open your project. Drag an empty `Actor` into the scene and add your `ActorSpawnerComponent` to it. Select your new Component in the **Details** panel and assign a value to `ActorToSpawn`.

Now, whenever `Spawn()` is called on an instance of your component, it will instantiate a copy of the `Actor` class that's specified in `ActorToSpawn`.

How it works...

We create the `Spawn` `UFUNCTION` and a variable called `ActorToSpawn`. The
`ActorToSpawnUPROPERTY` is of the `TSubclassOf< >` type, a template type that
allows us to restrict a pointer to either a base class or subclasses thereof. This also
means that within the editor, we will get a pre-filtered list of classes to pick from,
preventing us from accidentally assigning an invalid value:

Inside the `Spawn` function's implementation, we get access to our world. From here,
we check it for validity.

`SpawnActor` wants an `FTransform*` to specify the location to spawn the new actor to, so we create a new stack variable to contain a copy of the current component's transform.

If `TheWorld` is valid, we request it to spawn an instance of the specified `ActorToSpawn` subclass, passing in the address of the `FTransform` we just created, which now contains the desired location for the new actor.

See also

- `Chapter 8`, *Integrating C++ and the Unreal Editor*, contains a much more detailed investigation into how you can make things Blueprint-accessible

Creating an InventoryComponent for an RPG

An `InventoryComponent` enables its containing `Actor` to store `InventoryActors` in its inventory, and place them back into the game world.

Getting ready

Make sure you've followed the *Axis mappings – keyboard, mouse, and gamepad directional input for an FPS character* recipe in `Chapter 6`, *Input and Collision*, before continuing with this recipe, as it shows you how to create a simple character.

Also, the *Instantiating an Actor using SpawnActor* recipe in this chapter shows you how to create a custom `GameMode`.

How to do it...

1. Create an `ActorComponent` subclass using the engine called `InventoryComponent`:

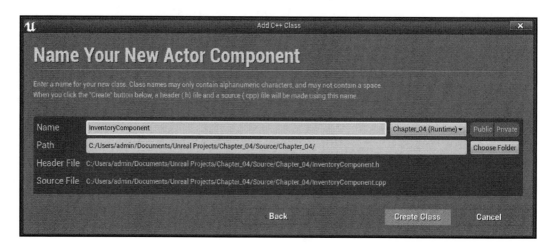

2. Inside of the `InventoryComponent.h` file, add the following code:

```
#pragma once

#include "CoreMinimal.h"
#include "Components/ActorComponent.h"
#include "InventoryComponent.generated.h"


UCLASS( ClassGroup=(Custom),
meta=(BlueprintSpawnableComponent) )
class CHAPTER_04_API UInventoryComponent : public
UActorComponent
{
    GENERATED_BODY()

public:
    // Sets default values for this component's properties
    UInventoryComponent();

    UPROPERTY()
    TArray<AInventoryActor*> CurrentInventory;

    UFUNCTION()
    int32 AddToInventory(AInventoryActor* ActorToAdd);
```

```
UFUNCTION()
void RemoveFromInventory(AInventoryActor* ActorToRemove);

protected:
    // Called when the game starts
    virtual void BeginPlay() override;

public:
    // Called every frame
    virtual void TickComponent(float DeltaTime, ELevelTick
TickType, FActorComponentTickFunction* ThisTickFunction)
override;

};
```

3. Add the following function implementation to the source file:

```
int32 UInventoryComponent::AddToInventory(AInventoryActor*
ActorToAdd)
{
    return CurrentInventory.Add(ActorToAdd);
}

void UInventoryComponent::RemoveFromInventory(AInventoryActor*
ActorToRemove)
{
    CurrentInventory.Remove(ActorToRemove);
}
```

4. Next, create a new `StaticMeshActor` subclass called `InventoryActor`. Remember to check **Show All Classes** to see the `StaticMeshActor` class:

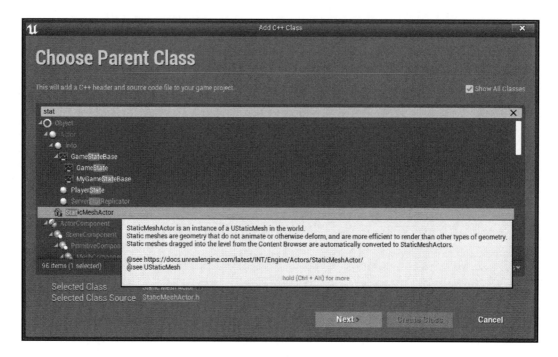

5. Now that we have the file, go to the `InventoryComponent.h` file and add the following includes:

```
#pragma once

#include "CoreMinimal.h"
#include "Components/ActorComponent.h"
#include "InventoryActor.h"
#include "InventoryComponent.generated.h"


UCLASS( ClassGroup=(Custom),
meta=(BlueprintSpawnableComponent) )
class CHAPTER_04_API UInventoryComponent : public
UActorComponent
```

6. Return to the `InventoryActor.h` file and add the following to its declaration:

```
UCLASS()
class CHAPTER_04_API AInventoryActor : public AStaticMeshActor
{
  GENERATED_BODY()

public:
    virtual void PickUp();
    virtual void PutDown(FTransform TargetLocation);
};
```

7. Implement the new functions in the implementation file:

```
void AInventoryActor::PickUp()
{
  SetActorTickEnabled(false);
  SetActorHiddenInGame(true);
  SetActorEnableCollision(false);
}

void AInventoryActor::PutDown(FTransform TargetLocation)
{
  SetActorTickEnabled(true);
  SetActorHiddenInGame(false);
  SetActorEnableCollision(true);
  SetActorLocation(TargetLocation.GetLocation());
}
```

8. Also, change the constructor to look like the following:

```
AInventoryActor::AInventoryActor()
    :Super()
{
    PrimaryActorTick.bCanEverTick = true;
    auto MeshAsset =
ConstructorHelpers::FObjectFinder<UStaticMesh>(TEXT("StaticMes
h'/Engine/BasicShapes/Cube.Cube'"));

    if (MeshAsset.Object != nullptr)
    {
GetStaticMeshComponent()->SetStaticMesh(MeshAsset.Object);
        GetStaticMeshComponent()->SetCollisionProfileName(
UCollisionProfile::Pawn_ProfileName);
    }

    GetStaticMeshComponent()->SetMobility(EComponentMobility::Mova
```

```
ble);

    SetActorEnableCollision(true);
}
```

9. Afterwards, we need to add the following #includes for `InventoryActor.cpp`:

   ```
   #include "InventoryActor.h"
   #include "ConstructorHelpers.h"
   #include "Engine/CollisionProfile.h"
   ```

10. We need to add an `InventoryComponent` to our character so that we have an inventory that we can store items in. Create a class that's derived from the `Character` class called `InventoryCharacter`:

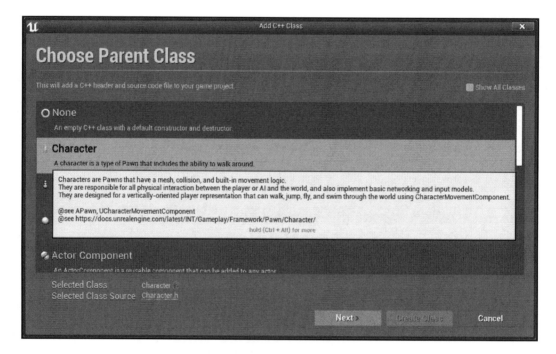

11. Add the following to the #includes:

    ```
    #pragma once

    #include "CoreMinimal.h"
    #include "GameFramework/Character.h"
    #include "InventoryComponent.h"
    ```

```
#include "InventoryActor.h"
#include "InventoryCharacter.generated.h"

UCLASS()
class CHAPTER_04_API AInventoryCharacter : public ACharacter
```

12. Then, add the following to the `InventoryCharacter` class's declaration:

```
UCLASS()
class CHAPTER_04_API AInventoryCharacter : public ACharacter
{
    GENERATED_BODY()

public:
    // Sets default values for this character's properties
    AInventoryCharacter();

    UPROPERTY()
    UInventoryComponent* MyInventory;

    UFUNCTION()
    void DropItem();

    UFUNCTION()
    void TakeItem(AInventoryActor* InventoryItem);

    UFUNCTION()
    virtual void NotifyHit(class UPrimitiveComponent* MyComp,
        AActor* Other, class UPrimitiveComponent* OtherComp,
        bool bSelfMoved, FVector HitLocation, FVector
        HitNormal, FVector NormalImpulse, const FHitResult&
        Hit) override;

    UFUNCTION()
    void MoveForward(float AxisValue);
    void MoveRight(float AxisValue);
    void PitchCamera(float AxisValue);
    void YawCamera(float AxisValue);

protected:
    // Called when the game starts or when spawned
    virtual void BeginPlay() override;

public:
    // Called every frame
    virtual void Tick(float DeltaTime) override;

    // Called to bind functionality to input
```

```
        virtual void SetupPlayerInputComponent(class
UInputComponent* PlayerInputComponent) override;

private:
    FVector MovementInput;
    FVector CameraInput;

};
```

13. Add the following line to the character's constructor implementation:

```
AInventoryCharacter::AInventoryCharacter()
{
    // Set this character to call Tick() every frame. You can
turn this
    // off to improve performance if you don't need it.
    PrimaryActorTick.bCanEverTick = true;

    MyInventory =
CreateDefaultSubobject<UInventoryComponent>("MyInventory");
}
```

14. Add the following code to the overridden SetupPlayerInputComponent:

```
// Called to bind functionality to input
void
AInventoryCharacter::SetupPlayerInputComponent(UInputComponent
* PlayerInputComponent)
{
    Super::SetupPlayerInputComponent(PlayerInputComponent);

    PlayerInputComponent->BindAction("DropItem",
                                     EInputEvent::IE_Pressed,
this,
&AInventoryCharacter::DropItem);

    // Movement
    PlayerInputComponent->BindAxis("MoveForward", this,
&AInventoryCharacter::MoveForward);
    PlayerInputComponent->BindAxis("MoveRight", this,
&AInventoryCharacter::MoveRight);
    PlayerInputComponent->BindAxis("CameraPitch", this,
&AInventoryCharacter::PitchCamera);
    PlayerInputComponent->BindAxis("CameraYaw", this,
&AInventoryCharacter::YawCamera);
}
```

15. Next, add in the `MoveForward`, `MoveRight`, `CameraPitch`, and `CameraYaw` axes and `DropItem` action to the `Input` menu. If you do not recall how to do this, read `Chapter 6`, *Input and Collision*, where we go into detail on this. Here are the settings that I used for this particular example:

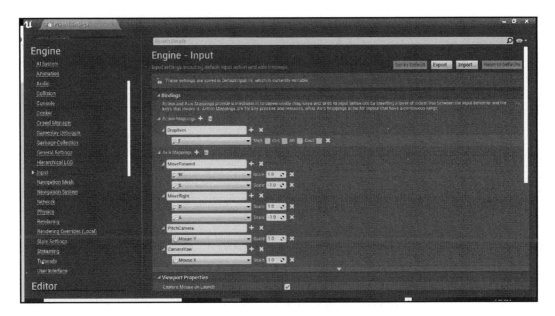

16. Finally, add the following function implementations:

```
void AInventoryCharacter::DropItem()
{
    if (MyInventory->CurrentInventory.Num() == 0)
    {
        return;
    }
    AInventoryActor* Item =
MyInventory->CurrentInventory.Last();
    MyInventory->RemoveFromInventory(Item);


    FVector ItemOrigin;
    FVector ItemBounds;
    Item->GetActorBounds(false, ItemOrigin, ItemBounds);

    FTransform PutDownLocation = GetTransform() +
FTransform(RootComponent->GetForwardVector() *
ItemBounds.GetMax());
```

```
        Item->PutDown(PutDownLocation);
    }


    void AInventoryCharacter::NotifyHit(class UPrimitiveComponent*
    MyComp, AActor* Other, class UPrimitiveComponent* OtherComp,
    bool bSelfMoved, FVector HitLocation, FVector HitNormal,
    FVector NormalImpulse, const FHitResult& Hit)
    {
        AInventoryActor* InventoryItem =
    Cast<AInventoryActor>(Other);
        if (InventoryItem != nullptr)
        {
            TakeItem(InventoryItem);
        }

    }

    void AInventoryCharacter::TakeItem(AInventoryActor*
    InventoryItem)
    {
        InventoryItem->PickUp();
        MyInventory->AddToInventory(InventoryItem);
    }

    //Movement
    void AInventoryCharacter::MoveForward(float AxisValue)
    {
        MovementInput.X = FMath::Clamp<float>(AxisValue, -1.0f,
    1.0f);
    }

    void AInventoryCharacter::MoveRight(float AxisValue)
    {
        MovementInput.Y = FMath::Clamp<float>(AxisValue, -1.0f,
    1.0f);
    }

    void AInventoryCharacter::PitchCamera(float AxisValue)
    {
        CameraInput.Y = AxisValue;
    }

    void AInventoryCharacter::YawCamera(float AxisValue)
    {
        CameraInput.X = AxisValue;
    }
```

17. To handle the movement functions, update the `Tick` function to the
following:

```
// Called every frame
void AInventoryCharacter::Tick(float DeltaTime)
{
    Super::Tick(DeltaTime);

    if (!MovementInput.IsZero())
    {
        MovementInput *= 100;

        //Scale our movement input axis values by 100 units
        // per second
        FVector InputVector = FVector(0, 0, 0);
        InputVector += GetActorForwardVector()*
MovementInput.X *
        DeltaTime;
        InputVector += GetActorRightVector()* MovementInput.Y
*
        DeltaTime;
        /* GEngine->AddOnScreenDebugMessage(-1, 1,
            FColor::Red,
            FString::Printf(TEXT("x- %f, y - %f, z - %f"),
        InputVector.X, InputVector.Y, InputVector.Z)); */
    }

    if (!CameraInput.IsNearlyZero())
    {
        FRotator NewRotation = GetActorRotation();
        NewRotation.Pitch += CameraInput.Y;
        NewRotation.Yaw += CameraInput.X;

        APlayerController* MyPlayerController =
        Cast<APlayerController>(GetController());
        if (MyPlayerController != nullptr)
        {
            MyPlayerController->AddYawInput(CameraInput.X);
            MyPlayerController->AddPitchInput(CameraInput.Y);
        }
        SetActorRotation(NewRotation);
    }
}
```

18. Then, add the following #include:

```
#include "InventoryCharacter.h"
#include "GameFramework/CharacterMovementComponent.h"
```

19. Compile your code and test it in the Editor. Create a new level and drag a few instances of InventoryActor out into your scene.

20. Refer to the *Instantiating an Actor using SpawnActor* recipe if you need a reminder of how to override the current game mode. Add the following line to the constructor of your Game Mode from that recipe, and then set your level's GameMode to the one you created in that recipe:

```
#include "Chapter_04GameModeBase.h"
#include "InventoryCharacter.h"

AChapter_04GameModeBase::AChapter_04GameModeBase()
{
    DefaultPawnClass = AInventoryCharacter::StaticClass();
}
```

21. Of course, we will also need to update the GameMode's .h file:

```
UCLASS()
class CHAPTER_04_API AChapter_04GameModeBase : public
AGameModeBase
{
    GENERATED_BODY()
    AChapter_04GameModeBase();
};
```

22. Compile and launch your project. If all went well, you should be able to pick up objects by walking on them:

23. Then, you can drop the items whenever you hit the key that's assigned for `DropItem` in front of you:

How it works...

Our new component contains an array of actors, storing them by pointer as well as declaring functions that add or remove items to the array. These functions are simple wrappers around the TArray add/remove functionality, but allow us to optionally do things such as checking whether the array is within a specified size limit before going ahead with storing the item.

InventoryActor is a base class that can be used for all of the items that can be taken by a player.

In the PickUp function, we need to disable the actor when it is picked up. To do that, we have to do the following:

- Disable actor ticking
- Hide the actor
- Disable collision

We do this with the SetActorTickEnabled, SetActorHiddenInGame, and SetActorEnableCollision functions.

The PutDown function is the reverse of this. We enable actor ticking, unhide the actor, and then turn its collision back on, and we transport the actor to the desired location.

We add an InventoryComponent to our new character as well as a function to take items.

In the constructor for our character, we create a default subobject for our InventoryComponent. We also add a NotifyHit override so that we are notified when the character hits other Actors.

Inside this function, we cast the other actor to an InventoryActor. If the cast is successful, then we know our Actor was an InventoryActor, and so we can call the TakeItem function to take it.

In the `TakeItem` function, we notify the Inventory item actor that we want to pick it up, and then we add it to our inventory.

The last piece of functionality in the `InventoryCharacter` is the `DropItem` function. This function checks whether we have any items in our inventory. If it has any items, we remove it from our inventory, and then we calculate a safe distance in front of our player character to drop the item using the Item Bounds to get its maximum bounding box dimension.

We then inform the item that we are placing it in the world at the desired location.

See also

- `Chapter 5`, *Handling Events and Delegates,* has a detailed explanation of how events and input handling work together within the Engine, as well as a recipe for the `SimpleCharacter` class we mentioned in this recipe
- `Chapter 6`, *Input and Collision,* also has recipes concerning the binding of input actions and axes

Creating an OrbitingMovement Component

This component is similar to `RotatingMovementComponent` in that it is designed to make the components parented to it move in a particular way. In this instance, it will move any attached components in an orbit around a fixed point at a fixed distance.

This could be used, for example, for a shield that orbits around a character in an **Action RPG**.

How to do it...

1. Create a new `SceneComponent` subclass called `OrbitingMovementComponent`:

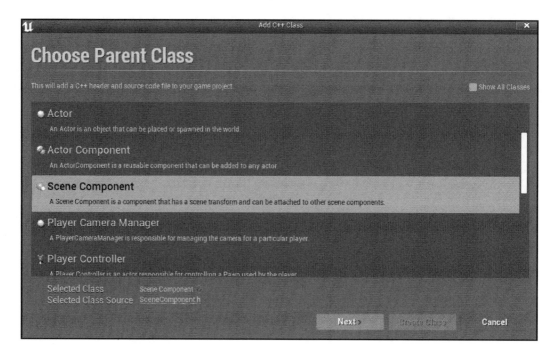

2. Add the following properties to the class declaration:

```
UCLASS( ClassGroup=(Custom),
meta=(BlueprintSpawnableComponent) )
class CHAPTER_04_API UOrbitingMovementComponent : public
USceneComponent
{
    GENERATED_BODY()

public:
    // Sets default values for this component's properties
    UOrbitingMovementComponent();

    UPROPERTY()
    bool RotateToFaceOutwards;
    UPROPERTY()
    float RotationSpeed;
```

```
UPROPERTY()
float OrbitDistance;

float CurrentValue;

protected:
  // Called when the game starts
  virtual void BeginPlay() override;

public:
  // Called every frame
  virtual void TickComponent(float DeltaTime, ELevelTick
TickType, FActorComponentTickFunction* ThisTickFunction)
override;
```

3. Add the following code to the constructor:

```
// Sets default values for this component's properties
UOrbitingMovementComponent::UOrbitingMovementComponent()
{
    // Set this component to be initialized when the game
    // starts, and to be ticked every frame. You can turn
    // these features off to improve performance if you
    // don't need them.
    PrimaryComponentTick.bCanEverTick = true;
    // ...
    RotationSpeed = 5;
    OrbitDistance = 100;
    CurrentValue = 0;
    RotateToFaceOutwards = true;
}
```

4. Add the following code to the `TickComponent` function:

```
// Called every frame
void UOrbitingMovementComponent::TickComponent(float
DeltaTime,
                                               ELevelTick
TickType,
FActorComponentTickFunction*
                                          ThisTickFunction)
{
    Super::TickComponent(DeltaTime, TickType,
ThisTickFunction);

    // ...
    float CurrentValueInRadians =
FMath::DegreesToRadians<float>(
```

```
                                                    CurrentValue);

            SetRelativeLocation(
                    FVector(OrbitDistance *
        FMath::Cos(CurrentValueInRadians),
                        OrbitDistance *
        FMath::Sin(CurrentValueInRadians),
                            RelativeLocation.Z)
                            );

            if (RotateToFaceOutwards)
            {
                FVector LookDir = (RelativeLocation).GetSafeNormal();
                FRotator LookAtRot = LookDir.Rotation();
                SetRelativeRotation(LookAtRot);
            }

            CurrentValue = FMath::Fmod(CurrentValue + (RotationSpeed *
                            DeltaTime), 360);
    }
```

5. You can test this component by creating a simple `Actor` Blueprint.

6. Add an `OrbitingMovement` Component to your `Actor`, and then add a few meshes using the `Cube` component. Parent them to the `OrbitingMovement` component by dragging them onto it in the **Components** panel. The resulting hierarchy should look as follows:

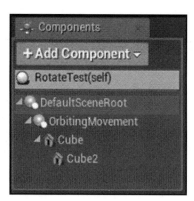

7. Refer to the *Creating a custom Actor Component* recipe if you're unsure of the process.

8. Hit play to see the meshes moving around in a circular pattern around the center of the `Actor`.

How it works...

The properties that are added to the component are the basic parameters that we use to customize the circular motion of the component.

`RotateToFaceOutwards` specifies whether the component will orient to face away from the center of rotation on every update. `RotationSpeed` is the number of degrees the component rotates every second.

`OrbitDistance` indicates the distance that the components that rotate must be moved from the origin. `CurrentValue` is the current rotation position in degrees.

Inside our constructor, we establish some sane defaults for our new component.

In the `TickComponent` function, we calculate the location and rotation of our component.

The formula in the next step requires our angles to be expressed in radians rather than degrees. Radians describe an angle in terms of π. First, we use the `DegreesToRadians` function to convert our current value in degrees to radians.

The `SetRelativeLocation` function uses the general equation for circular motion, that is, *Pos(θ) = cos(θ in radians), sin(θ in radians)*. We preserve the Z axis position of each object.

The next step is to rotate the object back toward the origin (or directly away from it). This is only calculated if `RotateToFaceOutwards` is `true`, and involves getting the relative offset of the component to its parent and creating a rotator based on a vector pointing from the parent to the current relative offset. We then set the relative rotation to the resulting rotator.

Lastly, we increment the current value in degrees so that it moves `RotationSpeed` units per second, clamping the resulting value between 0 and 360 to allow the rotation to loop.

Creating a building that spawns units

For this recipe, we will create a building that spawns units at a fixed time interval at a particular location.

How to do it...

1. Create a new `Actor` subclass in the editor, which we will name `Barracks`:

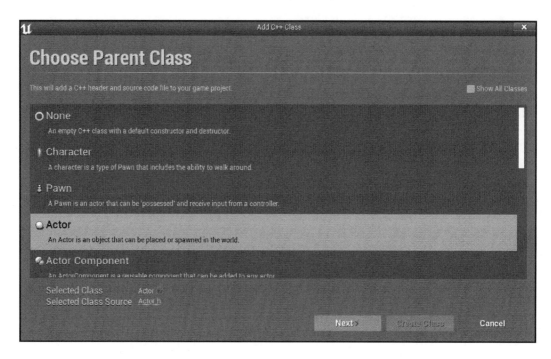

2. Then, add the following implementation to the class:

```
UCLASS()
class CHAPTER_04_API ABarracks : public AActor
{
    GENERATED_BODY()
public:
    // Sets default values for this actor's properties
    ABarracks();

protected:
    // Called when the game starts or when spawned
    virtual void BeginPlay() override;

public:
    // Called every frame
    virtual void Tick(float DeltaTime) override;

    UPROPERTY()
```

```
        UStaticMeshComponent* BuildingMesh;

        UPROPERTY()
        UParticleSystemComponent* SpawnPoint;
        UPROPERTY()
        UClass* UnitToSpawn;
        UPROPERTY()
        float SpawnInterval;
        UFUNCTION()
        void SpawnUnit();
        UFUNCTION()
        void EndPlay(const EEndPlayReason::Type EndPlayReason)
override;
        UPROPERTY()
        FTimerHandle SpawnTimerHandle;

    };
```

3. Add the following code to the constructor:

```
#include "Barracks.h"
#include "Particles/ParticleSystemComponent.h"
#include "BarracksUnit.h"

// Sets default values
ABarracks::ABarracks()
{
    // Set this actor to call Tick() every frame. You can turn
    // this off to improve performance if you don't need it.
    PrimaryActorTick.bCanEverTick = true;

    BuildingMesh =
CreateDefaultSubobject<UStaticMeshComponent>(
                    "BuildingMesh");

    SpawnPoint =
CreateDefaultSubobject<UParticleSystemComponent>(
                    "SpawnPoint");

    SpawnInterval = 10;

    auto MeshAsset =
ConstructorHelpers::FObjectFinder<UStaticMesh>(
                        TEXT("Static
                        Mesh'/Engine/BasicShapes/Cube.Cube'"));

    if (MeshAsset.Object != nullptr)
    {
```

```
            BuildingMesh->SetStaticMesh(MeshAsset.Object);
        }

        auto ParticleSystem =
        ConstructorHelpers::FObjectFinder<UParticleSystem>
    (TEXT("ParticleSystem'/Engine/Tutorial/SubEditors/TutorialAsse
    ts
        /TutorialParticleSystem.TutorialParticleSystem'"));
        if (ParticleSystem.Object != nullptr)
        {
          SpawnPoint->SetTemplate(ParticleSystem.Object);
        }

        SpawnPoint->SetRelativeScale3D(FVector(0.5, 0.5, 0.5));
        UnitToSpawn = ABarracksUnit::StaticClass();
    }
```

Currently, we do not have the `BarracksUnit` class created, so you'll see Visual Studio complain. We'll implement that as soon as we finish up the `Barracks` class.

4. Add the following code to the `BeginPlay` function:

```
// Called when the game starts or when spawned
void ABarracks::BeginPlay()
{
    Super::BeginPlay();

    RootComponent = BuildingMesh;
    SpawnPoint->AttachTo(RootComponent);
    SpawnPoint->SetRelativeLocation(FVector(150, 0, 0));
    GetWorld()->GetTimerManager().SetTimer(SpawnTimerHandle,
    this, &ABarracks::SpawnUnit, SpawnInterval, true);
}
```

5. Create the implementation for the `SpawnUnit` function:

```
void ABarracks::SpawnUnit()
{
  FVector SpawnLocation = SpawnPoint->GetComponentLocation();
  GetWorld()->SpawnActor(UnitToSpawn, &SpawnLocation);
}
```

6. Implement the overridden EndPlay function:

```
void ABarracks::EndPlay(const EEndPlayReason::Type
EndPlayReason)
{
  Super::EndPlay(EndPlayReason);
  GetWorld()->GetTimerManager().ClearTimer(SpawnTimerHandle);
}
```

7. Next, create a new character subclass, BarracksUnit, and add one property:

```
UPROPERTY()
UParticleSystemComponent* VisualRepresentation;
```

8. You'll need to add the following #include to get access to the UParticleSystemComponent class:

```
#include "Particles/ParticleSystemComponent.h"
```

9. Initialize the component in the constructor implementation:

```
VisualRepresentation =
CreateDefaultSubobject<UParticleSystemComponent>("SpawnPoin
t");auto ParticleSystem =
ConstructorHelpers::FObjectFinder<UParticleSystem>(TEXT("Pa
rticleSystem'/Engine/Tutorial/SubEditors/TutorialAssets/Tut
orialParticleSystem.TutorialParticleSystem'"));
if (ParticleSystem.Object != nullptr)
{
  SpawnPoint->SetTemplate(ParticleSystem.Object);
}
SpawnPoint->SetRelativeScale3D(FVector(0.5, 0.5, 0.5));
SpawnCollisionHandlingMethod =
ESpawnActorCollisionHandlingMethod::AlwaysSpawn;
```

10. Attach the visual representation to the root component:

```
void ABarracksUnit::BeginPlay()
{
  Super::BeginPlay();
  SpawnPoint->AttachTo(RootComponent);
}
```

11. Lastly, add the following to the `Tick` function to get the spawned actor moving:

```
SetActorLocation(GetActorLocation() + FVector(10, 0, 0));
```

12. Compile your project. Place a copy of the barracks actor into the level. You can then observe it spawning the character at fixed intervals.

    If all went well, you should be able to drag and drop a `Barracks` object into the world and play the game. Afterwards, you'll notice objects (`BarracksUnit` objects) being spawned from a singular point and continually moving in a direction!

How it works...

First, we create the barracks actor. We add a particle system component to indicate where the new units will be spawning and a static mesh for the visual representation of the building.

In the constructor, we initialize the components and then set their values using `FObjectFinder`. We also set the class to spawn using the `StaticClass` function to retrieve a `UClass*` instance from a class type.

In the `BeginPlay` function of the barracks, we create a timer that calls our `SpawnUnit` function at fixed intervals. We store the timer handle in a member variable in the class so that when our instance is being destroyed, we can halt the timer; otherwise, when the timer triggers again, we'll encounter a crash where the object pointer is dereferenced.

The `SpawnUnit` function gets the world space location of the `SpawnPoint` object, and then asks the world to spawn an instance of our unit class at that location.

`BarracksUnit` has code in its `Tick()` function to move forward by 10 units every frame so that each spawned unit will move to make room for the next one.

The `EndPlay` function override calls the parent class implementation of the function, which is important if there are timers to cancel or perform deinitialization in the parent class. It then uses the timer handle stored in `BeginPlay` to cancel the timer.

5
Handling Events and Delegates

We will cover the following recipes in this chapter:

- Handling events that have been implemented via virtual functions
- Creating a delegate that is bound to a UFUNCTION
- Unregistering a delegate
- Creating a delegate that takes input parameters
- Passing payload data with a delegate binding
- Creating a multicast delegate
- Creating a custom Event
- Creating a Time of Day handler
- Creating a respawning pickup for a First Person Shooter

Introduction

Unreal uses events to notify objects about things that happen in the game world in an efficient manner. Events and delegates are useful to ensure that these notifications can be issued in a way that minimizes class coupling, and allows arbitrary classes to subscribe to be notified.

Technical requirements

This chapter requires the use of Unreal Engine 4 and uses Visual Studio 2017 as the IDE. Instructions on how to install both pieces of software and their requirements can be found in Chapter 1, *UE4 Development Tools*, of this book.

Handling events that have been implemented via virtual functions

Some `Actor` and `Component` classes provided with Unreal include event handlers in the form of `virtual` functions. This recipe will show you how to customize those handlers by overriding the `virtual` functions in question.

How to do it...

1. Create an empty `Actor` in the Editor. Call it `MyTriggerVolume`:

2. Add the following code to the class header:

```
UPROPERTY()
UBoxComponent* TriggerZone;

UFUNCTION()
virtual void NotifyActorBeginOverlap(AActor* OtherActor)
override;

UFUNCTION()
virtual void NotifyActorEndOverlap(AActor* OtherActor)
override;
```

3. Because we are referencing a class that's isn't a part of our project already, we also need to add an #include:

```
#include "CoreMinimal.h"
#include "GameFramework/Actor.h"
#include "Components/BoxComponent.h"
#include "MyTriggerVolume.generated.h"
```

Remember to place the include above the .generated.h file.

4. Add the following script to the constructor to create the BoxComponent. This will trigger our events:

```
// Sets default values
AMyTriggerVolume::AMyTriggerVolume()
{
    // Set this actor to call Tick() every frame. You can turn
    // this off to improve performance if you don't need it.
    PrimaryActorTick.bCanEverTick = true;

    // Create a new component for the instance and initialize
        it
    TriggerZone =
CreateDefaultSubobject<UBoxComponent>("TriggerZone");
    TriggerZone->SetBoxExtent(FVector(200, 200, 100));
}
```

5. Add the implementation for the preceding additional functions to the .cpp file:

```
void AMyTriggerVolume::NotifyActorBeginOverlap(AActor*
OtherActor)
{
    auto Message = FString::Printf(TEXT("%s entered me"),
                *(OtherActor->GetName()));

    GEngine->AddOnScreenDebugMessage(-1, 1, FColor::Red,
Message);
}

void AMyTriggerVolume::NotifyActorEndOverlap(AActor*
OtherActor)
{
    auto Message = FString::Printf(TEXT("%s left me"),
                *(OtherActor->GetName()));

    GEngine->AddOnScreenDebugMessage(-1, 1, FColor::Red,
```

```
Message);
  }
```

6. Compile your project and place an instance of `MyTriggerActor` into the level:

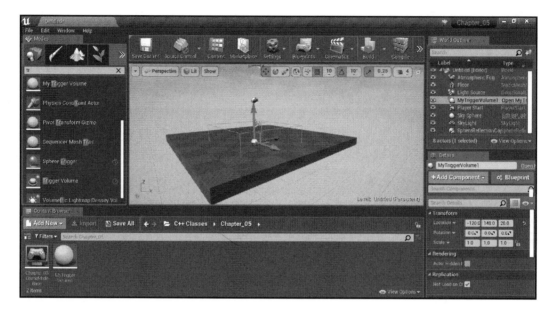

Trigger Volume placed in the level

You should see the lines around the object, indicating where collisions would take place. Feel free to move it around and/or adjust the properties as needed so that they fit where you want.

7. Then, verify that overlap/touch events are handled by walking into the volume and viewing the output that's printed to the screen:

How it works...

As always, we first declare a UPROPERTY to hold a reference to our component subobject. We then create two UFUNCTION declarations. These are marked as virtual and override so that the compiler understands that we want to replace the parent implementation, and that our function implementations can be replaced in turn.

In the constructor for the object, we create the subobject using the CreateDefaultSubobject function. Afterwards, we set the extents (size) of the box via the SetBoxExtent function using a FVector holding the X, Y, and Z sizes we want the box to have, respectively.

In the implementation of the functions, we create an FString from some preset text and substitute some data parameters using the FString::Printf function. Note that the Actor->GetName() function returns an FString as well, and is dereferenced using the * operator before being passed into FString::Printf. Not doing this results in an error.

This FString is then passed to a global engine function, AddOnScreenDebugMessage, to display this information on the screen.

The first argument of -1 tells the engine that duplicate strings are allowed, the second parameter is the length of time the message should be displayed for in seconds, the third argument is the color, and the fourth is the actual string to print itself. While it would be possible to not create an additional variable and just put the information within the function call, it makes the code more difficult to read.

Now, when a component of our actor overlaps something else, its UpdateOverlaps function will call NotifyActorBeginOverlap, and the virtual function dispatch will call our custom implementation.

There's more...

Unreal's documentation contains information on all of the variables and functions that all of their built-in classes have. For instance, the Actor class can be found at https://api.unrealengine.com/INT/API/Runtime/Engine/GameFramework/AActor/index.html, as shown in the following screenshot:

If you scroll down to the functions we used in this recipe, you can see more information on them (feel free to use *Ctrl + F* to find a particular item):

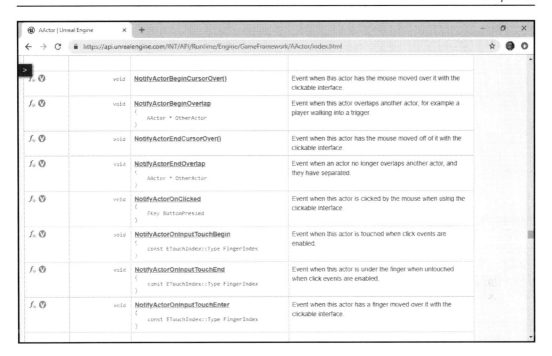

On the left-most tab, you'll see some icons where the blue circle with the **V** inside it indicates that the function is `virtual` and can be overwritten in your own class. If you haven't gotten a chance to yet, it would also be a good idea to look at all of the events so that you are familiar with what's already been included.

Creating a delegate that is bound to a UFUNCTION

Pointers are great since we are able to assign them at runtime and can change where in memory they are pointing to. In addition to standard types, we can also create pointers to functions as well, but these raw function pointers are unsafe to use for a number of reasons. Delegates are a much safer version of function pointers that gives us the flexibility to call a function without knowing which function is assigned until the moment it is called. This flexibility is one of the main reasons to prefer delegates over static functions. This recipe shows you how to associate a `UFUNCTION` to a delegate so that it will be called when the delegate is executed.

Getting ready

Ensure you've followed the previous recipe in order to create the `MyTriggerVolume` class because we will be using that to call our delegate.

How to do it...

1. Inside our Unreal project's `GameMode` header, declare the delegate with the following macro, just before the class declaration:

```
DECLARE_DELEGATE(FStandardDelegateSignature)
UCLASS()
class CHAPTER_05_API AChapter_05GameModeBase : public
AGameModeBase
```

2. Add a new member to our game mode:

```
DECLARE_DELEGATE(FStandardDelegateSignature)
UCLASS()
class CHAPTER_05_API AChapter_05GameModeBase : public
AGameModeBase
{
  GENERATED_BODY()

public:
    FStandardDelegateSignature MyStandardDelegate;
};
```

3. Create a new `Actor` class called `DelegateListener`:

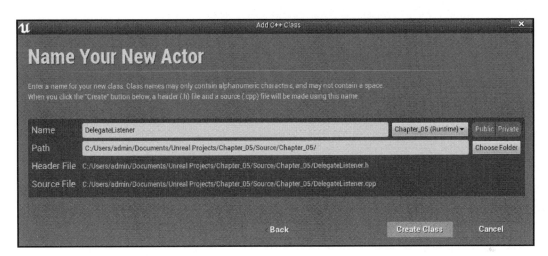

4. Add the following to the declaration of that class:

```
UFUNCTION()
void EnableLight();

UPROPERTY()
UPointLightComponent* PointLight;
```

5. Since the script doesn't know what the `UPointLightComponent` class is, we will also need to add the following new `#include` above the generated `.h` file:

```
#include "CoreMinimal.h"
#include "GameFramework/Actor.h"
#include "Components/PointLightComponent.h"
#include "DelegateListener.generated.h"
```

6. In the class implementation `.cpp` file, add the following code, in bold, to the constructor:

```
ADelegateListener::ADelegateListener()
{
  // Set this actor to call Tick() every frame. You can turn
this
  // off to improve performance if you don't need it.
  PrimaryActorTick.bCanEverTick = true;

  // Create a point light
```

```
    PointLight =
CreateDefaultSubobject<UPointLightComponent>("PointLight");
    RootComponent = PointLight;

    // Turn it off at the beginning so we can turn it on later
    //    through code
    PointLight->SetVisibility(false);

    // Set the color to blue to make it easier to see
    PointLight->SetLightColor(FLinearColor::Blue);

}
```

7. Inside the `ADelegateListener::BeginPlay` implementation, add the following code:

```
void ADelegateListener::BeginPlay()
{
    Super::BeginPlay();

    UWorld* TheWorld = GetWorld();
    if (TheWorld != nullptr)
    {
        AGameModeBase* GameMode =
UGameplayStatics::GetGameMode(TheWorld);

        AChapter_05GameModeBase * MyGameMode =
Cast<AChapter_05GameModeBase>(GameMode);

        if (MyGameMode != nullptr)
        {
            MyGameMode->MyStandardDelegate.BindUObject(this,
&ADelegateListener::EnableLight);
        }
    }
}
```

8. Since the script does not know about the `UGameplayStatics` class or our GameMode in the `DelegateListener.cpp` file, add the following #includes:

```
#include "DelegateListener.h"
#include "Chapter_05GameModeBase.h"
#include "Kismet/GameplayStatics.h"
```

9. Lastly, implement `EnableLight`:

```
void ADelegateListener::EnableLight()
{
   PointLight->SetVisibility(true);
}
```

10. Put the following code in our `NotifyActorBeginOverlap` function of `TriggerVolume`:

```
void AMyTriggerVolume::NotifyActorBeginOverlap(AActor*
OtherActor)
{
    auto Message = FString::Printf(TEXT("%s entered me"),
                    *(OtherActor->GetName()));

    GEngine->AddOnScreenDebugMessage(-1, 1, FColor::Red,
Message);

    // Call our delegate
    UWorld* TheWorld = GetWorld();

    if (TheWorld != nullptr)
    {
        AGameModeBase* GameMode =
UGameplayStatics::GetGameMode(TheWorld);
        AChapter_05GameModeBase * MyGameMode =
Cast<AChapter_05GameModeBase>(GameMode);

        if(MyGameMode != nullptr)
        {
            MyGameMode->MyStandardDelegate.ExecuteIfBound();
        }
    }
}
```

11. Just like we previously included, be sure that you add the following code to your CPP file too so that the compiler knows about the class before we use it:

```
#include "MyTriggerVolume.h"
#include "Chapter_05GameModeBase.h"
#include "Kismet/GameplayStatics.h"
```

12. Compile your game. Make sure that your game mode is set in the current level (refer to the *Instantiating an Actor using SpawnActor* recipe in `Chapter 4`, *Actors and Components*, if you don't know how), and drag a copy of your `MyTriggerVolume` out into the level. Also, drag a copy of `DelegateListener` out into the level, and place it about 100 units above a flat surface so that we can see the light when playing the game:

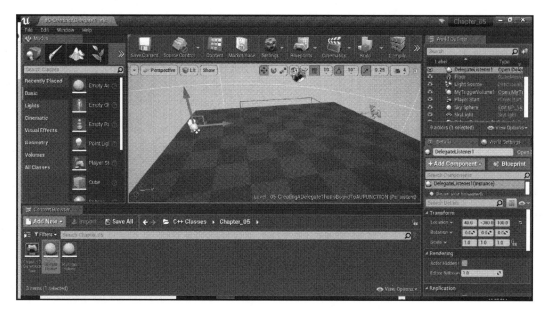

The DelegateListener positioned above the ground plane

13. When you hit **Play** and walk into the area covered by the Trigger volume, you should see the `PointLight` component, which we added to `DelegateListener`, turn on:

How it works...

Inside our GameMode header, we declare a type of delegate that doesn't take any parameters, called FStandardDelegateSignature. We then create an instance of the delegate as a member of our GameModeBase class.

We add a PointLight component inside of the DelegateListener so that we have a visual representation of the delegate being executed that we can turn on later on. In the constructor, we initialize our PointLight, and then disable it. To make it easier to see, we also change the color to blue.

We override BeginPlay. We first call the parent class's implementation of BeginPlay(). Then, we get the game world, retrieving the GameMode class using GetGameMode(). Casting the resulting AGameMode* to a pointer of our GameMode class requires the use of the Cast template function. We can then access the delegate instance member of the GameMode and bind our EnableLight function to the delegate so that it will be called when the delegate is executed. In this case, we are binding to UFUNCTION(), so we use BindUObject.

If we had wanted to bind to a plain C++ class function, we would have used `BindRaw`. If we had wanted to bind to a static function, we would have used `BindStatic()`. If you're using these, you must be very careful and unbind them manually when an object is being destroyed. It's the same as using naked C++ memory allocation. When it comes to UE4, the general rule of thumb is to use a `UObject` wherever possible. It saves a lot of headaches!

When `TriggerVolume` overlaps the player, it retrieves `GameMode`, then calls `ExecuteIfBound` on the delegate. `ExecuteIfBound` checks that there's a function bound to the delegate, and then invokes it for us. The `EnableLight` function enables the `PointLight` component when it's invoked by the delegate object.

See also

- The next recipe, *Unregistering a delegate,* shows you how to safely unregister your delegate binding in the event of the `Listener` being destroyed before the delegate is called

 To learn more about this and additional options for working with delegates, check out `https://docs.unrealengine.com/en-us/ Programming/UnrealArchitecture/Delegates`.

Unregistering a delegate

Sometimes, it is necessary to remove a delegate binding. This is like setting a function pointer to `nullptr` so that it no longer references an object that has been deleted.

Getting ready

You'll need to follow the previous recipe so that you have a delegate to unregister.

How to do it...

1. In the `DelegateListener` class, add the following overridden function declaration:

```
UFUNCTION()
virtual void EndPlay(const EEndPlayReason::Type EndPlayReason)
override;
```

2. Implement the function like this:

```
void ADelegateListener::EndPlay(const EEndPlayReason::Type
EndPlayReason)
{
    Super::EndPlay(EndPlayReason);
    UWorld* TheWorld = GetWorld();

    if (TheWorld != nullptr)
    {
        AGameModeBase* GameMode =
UGameplayStatics::GetGameMode(TheWorld);

        AChapter_05GameModeBase * MyGameMode =
Cast<AChapter_05GameModeBase>(GameMode);

        if (MyGameMode != nullptr)
        {
            MyGameMode->MyStandardDelegate.Unbind();
        }
    }
}
```

How it works...

This recipe combines both of the previous recipes in this chapter so far. We override `EndPlay`, which is an event that's implemented as a virtual function, so that we can execute code when our `DelegateListener` leaves play.

In that overridden implementation, we call the `Unbind()` method on the delegate, which unlinks the member function from the `DelegateListener` instance.

Without this being done, the delegate dangles like a pointer, leaving it in an invalid state when the `DelegateListener` leaves the game. Using `BindUObject()` helps avoid most of these situations, and just a few unfortunate timing situations could cause calls on objects to be marked for destruction. It is still a good practice to unbind delegates manually, even when using `BindUObject()`, because when these timing mishaps cause bugs, they're almost impossible to track down.

Creating a delegate that takes input parameters

So far, the delegates that we've used haven't taken any input parameters. This recipe shows you how to change the signature of the delegate so that it accepts some input.

Getting ready

Ensure that you followed the recipe at the beginning of this chapter, which showed you how to create a `TriggerVolume` and the other infrastructure that we require for this recipe.

How to do it...

1. Add a new delegate declaration to `GameMode`:

```
DECLARE_DELEGATE(FStandardDelegateSignature)
DECLARE_DELEGATE_OneParam(FParamDelegateSignature,
FLinearColor)

UCLASS()
class CHAPTER_05_API AChapter_05GameModeBase : public
AGameModeBase
```

2. Add a new member to `GameMode`:

```
DECLARE_DELEGATE(FStandardDelegateSignature)
DECLARE_DELEGATE_OneParam(FParamDelegateSignature,
FLinearColor)

UCLASS()
class CHAPTER_05_API AChapter_05GameModeBase : public
```

```
AGameModeBase
{
  GENERATED_BODY()

public:
    FStandardDelegateSignature MyStandardDelegate;

    FParamDelegateSignature MyParameterDelegate;

};
```

3. Create a new `Actor` class called `ParamDelegateListener`. Add the following to the declaration:

```
#pragma once

#include "CoreMinimal.h"
#include "GameFramework/Actor.h"
#include "Components/PointLightComponent.h"
#include "ParamDelegateListener.generated.h"

UCLASS()
class CHAPTER_05_API AParamDelegateListener : public AActor
{
    GENERATED_BODY()
public:
    // Sets default values for this actor's properties
    AParamDelegateListener();

    UFUNCTION()
    void SetLightColor(FLinearColor LightColor);

    UPROPERTY()
    UPointLightComponent* PointLight;

protected:
    // Called when the game starts or when spawned
    virtual void BeginPlay() override;

public:
    // Called every frame
    virtual void Tick(float DeltaTime) override;

};
```

4. In the class implementation, add the following to the constructor:

```
// Sets default values
AParamDelegateListener::AParamDelegateListener()
{
    // Set this actor to call Tick() every frame. You can turn
this off
    // to improve performance if you don't need it.
    PrimaryActorTick.bCanEverTick = true;

    PointLight =
CreateDefaultSubobject<UPointLightComponent>("PointLight");
    RootComponent = PointLight;

}
```

5. In the `ParamDelegateListener.cpp` file, add the following `#includes`:

```
#include "ParamDelegateListener.h"
#include "Chapter_05GameModeBase.h"
#include "Kismet/GameplayStatics.h"
```

6. Inside the `AParamDelegateListener::BeginPlay` implementation, add the following code:

```
// Called when the game starts or when spawned
void AParamDelegateListener::BeginPlay()
{
    Super::BeginPlay();

    UWorld* TheWorld = GetWorld();

    if (TheWorld != nullptr)
    {
        AGameModeBase* GameMode =
UGameplayStatics::GetGameMode(TheWorld);

        AChapter_05GameModeBase * MyGameMode =
Cast<AChapter_05GameModeBase>(GameMode);

        if (MyGameMode != nullptr)
        {
            MyGameMode->MyParameterDelegate.BindUObject(this,
&AParamDelegateListener::SetLightColor);
        }
    }
}
```

7. Lastly, implement `SetLightColor`:

```
void AParamDelegateListener::SetLightColor(FLinearColor
LightColor)
{
    PointLight->SetLightColor(LightColor);
}
```

8. Inside our `TriggerVolume`, in `NotifyActorBeginOverlap`, add the following new code:

```
void AMyTriggerVolume::NotifyActorBeginOverlap(AActor*
OtherActor)
{
    auto Message = FString::Printf(TEXT("%s entered me"),
                    *(OtherActor->GetName()));

    GEngine->AddOnScreenDebugMessage(-1, 1, FColor::Red,
Message);

    // Call our delegate
    UWorld* TheWorld = GetWorld();

    if (TheWorld != nullptr)
    {
        AGameModeBase* GameMode =
UGameplayStatics::GetGameMode(TheWorld);
        AChapter_05GameModeBase * MyGameMode =
Cast<AChapter_05GameModeBase>(GameMode);

        if(MyGameMode != nullptr)
        {
            MyGameMode->MyStandardDelegate.ExecuteIfBound();

            // Call the function using a parameter
            auto Color = FLinearColor(1, 0, 0, 1);
MyGameMode->MyParameterDelegate.ExecuteIfBound(Color);
        }
    }
}
```

9. Save your script and then go back to the Unreal Editor and compile your code. Add the `MyTriggerVolume` and `ParamDelegateListener` objects to your scene and then run the game and confirm that the light starts off as white and, upon collision, changes to red:

How it works...

Our new delegate signature uses a slightly different macro for declaration. Note the `_OneParam` suffix at the end of `DECLARE_DELEGATE_OneParam`. As you'd expect, we also need to specify what type our parameter will be. Just like when we created a delegate without parameters, we can create an instance of the delegate as a member of our `GameMode` class.

 Delegate signatures can have either a global or class scope, but not a function body (as the documentation states). You can find more information about this at `https://docs.unrealengine.com/en-US/Programming/UnrealArchitecture/Delegates`.

Then, we create a new type of `DelegateListener`: one that is expecting a parameter to be passed into the function that it binds to the delegate. When we call the `ExecuteIfBound()` method for the delegate, we need to pass in the value that will be inserted into the function parameter.

Inside the function that we have bound, we use the parameter to set the color of our light. This means that `TriggerVolume` doesn't need to know anything about `ParamDelegateListener` to call functions on it. The delegate has allowed us to minimize coupling between the two classes.

See also

- The *Unregistering a delegate* recipe shows you how to safely unregister your delegate binding in the event of the Listener being destroyed before the delegate is called

Passing payload data with a delegate binding

With only minimal changes, parameters can be passed through to a delegate at creation time. This recipe shows you how to specify data to be always passed as parameters to a delegate invocation. The data is calculated when the binding is created, and doesn't change from that point forward.

Getting ready

Ensure that you've followed the previous recipe. We will be extending the functionality of the previous recipe to pass additional creation-time parameters to our bound delegate function.

How to do it...

1. Inside your `AParamDelegateListener::BeginPlay` function, change the call to `BindUObject` to the following:

   ```
   // Called when the game starts or when spawned
   void AParamDelegateListener::BeginPlay()
   {
       Super::BeginPlay();

       UWorld* TheWorld = GetWorld();
   ```

```
        if (TheWorld != nullptr)
        {
            AGameModeBase* GameMode =
    UGameplayStatics::GetGameMode(TheWorld);

            AChapter_05GameModeBase * MyGameMode =
                            Cast<AChapter_05GameModeBase>
                            (GameMode);

            if (MyGameMode != nullptr)
            {
                MyGameMode->MyParameterDelegate.BindUObject(this,
    &AParamDelegateListener::SetLightColor,
                            false);
            }
        }
    }
```

2. In the `ParamDelegateListener.h` file, change the declaration of `SetLightColor` to the following:

```
UCLASS()
class CHAPTER_05_API AParamDelegateListener : public AActor
{
    GENERATED_BODY()
public:
    // Sets default values for this actor's properties
    AParamDelegateListener();

    UFUNCTION()
    void SetLightColor(FLinearColor LightColor, bool
EnableLight);

    UPROPERTY()
    UPointLightComponent* PointLight;

protected:
    // Called when the game starts or when spawned
    virtual void BeginPlay() override;

public:
    // Called every frame
    virtual void Tick(float DeltaTime) override;

};
```

3. Alter the implementation of `SetLightColor`, as follows:

```
void AParamDelegateListener::SetLightColor(FLinearColor
LightColor, bool EnableLight)
{
    PointLight->SetLightColor(LightColor);
    PointLight->SetVisibility(EnableLight);
}
```

4. Compile and run your project. Verify that, when you walk into `TriggerVolume`, the light turns off because of the false payload parameter that was passed in when you bound the function.

How it works...

When we bind the function to the delegate, we specify some additional data (in this case, a Boolean of value `false`). You can pass up to four "payload" variables in this fashion. They are applied to your function after any parameters are declared in the `DECLARE_DELEGATE_*` macro that you used.

We change the function signature of our delegate so that it can accept the extra argument.

Inside the function, we use the extra argument to turn the light on or off, depending on the value being `true` or `false` at compile time.

We don't need to change the call to `ExecuteIfBound`: the delegate system automatically applies the delegate parameters, which are passed in through `ExecuteIfBound` first. It then applies any payload parameters, which are always specified after the function reference in a call to `BindUObject`.

See also

- The *Unregistering a delegate* recipe shows you how to safely unregister your delegate binding in the event of the Listener being destroyed before the delegate is called

Creating a multicast delegate

The standard delegates that we've used so far in this chapter are essentially function pointers : they allow you to call one particular function on one particular object instance. Multicast delegates are a collection of function pointers, each potentially on different objects, all of which will be invoked when the delegate is **broadcast**.

Getting ready

This recipe assumes that you have followed the initial recipe in this chapter, *Handling events that have been implemented via virtual functions*, as it shows you how to create `TriggerVolume`, which is used to broadcast the multicast delegate.

How to do it...

1. Add a new delegate declaration to the `GameMode` header:

```
DECLARE_DELEGATE(FStandardDelegateSignature)
DECLARE_DELEGATE_OneParam(FParamDelegateSignature,
FLinearColor)
DECLARE_MULTICAST_DELEGATE(FMulticastDelegateSignature)

UCLASS()
class CHAPTER_05_API AChapter_05GameModeBase : public
AGameModeBase
{
  GENERATED_BODY()

public:
    FStandardDelegateSignature MyStandardDelegate;

    FParamDelegateSignature MyParameterDelegate;

    FMulticastDelegateSignature MyMulticastDelegate;

};
```

2. Create a new `Actor` class called `MulticastDelegateListener`. Add the following to the declaration:

```cpp
#pragma once

#include "CoreMinimal.h"
#include "GameFramework/Actor.h"
#include "Components/PointLightComponent.h"
#include "MulticastDelegateListener.generated.h"

UCLASS()
class CHAPTER_05_API AMulticastDelegateListener : public
AActor
{
  GENERATED_BODY()
public:
  // Sets default values for this actor's properties
  AMulticastDelegateListener();

    UFUNCTION()
    void ToggleLight();

    UFUNCTION()
    virtual void EndPlay(const EEndPlayReason::Type
EndPlayReason)
    override;

    UPROPERTY()
    UPointLightComponent* PointLight;

    FDelegateHandle MyDelegateHandle;

protected:
  // Called when the game starts or when spawned
  virtual void BeginPlay() override;

public:
  // Called every frame
  virtual void Tick(float DeltaTime) override;

};
```

3. In the class implementation, add the following code to the constructor:

```
// Sets default values
AMulticastDelegateListener::AMulticastDelegateListener()
{
    // Set this actor to call Tick() every frame. You can turn
this
    //off to improve performance if you don't need it.
  PrimaryActorTick.bCanEverTick = true;

    PointLight = CreateDefaultSubobject<UPointLightComponent>
    ("PointLight");
    RootComponent = PointLight;
}
```

4. In the `MulticastDelegateListener.cpp` file, add the following #includes:

```
#include "MulticastDelegateListener.h"
#include "Chapter_05GameModeBase.h"
#include "Kismet/GameplayStatics.h"
```

5. Inside the `MulticastDelegateListener::BeginPlay` implementation, add the following code:

```
// Called when the game starts or when spawned
void AMulticastDelegateListener::BeginPlay()
{
  Super::BeginPlay();
    UWorld* TheWorld = GetWorld();

    if (TheWorld != nullptr)
    {
        AGameModeBase* GameMode =
UGameplayStatics::GetGameMode(TheWorld);

        AChapter_05GameModeBase * MyGameMode =
                            Cast<AChapter_05GameModeBase>
                            (GameMode);

        if (MyGameMode != nullptr)
        {
            MyDelegateHandle = MyGameMode-
            >MyMulticastDelegate.AddUObject(this,
            &AMulticastDelegateListener::ToggleLight);
        }
    }
```

```
}
```

6. Implement `ToggleLight`:

```cpp
void AMulticastDelegateListener::ToggleLight()
{
  PointLight->ToggleVisibility();
}
```

7. Implement our `EndPlay` overridden function:

```cpp
void AMulticastDelegateListener::EndPlay (const
EEndPlayReason::Type EndPlayReason)
{
    Super::EndPlay(EndPlayReason);

    UWorld* TheWorld = GetWorld();

    if (TheWorld != nullptr)
    {
        AGameModeBase* GameMode =
UGameplayStatics::GetGameMode(TheWorld);

        AChapter_05GameModeBase * MyGameMode =
                        Cast<AChapter_05GameModeBase>
                        (GameMode);

        if (MyGameMode != nullptr)
        {
            MyGameMode-
            >MyMulticastDelegate.Remove(MyDelegateHandle);
        }
    }

}
```

8. Add the following line to
   `TriggerVolume::NotifyActorBeginOverlap()`:

```cpp
MyGameMode->MyMulticastDelegate.Broadcast();
```

9. Compile and load your project. Set the `GameMode` in your level as our
   cookbook game mode, and then drag four or five instances
   of `MulticastDelegateListener` into the scene.

10. Step into `TriggerVolume` to see all of the `MulticastDelegateListener` toggle their light's visibility:

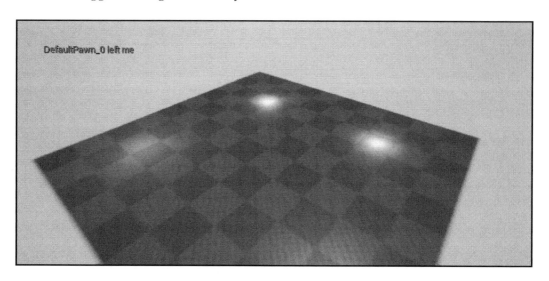

How it works...

As you might expect, the delegate type needs to be explicitly declared as a multicast delegate rather than a standard single-binding one. Our new `Listener` class is very similar to our original `DelegateListener`. The primary difference is that we need to store a reference to our delegate instance in `FDelegateHandle`.

When the actor is destroyed, we safely remove ourselves from the list of functions that are bound to the delegate by using the stored `FDelegateHandle` as a parameter to `Remove()`.

The `Broadcast()` function is the multicast equivalent of `ExecuteIfBound()`. Unlike standard delegates, there is no need to check whether the delegate bound either in advance or with a call such as `ExecuteIfBound`. `Broadcast()` is safe to run, no matter how many functions are bound, or even if none are.

When we have multiple instances of our multicast listener in the scene, they each register themselves with the multicast delegate that's implemented in the `GameMode`. Then, when the `TriggerVolume` overlaps a player, it broadcasts the delegate, and each Listener is notified, causing it to toggle the visibility of its associated point light.

Multicast delegates can take parameters in exactly the same way that a standard delegate can.

Creating a custom Event

Custom delegates are quite useful, but one of their limitations is that they can be broadcast externally by some other third-party class; that is, their Execute/Broadcast methods are publically accessible.

At times, you may want a delegate that is externally assignable by other classes, but can only be broadcast by the class that contains them. This is the primary purpose of Events.

Getting ready

Make sure you've followed the initial recipe in this chapter so that you have the MyTriggerVolume and Chapter_05GameModeBase implementations.

How to do it...

1. Add the following event declaration macro to the header of your MyTriggerVolume class:

   ```
   DECLARE_EVENT(AMyTriggerVolume, FPlayerEntered)
   ```

2. Add an instance of the declared event signature to the class:

   ```
   FPlayerEntered OnPlayerEntered;
   ```

3. In AMyTriggerVolume::NotifyActorBeginOverlap, add the following code:

   ```
   OnPlayerEntered.Broadcast();
   ```

4. Create a new `Actor` class called `TriggerVolEventListener`:

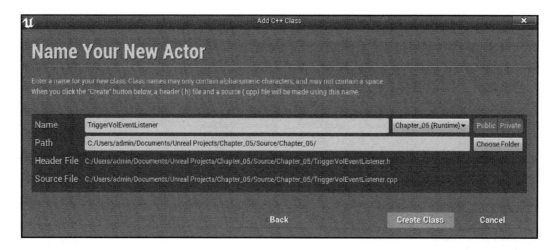

5. Add the following class members to its declaration:

```cpp
#pragma once

#include "CoreMinimal.h"
#include "GameFramework/Actor.h"
#include "Components/PointLightComponent.h"
#include "MyTriggerVolume.h"
#include "TriggerVolEventListener.generated.h"

UCLASS()
class CHAPTER_05_API ATriggerVolEventListener : public AActor
{
    GENERATED_BODY()
public:
    // Sets default values for this actor's properties
    ATriggerVolEventListener();

    UPROPERTY()
    UPointLightComponent* PointLight;

    UPROPERTY(EditAnywhere)
    AMyTriggerVolume* TriggerEventSource;

    UFUNCTION()
    void OnTriggerEvent();

protected:
    // Called when the game starts or when spawned
```

```
        virtual void BeginPlay() override;

public:
    // Called every frame
    virtual void Tick(float DeltaTime) override;

};
```

6. Initialize `PointLight` in the class constructor:

```
// Sets default values
ATriggerVolEventListener::ATriggerVolEventListener()
{
    // Set this actor to call Tick() every frame. You can turn this
    //off to improve performance if you don't need it.
    PrimaryActorTick.bCanEverTick = true;

    PointLight = CreateDefaultSubobject<UPointLightComponent>
    ("PointLight");
    RootComponent = PointLight;
}
```

7. Inside `BeginPlay`, add the following code:

```
// Called when the game starts or when spawned
void ATriggerVolEventListener::BeginPlay()
{
    Super::BeginPlay();

    if (TriggerEventSource != nullptr)
    {
        TriggerEventSource->OnPlayerEntered.AddUObject(this,
        &ATriggerVolEventListener::OnTriggerEvent);
    }
}
```

8. Lastly, implement `OnTriggerEvent()`:

```
void ATriggerVolEventListener::OnTriggerEvent()
{
  PointLight->SetLightColor(FLinearColor(0, 1, 0, 1));
}
```

9. Compile your project and launch the editor. Create a level with the game mode set to our `Chapter_05GameModeBase`, and then drag an instance of `ATriggerVolEventListener` and `AMyTriggerVolume` out into the level.

10. Select `TriggerVolEventListener`, and you'll see `TriggerVolEventListener` listed as a category in the **Details** panel, with the property as **Trigger Event Source**:

The Trigger Vol Event Listener category

11. Use the drop-down menu to select your instance of `AMyTriggerVolume` so that the Listener knows which event to bind to:

12. Play your game and enter the trigger volume's zone of effect. Verify that the color of your `EventListener` changes to green:

How it works...

As with all of the other types of delegate, Events require their own special macro function. The first parameter is the class that the event will be implemented into. This will be the only class able to call `Broadcast()`, so make sure it is the right one. The second parameter is the type name for our new event function signature. We add an instance of this type to our class. The Unreal documentation suggests `On<x>` as a naming convention.

When something overlaps our `TriggerVolume`, we call `Broadcast()` on our own event instance. Inside the new class, we create a point light as a visual representation of the event being triggered.

We also create a pointer to `TriggerVolume` to listen to events. We mark the `UPROPERTY` as `EditAnywhere`, because this allows us to set it in the Editor rather than having to acquire the reference programmatically using `GetAllActorsOfClass` or something else.

Last is our event handler for when something enters the `TriggerVolume`. We create and initialize our point light in the constructor as usual. When the game starts, the Listener checks that our `TriggerVolume` reference is valid, and then binds our `OnTriggerEvent` function to the `TriggerVolume` event. Inside `OnTriggerEvent`, we change our light's color to green. When something enters `TriggerVolume`, it causes `TriggerVolume` to call a broadcast on its own event. Our `TriggerVolEventListener` then has its bound method invoked, changing our light's color.

Creating a Time of Day handler

This recipe shows you how to use the concepts that were introduced in the previous recipes to create an actor that informs other actors of the passage of time within your game.

How to do it...

1. Create a new `Actor` class called `TimeOfDayHandler`, as shown in the following screenshot:

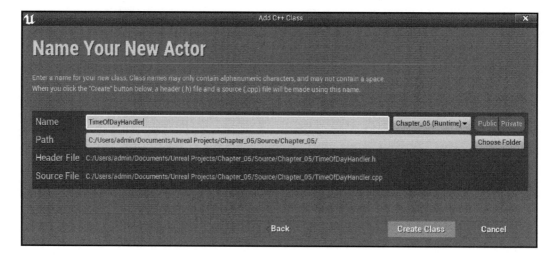

2. Add a multicast delegate declaration to the header:

```
DECLARE_MULTICAST_DELEGATE_TwoParams(FOnTimeChangedSignature,
int32,
                                     int32)
UCLASS()
class CHAPTER_05_API ATimeOfDayHandler : public AActor
```

3. Add an instance of our delegate to the class declaration in the `public` section:

```
FOnTimeChangedSignature OnTimeChanged;
```

4. Add the following properties to the class:

```
UPROPERTY()
int32 TimeScale;

UPROPERTY()
int32 Hours;
UPROPERTY()
int32 Minutes;

UPROPERTY()
float ElapsedSeconds;
```

5. Add the initialization of these properties to the constructor:

```
// Sets default values
ATimeOfDayHandler::ATimeOfDayHandler()
{
    // Set this actor to call Tick() every frame. You can turn this
    //  off to improve performance if you don't need it.
    PrimaryActorTick.bCanEverTick = true;

    TimeScale = 60;
    Hours = 0;
    Minutes = 0;
    ElapsedSeconds = 0;
}
```

6. Inside `Tick`, add the following code:

```
// Called every frame
void ATimeOfDayHandler::Tick(float DeltaTime)
{
    Super::Tick(DeltaTime);
```

```
        ElapsedSeconds += (DeltaTime * TimeScale);

        if(ElapsedSeconds > 60)
        {
            ElapsedSeconds -= 60;
            Minutes++;

            if (Minutes > 60)
            {
                Minutes -= 60;
                Hours++;
            }

            OnTimeChanged.Broadcast(Hours, Minutes);
        }

    }
```

7. Create a new `Actor` class called `Clock`, as shown in the following screenshot:

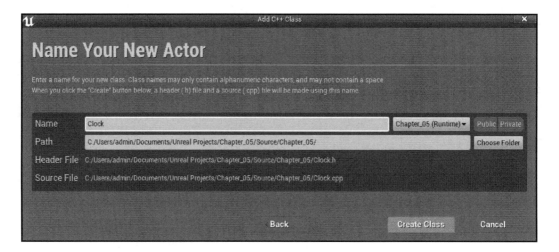

8. Add the following properties to the class header:

```
#pragma once

#include "CoreMinimal.h"
#include "GameFramework/Actor.h"
#include "Clock.generated.h"

UCLASS()
```

```
class CHAPTER_05_API AClock : public AActor
{
    GENERATED_BODY()
public:
    // Sets default values for this actor's properties
    AClock();

    UPROPERTY()
    USceneComponent* RootSceneComponent;

    UPROPERTY()
    UStaticMeshComponent* ClockFace;

    UPROPERTY()
    USceneComponent* HourHandle;

    UPROPERTY()
    UStaticMeshComponent* HourHand;

    UPROPERTY()
    USceneComponent* MinuteHandle;

    UPROPERTY()
    UStaticMeshComponent* MinuteHand;

    UFUNCTION()
    void TimeChanged(int32 Hours, int32 Minutes);

    FDelegateHandle MyDelegateHandle;

protected:
    // Called when the game starts or when spawned
    virtual void BeginPlay() override;

public:
    // Called every frame
    virtual void Tick(float DeltaTime) override;

};
```

9. Initialize and transform the components in the constructor:

```
#include "TimeOfDayHandler.h"
#include "Kismet/GameplayStatics.h"

// Sets default values
AClock::AClock()
{
```

```cpp
    // Set this actor to call Tick() every frame. You can turn
this off to improve performance if you don't need it.
    PrimaryActorTick.bCanEverTick = true;

    RootSceneComponent =
CreateDefaultSubobject<USceneComponent>("RootSceneComponent");
    ClockFace =
CreateDefaultSubobject<UStaticMeshComponent>("ClockFace");
    HourHand =
CreateDefaultSubobject<UStaticMeshComponent>("HourHand");
    MinuteHand =
CreateDefaultSubobject<UStaticMeshComponent>("MinuteHand");
    HourHandle =
CreateDefaultSubobject<USceneComponent>("HourHandle");
    MinuteHandle =
CreateDefaultSubobject<USceneComponent>("MinuteHandle");
    auto MeshAsset =
ConstructorHelpers::FObjectFinder<UStaticMesh>(TEXT("StaticMes
h'/Engine/BasicShapes/Cylinder.Cylinder'"));

    if (MeshAsset.Object != nullptr)
    {
        ClockFace->SetStaticMesh(MeshAsset.Object);
        HourHand->SetStaticMesh(MeshAsset.Object);
        MinuteHand->SetStaticMesh(MeshAsset.Object);
    }

    RootComponent = RootSceneComponent;

    HourHand->AttachToComponent(HourHandle,
FAttachmentTransformRules::KeepRelativeTransform);

    MinuteHand->AttachToComponent(MinuteHandle,
FAttachmentTransformRules::KeepRelativeTransform);

    HourHandle->AttachToComponent(RootSceneComponent,
FAttachmentTransformRules::KeepRelativeTransform);

    MinuteHandle->AttachToComponent(RootSceneComponent,
FAttachmentTransformRules::KeepRelativeTransform);

    ClockFace->AttachToComponent(RootSceneComponent,
FAttachmentTransformRules::KeepRelativeTransform);

    ClockFace->SetRelativeTransform(FTransform(FRotator(90, 0,
0),
                                              FVector(10, 0, 0),
                                              FVector(2, 2, 0.1)));
```

```
       HourHand->SetRelativeTransform(FTransform(FRotator(0, 0,
0),
                                      FVector(0, 0, 25),
                                      FVector(0.1, 0.1, 0.5)));

       MinuteHand->SetRelativeTransform(FTransform(FRotator(0, 0,
0),
                                        FVector(0, 0, 50),
                                        FVector(0.1, 0.1, 1)));

   }
```

10. Add the following code to `BeginPlay`:

```
// Called when the game starts or when spawned
void AClock::BeginPlay()
{
    Super::BeginPlay();

    TArray<AActor*> TimeOfDayHandlers;

    UGameplayStatics::GetAllActorsOfClass(GetWorld(),
ATimeOfDayHandler::StaticClass(),
                                          TimeOfDayHandlers);

    if (TimeOfDayHandlers.Num() != 0)
    {
        auto TimeOfDayHandler = Cast<ATimeOfDayHandler>
        (TimeOfDayHandlers[0]);
        MyDelegateHandle =
        TimeOfDayHandler->OnTimeChanged.AddUObject(this,
        &AClock::TimeChanged);
    }
}
```

11. Lastly, implement `TimeChanged` as your event handler:

```
void AClock::TimeChanged(int32 Hours, int32 Minutes)
{
    HourHandle->SetRelativeRotation(FRotator(0, 0, 30 *
Hours));
    MinuteHandle->SetRelativeRotation(FRotator(0, 0, 6 *
Minutes));
}
```

12. Place an instance of `TimeOfDayHandler` and the `AClock` into your level. Then, play it to see the hands on the clock rotate:

How it works...

`TimeOfDayHandler` contains a delegate that takes two parameters, hence the use of the `TwoParams` variant of the macro. Our class contains variables to store hours, minutes, and seconds, as well as `TimeScale`, which is an acceleration factor that's used to speed up time for testing purposes. Inside the handler's `Tick` function, we accumulate elapsed seconds based on the time elapsed since the last frame. We check if the elapsed seconds have gone over 60. If so, we subtract 60, and increment `Minutes`. The same happens with `Minutes`: if they go over 60, we subtract 60, and increment `Hours`. If `Minutes` or `Hours` was updated, we broadcast our delegate to let any object that has subscribed to the delegate know that the time has changed.

The `Clock` actor uses a series of Scene components and Static meshes to build a mesh hierarchy that resembles a clock face. In the `Clock` constructor, we parent the components in the hierarchy and set their initial scale and rotations. In `BeginPlay`, the clock uses `GetAllActorsOfClass()` to fetch all of the time of day handlers in the level. If there's at least one `TimeOfDayHandler` in the level, the `Clock` accesses the first one, and subscribes to its `TimeChanged` event. When the `TimeChanged` event fires, the clock rotates the hour and minute hands based on how many hours and minutes the time is currently set at.

Creating a respawning pickup for a First Person Shooter

This recipe shows you how to create a placeable pickup that will respawn after a certain amount of time, suitable as an ammo or other pickup for a **First Person Shooter (FPS)**.

How to do it...

1. Create a new `Actor` class called `Pickup`:

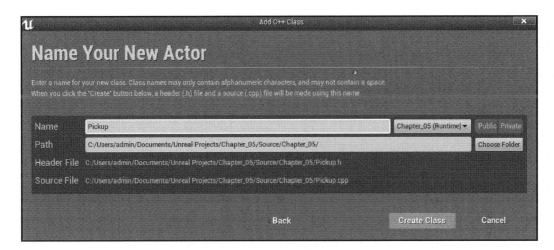

2. Declare the following delegate type in `Pickup.h`:

   ```
   DECLARE_DELEGATE(FPickedupEventSignature)
   ```

3. Add the following properties to the class header:

   ```
   // Fill out your copyright notice in the Description page of
   Project Settings.

   #pragma once

   #include "CoreMinimal.h"
   #include "GameFramework/Actor.h"
   #include "GameFramework/RotatingMovementComponent.h"
   #include "Pickup.generated.h"
   ```

```
DECLARE_DELEGATE(FPickedupEventSignature)
UCLASS()
class CHAPTER_05_API APickup : public AActor
{
    GENERATED_BODY()
public:
    // Sets default values for this actor's properties
    APickup();

    virtual void NotifyActorBeginOverlap(AActor* OtherActor)
    override;

    UPROPERTY()
    UStaticMeshComponent* MyMesh;

    UPROPERTY()
    URotatingMovementComponent* RotatingComponent;

    FPickedupEventSignature OnPickedUp;

protected:
    // Called when the game starts or when spawned
    virtual void BeginPlay() override;

public:
    // Called every frame
    virtual void Tick(float DeltaTime) override;

};
```

4. The class will be using the `ConstructorHelpers` struct, so we need to add the following `#include` to the `Pickup.cpp` file:

    ```
    #include "ConstructorHelpers.h"
    ```

5. Add the following code to the constructor:

    ```
    // Sets default values
    APickup::APickup()
    {
        // Set this actor to call Tick() every frame. You can turn
    this
        // off to improve performance if you don't need it.
      PrimaryActorTick.bCanEverTick = true;

        MyMesh =
    CreateDefaultSubobject<UStaticMeshComponent>("MyMesh");
    ```

```
    RotatingComponent =
    CreateDefaultSubobject<URotatingMovementComponent>
    ("RotatingComponent");
    RootComponent = MyMesh;

    auto MeshAsset =
ConstructorHelpers::FObjectFinder<UStaticMesh>
    (TEXT("StaticMesh'/Engine/BasicShapes/Cube.Cube'"));

    if (MeshAsset.Object != nullptr)
    {
        MyMesh->SetStaticMesh(MeshAsset.Object);
    }

MyMesh->SetCollisionProfileName(TEXT("OverlapAllDynamic"));
    RotatingComponent->RotationRate = FRotator(10, 0, 10);
}
```

6. Implement the overridden `NotifyActorBeginOverlap`:

```
void APickup::NotifyActorBeginOverlap(AActor* OtherActor)
{
    OnPickedUp.ExecuteIfBound();
}
```

7. Create a second `Actor` class called `PickupSpawner`:

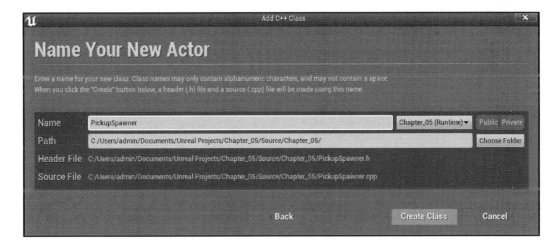

8. Add the following code to the class header:

```
#pragma once

#include "CoreMinimal.h"
#include "GameFramework/Actor.h"
#include "Pickup.h"
#include "PickupSpawner.generated.h"

UCLASS()
class CHAPTER_05_API APickupSpawner : public AActor
{
    GENERATED_BODY()
public:
    // Sets default values for this actor's properties
    APickupSpawner();

    UPROPERTY()
    USceneComponent* SpawnLocation;
    UFUNCTION()
    void PickupCollected();
    UFUNCTION()
    void SpawnPickup();
    UPROPERTY()
    APickup* CurrentPickup;
    FTimerHandle MyTimer;

protected:
    // Called when the game starts or when spawned
    virtual void BeginPlay() override;

public:
    // Called every frame
    virtual void Tick(float DeltaTime) override;

};
```

9. Initialize our root component in the constructor:

```
SpawnLocation =
  CreateDefaultSubobject<USceneComponent>("SpawnLocation");
```

10. Spawn a pickup when gameplay starts with the SpawnPickup function in BeginPlay:

```
// Called when the game starts or when spawned
void APickupSpawner::BeginPlay()
{
```

```
        Super::BeginPlay();

        SpawnPickup();

    }
```

11. **Implement** `PickupCollected`:

```
    void APickupSpawner::PickupCollected()
    {
        GetWorld()->GetTimerManager().SetTimer(MyTimer,
                                               this,
    &APickupSpawner::SpawnPickup,
                                                10,
                                                false);

        CurrentPickup->OnPickedUp.Unbind();
        CurrentPickup->Destroy();
    }
```

12. **Create the following code for** `SpawnPickup`:

```
void APickupSpawner::SpawnPickup()
{
    UWorld* MyWorld = GetWorld();

    if (MyWorld != nullptr)
    {
        CurrentPickup = MyWorld->SpawnActor<APickup>(
APickup::StaticClass(),
                                                GetTransform());

        CurrentPickup->OnPickedUp.BindUObject(this,
&APickupSpawner::PickupCollected);
    }
}
```

13. Compile and launch the editor, and then drag an instance of `PickupSpawner` out into the level. Walk into the pickup that's represented by the spinning cube and verify that it spawns again 10 seconds later:

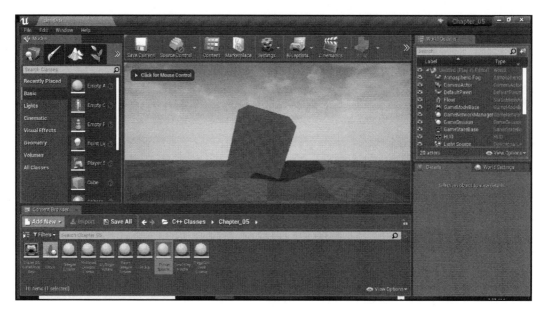

The result of completing the recipe

How it works...

As usual, we need to create a delegate inside our `Pickup` that our Spawner can subscribe to so that it knows when the player collects the pickup. The `Pickup` also contains a Static mesh as a visual representation, and a `RotatingMovementComponent` so that the mesh will spin as a way to attract the attention of the players. Inside the `Pickup` constructor, we load one of the engine's inbuilt meshes as our visual representation. We specify that the mesh will overlap with other objects, then set the rotation rate of our mesh at 10 units per second in the X and Z axes. When the player overlaps the `Pickup`, it fires off its `PickedUp` delegate from the first step.

The `PickupSpawner` used

a Scene component to specify where to spawn the pickup actor. It has a function for doing so, and a tagged UPROPERTY reference to the currently spawned `Pickup`. In the `PickupSpawner` constructor, we initialize our components as always. When play begins, the Spawner runs its `SpawnPickup` function. This function spawns an instance of our `Pickup`, then binds `APickupSpawner::PickupCollected` to the `OnPickedUp` function on the new instance. It also stores a reference to that current instance.

When `PickupCollected` runs after the player has overlapped the `Pickup`, a timer is created to respawn the pickup after 10 seconds. The existing delegate binding to the collected pickup is removed, and then the pickup is destroyed. After 10 seconds, the timer fires, running `SpawnActor` again, which creates a new `Pickup`.

6
Input and Collision

This chapter covers recipes surrounding game control input (keyboard, mouse, and gamepad), and collisions with obstacles.

The following recipes will be covered in this chapter:

- Axis Mappings – keyboard, mouse, and gamepad directional input for an FPS character
- Axis Mappings – normalized input
- Action Mappings – one-button responses for an FPS character
- Adding Axis and Action Mappings from C++
- Mouse UI input handling
- UMG keyboard UI shortcut keys
- Collision – letting objects pass through one another using Ignore
- Collision – picking up objects using Overlap
- Collision – preventing interpenetration using Block

Introduction

Good input controls are extremely important in your game. Providing all of the keyboard, mouse, and especially gamepad input is going to make your game much more palatable to users.

 You can use Xbox 360 and PlayStation controllers on your Windows PC – they have USB input. Check your local electronics shops for USB game controllers to find some good ones. You can also use a wireless controller with the proper receiver to connect to your PC.

Technical requirements

This chapter requires the use of Unreal Engine 4 and uses Visual Studio 2017 as the IDE. Instructions on how to install both pieces of software and the requirements for them can be found in Chapter 1, *UE4 Development Tools*, of this book.

Axis Mappings – keyboard, mouse, and gamepad directional input for an FPS character

There are two types of input mapping: **Axis mappings** and **Action mappings**. Axis mappings are inputs that you hold down for an extended period of time to get their effect (for example, holding the *W* key to move the player forward), while Action mappings are one-off inputs (such as pressing the *A* button on the gamepad or spacebar on the keyboard to make the player jump). In this recipe, we'll cover how to set up keyboard, mouse, and gamepad axis-mapped input controls to move an FPS character.

Getting ready

You must have a UE4 project, which has a main character player in it and a ground plane to walk on, ready for this recipe.

How to do it...

1. Create a C++ class and select Character as the parent class. Then, hit Next:

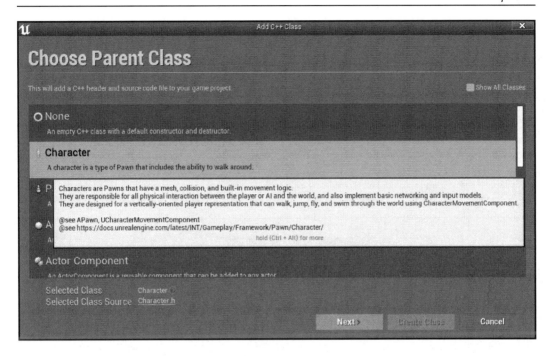

2. Under the **Name** property, type in `Warrior`, and then click on **Create Class**:

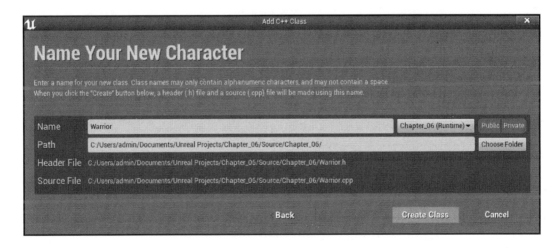

We will dive into doing the implementation after we do some setup inside UE4.

3. Launch UE4 and right-click on the **Warrior** class. Then, select **Create Blueprint class based on Warrior**:

4. From the menu that pops up, set the name to `BP_Warrior` and then select **Create Blueprint Class**:

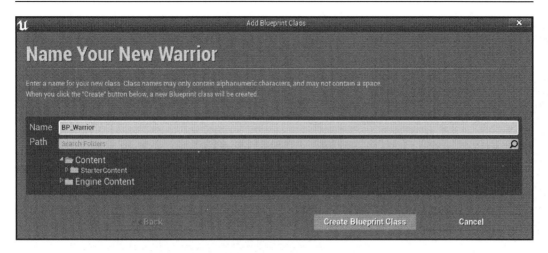

5. Close the Blueprints menu that was just opened.
6. Create and select a new Blueprint for your GameMode class, by going to **Settings | Project Settings | Maps & Modes**:

7. Click on the + icon beside the default **GameMode** drop-down menu, which will create a new Blueprint of the GameMode class. Put a name of your choice (say, BP_GameMode):

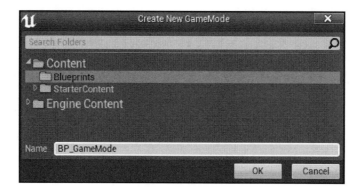

8. Double-click the new BP_GameMode Blueprint class that you created to edit it. It can be found in the Contents\Blueprints folder from the **Content Browser**.

9. Once your BP_GameMode blueprint is opened, select your Blueprinted BP_Warrior class as the **Default Pawn Class**:

The location of the **Default Pawn Class** property.

10. To set up the keyboard's input, which will drive the player, open **Settings** | **Project Settings** | **Input**. (**Input** can be found under the **Engine** subsection.) In the following steps, we will complete the process that drives the player forward in the game.

11. Click on the + icon beside the **Axis Mappings** heading:

Axis Mappings supports continuous (button-held) input, while **Action Mappings** supports one-off events.

12. Give a name to the Axis mapping. This first example will show how to move the player forward, so name it something like Forward.

13. Underneath **Forward**, select a keyboard key to assign to this Axis mapping, such as *W*.

14. Click on the + icon beside **Forward** and select a game controller input to map so that you can move the player forward (such as **Gamepad Left Thumbstick Up**):

15. Complete **Axis Mappings** for Back, Left, and Right with keyboard, gamepad, and, optionally, mouse input bindings for each:

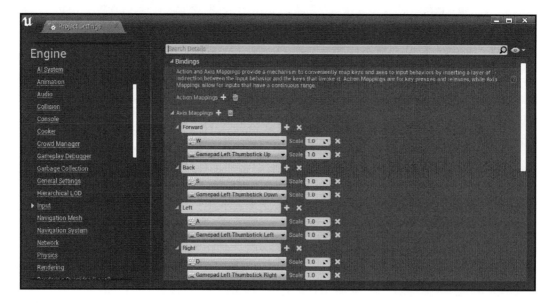

16. Now, return to the `.h` file. We will need to add some new function definitions, which we will be writing:

```
#pragma once

#include "CoreMinimal.h"
#include "GameFramework/Character.h"
#include "Warrior.generated.h"

UCLASS()
class CHAPTER_06_API AWarrior : public ACharacter
{
    GENERATED_BODY()

public:
    // Sets default values for this character's properties
    AWarrior();

protected:
    // Called when the game starts or when spawned
    virtual void BeginPlay() override;

public:
    // Called every frame
    virtual void Tick(float DeltaTime) override;

    // Called to bind functionality to input
    virtual void SetupPlayerInputComponent(class
UInputComponent*
                                        PlayerInputComponent)
override;

    // Movement functions
    void Forward(float amount);
    void Back(float amount);
    void Right(float amount);
    void Left(float amount);

};
```

17. From your C++ code, override the `SetupPlayerInputComponent` function for the `AWarrior` class, as follows:

```
#include "Components/InputComponent.h"

// ...

// Called to bind functionality to input
```

```
void AWarrior::SetupPlayerInputComponent(UInputComponent*
PlayerInputComponent)
{
    Super::SetupPlayerInputComponent(PlayerInputComponent);

    check(PlayerInputComponent);
    PlayerInputComponent->BindAxis("Forward", this,
                                    &AWarrior::Forward);
    PlayerInputComponent->BindAxis("Back", this,
&AWarrior::Back);
    PlayerInputComponent->BindAxis("Right", this,
&AWarrior::Right);
    PlayerInputComponent->BindAxis("Left", this,
&AWarrior::Left);
}
```

18. Provide a `Forward` function inside your `AWarrior` class, as follows:

```
void AWarrior::Forward(float amount)
{
    // Moves the player forward by an amount in forward
    // direction
    AddMovementInput(GetActorForwardVector(), amount);
}
```

19. Write and complete functions for the rest of the input directions, that is, `AWarrior::Back`, `AWarrior::Left`, and `AWarrior::Right`:

```
void AWarrior::Back(float amount)
{
    AddMovementInput(-GetActorForwardVector(), amount);
}

void AWarrior::Right(float amount)
{
    AddMovementInput(GetActorRightVector(), amount);
}

void AWarrior::Left(float amount)
{
    AddMovementInput(-GetActorRightVector(), amount);
}
```

20. Return to Unreal and compile your code. Afterwards, play and game and confirm that you can now move with both the keyboard and the left thumbstick on your gamepad:

How it works...

The UE4 Engine allows wire-up input events directly to C++ function calls. The functions that are called by an input event are member functions of some class. In the preceding example, we routed both the pressing of the *W* key and holding of the gamepad's Left Thumbstick Up to the AWarrior::Forward C++ function. The instance to call AWarrior::Forward on is the instance that routed the controller's input. That is controlled by the object set as the player's avatar in the GameMode class.

See also

- Instead of entering the input axis bindings in the UE4 editor, you can actually code it in from C++. We'll describe this in detail in a later recipe, *Adding Axis and Action Mappings from C++*.

Axis Mappings – normalized input

As you may have noticed, inputs of 1.0 right and 1.0 forward will actually sum to a total of 2.0 units of speed. This means it is possible to move faster diagonally than it is to move in purely forward, backward, left, or right directions. What we really should do is clamp off any input value that results in speed in excess of 1.0 units while maintaining the direction of input indicated. We can do this by storing the previous input values and overriding the ::Tick() function.

Getting ready

To work on this recipe, you must have completed the previous one with our `Warrior` class as we will be adding to it.

How to do it...

1. Go to your `Warrior.h` file and add the following property:

```
protected:
    // Called when the game starts or when spawned
    virtual void BeginPlay() override;

    // The movement from the previous frame
    FVector2D lastInput;
```

2. We will then need to initialize the variable inside of the class constructor:

```
// Sets default values
AWarrior::AWarrior()
{
    // Set this character to call Tick() every frame. You can
turn
    // this off to improve performance if you don't need it.
    PrimaryActorTick.bCanEverTick = true;

    lastInput = FVector2D::ZeroVector;
}
```

3. Update the `::Forward`, `::Back`, `::Right`, and `::Left` functions, as follows:

```
void AWarrior::Forward(float amount)
{
    // We use a += of the amount added so that when the other
    // function modifying .Y (::Back()) affects lastInput, it
won't
    // overwrite with 0's
    lastInput.Y += amount;
}

void AWarrior::Back(float amount)
{
    // In this case we are using -= since we are moving
backwards
```

```
        lastInput.Y -= amount;
    }

    void AWarrior::Right(float amount)
    {
        lastInput.X += amount;
    }

    void AWarrior::Left(float amount)
    {
        lastInput.X -= amount;
    }
```

4. In the `AWarrior::Tick()` function, modify the input values after normalizing any oversize in the input vector:

```
    // Called every frame
    void AWarrior::Tick(float DeltaSeconds)
    {
        Super::Tick(DeltaSeconds);

        float len = lastInput.Size();

        // If the player's input is greater than 1, normalize it
        if (len > 1.f)
        {
            lastInput /= len;
        }
        AddMovementInput(GetActorForwardVector(), lastInput.Y);
        AddMovementInput(GetActorRightVector(), lastInput.X);

        // Zero off last input values
        lastInput = FVector2D(0.f, 0.f);
    }
```

How it works...

We normalize the input vector when it is over a magnitude of 1.0. This constricts the maximum input velocity to 1.0 units (rather than 2.0 units when full up and full right are pressed, for example).

Action Mappings – one-button responses for an FPS character

An Action mapping is for handling single-button pushes (not buttons that are held down). For buttons that should be held down, be sure to use an Axis mapping instead.

Getting ready

Have a UE4 project ready with the actions that you need to complete, such as Jump or ShootGun.

How to do it...

1. Open **Settings** | **Project Settings** | **Input**.
2. Go to the **Action Mappings** heading and click on the + icon beside it:

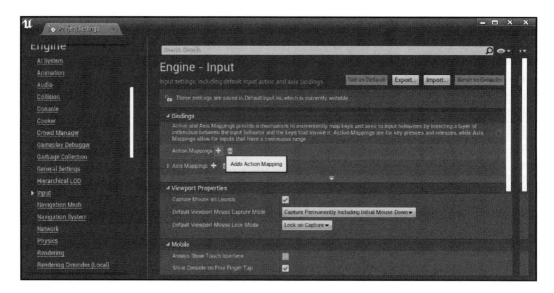

3. Start to type in the actions that should be mapped to button pushes. For example, type in Jump for the first Action.

4. Click on the arrow to the left of the action to open up the menu and then select a key to press for that action to occur, for example, **Space Bar**.

5. If you would like the same action triggered by another key push, click on the + beside your **Action Mappings** name and select another key to trigger the Action.

6. If you want the **Shift**, **Ctrl**, **Alt**, or **Cmd** keys to be held down for the Action to occur, be sure to indicate that in the checkboxes to the right of the key selection box:

7. To link your Action to a C++ code function, you need to override the SetupPlayerInputComponent(UInputControl* control) function. Enter the following code inside that function:

```cpp
// Called to bind functionality to input
void AWarrior::SetupPlayerInputComponent(UInputComponent*
PlayerInputComponent)
{
    Super::SetupPlayerInputComponent(PlayerInputComponent);

    check(PlayerInputComponent);
    PlayerInputComponent->BindAxis("Forward", this,
&AWarrior::Forward);
    PlayerInputComponent->BindAxis("Back", this,
&AWarrior::Back);
    PlayerInputComponent->BindAxis("Right", this,
&AWarrior::Right);
    PlayerInputComponent->BindAxis("Left", this,
&AWarrior::Left);

    PlayerInputComponent->BindAction("Jump", IE_Pressed, this,
&AWarrior::Jump);
}
```

8. Compile your script and play the game. Whenever you press the *spacebar*, you should see the player jump in the air! Refer to the following screenshot:

How it works...

Action Mappings are single-button-push events that fire off C++ code to run in response to them. You can define any number of actions that you wish in the UE4 Editor, but be sure to tie up **Action Mappings** to actual key pushes in C++.

You may notice that the Jump function we are calling, when we use our action, already exists when we added a reference to it. That is because the Character class already contains an implementation for it. Note that the default implementation doesn't feel like a usual jump – it's more of a rise and float action.

You can find more information on the Character class and the pre-built functions it has at https://api.unrealengine.com/INT/API/Runtime/Engine/GameFramework/ACharacter/index.html.

See also

- You can list the Actions that you want mapped from C++ code. See the following recipe, *Adding Axis and Action Mappings from C++*, for this.

Adding Axis and Action Mappings from C++

Axis Mappings and Action Mappings can be added to your game via the UE4 Editor and is often how designers will do it, but we can also add them directly from C++ code. Since the connections to C++ functions is from C++ code anyway, you may find it more convenient to define your Axis and Action Mappings in C++ as well.

Getting ready

You need a UE4 project that you'd like to add some Axis and Action mappings to. You can delete the existing Axis and Action mappings listed in **Settings** | **Project Settings** | **Input** if you are adding them via C++ code.

To add your custom Axis and Action Mappings, there are two C++ functions that you need to know about: `UPlayerInput::AddAxisMapping` and `UPlayerInput::AddActionMapping`. These are member functions that are available on the `UPlayerInput` object. The `UPlayerInput` object is inside the `PlayerController` object, and is accessible via the following code:

```
GetWorld()->GetFirstPlayerController()->PlayerInput
```

You can also use the two static member functions of `UPlayerInput` to create your Axis and Action Mappings if you'd prefer not to access player controllers individually:

```
UPlayerInput::AddEngineDefinedAxisMapping()
UPlayerInput::AddEngineDefinedActionMapping()
```

How to do it...

1. To begin, we need to define our `FInputAxisKeyMapping` or `FInputActionKeyMapping` objects, depending on whether you are hooking up an Axis key mapping (for buttons that are held down for input) or an Action key mapping (for one-off-event buttons that are pressed once for input).

    1. To use either of the following classes, we will need to include the following `.h` file:

        ```
        #include "GameFramework/PlayerInput.h"
        ```

    2. For Axis key mappings, we define an `FInputAxisKeyMapping` object, as follows:

        ```
        FInputAxisKeyMapping backKey( "Back", EKeys::S, 1.f );
        ```

    3. This will include the string name for the action, the key to press (use the EKeys enum), and whether or not *Shift, Ctrl, Alt,* or *cmd* (Mac) should be held to trigger the event.

    4. For action key mappings, define `FInputActionKeyMapping`, as follows:

        ```
        FInputActionKeyMapping jump("Jump", EKeys::SpaceBar, 0, 0, 0, 0);
        ```

    5. This will include the string name for the action, the key to press, and whether or not *Shift, Ctrl, Alt,* or *cmd* (Mac) should be held to trigger the event.

2. In your player `Pawn` class's `SetupPlayerInputComponent` function, register your Axis and Action key mappings to the following:

    1. The `PlayerInput` object connected to a specific controller:

        ```
        GetWorld()->GetFirstPlayerController()->PlayerInput
          ->AddAxisMapping( backKey ); // specific to a controller
        ```

    2. Alternatively, you could register to the static member functions of the `UPlayerInput` object directly:

        ```
        UPlayerInput::AddEngineDefinedActionMapping(jump );
        ```

Ensure that you're using the correct function for Axis versus Action Mappings!

3. Register your Action and Axis Mappings to C++ functions using C++ code, just like we did in the preceding two recipes, for example:

```
PlayerInputComponent->BindAxis("Back", this, &AWarrior::Back);
PlayerInputComponent->BindAction("Jump", IE_Pressed, this,
&AWarrior::Jump
    );
```

How it works...

The Action and Axis Mapping registration functions allow you to set up your input mappings from C++ code directly. The C++ coded input mappings are essentially the same as entering the input mappings in the **Settings** | **Project Settings** | **Input** dialog.

Mouse UI input handling

When using the **Unreal Motion Graphics (UMG)** toolkit, you will find that mouse events are very easy to handle. We can register C++ functions to run after mouse clicks or other types of interactions with the UMG components.

Usually, event registration will be via Blueprints; however, in this recipe, we will outline how to write and wire up C++ functions to UMG events.

Getting ready

Create a UMG canvas in your UE4 project. From there, we'll register event handlers for the `OnClicked`, `OnPressed`, and `OnReleased` events.

How to do it...

1. Right-click in your **Content Browser** (or click on **Add New**) and select **User Interface | Widget Blueprint,** as shown in the following screenshot. This will add an editable widget blueprint to your project:

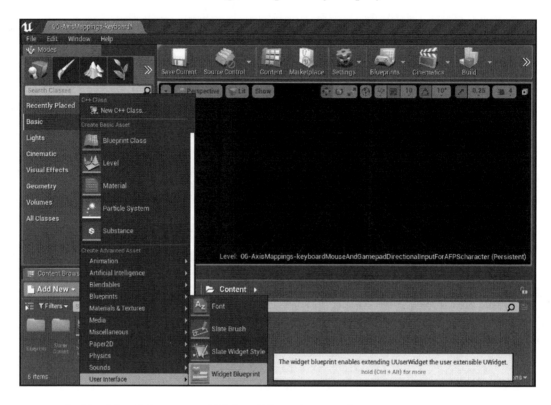

2. Double-click on your **Widget Blueprint** to edit it.
3. Add a button to the interface by dragging it from the palette on the left:

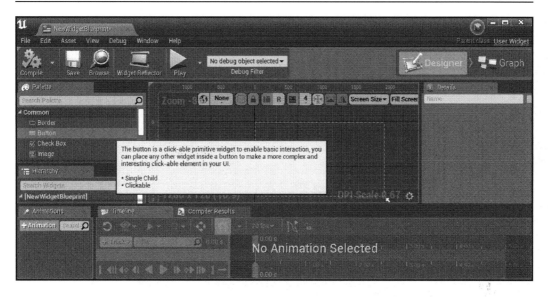

4. Scroll down the **Details** panel for your button until you find the **Events** subsection.

5. Click on the + icon beside any event that you'd like to handle:

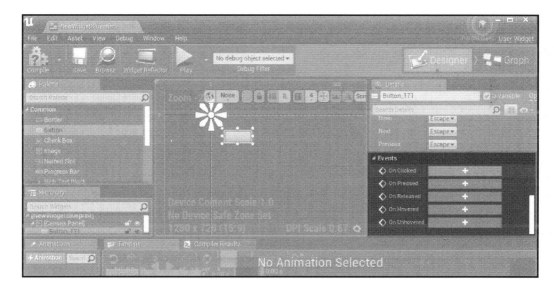

6. Connect the event that appears in Blueprints to any C++ UFUNCTION() that has the BlueprintCallable tag in the macro. For example, in your GameModeBase class derivative, you could include a function such as the following one:

```
UCLASS()
class CHAPTER_06_API AChapter_06GameModeBase : public
AGameModeBase
{
    GENERATED_BODY()
public:
    UFUNCTION(BlueprintCallable, Category = UIFuncs)
    void ButtonClicked()
    {
        UE_LOG(LogTemp, Warning, TEXT("UI Button Clicked"));
    }
};
```

7. Trigger the function call by routing to it in the Blueprint diagram under the event of your choice. For example, I used the OnClick function. Once created, I used the **Get Game Mode** node to get our current game mode and then Cast to Chapter06_GameModeBase to gain access to the ButtonClicked function:

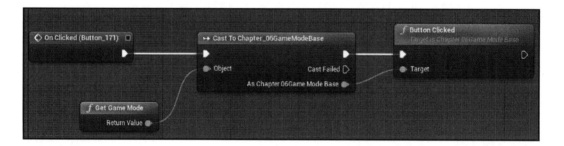

 Note that for this to work, ensure that you have set the Game Mode for the level/project as Chapter_06GameModeBase.

8. Construct and display your UI by calling **Create Widget**, followed by **Add to Viewport** in the BeginPlay function of your GameModeBase (or any such main object) or through the Level Blueprint.

9. To do this via C++, you'll need to go to the `Chapter_06.Build.cs` file and modify the following line:

```
PublicDependencyModuleNames.AddRange(new string[] { "Core",
"CoreUObject", "Engine", "InputCore", "UMG", "Slate",
"SlateCore" });
```

10. Afterwards, add the following property and function to the `Chapter_06GameModeBase.h` file:

```
public:
    UFUNCTION(BlueprintCallable, Category = UIFuncs)
    void ButtonClicked()
    {
        UE_LOG(LogTemp, Warning, TEXT("UI Button Clicked"));
    }

    void BeginPlay();

    UPROPERTY(EditAnywhere, BlueprintReadWrite, Category =
"UI")
    TSubclassOf<class UUserWidget> Widget;
```

11. Then, update the C++ file:

```
#include "Chapter_06GameModeBase.h"
#include "Blueprint/UserWidget.h"

void AChapter_06GameModeBase::BeginPlay()
{
    Super::BeginPlay();

    if(Widget)
    {
        UUserWidget* Menu =
CreateWidget<UUserWidget>(GetWorld(),
        Widget);

        if(Menu)
        {
            Menu->AddToViewport();
GetWorld()->GetFirstPlayerController()->bShowMouseCursor =
        true;
        }
    }
}
```

12. Now, we need to set **Widget** to our created menu. To do that, from the **Content Browser**, right-click on the Chapter06_GameModeBase from the C++ Classes\Chapter_06 folder and create a new Blueprint from it. Once at the **Blueprints** menu, go to the **Details** tab and under the **UI** section, set the **Widget** to the item you wish to display:

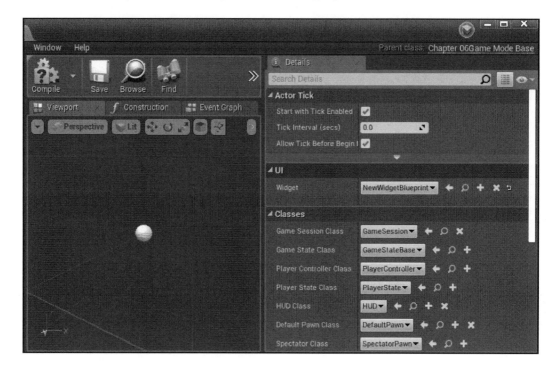

13. Finally, go to **Settings** | **World Settings**. From there, change the **Game Mode Override** to your Blueprint version of the GameMode:

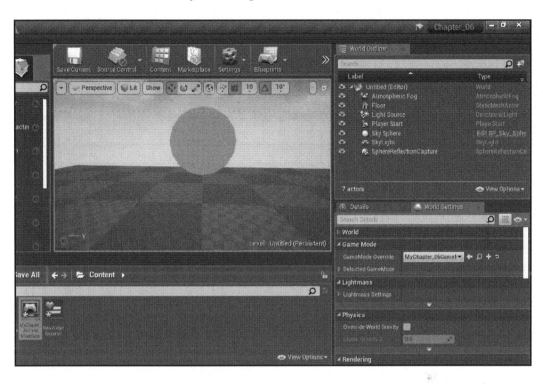

14. Then, open the **Output Log** by going to **Window | Developer Tools | Output Log** and then play the game. You should see the button displayed on your screen. If you click on it, you should see a message displayed on the **Output Log**!

How it works...

Your widget's Blueprint button events can be easily connected to Blueprint events, or C++ functions by creating a UFUNCTION() that has the BlueprintCallable tag in the macro.

For more information on using UMG and building simple menus and displaying them using Blueprints, check out `https://docs.` `unrealengine.com/en-us/Engine/UMG/HowTo/CreatingWidgets`.

UMG keyboard UI shortcut keys

Every user interface needs shortcut keys associated with it. To program these into your UMG interface, you can simply wire up certain key combinations to an Action Mapping. When the Action triggers, just invoke the same Blueprints function that the UI button itself triggers.

Getting ready

You should have a UMG interface created already, as shown in the previous recipe.

How to do it...

1. In **Settings** | **Project Settings** | **Input**, define a new Action Mapping for your hot key event, for example, `HotKey_UIButton_Spell`:

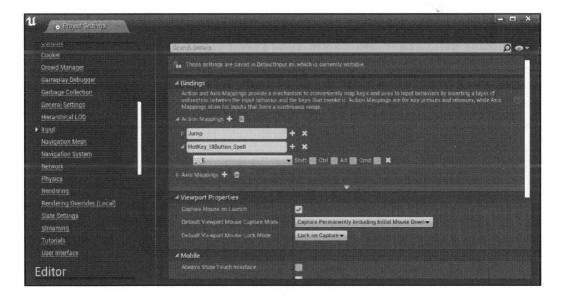

2. Wire up the event to your UI's function call either in Blueprints or in C++ code. In our case, I will add it to the `AWarrior` class we created previously by adding it to the `SetupPlayerInputComponent` function:

```
#include "Chapter_06GameModeBase.h"

// ...

// Called to bind functionality to input
void AWarrior::SetupPlayerInputComponent(UInputComponent*
PlayerInputComponent)
{
    Super::SetupPlayerInputComponent(PlayerInputComponent);

    check(PlayerInputComponent);
    PlayerInputComponent->BindAxis("Forward", this,
    &AWarrior::Forward);
    PlayerInputComponent->BindAxis("Back", this,
&AWarrior::Back);
    PlayerInputComponent->BindAxis("Right", this,
&AWarrior::Right);
    PlayerInputComponent->BindAxis("Left", this,
&AWarrior::Left);

    PlayerInputComponent->BindAction("Jump", IE_Pressed, this,
    &AWarrior::Jump);

    // Example of adding bindings via code instead of the
    //   editor
    FInputAxisKeyMapping backKey("Back", EKeys::S, 1.f);
    FInputActionKeyMapping jump("Jump", EKeys::SpaceBar, 0, 0,
    0, 0);

    GetWorld()->GetFirstPlayerController()->PlayerInput-
    >AddAxisMapping(backKey);
    GetWorld()->GetFirstPlayerController()->PlayerInput-
    >AddActionMapping(jump);

    // Calling function for HotKey
    auto GameMode = Cast<AChapter_06GameModeBase>(GetWorld()-
    >GetAuthGameMode());
    auto Func = &AChapter_06GameModeBase::ButtonClicked;

    if(GameMode && Func)
    {
PlayerInputComponent->BindAction("HotKey_UIButton_Spell",
                                    IE_Pressed, GameMode,
                                    Func);
```

```
        }
    }
```

3. Compile your script and then open the World Settings by going to **Settings | World Settings**. Under **Selected GameMode**, set the **Default Pawn Class** to BP_Warrior. You should now notice that you can either press your key or press the button to execute the ButtonClicked function we created in the previous recipe!

How it works...

Wiring up an Action Mapping with a short circuit to the function that's called by the UI will allow you to implement hot keys in your game program nicely.

Collision – letting objects pass through one another using Ignore

Collision settings are fairly easy to get started with. There are three classes of intersection for collisions:

- Ignore: Collisions that pass through each other without any notification.
- Overlap: Collisions that trigger the OnBeginOverlap and OnEndOverlap events. Interpenetration of objects with an Overlap setting is allowed.
- Block: Collisions that prevent all interpenetration, and prevent objects from overlapping each other at all.

Objects are classed into one of many **Object Types**. The **Collision** settings for a particular Blueprint's Component allow you to class the object as an **Object Type** of your choice, as well as specify how that object collides with all other objects of all other types. This takes a tabular format in the **Details | Collision** section of the Blueprint Editor.

For example, the following screenshot shows the **Collision** settings for a character's
`CapsuleComponent`:

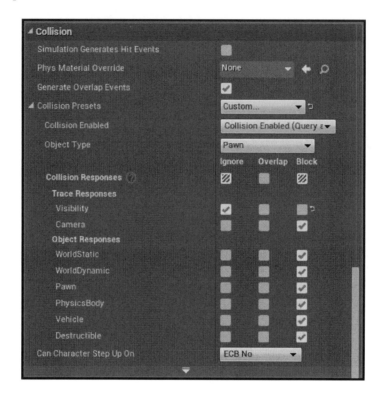

Getting ready

You should have a UE4 project with some objects that you'd like to program
intersections for.

How to do it...

1. Open the Blueprint Editor for the object that you'd like other objects to
   simply pass through and ignore. Under the **Components** listing, select the
   component that you'd like to program settings for.

2. With your component selected, see your **Details** tab (usually on the right). Under **Collision Presets**, select either the **NoCollision** or **Custom...** presets:

- If you select the **NoCollision** preset, you can just leave it at that, and all collisions will be ignored.
- If you select the **Custom...** preset, then choose either of the following:
    - **NoCollision** under the **Collision Enabled** drop-down menu.
    - Select a collision mode under **Collision Enabled** involving **Queries**, and be sure to check the **Ig**

- **nore** checkbox for each **Object Type** that you'd like it to ignore collisions with.

How it works...

Ignored collisions will not fire any events or prevent interpenetrations between objects marked as such. Note that if Object A is set to ignore Object B, it does not matter whether Object B is set to ignore Object A or not. They will ignore each other as long as one of them is set to ignore the other.

Collision – picking up objects using Overlap

Item pickup is a pretty important thing to do cleanly. In this recipe, we'll outline how to get item pickups working using **Overlap** events on Actor Component primitives.

Getting ready

The previous recipe, *Collisions – Letting objects pass through each other using Ignore*, describes the basics of collisions. You should read it for background before beginning this recipe. What we'll do here is create a **New Object Channel...** to identify Item class objects so that they can be programmed for overlaps, but only with the player avatar's collision volume.

How to do it...

1. Start by creating a unique collision Channel for the `Item` object's collision primitive. This is under **Settings** | **Project Settings** | **Collision:**

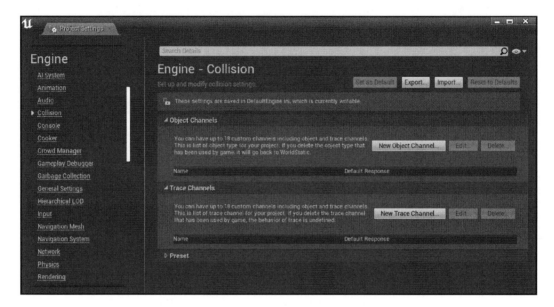

2. Once there, create a new Object Channel by going to **New Object Channel....**

3. Name the new Object Channel `Item` and set the **Default Response** to **Overlap**. Afterwards, hit the **Accept** button:

4. Take your `Item` actor and select the primitive component on it that is used to intersect for pickup with the player avatar. From the **Details** tab, go to the **Collision** section and under **Collision Presets**, change the option to **Custom...**. Afterwards, set the **Object Type** of that primitive to `Item`.

5. Check the **Overlap** checkbox against the `Pawn` class **Object Type**, as shown in the following screenshot:

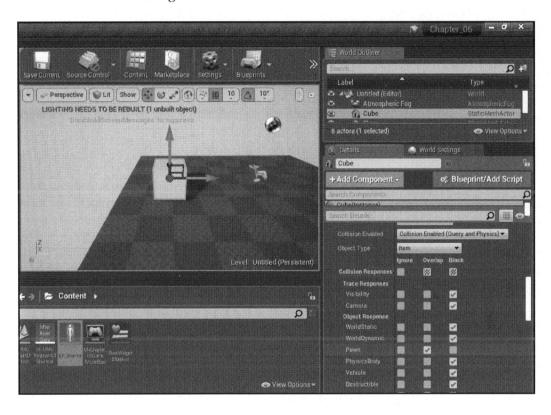

6. Ensure that the **Generate Overlap Events** checkbox is checked:

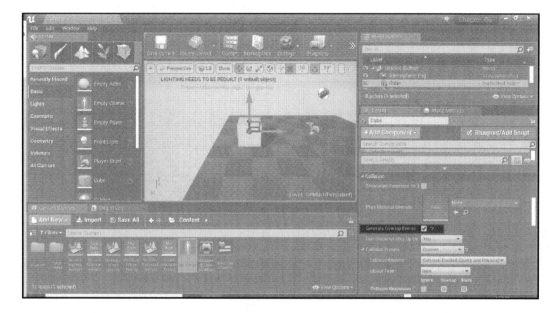

Location of the **Generate Overlap Events** property.

7. Take the player actor who will pick up the items (**BP_Warrior** for this example) and select the component on them that feels for the items. Usually, this will be their `CapsuleComponent`. Check **Overlap** with the `Item` object:

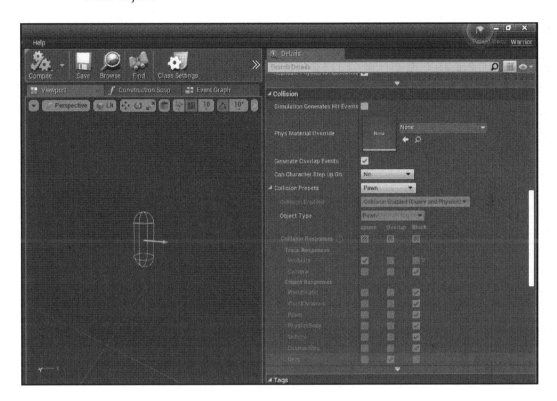

8. Now, the Player overlaps the item, and the item overlaps the player pawn. We do have to signal overlaps both ways (`Item` overlaps `Pawn` and `Pawn` Overlaps `Item`) for it to work properly. Ensure that **Generate Overlap Events** is also checked for the `Pawn` intersecting component.

9. Next, we have to complete the `OnComponentBeginOverlap` event for either the item or the Player's pickup volume, using either Blueprints or C++ code:

   1. If you prefer Blueprints, in the **Events** section of the **Details** pane of the Items's intersectable Component, click on the + icon beside the **On Component Begin Overlap** event:

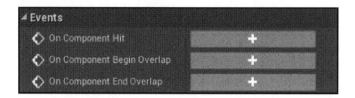

   2. Use the `OnComponentBeginOverlap` event that appears in your `Actor` Blueprint diagram to wire in Blueprints code to run when an overlap with the Player's capsule volume occurs.

   3. If you prefer C++, you can write and attach a C++ function to the `CapsuleComponent`. Write a member function in your player's `Character` class (for example, the `Warrior.h` file) with a signature, as follows:

```
UFUNCTION(BlueprintNativeEvent, Category = Collision)
void OnOverlapsBegin(UPrimitiveComponent* Comp,
                     AActor* OtherActor,
                     UPrimitiveComponent* OtherComp,
                     int32 OtherBodyIndex,
                     bool bFromSweep,
                     const FHitResult&SweepResult);

UFUNCTION(BlueprintNativeEvent, Category = Collision)
void OnOverlapsEnd(UPrimitiveComponent* Comp,
                   AActor* OtherActor,
                   UPrimitiveComponent* OtherComp,
                   int32 OtherBodyIndex);

virtual void PostInitializeComponents() override;
```

4. Complete the implementation of the `OnOverlapsBegin()` function in your `.cpp` file, making sure to end the function name with `_Implementation`:

```
void AWarrior::OnOverlapsBegin_Implementation(
    UPrimitiveComponent* Comp,
    AActor* OtherActor, UPrimitiveComponent* OtherComp,
    int32 OtherBodyIndex,
    bool bFromSweep, const FHitResult&SweepResult)
{
    UE_LOG(LogTemp, Warning, TEXT("Overlaps warrior
    began"));
}

void AWarrior::OnOverlapsEnd_Implementation(
    UPrimitiveComponent* Comp,
    AActor* OtherActor, UPrimitiveComponent* OtherComp,
    int32 OtherBodyIndex)
{
    UE_LOG(LogTemp, Warning, TEXT("Overlaps warrior
    ended"));
}
```

5. Then, provide a `PostInitializeComponents()` override to connect the `OnOverlapsBegin()` function with overlaps to the capsule in your avatar's class, as follows:

```
#include "Components/CapsuleComponent.h"

// ...

void AWarrior::PostInitializeComponents()
{
    Super::PostInitializeComponents();

    if (RootComponent)
    {
        // Attach contact function to all bounding
components.
GetCapsuleComponent()->OnComponentBeginOverlap.AddDynamic(
this, &AWarrior::OnOverlapsBegin);
GetCapsuleComponent()->OnComponentEndOverlap.AddDynamic(th
is, &AWarrior::OnOverlapsEnd);
    }
}
```

10. Compile your script and then run your project. You should see log messages when you enter and leave the object! Refer to the following screenshot:

How it works...

The **Overlap** event that's raised by the engine allows code to run when two UE4 `Actor` Components overlap, without preventing interpenetration of the objects.

Collision – preventing interpenetration using Block

Blocking means that the `Actor` components will be prevented from interpenetration in the engine, and any collision between two primitive shapes will be resolved, and not overlapping, after collisions are found.

Getting ready

Begin with a UE4 project that has some objects with Actors that have collision primitives attached to them (`SphereComponents`, `CapsuleComponents`, or `BoxComponents`).

How to do it...

1. Open the Blueprint of an actor that you want to block another actor with. For example, we want the Player actor to block other Player actor instances.
2. Mark primitives inside the actor that you do not want interpenetrating with other components as blocking those components in the **Details** pane:

How it works...

When objects b

lock one another, they will not be allowed to interpenetrate. Any interpenetration will be automatically resolved, and the objects will be pushed off each other. This is one of the details that often causes lots of headaches. For objects to actually block each other, they both have to be set to block.

 For more information, check out the official UE4 blog post on the subject: `https://www.unrealengine.com/en-US/blog/collision-filtering`.

There's more...

You can override the `OnComponentHit` function to run code when two objects hit each other. This is distinct from the `OnComponentBeginOverlap` event.

7
Communication Between Classes and Interfaces: Part I

The following recipes will be covered in this chapter:

- Creating a UInterface
- Implementing a UInterface on an object
- Checking if a class implements a UInterface
- Casting to a UInterface implemented in native code
- Calling native UInterface functions from C++
- Inheriting UInterfaces from one another
- Overriding UInterface functions in C++
- Implementing a simple interaction system with UInterfaces

Introduction

This chapter shows you how to write your own UInterfaces, and demonstrates how to take advantage of them within C++ to minimize class coupling and help keep your code clean.

In your game projects, you will sometimes require a series of potentially disparate objects to share a common functionality, but it would be inappropriate to use inheritance because there is no *is-a* relationship between the different objects in question. Languages such as C++ tend to use multiple inheritance to solve this issue.

However, in Unreal, if you wanted functions from both parent classes to be accessible to Blueprint, you would need to make both of them UCLASS. This is a problem for two reasons. Inheriting from UClass twice in the same object would break the concept that UObject should form a neatly traversable hierarchy. It also means that there are two instances of the UClass methods on the object, and they would have to be explicitly differentiated between within the code. The Unreal codebase solves this issue by borrowing a concept from C#: that of an explicit Interface type.

The reason for using this approach, instead of composition, is that Components are only available on Actors, not on UObjects in general. Interfaces can be applied to any UObject. Furthermore, it means that we are no longer modeling an *is-a* relationship between the object and the component; instead, it would only be able to represent *has-a* relationships.

Technical requirements

This chapter requires the use of Unreal Engine 4 and uses Visual Studio 2017 as the IDE. Instructions on how to install both pieces of software and the requirements for them can be found in Chapter 1, *UE4 Development Tools*, of this book.

Creating a UInterface

UInterfaces are pairs of classes that work together to enable classes to exhibit polymorphic behavior among multiple class hierarchies. This recipe shows you the basic steps involved in creating a UInterface purely in code.

How to do it...

1. From the Content Browser, go to **Add New** | **New C++ Class**. From the menu that pops up, scroll down all the way until you see the **Unreal Interface** selection and select it. Afterward, click on the **Next** button:

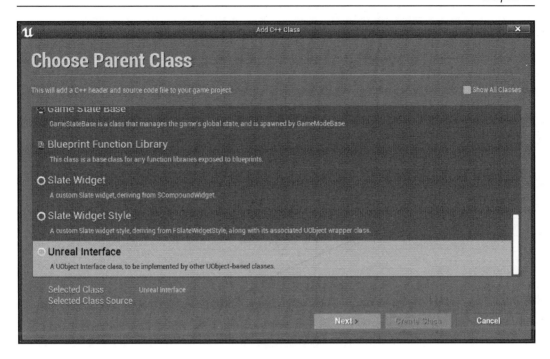

2. From there, verify that the **Name** of the class is `MyInterface` and then click on the **Create Class** button:

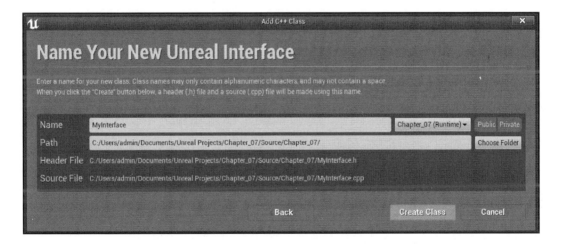

3. Add the following code to the header file:

```
#pragma once

#include "CoreMinimal.h"
#include "UObject/Interface.h"
#include "MyInterface.generated.h"

// This class does not need to be modified.
UINTERFACE(MinimalAPI)
class UMyInterface : public UInterface
{
    GENERATED_BODY()
};

class CHAPTER_07_API IMyInterface
{
    GENERATED_BODY()

    // Add interface functions to this class. This is the class
that
    //will be inherited to implement this interface.

public:
    virtual FString GetTestName();
};
```

4. Implement the class with this code in the .cpp file:

```
#include "MyInterface.h"

// Add default functionality here for any IMyInterface
functions that are not pure virtual.
FString IMyInterface::GetTestName()
{
    unimplemented();
    return FString();
}
```

5. Compile your project to verify that the code was written without errors.

How it works...

UInterfaces are implemented as pairs of classes that are declared in the interface's header.

As always, because we are leveraging Unreal's reflection system, we need to include our generated header file. Refer to the *Handling events implemented via virtual functions* recipe in `Chapter 5`, *Handling Events and Delegates*, for more information.

As with classes that inherit from `UObject`, which uses `UCLASS`, we need to use the `UINTERFACE` macro to declare our new `UInterface`. Passing in the class specifier of `MinimalAPI` causes only the class's type information to be exported for use by other modules.

 For more information on this and other class specifiers, check out: `https://docs.unrealengine.com/en-US/Programming/UnrealArchitecture/Reference/Classes/Specifiers`.

The class is tagged as `UE4COOKBOOK_API` to help with exporting library symbols.

The base class for the `UObject` portion of the interface is `UInterface`.

Just like `UCLASS` types, we require a macro to be placed inside the body of our class so that the auto-generated code is inserted into it. That macro is `GENERATED_BODY()` for UInterfaces. The macro must be placed at the very start of the class body.

The second class is also tagged as `UE4COOKBOOK_API`, and is named in a specific way.

Note that the `UInterface` derived class and the standard class have the same name but a different prefix. The `UInterface` derived class has the prefix `U`, and the standard class has the prefix `I`. This is important as this is how the Unreal Header Tool expects classes to be named for the code it generates to work properly.

The plain native Interface class requires its own autogenerated content, which we include using the `GENERATED_BODY()` macro.

We declare functions that classes inheriting the interface should implement inside `IInterface`.

Within the implementation file, we implement the constructor for our `UInterface`, as it is declared by the Unreal Header Tool and requires an implementation.

We also create a default implementation for our `GetTestName()` function. Without this, the linking phase in the compilation will fail. This default implementation uses the `unimplemented()` macro, which will issue a debug assert when the line of code is executed.

 For more information on creating interfaces, check out the following link: `https://docs.unrealengine.com/en-us/Programming/ UnrealArchitecture/Reference/Interfaces`.

See also

- Refer to the *Passing payload data with a delegate binding* recipe in `Chapter 5`, *Handling Events and Delegates*; the first recipe, in particular, explains some of the principles that we've applied here

Implementing a UInterface on an object

Now that we have created a UInterface, we can say that an object has all of the functions defined or implements them. In this recipe, we will see exactly how to do that.

Getting ready

Ensure that you've followed the previous recipe so that you have a `UInterface` ready to be implemented.

How to do it...

1. Create a new `Actor` class using the Unreal Wizard, called `SingleInterfaceActor`:

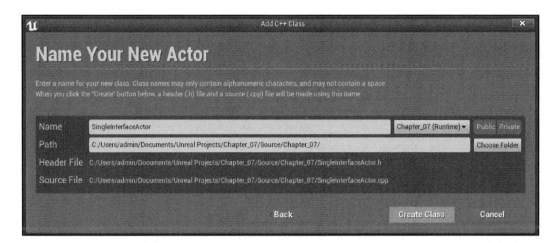

2. Add `IInterface`—in this case, `IMyInterface`—to the public inheritance list for our new `Actor` class:

```
#pragma once

#include "CoreMinimal.h"
#include "GameFramework/Actor.h"
#include "MyInterface.h"
#include "SingleInterfaceActor.generated.h"

UCLASS()
class CHAPTER_07_API ASingleInterfaceActor : public AActor,
public IMyInterface
{
  GENERATED_BODY()
```

3. Add an `override` declaration to the class for the `IInterface` function(s) that we wish to override:

```
UCLASS()
class CHAPTER_07_API ASingleInterfaceActor : public AActor,
public IMyInterface
{
  GENERATED_BODY()
```

```
public:
  // Sets default values for this actor's properties
  ASingleInterfaceActor();

protected:
  // Called when the game starts or when spawned
  virtual void BeginPlay() override;

public:
  // Called every frame
  virtual void Tick(float DeltaTime) override;

  FString GetTestName() override;

};
```

4. Implement the overridden function in the implementation file by adding the following code:

```
FString ASingleInterfaceActor::GetTestName()
{
    return IMyInterface::GetTestName();
}
```

How it works...

C++ uses multiple inheritance in the way it implements interfaces, so we leverage that mechanism here with the declaration of our SingleInterfaceActor class, where we add public IMyInterface.

We inherit from IInterface rather than UInterface to prevent SingleInterfaceActor from inheriting two copies of UObject.

Given that the interface declares a virtual function, we need to redeclare that function with the override specifier if we wish to implement it ourselves.

In our implementation file, we implement our overridden virtual function.

Inside our function override, for demonstration purposes, we call the base IInterface implementation of the function. Alternatively, we could write our own implementation and avoid calling the base class one altogether.

We use `IInterface::` specifier rather than `Super`, because `Super` refers to the `UClass` that is the parent of our class, and `IInterfaces` aren't UClasses (hence there's no `U` prefix).

You can implement a second, or multiple, `IInterfaces` on your object, as needed.

Checking if a class implements a UInterface

When writing C++ code, it's always a good idea to make sure that something exists before using it. In this recipe, we will see how we can check whether a particular object implements a specific `UInterface`.

Getting ready

Follow the first two recipes so that you have a `UInterface` we can check for, and a class implementing the interface that can be tested against.

How to do it...

1. Inside your Game Mode implementation, add the following code to the `BeginPlay` function:

```
void AChapter_07GameModeBase::BeginPlay()
{
    Super::BeginPlay();

    // Spawn a new actor using the ASingleInterfaceActor class at
    //the default location
    FTransform SpawnLocation;
    ASingleInterfaceActor* SpawnedActor =
GetWorld()->SpawnActor<ASingleInterfaceActor>(
ASingleInterfaceActor::StaticClass(),
                                        SpawnLocation);
    // Get a reference to the class the actor has
    UClass* ActorClass = SpawnedActor->GetClass();

    // If the class implements the interface, display a
```

```
message
    if (ActorClass-
    >ImplementsInterface(UMyInterface::StaticClass()))
    {
        GEngine->AddOnScreenDebugMessage(-1, 10, FColor::Red,
                            TEXT("Spawned actor implements
                                    interface!"));
    }
}
```

2. Given that we are referencing both `ASingleInterfaceActor` and `IMyInterface`, we need to `#include` both `MyInterface.h` and `SingleInterfaceActor.h` in our source file:

```
#include "Chapter_07GameModeBase.h"
#include "MyInterface.h"
#include "SingleInterfaceActor.h"
```

3. Save your script and compile your code. Afterward, from the **World Settings** menu, set the **GameMode Override** property to your `GameModeBase` class and play the game. If all went well, you should see a message stating that you've implemented the interface:

How it works...

Inside `BeginPlay`, we create an empty `FTransform` object, which has the default value of `0` for all translation and rotation components, so we don't need to explicitly set any of them.

We then use the `SpawnActor` function from `UWorld` so that we can create an instance of our `SingleActorInterface`, storing the pointer to the instance into a temporary variable.

We then use `GetClass()` on our instance to get a reference to its associated `UClass`. We need a reference to `UClass` because that object is the one that holds all of the reflection data for the object.

Reflection data includes the names and types of all `UPROPERTY` on the object, the inheritance hierarchy for the object, and a list of all the interfaces that it implements.

As a result, we can call `ImplementsInterface()` on `UClass`, and it will return `true` if the object implements the `UInterface` in question.

If the object implements the interface, and therefore returns `true` from `ImplementsInterface`, we then print a message to the screen.

See also

- `Chapter 4`, Actors and Components, has a number of recipes relating to the spawning of actors (such as Instantiating an Actor using SpawnActor)

Casting to a UInterface implemented in native code

One advantage that UInterfaces provide you with as a developer is the ability to treat a collection of heterogeneous objects that implement a common interface as a collection of the same object, using `Cast< >` to handle the conversion.

Please note that this won't work if your class implements the interface through a Blueprint.

Getting ready

You should have a `UInterface` and an `Actor` implementing the interface ready for this recipe.

Create a new game mode using the wizard within Unreal, or reuse a project and `GameMode` from a previous recipe.

How to do it...

1. Open your game mode's declaration and add a new property to the class:

```
UCLASS()
class CHAPTER_07_API AChapter_07GameModeBase : public
AGameModeBase
{
    GENERATED_BODY()

public:
    virtual void BeginPlay() override;

    TArray<IMyInterface*> MyInterfaceInstances;
};
```

2. Add `#include "MyInterface.h"` to the header's include section:

```
#pragma once

#include "CoreMinimal.h"
#include "GameFramework/GameModeBase.h"
#include "MyInterface.h"
#include "Chapter_07GameModeBase.generated.h"
```

3. Add the following within the game mode's `BeginPlay` implementation:

```
for (TActorIterator<AActor> It (GetWorld(),
AActor::StaticClass());
    It;
    ++It)
{
    AActor* Actor = *It;

    IMyInterface* MyInterfaceInstance =
Cast<IMyInterface>(Actor);
```

```
        // If the pointer is valid, add it to the list
        if (MyInterfaceInstance)
        {
            MyInterfaceInstances.Add(MyInterfaceInstance);
        }
    }

    // Print out how many objects implement the interface
    FString Message = FString::Printf(TEXT("%d actors implement
    the
                                interface"),
    MyInterfaceInstances.Num());

    GEngine->AddOnScreenDebugMessage(-1, 10, FColor::Red,
    Message);
```

4. Since we are using the `TActorIterator` class, we will need to add the following `#include` to the top of our `GameModeBase` class' implementation file:

```
#include "Chapter_07GameModeBase.h"
#include "MyInterface.h"
#include "SingleInterfaceActor.h"
#include "EngineUtils.h" // TActorIterator
```

5. If you haven't done so already, set the level's game mode override to your game mode, then drag a few instances of your custom Interface-implementing actor into the level.

6. When you play your level, a message should be printed on screen that indicates the number of instances of the interface that have been implemented in Actors in the level:

How it works...

We create an array of pointers to `MyInterface` implementations.

Inside `BeginPlay`, we use `TActorIterator<AActor>` to get all of the `Actor` instances in our level.

`TActorIterator` has the following constructor:

```
explicit TActorIterator( UWorld* InWorld,
  TSubclassOf<ActorType>InClass = ActorType::StaticClass() )
: Super(InWorld, InClass )
```

`TActorIterator` expects a world to act on, as well as a `UClass` instance to specify what types of Actor we are interested in.

`ActorIterator` is an iterator like the STL iterator type. This means that we can write a `for` loop in the following form:

```
for (iterator-constructor;iterator;++iterator)
```

Inside the loop, we dereference the iterator to get an `Actor` pointer.

We then attempt to cast it to our interface; this will return a pointer to the interface if it does implement it, otherwise it will return `nullptr`.

As a result, we can check if the interface pointer is `null`, and if not, we can add the interface pointer reference to our array.

Finally, once we've iterated through all the actors in `TActorIterator`, we can display a message on the screen that displays the count of items that implemented the interface.

Calling native UInterface functions from C++

We can use C++ to call native `UInterface` functions from other classes as well. For example, in this recipe, we will make a volume call a function on an object if it implements a particular interface.

Getting ready

Follow the previous recipe to get an understanding of casting an `Actor` pointer to an Interface pointer.

 Note that as this recipe relies on the casting technique we used in the previous recipe, it will only work with objects that implement the interface using C++ rather than Blueprint. This is because Blueprint classes are not available at compile time, and so, technically, don't inherit the interface.

How to do it...

1. Create a new `Actor` class using the editor wizard. Call it `AntiGravityVolume`:

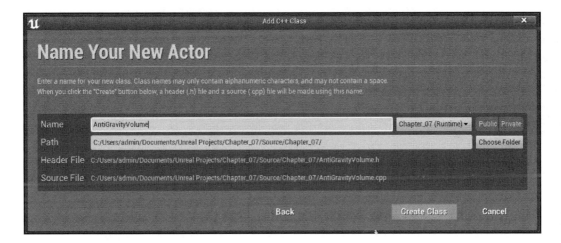

2. Update the header file to add a `BoxComponent` to the new `Actor` and two virtual functions:

```cpp
#pragma once

#include "CoreMinimal.h"
#include "GameFramework/Actor.h"
#include "Components/BoxComponent.h"
#include "AntiGravityVolume.generated.h"

UCLASS()
```

```
class CHAPTER_07_API AAntiGravityVolume : public AActor
{
    GENERATED_BODY()
public:
    // Sets default values for this actor's properties
    AAntiGravityVolume();

protected:
    // Called when the game starts or when spawned
    virtual void BeginPlay() override;

public:
    // Called every frame
    virtual void Tick(float DeltaTime) override;

    UPROPERTY()
    UBoxComponent* CollisionComponent;

    virtual void NotifyActorBeginOverlap(AActor* OtherActor)
override;
    virtual void NotifyActorEndOverlap(AActor* OtherActor)
override;


};
```

3. Create an implementation within your source file, as follows:

```
void AAntiGravityVolume::NotifyActorBeginOverlap(AActor*
OtherActor)
{
    IGravityObject* GravityObject =
Cast<IGravityObject>(OtherActor);

    if (GravityObject != nullptr)
    {
        GravityObject->DisableGravity();
    }
}

void AAntiGravityVolume::NotifyActorEndOverlap(AActor*
OtherActor)
{
    IGravityObject* GravityObject =
Cast<IGravityObject>(OtherActor);

    if (GravityObject != nullptr)
    {
```

```
                GravityObject->EnableGravity();
        }
    }
```

4. Initialize the `BoxComponent` in your constructor:

```
// Sets default values
AAntiGravityVolume::AAntiGravityVolume()
{
    // Set this actor to call Tick() every frame. You can turn
this off
    // to improve performance if you don't need it.
    PrimaryActorTick.bCanEverTick = true;

    CollisionComponent =
CreateDefaultSubobject<UBoxComponent>("CollisionComponent");

    CollisionComponent->SetBoxExtent(FVector(200, 200, 400));
    RootComponent = CollisionComponent;
}
```

The script will not compile since `GravityObject` doesn't exist. Let's fix that:

5. Create an interface called `GravityObject`:

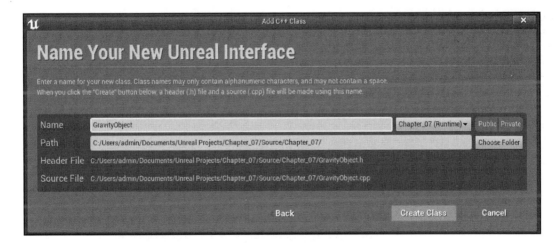

6. Add the following `virtual` functions to `IGravityObject`:

```
class CHAPTER_07_API IGravityObject
{
    GENERATED_BODY()
```

```
        // Add interface functions to this class. This is the
    class that
        // will be inherited to implement this interface.
    public:
        virtual void EnableGravity();
        virtual void DisableGravity();
    };
```

7. Create the default implementation of the `virtual` functions inside the `IGravityObject` implementation file:

```
#include "GravityObject.h"

// Add default functionality here for any IGravityObject
functions that are not pure virtual.
void IGravityObject::EnableGravity()
{
    AActor* ThisAsActor = Cast<AActor>(this);
    if (ThisAsActor != nullptr)
    {
        TArray<UPrimitiveComponent*> PrimitiveComponents;

        ThisAsActor->GetComponents(PrimitiveComponents);

        for (UPrimitiveComponent* Component :
PrimitiveComponents)
        {
            Component->SetEnableGravity(true);
        }

        GEngine->AddOnScreenDebugMessage(-1, 1, FColor::Red,
        TEXT("Enabling Gravity"));
    }
}

void IGravityObject::DisableGravity()
{
    AActor* ThisAsActor = Cast<AActor>(this);
    if (ThisAsActor != nullptr)
    {
        TArray<UPrimitiveComponent*> PrimitiveComponents;

        ThisAsActor->GetComponents(PrimitiveComponents);

        for (UPrimitiveComponent* Component :
PrimitiveComponents)
        {
            Component->SetEnableGravity(false);
```

```
        }

        GEngine->AddOnScreenDebugMessage(-1, 1, FColor::Red,
        TEXT("Disabling Gravity"));
    }
}
```

8. Afterward, go back to the `AntiGravityVolume.cpp` file and add the following `#include`:

```
#include "AntiGravityVolume.h"
#include "GravityObject.h"
```

At this point, our code will compile, but there's nothing using the interface. Let's add a new class that will.

9. Create a subclass of `Actor` called `PhysicsCube`:

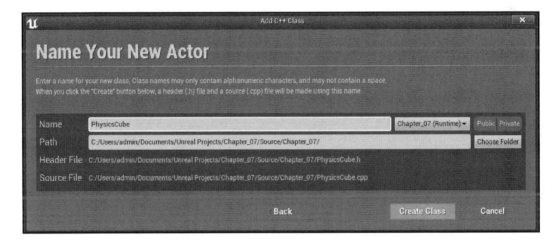

10. Add a static mesh property to the header:

```
#pragma once

#include "CoreMinimal.h"
#include "GameFramework/Actor.h"
#include "Components/StaticMeshComponent.h"
#include "PhysicsCube.generated.h"

UCLASS()
class CHAPTER_07_API APhysicsCube : public AActor
{
    GENERATED_BODY()
```

```
public:
  // Sets default values for this actor's properties
  APhysicsCube();

protected:
  // Called when the game starts or when spawned
  virtual void BeginPlay() override;

public:
  // Called every frame
  virtual void Tick(float DeltaTime) override;

    UPROPERTY()
    UStaticMeshComponent* MyMesh;

};
```

11. Initialize the component in your constructor:

```
#include "PhysicsCube.h"
#include "ConstructorHelpers.h"

// Sets default values
APhysicsCube::APhysicsCube()
{
   // Set this actor to call Tick() every frame. You can turn this
   //off
   // to improve performance if you don't need it.
  PrimaryActorTick.bCanEverTick = true;

    MyMesh =
CreateDefaultSubobject<UStaticMeshComponent>("MyMesh");

    auto MeshAsset =
ConstructorHelpers::FObjectFinder<UStaticMesh>
    (TEXT("StaticMesh'/Engine/BasicShapes/Cube.Cube'"));

    if (MeshAsset.Object != nullptr)
    {
        MyMesh->SetStaticMesh(MeshAsset.Object);
    }

    MyMesh->SetMobility(EComponentMobility::Movable);
    MyMesh->SetSimulatePhysics(true);
    SetActorEnableCollision(true);
}
```

12. To have `PhysicsCube` implement `GravityObject`, first `#include` `"GravityObject.h"` in the header file, then modify the class declaration:

```
#pragma once

#include "CoreMinimal.h"
#include "GameFramework/Actor.h"
#include "Components/StaticMeshComponent.h"
#include "GravityObject.h"
#include "PhysicsCube.generated.h"


UCLASS()
class CHAPTER_07_API APhysicsCube : public AActor, public
IGravityObject
```

13. Compile your project.
14. Create a new level and place an instance of our gravity volume in the scene.
15. Place an instance of `PhysicsCube` above the gravity volume, then rotate it slightly so that it has one corner lower than the others, as shown in the following screenshot:

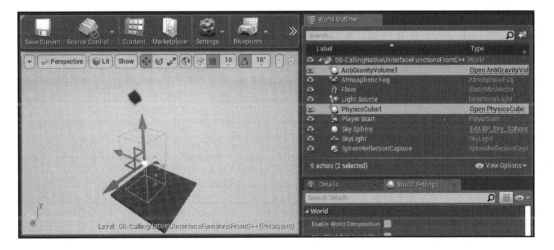

16. Verify that the gravity is turned off on the object when it enters the volume and then turns back on again:

Note that the gravity volume doesn't need to know anything about your `PhysicsCube` actor, just the `GravityObject` interface.

How it works...

We create a new `Actor` class and add a box component to give the actor something that will collide with the character. Alternatively, you could subclass `AVolume` if you wanted to use the **Binary Space Partitioning (BSP)** functionality to define the volume's shape (found under **Geometry** in the **Place** section of the **Modes** tab).

`NotifyActorBeginOverlap` and `NotifyActorEndOverlap` are overridden so that we can perform an operation when an object enters or leaves the `AntiGravityVolume` area.

Inside the `NotifyActorBeginOverlap` implementation, we attempt to cast the object that overlapped us into an `IGravityObject` pointer. This tests whether the object in question implements the interface. If the pointer is valid, then the object does implement the interface, so it is safe to use the interface pointer to call Interface methods on the object.

Given that we are inside `NotifyActorBeginOverlap`, we want to disable gravity on the object, so we call `DisableGravity()`. Inside `NotifyActorEndOverlap`, we perform the same check, but we re-enable gravity on the object. Within the default implementation of `DisableGravity`, we cast our own pointer (the `this` pointer) to `AActor`. This allows us to confirm that the interface has been implemented only on the `Actor` subclasses, and to call methods defined in `AActor`.

If the pointer is valid, we know we are an `Actor`, so we can use `GetComponents<class ComponentType>()` to get a `TArray` of all components of a specific type from ourselves. `GetComponents` is a `template` function. It expects some template parameters, as follows:

```
template<class T, class AllocatorType>
  voidGetComponents(TArray<T*, AllocatorType>&OutComponents)
  const
```

Since the 2014 version of the standard, C++ supports compile-time deduction of template parameters. This means that we don't need to actually specify the template parameters when we call the function if the compiler can work them out from the normal function parameters that we provide.

The default implementation of `TArray` is `template<typename T, typename Allocator = FDefaultAllocator> class TArray;`. This means that we don't need to specify an allocator by default, so we just use `TArray<UPrimitiveComponent*>` when we declare the array.

When `TArray` is passed into the `GetComponents` function, the compiler knows it is actually `TArray<UPrimitiveComponent*, FDefaultAllocator>`, and it is able to fill in the template parameters `T` and `AllocatorType` with `UPrimitiveComponent` and `FDefaultAllocator`, so neither of those are required as template parameters for the function's invocation.

`GetComponents` iterates through the components that `Actor` has, and any components that inherit from `typename T` have pointers to them stored inside the `PrimitiveComponents` array.

Using a range-based `for` loop, another new feature of C++, we can iterate over the components that the function placed into our `TArray` without needing to use the traditional `for` loop structure.

Each of the components has `SetEnableGravity(false)` called on them, which disables gravity.

Likewise, the `EnableGravity` function iterates over all the primitive components contained in the actor, and enables gravity with `SetEnableGravity(true)`.

See also

- Look at `Chapter 4`, *Actors and Components,* for extensive discussions on Actors and Components
- `Chapter 5`, *Handling Events and Delegates,* discusses events such as `NotifyActorOverlap`

Inheriting UInterfaces from one another

Sometimes, you may need to create a `UInterface` that specializes on a more general `UInterface`. This recipe shows you how to use inheritance with UInterfaces to specialize a `Killable` interface with an `Undead` interface that cannot be killed by normal means.

How to do it...

1. Create a `UInterface`/`IInterface` called `Killable`:

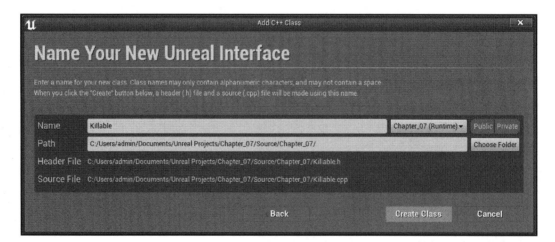

2. Add `UINTERFACE(meta=(CannotImplementInterfaceInBlueprint))` to the `UInterface` declaration:

```
// This class does not need to be modified.
UINTERFACE(meta = (CannotImplementInterfaceInBlueprint))
class UKillable : public UInterface
{
  GENERATED_BODY()
};
```

3. Add the following functions to the header file under the `IKillable` class:

```
class CHAPTER_07_API IKillable
{
    GENERATED_BODY()

    // Add interface functions to this class. This is the
class that
    // will be inherited to implement this interface.
public:
    UFUNCTION(BlueprintCallable, Category = Killable)
    virtual bool IsDead();
    UFUNCTION(BlueprintCallable, Category = Killable)
    virtual void Die();
};
```

4. Provide default implementations for the interface inside the implementation file:

```
#include "Killable.h"

// Add default functionality here for any IKillable functions
that are
// not pure virtual.
bool IKillable::IsDead()
{
    return false;
}

void IKillable::Die()
{
    GEngine->AddOnScreenDebugMessage(-1, 1, FColor::Red,
"Arrrgh");

    AActor* Me = Cast<AActor>(this);

    if (Me)
    {
```

```
            Me->Destroy();
        }

    }
```

5. Create a new UINTERFACE/IInterface **called** Undead:

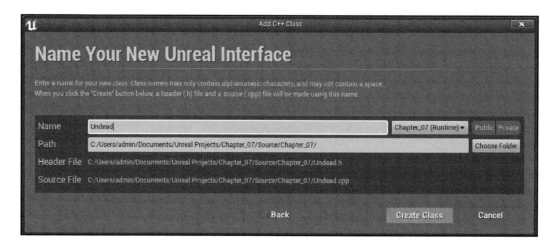

6. Modify them so they inherit from UKillable/IKillable:

```
#pragma once

#include "CoreMinimal.h"
#include "UObject/Interface.h"
#include "Killable.h"
#include "Undead.generated.h"

// This class does not need to be modified.
UINTERFACE(MinimalAPI)
class UUndead : public UKillable
{
    GENERATED_BODY()
};

/**
 *
 */
class CHAPTER_07_API IUndead : public IKillable
{
    GENERATED_BODY()

    // Add interface functions to this class. This is the class
```

```
that will
    // be inherited to implement this interface.
public:
};
```

Ensure that you include the header defining the `Killable` interface.

7. Add some overrides and new method declarations to the new interface:

```
class CHAPTER_07_API IUndead : public IKillable
{
    GENERATED_BODY()

    // Add interface functions to this class. This is the
class that
    // will be inherited to implement this interface.
public:
    virtual bool IsDead() override;
    virtual void Die() override;
    virtual void Turn();
    virtual void Banish();
};
```

8. Create implementations for the functions:

```
#include "Undead.h"

// Add default functionality here for any IUndead functions
that are
// not pure virtual.
bool IUndead::IsDead()
{
    return true;
}

void IUndead::Die()
{
    GEngine->AddOnScreenDebugMessage(-1, 1, FColor::Red, "You
can't kill what is already dead. Mwahaha");
}

void IUndead::Turn()
{
    GEngine->AddOnScreenDebugMessage(-1, 1, FColor::Red, "I'm
fleeing!");

}
```

```
void IUndead::Banish()
{
    AActor* Me = Cast<AActor>(this);
    if (Me)
    {
        Me->Destroy();
    }
}
```

9. Create two new `Actor` classes in C++: one called `Snail`, and another called `Zombie`.

10. Set the `Snail` class to implement the `IKillable` interface, and add the appropriate header file, #include:

```
#pragma once

#include "CoreMinimal.h"
#include "GameFramework/Actor.h"
#include "Killable.h"
#include "Snail.generated.h"

UCLASS()
class CHAPTER_07_API ASnail : public AActor, public IKillable
```

11. Likewise, set the `Zombie` class to implement `IUndead`, and #include "Undead.h":

```
#pragma once

#include "CoreMinimal.h"
#include "GameFramework/Actor.h"
#include "Undead.h"
#include "Zombie.generated.h"

UCLASS()
class CHAPTER_07_API AZombie : public AActor, public IUndead
```

12. Compile your project and drag an instance of both `Zombie` and `Snail` into your level:

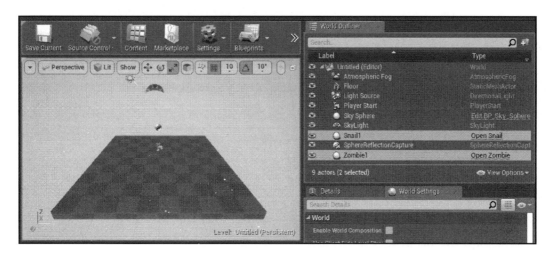

13. Open the Level Blueprint by going to **Blueprints | Level Blueprint**. Afterward, add references to each of the newly created objects in the **Level Blueprint** by dragging and dropping them from the **World Outliner** into the **Level Blueprint** and releasing them, one at a time:

14. Afterward, call Die (Interface Call) on each reference:

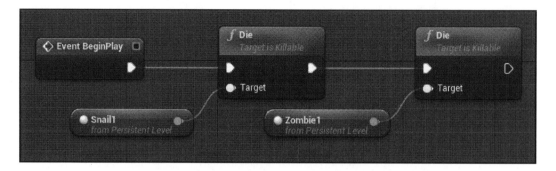

15. Connect the execution pins of the two message calls, then wire it up to Event BeginPlay. Run the game, and then verify that the Zombie is disdainful of your efforts to kill it, but the Snail groans and then dies (it is removed from the world outliner):

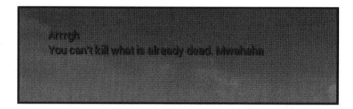

How it works...

To make it possible to test this recipe in the **Level Blueprint**, we need to make the interface functions callable via Blueprint, so we need the BlueprintCallable specifier on our UFUNCTION.

However, in a UInterface, the compiler expects the interface to be implementable via both C++ and Blueprint by default. This conflicts with BlueprintCallable, which is merely saying that the function can be invoked from Blueprint, not that it can be overridden in it.

We can resolve this conflict by marking the interface as CannotImplementInterfaceInBlueprint. This enables the use of BlueprintCallable as our UFUNCTION specifier, rather than BlueprintImplementableEvent (which has extra overhead due to the extra code allowing for the function to be overridden via Blueprint).

We define `IsDead` and `Die` as `virtual` to allow them to be overridden in another C++ class that inherits this one. In our default interface implementation, `IsDead` always returns `false`. The default implementation of `Die` prints a death message to the screen, and then destroys the object implementing this interface if it is an `Actor`.

We can now create a second interface called `Undead`, which inherits from `Killable`. We use `public UKillable`/`public IKillable` in the class declarations to express this.

Of course, as a result, we need to include the header file that defines the `Killable` interface. Our new interface overrides the two functions that `Killable` defines to provide more appropriate definitions of `IsDead`/`Die` for `Undead`. Our overridden definitions have `Undead` already dead by returning `true` from `IsDead`. When `Die` is called on `Undead`, we simply print a message with `Undead` laughing at our feeble attempt to kill it again, and do nothing.

We can also specify default implementations for our Undead-specific functions, namely `Turn()` and `Banish()`. When the `Undead` are Turned, they flee, and for demonstration purposes, we print a message to the screen. If an `Undead` is Banished, however, they are annihilated and destroyed without a trace.

To test our implementation, we create two `Actors` that each inherit from one of the two interfaces. After we add an instance of each actor to our level, we use the **Level Blueprint** to access the level's `BeginPlay` event. When the level begins to play, we use a message call to try and call the `Die` function on our instances.

The messages that print out are different and correspond to the two function implementations, showing that the Zombie's implementation of `Die` is different, and has overridden the Snail's.

Overriding UInterface functions in C++

One side-effect of UInterfaces allowing inheritance in C++ is that we can override default implementations in subclasses as well as in Blueprint. This recipe shows you how to do so.

Getting ready

Follow the *Calling native UInterface functions from C++* recipe in which a Physics Cube has already been created so that you have the class ready.

How to do it...

1. Create a new Interface called `Selectable`:

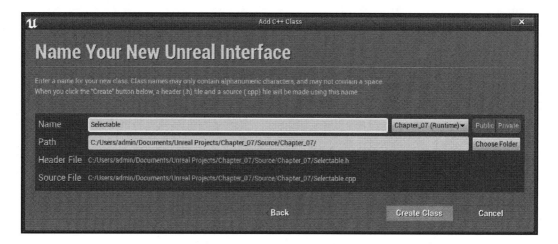

2. Define the following functions inside `ISelectable`:

```
class CHAPTER_07_API ISelectable
{
  GENERATED_BODY()

  // Add interface functions to this class. This is the class
that will
  // be inherited to implement this interface.
public:
    virtual bool IsSelectable();
    virtual bool TrySelect();
    virtual void Deselect();
};
```

3. Provide a default implementation for the functions, like so:

```cpp
#include "Selectable.h"

// Add default functionality here for any ISelectable
functions that are not pure virtual.
bool ISelectable::IsSelectable()
{
    GEngine->AddOnScreenDebugMessage(-1, 1, FColor::Red,
"Selectable");
    return true;
}

bool ISelectable::TrySelect()
{
    GEngine->AddOnScreenDebugMessage(-1, 1, FColor::Red,
"Accepting Selection");
    return true;
}

void ISelectable::Deselect()
{
    unimplemented();
}
```

4. Create a class based on `APhysicsCube` by right-clicking on the **Physics Cube** script from the **Content Browser** and selecting **Create C++ class derived from PhysicsCube**:

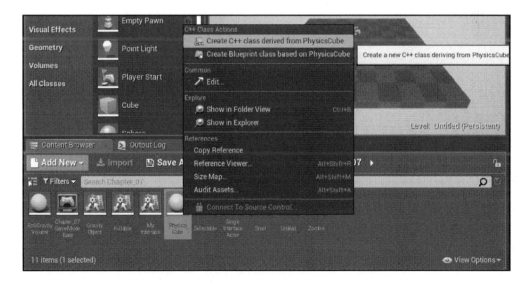

---

5. Once you're done, change the **Name** of the new cube to `SelectableCube` and click on the **Create Class** option:

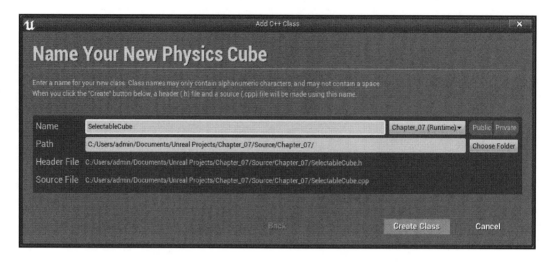

6. Add `#include "Selectable.h"` inside the `SelectableCube` class' header.

7. Modify the `ASelectableCube` declaration, like so:

```
#pragma once

#include "CoreMinimal.h"
#include "PhysicsCube.h"
#include "Selectable.h"
#include "SelectableCube.generated.h"

UCLASS()
class CHAPTER_07_API ASelectableCube : public APhysicsCube,
public ISelectable
```

8. Add the following functions to the header:

```
UCLASS()
class CHAPTER_07_API ASelectableCube : public APhysicsCube,
public ISelectable
{
    GENERATED_BODY()
public:
    ASelectableCube();
    virtual void NotifyHit(class UPrimitiveComponent* MyComp,
                           AActor* Other,
                           class UPrimitiveComponent*
OtherComp,
                           bool bSelfMoved, FVector
HitLocation,
                           FVector HitNormal, FVector
NormalImpulse,
                           const FHitResult& Hit) override;

};
```

9. Implement the functions:

```
#include "SelectableCube.h"

ASelectableCube::ASelectableCube() : Super()
{
    MyMesh->SetNotifyRigidBodyCollision(true);
}

void ASelectableCube::NotifyHit(class UPrimitiveComponent*
MyComp,
                                AActor* Other,
                                class UPrimitiveComponent*
OtherComp,
                                bool bSelfMoved, FVector
HitLocation,
                                FVector HitNormal,
                                FVector NormalImpulse,
                                const FHitResult& Hit)
{
    if (ISelectable::IsSelectable())
    {
        TrySelect();
    }
}
```

10. Create a new class called `NonSelectableCube`, which inherits from `SelectableCube`, in the same manner that we did with the `Physics Cube` to create the `SelectableCube` class:

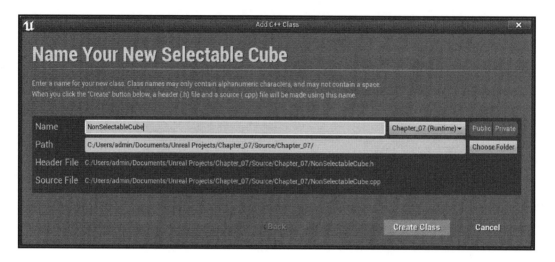

11. `NonSelectableCube` should override the functions from `SelectableInterface`:

```
#pragma once

#include "CoreMinimal.h"
#include "SelectableCube.h"
#include "NonSelectableCube.generated.h"

UCLASS()
class CHAPTER_07_API ANonSelectableCube : public
ASelectableCube
{
    GENERATED_BODY()
public:
    virtual bool IsSelectable() override;
    virtual bool TrySelect() override;
    virtual void Deselect() override;
};
```

12. The implementation file should be altered to include the following:

```
#include "NonSelectableCube.h"

bool ANonSelectableCube::IsSelectable()
```

```
{
    GEngine->AddOnScreenDebugMessage(-1, 1, FColor::Red, "Not
Selectable");
    return false;
}

bool ANonSelectableCube::TrySelect()
{
    GEngine->AddOnScreenDebugMessage(-1, 1, FColor::Red,
"Refusing Selection");
    return false;
}

void ANonSelectableCube::Deselect()
{
    unimplemented();
}
```

13. Place an instance of SelectableCube into the level at a certain range above the ground, and then play your game. You should get messages verifying that the actor is selectable, and that it has accepted the selection when the cube hits the ground:

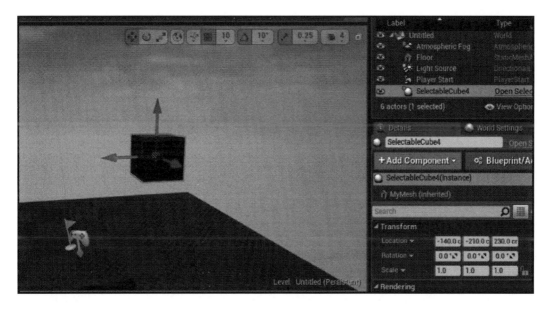

14. Remove SelectableCube and replace it with an instance of NonSelectableCube to see the alternative messages indicating that this actor isn't selectable and has refused selection.

How it works...

We create three functions inside the `Selectable` interface. `IsSelectable` returns a Boolean to indicate whether the object is selectable. You could avoid this and simply use `TrySelect`, given that it returns a Boolean value to indicate success, but, for example, you might want to know if the object inside your UI is a valid selection without having to actually try it.

`TrySelect` actually attempts to select the object. There's no explicit contract forcing users to respect `IsSelectable` when trying to select the object, so `TrySelect` is named to communicates that the selection may not always succeed.

Lastly, `Deselect` is a function that's added to allow objects to handle losing the player selection. This could involve changing the UI elements, halting sounds or other visual effects, or simply removing a selection outline from around the unit.

The default implementations of the functions return `true` for `IsSelectable` (the default is for any object to be selectable), `true` for `TrySelect` (selection attempts always succeed), and issue a debug assert if `Deselect` is called without being implemented by the class.

You could also implement `Deselect` as a pure `virtual` function if you wish. `SelectableCube` is a new class inheriting from `PhysicsCube`, but also implementing the `ISelectable` interface. It also overrides `NotifyHit`, a `virtual` function defined in `AActor` that triggers when the actor undergoes a **RigidBody** collision.

We call the constructor from `PhysicsCube` with the `Super()` constructor call inside the implementation of `SelectableCube`. We then add our own implementation, which calls `SetNotifyRigidBodyCollision(true)` on our static mesh instance. This is necessary, because by default, `RigidBodies` (such as `PrimitiveComponents` with a collision) don't trigger `Hit` events as a performance optimization. As a result, our overridden `NotifyHit` function would never be called.

Within the implementation of `NotifyHit`, we call some of the `ISelectable` interface functions on ourselves. Given that we know we are an object that inherits from `ISelectable`, we don't need to cast to an `ISelectable*` to call them.

We check to see if the object is selectable with `IsSelectable` and, if so, we try to actually perform the selection using `TrySelect`. `NonSelectableCube` inherits from `SelectableCube`, so we can force the object to never be selectable.

We accomplish this by overriding the `ISelectable` interface functions again. Within `ANonSelectableCube::IsSelectable()`, we print a message to the screen so that we can verify that the function is being called, and then return `false` to indicate that the object isn't selectable at all.

In case the user doesn't respect `IsSelectable()`, `ANonSelectableCube::TrySelect()` always returns `false` to indicate that the selection wasn't successful.

Given that it is impossible for `NonSelectableCube` to be selected, `Deselect()` calls `unimplemented()`, which throws an assert warning that the function was not implemented.

Now, when playing your scene, each time `SelectableCube/NonSelectableCube` hits another object, causing a RigidBody collision, the actor in question will attempt to select itself, and print messages to the screen.

See also

- Refer to `Chapter 6`, *Input and Collision, and the Mouse UI input handling* recipe, which shows you how to **Raycast** from the mouse cursor into the game world to determine what is being clicked on. This could be used to extend this recipe to allow the player to click on items to select them.

Implementing a simple interaction system with UInterfaces

This recipe will show you how to combine a number of other recipes in this chapter to demonstrate a simple interaction system, and a door with an interactable doorbell to cause the door to open.

Getting ready...

This recipe requires the use of Action bindings. If you are unfamiliar with creating Action mappings, please refer to `Chapter 6`, *Input and Collision*, before continuing with this recipe.

How to do it...

1. Create a new interface called `Interactable`.

2. Add the following functions to the `IInteractable` class declaration:

```
class CHAPTER_07_API IInteractable
{
    GENERATED_BODY()

    // Add interface functions to this class. This is the
class that
    // will be inherited to implement this interface.
public:
    UFUNCTION(BlueprintNativeEvent, BlueprintCallable,
            Category = Interactable)
    bool CanInteract();

    UFUNCTION(BlueprintNativeEvent, BlueprintCallable,
            Category = Interactable)
    void PerformInteract();

};
```

3. Create a second interface, `Openable`.

4. Add this function to its declaration:

```
class CHAPTER_07_API IOpenable
{
  GENERATED_BODY()

  // Add interface functions to this class. This is the class
that
    // will be inherited to implement this interface.
public:
    UFUNCTION(BlueprintNativeEvent, BlueprintCallable,
            Category = Openable)
    void Open();
};
```

5. Create a new class, based on `StaticMeshActor`, called `DoorBell`.

6. Add `#include "Interactable.h"` in `DoorBell.h`, and add the following functions to the class declaration:

```
#pragma once

#include "CoreMinimal.h"
```

```
#include "Engine/StaticMeshActor.h"
#include "Interactable.h"
#include "DoorBell.generated.h"


UCLASS()
class CHAPTER_07_API ADoorBell : public AStaticMeshActor,
public IInteractable
{
   GENERATED_BODY()
public:
    ADoorBell();

    virtual bool CanInteract_Implementation() override;
    virtual void PerformInteract_Implementation() override;

    UPROPERTY(BlueprintReadWrite, EditAnywhere)
    AActor* DoorToOpen;

private:
    bool HasBeenPushed;
};
```

7. In the `.cpp` file for `DoorBell`, add `#include "Openable.h"`.

8. Load a static mesh for our `DoorBell` in the constructor:

```
ADoorBell::ADoorBell()
{
    HasBeenPushed = false;

    auto MeshAsset =
ConstructorHelpers::FObjectFinder<UStaticMesh>(TEXT("StaticMes
h'/Engine/BasicShapes/Cube.Cube'"));

    UStaticMeshComponent * SM = GetStaticMeshComponent();

    if (SM != nullptr)
    {
        if (MeshAsset.Object != nullptr)
        {
            SM->SetStaticMesh(MeshAsset.Object);
            SM->SetGenerateOverlapEvents(true);
        }

        SM->SetMobility(EComponentMobility::Movable);
        SM->SetWorldScale3D(FVector(0.5, 0.5, 0.5));
    }
```

```
        SetActorEnableCollision(true);

        SetActorEnableCollision(true);

        DoorToOpen = nullptr;
    }
```

9. Add the following function implementations to implement the `Interactable` **interface on our** `DoorBell`:

```
bool ADoorBell::CanInteract_Implementation()
{
    return !HasBeenPushed;
}

void ADoorBell::PerformInteract_Implementation()
{
    HasBeenPushed = true;
    if (DoorToOpen->GetClass()->ImplementsInterface(
UOpenable::StaticClass()))
    {
        IOpenable::Execute_Open(DoorToOpen);
    }
}
```

10. Now create a new StaticMeshActor-based class called `Door`.

11. `#include` the `Openable` and `Interactable` interfaces into the class header, and then modify Door's declaration:

```
#pragma once

#include "CoreMinimal.h"
#include "Engine/StaticMeshActor.h"
#include "Interactable.h"
#include "Openable.h"
#include "Door.generated.h"

UCLASS()
class CHAPTER_07_API ADoor : public AStaticMeshActor, public
IInteractable, public IOpenable
{
    GENERATED_BODY()
};
```

12. Add interface functions and a constructor to `Door`:

```
UCLASS()
class CHAPTER_07_API ADoor : public AStaticMeshActor, public
IInteractable, public IOpenable
{
    GENERATED_BODY()
public:
    ADoor();

    UFUNCTION()
    virtual bool CanInteract_Implementation() override;

    UFUNCTION()
    virtual void PerformInteract_Implementation() override;

    UFUNCTION()
    virtual void Open_Implementation() override;
};
```

13. As with `DoorBell`, in the `Door` constructor, initialize our mesh component and load a model in it:

```
ADoor::ADoor()
{
    auto MeshAsset =
ConstructorHelpers::FObjectFinder<UStaticMesh>(TEXT("StaticMes
h'/Engine/BasicShapes/Cube.Cube'"));

    UStaticMeshComponent * SM = GetStaticMeshComponent();

    if (SM != nullptr)
    {
        if (MeshAsset.Object != nullptr)
        {
            SM->SetStaticMesh(MeshAsset.Object);
            SM->SetGenerateOverlapEvents(true);
        }

        SM->SetMobility(EComponentMobility::Movable);
        SM->SetWorldScale3D(FVector(0.3, 2, 3));
    }

    SetActorEnableCollision(true);
}
```

14. Implement interface functions:

```
bool ADoor::CanInteract_Implementation()
{
    return true;
}

void ADoor::PerformInteract_Implementation()
{
    GEngine->AddOnScreenDebugMessage(-1, 5, FColor::Red,
    TEXT("The door refuses to budge. Perhaps there is a hidden
    switch nearby ? "));
}

void ADoor::Open_Implementation()
{
    AddActorLocalOffset(FVector(0, 0, 200));
}
```

15. Create a new DefaultPawn-based class called `InteractingPawn`:

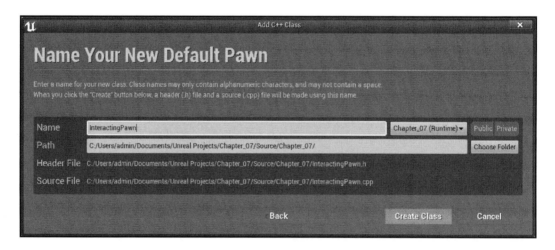

16. Add the following functions to the `Pawn` class header:

```
UCLASS()
class CHAPTER_07_API AInteractingPawn : public ADefaultPawn
{
    GENERATED_BODY()
public:
    void TryInteract();

private:
    virtual void SetupPlayerInputComponent( UInputComponent*
                                            InInputComponent)
override;
};
```

17. Inside the implementation file for the `Pawn`, add `#include "Interactable.h"`, and then provide implementations for both functions from the header:

```
#include "InteractingPawn.h"
#include "Interactable.h"
#include "Camera/PlayerCameraManager.h"
#include "CollisionQueryParams.h"
#include "WorldCollision.h"

void AInteractingPawn::TryInteract()
{
    APlayerController* MyController = Cast<APlayerController>(
Controller);

    if (MyController)
    {
        APlayerCameraManager* MyCameraManager =
MyController->PlayerCameraManager;

        auto StartLocation =
MyCameraManager->GetCameraLocation();
        auto EndLocation = StartLocation +
(MyCameraManager->GetActorForwardVector() *
                    100);

        FCollisionObjectQueryParams Params;
        FHitResult HitResult;

        GetWorld()->SweepSingleByObjectType(HitResult,
StartLocation,
                                            EndLocation,
                                            FQuat::Identity,
```

```
FCollisionObjectQueryParams(FCollisionObjectQueryParams::AllOb
jects),
FCollisionShape::MakeSphere(25),
            FCollisionQueryParams(FName("Interaction"),
true, this));

        if (HitResult.Actor != nullptr)
        {
            auto Class = HitResult.Actor->GetClass();
            if (Class->ImplementsInterface(
UInteractable::StaticClass()))
            {
                if (IInteractable::Execute_CanInteract(
HitResult.Actor.Get()))
                {
                    IInteractable::Execute_PerformInteract(
HitResult.Actor.Get());
                }
            }
        }

    }


}

void
AInteractingPawn::SetupPlayerInputComponent(UInputComponent*
InInputComponent)
{
    Super::SetupPlayerInputComponent(InInputComponent);
    InInputComponent->BindAction("Interact", IE_Released,
this,
&AInteractingPawn::TryInteract);
}
```

18. Now, create a new GameMode in either C++ or Blueprint, and set InteractingPawn as our default Pawn class.

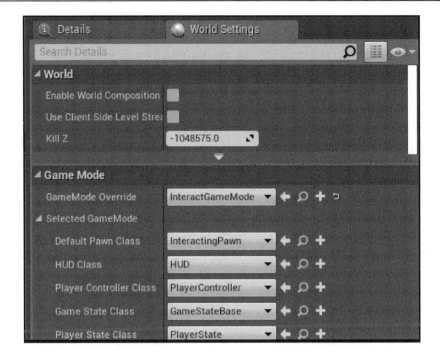

19. Drag a copy of both `Door` and `Doorbell` into the level:

20. Use the eyedropper beside doorbell's **Door to Open**, as shown in the following screenshot, then click on the door actor instance in your level:

Once you select the actor, you should see something similar to the following:

21. Create a new Action binding in the editor called Interact and bind it to a key of your choice:

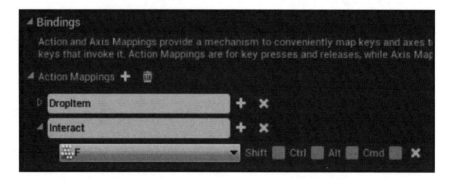

22. Play your level and walk up to the doorbell. Look at it, and press whatever key you bound Interact with. Verify that the door moves once. Refer to the following screenshot:

23. You can also interact with the door directly to receive some information about it:

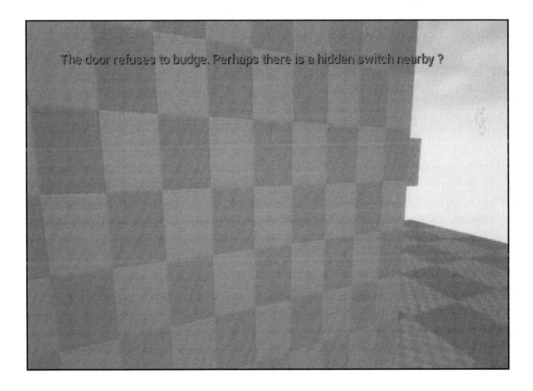

The door refuses to budge. Perhaps there is a hidden switch nearby ?

How it works...

As in previous recipes, we mark UFUNCTION as BlueprintNativeEvent and
BlueprintCallable to allow the UInterface to be implemented in either native
code or Blueprint, and allow the functions to be called with either method.

We create DoorBell based on StaticMeshActor for convenience, and have
DoorBell implement the Interactable interface. Inside the constructor for
DoorBell, we initialize HasBeenPushed and DoorToOpen to the default safe values.

Within the implementation for CanInteract, we return the inverse of
HasBeenPushed so that once the button has been pushed, it can't be interacted with.

Inside PerformInteract, we check if we have a reference to a door object to open. If
we have a valid reference, we verify that the door actor implements Openable, and
then we invoke the Open function on our door. Within Door, we implement both
Interactable and Openable, and override the functions from each.

We define the Door implementation of CanInteract to be the same as the default.
Within PerformInteract, we display a message to the user. Inside Open, we use
AddActorLocalOffset to move the door a certain distance away. With Timeline in
Blueprint or a linear interpolation, we could make this transition smooth rather than a
teleport.

Lastly, we create a new Pawn so that the player can actually interact with objects. We
create a TryInteract function, which we bind to the Interact input action in the
overridden SetupPlayerInputComponent function.

This means that when the player performs the input that is bound to Interact, our
TryInteract function will run. TryInteract gets a reference to
PlayerController, casting the generic controller reference that all Pawns have.

PlayerCameraManager is retrieved through PlayerController, so we can access
the current location and rotation of the player camera. We create start and end points
using the camera's location, then 100 units in the forward direction away from the
camera's location, and pass those into GetWorld::SweepSingleByObjectType.
This function takes in a number of parameters. HitResult is a variable that allows
the function to return information about any object hit by the trace.
CollisionObjectQueryParams allows us to specify whether we are interested in
dynamic, static items, or both.

We accomplish a sphere trace by passing the shape in using the `MakeSphere` function. Sphere traces allow for slightly more human error by defining a cylinder to check for objects rather than a straight line. Given that the players might not look directly at your object, you can tweak the sphere's radius as appropriate.

The final parameter, `SweepSingleByObjectType`, is a struct that gives the trace a name, lets us specify whether we are colliding against a complex collision geometry, and most importantly, allows us to specify that we want to ignore the object that is initiating the trace.

If `HitResult` contains an actor after the trace is done, we check whether the actor implements our interface, then attempt to call `CanInteract` on it. If the actor indicates yes, it can be interacted with, so we then tell it to actually perform the interaction.

8
Communication Between Classes and Interfaces: Part II

The following recipes will be covered in this chapter:

- Exposing UInterface methods to Blueprint from a native base class
- Implementing UInterface functions in Blueprint
- Creating C++ UInterface function implementations that can be overridden in Blueprint
- Calling Blueprint-defined interface functions from C++

Introduction

This chapter will show you ways in which you can use your C++ UInterfaces through Blueprints. This can be very helpful in letting designers access code that you've written without requiring them to dive into the C++ code of the project.

Technical requirements

This chapter requires the use of Unreal Engine 4 and uses Visual Studio 2017 as the IDE. Instructions on how to install both pieces of software and the requirements for them can be found in Chapter 1, *UE4 Development Tools*.

Exposing UInterface methods to Blueprint from a native base class

Being able to define `UInterface` methods in C++ is great, but they should be accessible from Blueprint too. Otherwise, designers or others who are using Blueprint won't be able to interact with your `UInterface`. This recipe shows you how to make a function from an interface callable within the Blueprint system.

How to do it...

1. Create a `UInterface` called `PostBeginPlay`:

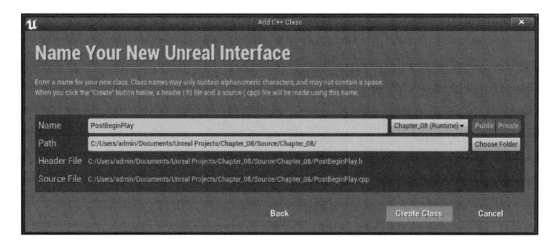

2. Open `PostBeginPlay.h` in Visual Studio and update the `UINTERFACE` of `UPostBeginPlay` and add the following `virtual` method in `IPostBeginPlay`:

```
#pragma once

#include "CoreMinimal.h"
#include "UObject/Interface.h"
#include "PostBeginPlay.generated.h"

UINTERFACE(meta = (CannotImplementInterfaceInBlueprint))
class UPostBeginPlay : public UInterface
{
    GENERATED_BODY()
```

```
};

/**
 *
 */
class CHAPTER_08_API IPostBeginPlay
{
    GENERATED_BODY()

    // Add interface functions to this class. This is the
    // class that will be inherited to implement
    // this interface.
public:
    UFUNCTION(BlueprintCallable, Category = Test)
    virtual void OnPostBeginPlay();
};
```

3. Provide an implementation of the function:

```
#include "PostBeginPlay.h"

// Add default functionality here for any IPostBeginPlay
// functions that are not pure virtual.
void IPostBeginPlay::OnPostBeginPlay()
{
    GEngine->AddOnScreenDebugMessage(-1, 1, FColor::Red,
"PostBeginPlay called");
}
```

4. Create a new `Actor` class called `APostBeginPlayTest`:

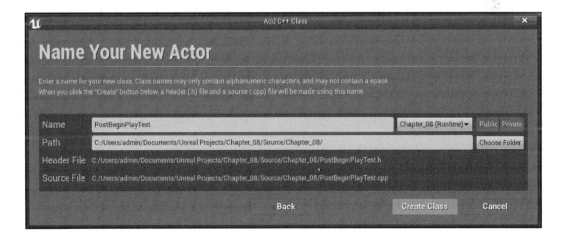

5. Modify the class declaration so that it also inherits `IPostBeginPlay`:

```
#pragma once

#include "CoreMinimal.h"
#include "GameFramework/Actor.h"
#include "PostBeginPlay.h"
#include "PostBeginPlayTest.generated.h"

UCLASS()
class CHAPTER_08_API APostBeginPlayTest : public AActor,
public IPostBeginPlay
```

6. Compile your project. Inside the editor, drag an instance of `APostBeginPlayTest` into your level:

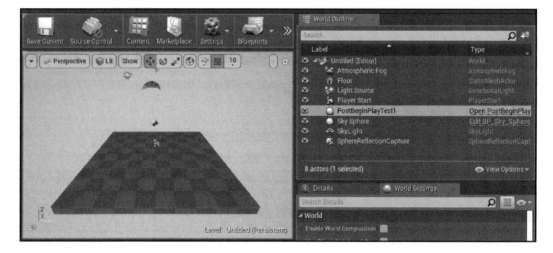

7. With the instance selected in the **World Outliner**, click on **Blueprints | Open Level Blueprint**:

8. Inside the Level Blueprint, right-click and **Create a Reference to PostBeginPlayTest1**:

 Note that you can also use the drag-and-drop method we discussed in the *Inheriting UInterfaces from one another* recipe from the previous chapter.

9. Drag away from the blue pin on the right-hand side of your actor reference, then search the context menu for `onpost` to see your new interface function. Click on it to insert a call to your native `UInterface` implementation from Blueprint:

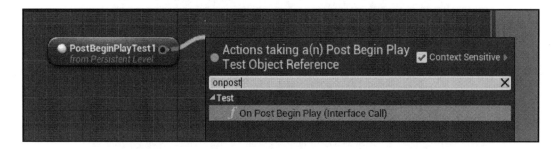

10. Finally, connect the execution pin (white arrow) from the `BeginPlay` node to the execution pin for `OnPostBeginPlay`:

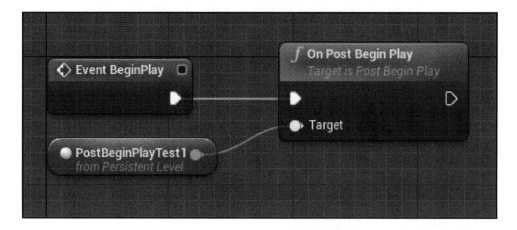

11. When you play your level, you should see the message **PostBeginPlay called** visible on screen for a short amount of time, verifying that Blueprint has successfully accessed and called through to your native code implementation of the `UInterface`.

How it works...

The UINTERFACE/IInterface pair function like they do in other recipes, with the UInterface containing reflection information and other data and the IInterface functioning as the actual interface class that can be inherited from.

The most significant element that allows the function inside IInterface to be exposed to Blueprint is the UFUNCTION specifier. BlueprintCallable marks this function as one that can be called from the Blueprint system.

Any functions exposed to Blueprint in any way require a Category value. This Category value specifies the heading under which the function will be listed in the context menu.

The function must also be marked virtual – this is so that a class that implements the interface via native code can override the implementations of the functions inside it. Without the virtual specifier, the Unreal Header Tool will give you an error, indicating that you have to either add virtual or BlueprintImplementableEvent as a UFUNCTION specifier.

The reason for this is that without either of those, the interface function wouldn't be overridable in C++ (due to the absence of virtual) or Blueprint (because BlueprintImplementableEvent was missing). An interface that can't be overridden, but only inherited, has limited utility, so Epic have chosen not to support it within UInterfaces.

We then provide a default implementation of the OnPostBeginPlay function, which uses the GEngine pointer to display a debug message, confirming that the function was invoked.

See also

- Refer to Chapter 8, *Communication Between Classes and Interfaces: Part II*, for a number of recipes that show you how you can integrate your C++ classes with Blueprint

Implementing UInterface functions in Blueprint

One of the key advantages of UInterface in Unreal is the ability for users to implement `UInterface` functions in the editor. This means that the interface can be implemented strictly in Blueprint without needing any C++ code, which is helpful to designers.

How to do it...

1. Create a new `UInterface` called `AttackAvoider`:

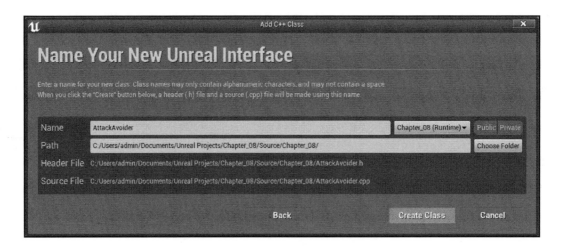

2. Add the following function declaration to the header:

```
#pragma once

#include "CoreMinimal.h"
#include "UObject/Interface.h"
#include "AttackAvoider.generated.h"

// This class does not need to be modified.
UINTERFACE(MinimalAPI)
class UAttackAvoider : public UInterface
{
  GENERATED_BODY()
};
```

```
class CHAPTER_08_API IAttackAvoider
{
  GENERATED_BODY()

  // Add interface functions to this class. This is the class
  // that will be inherited to implement this interface.
public:
    UFUNCTION(BlueprintImplementableEvent, BlueprintCallable,
  Category = AttackAvoider)
  void AttackIncoming(AActor* AttackActor);
};
```

3. Compile your project. From the **Content Browser**, open the **Content** folder and then create a new **Blueprint Class** within the Editor by selecting **Add New | Blueprint Class**:

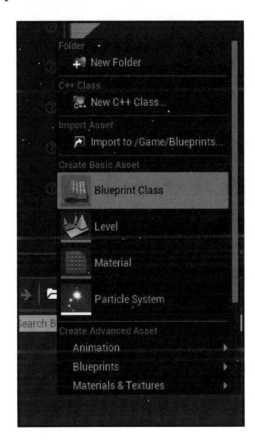

4. Base the class on **Actor**:

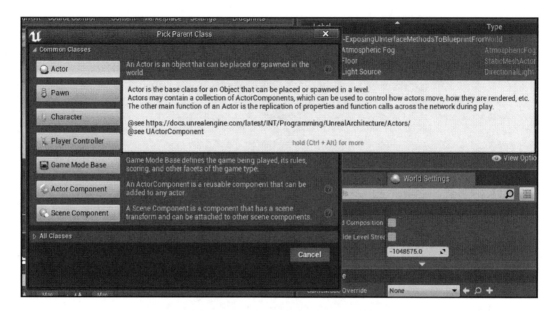

5. Name the blueprint `AvoiderBlueprint` and then double-click on it to open the Blueprint Editor. From there, open **Class Settings**:

6. Under the Details tab, click on the drop-down menu that says **Add** for **Implemented Interfaces**, and select **AttackAvoider**:

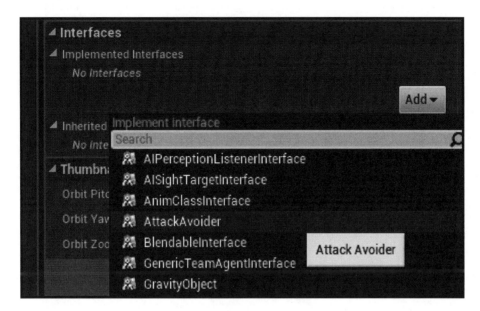

7. **Compile** your Blueprint:

8. Open the **Event Graph** by clicking on the **Event Graph** tab and then right-click within the graph and type `event attack`. Within the **Context Sensitive** menu, you should see **Event Attack Incoming**. Select it to place an event node in your graph:

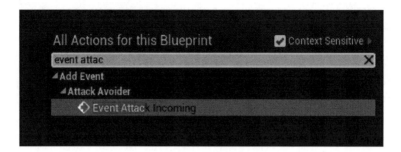

9. Drag this out from the execution pin on the new node and release. Type `print string` into the **Context Sensitive** menu to add a **Print String** node:

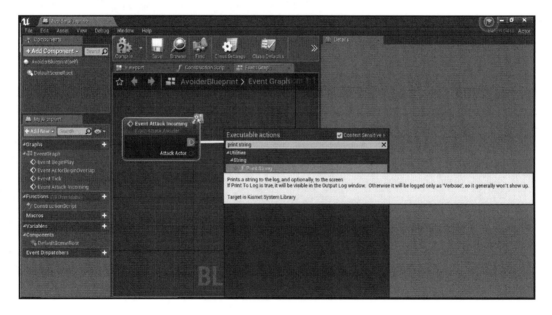

Selecting the Print String node

You have now implemented a `UInterface` function within Blueprint.

10. To see the event in action, drag the pin to the right of the **Event BeginPlay** event and call an **Attack Incoming** event:

11. Drag and drop an instance of your Blueprint class into the level and play the game:

If all went well, you should see the default message from **Print String**, or whatever you posted to happen when the event should happen!

How it works...

The `UINTERFACE`/`IInterface` are created in exactly the same way that we saw in the other recipes in this chapter. When we add a function to the interface, however, we use a new `UFUNCTION` specifier, `BlueprintImplementableEvent`.

`BlueprintImplementableEvent` tells the Unreal Header Tool to generate code that creates an empty stub function that can be implemented by Blueprint. We do not need to provide a default C++ implementation for the function.

We implement the interface inside Blueprint, which exposes the function for us in a way that allows us to define its implementation in Blueprint. The autogenerated code that's created by the header tool forwards the calls to the `UInterface` function to our Blueprint implementation.

See also

The *Overriding C++ UInterface functions through Blueprints* recipe shows you how to define a default implementation for your `UInterface` function in C++, then optionally override it in Blueprint if necessary.

Overriding C++ UInterface functions through Blueprints

Just like the previous recipe, UInterfaces are useful, but that utility is severely limited without their functionality being usable by designers.

The previous recipe, *Exposing UInterface methods to Blueprints from a native base class*, showed you how to call C++ `UInterface` functions from Blueprint; this recipe will show you how to replace the implementation of a `UInterface` function with your own custom Blueprint-only function.

How to do it...

1. Create a new interface called `Wearable` (Creating both `IWearable` & `UWearable`):

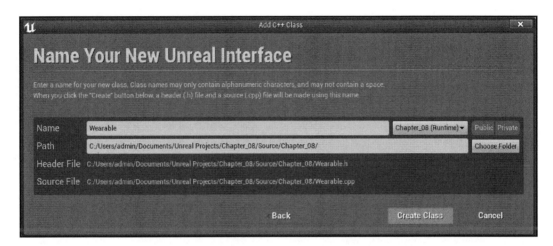

2. Add the following functions to the header of the `IWearable` class:

```
class CHAPTER_08_API IWearable
{
    GENERATED_BODY()

    // Add interface functions to this class. This is the
    // class that will be inherited to implement
    // this interface.
public:
    UFUNCTION(BlueprintNativeEvent, BlueprintCallable,
            Category = Wearable)
    int32 GetStrengthRequirement();

    UFUNCTION(BlueprintNativeEvent, BlueprintCallable,
            Category = Wearable)
    bool CanEquip(APawn* Wearer);

    UFUNCTION(BlueprintNativeEvent, BlueprintCallable,
            Category = Wearable)
    void OnEquip(APawn* Wearer);
};
```

UE 4.20 and above does not allow us to create a default implementation for a function if it is defined in an interface class, so we will have to use UE's default empty implementation, which gives us the default value as a return for each function. This is because, in C# and other languages that have interfaces, they are not supposed to have a default implementation.

3. Create a new `Actor` class called `Boots` inside the editor:

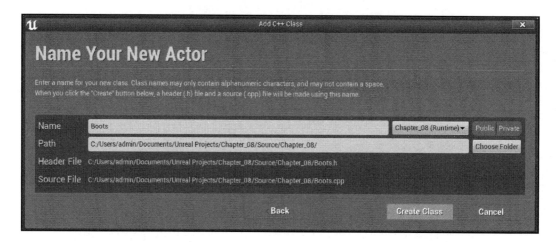

4. Add `#include "Wearable.h"` to the header file for `Boots` and modify the class declaration, as follows:

```
#pragma once

#include "CoreMinimal.h"
#include "GameFramework/Actor.h"
#include "Wearable.h"
#include "Boots.generated.h"

UCLASS()
class CHAPTER_08_API ABoots : public AActor, public IWearable
```

5. Add the following implementation of the pure `virtual` functions that were created by our Interface:

```
UCLASS()
class CHAPTER_08_API ABoots : public AActor, public IWearable
{
    GENERATED_BODY()
public:
    // Sets default values for this actor's properties
```

```
        ABoots();

protected:
        // Called when the game starts or when spawned
        virtual void BeginPlay() override;

public:
        // Called every frame
        virtual void Tick(float DeltaTime) override;

        // Implementing the functions needed for IWearable
        virtual void OnEquip_Implementation(APawn* Wearer)
override
        {
                GEngine->AddOnScreenDebugMessage(-1, 1, FColor::Red,
                                                "Item being worn");
        }

        virtual bool CanEquip_Implementation(APawn* Wearer)
override
        {
                return true;
        }

        virtual int32 GetStrengthRequirement_Implementation()
override
        {
                return 0;
        }

};
```

If you do not know how to do the following two steps, check out the previous recipe, *Implementing UInterface functions in Blueprint*.

6. Compile your script so that we will have access to the new functions we have created.
7. Create a new Blueprint class called `Gloves` based on `Actor` by going to the **Content Browser**, opening the `Content` folder, and then right clicking and then selecting **Blueprint Class**.

8. In the **Class Settings** menu, under the **Details** tab, scroll down to the **Implemented Interfaces** property and click on the **Add** button and select `Wearable` as the interface that the `Gloves` actor will implement:

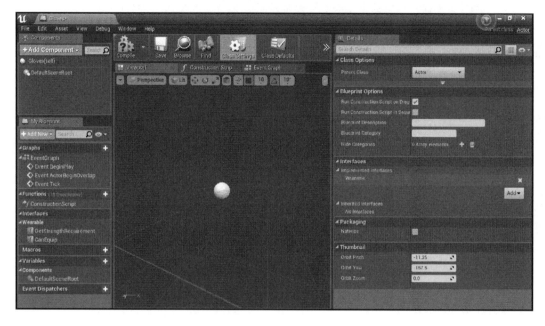

Adding the Wearable interface

9. Afterwards, hit the **Compile** button in order to apply the change.

10. Open the **Event Graph** and right-click it to create a new event. From the search bar, type in `on equip`, and you should see our event under the **Add Event** section:

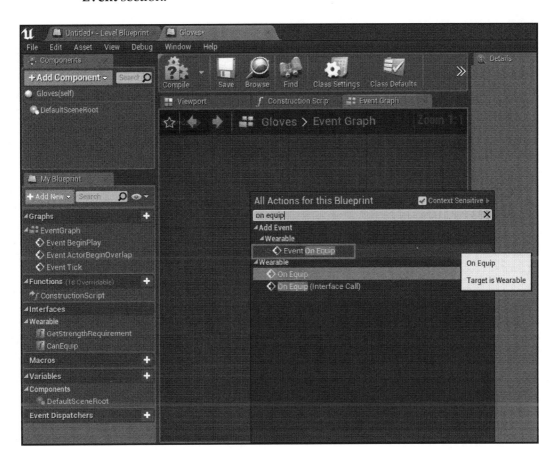

11. This allows us to override the `OnEquip` function from the default implementation to do whatever we want. For instance, add a **Print String** node with the **In String** being set to `Gloves being worn`:

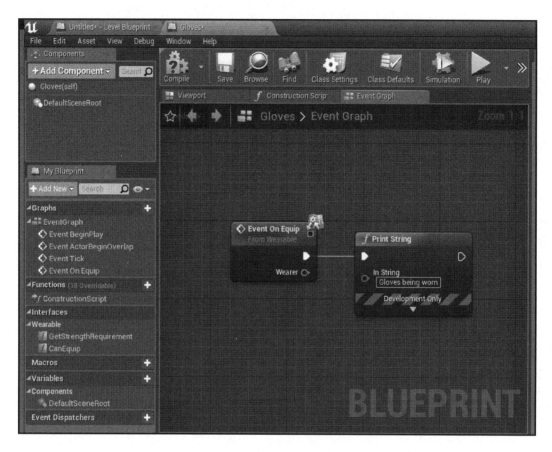

12. Click on the **Compile** button and then you can close the Blueprint. Drag a copy of both `Gloves` and `Boots` into your level for testing purposes.

13. Once added, add the following blueprint code to your level:

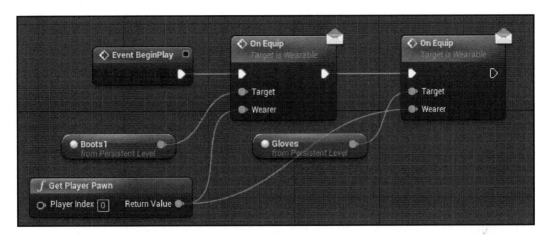

14. Verify that `Boots` performs the default behavior, but that `Gloves` performs the blueprint-defined behavior:

How it works...

This recipe uses two UFUNCTION specifiers together: BlueprintNativeEvent and BlueprintCallable. BlueprintCallable has been shown in previous recipes, and is a way of marking your UFUNCTION as visible and invokable in the Blueprint Editor.

BlueprintNativeEvent signifies a UFUNCTION that has a default C++ (native code) implementation, but is also overridable in Blueprint. It's a combination of a virtual function, along with BlueprintImplementableEvent.

For this mechanism to work, the Unreal Header Tool generates the body of your functions so that the Blueprint version of the function is called if it exists; otherwise, it dispatches the method call through to the native implementation.

The Boots class implements IWearable, overriding the default functionality. In contrast, Gloves also implements IWearable, but has an overridden implementation for OnEquip defined in Blueprint. This can be verified when we use **Level Blueprints** to call OnEquip for the two actors.

Calling Blueprint-defined interface functions from C++

While the previous recipes have focused on C++ being usable in Blueprint, such as being able to call functions from C++ in Blueprint, and override C++ functions with Blueprint, this recipe shows you the reverse: calling a Blueprint-defined interface function from C++.

How to do it...

1. Create a new `UInterface` called `Talker` (Creating the `UTalker`/`ITalker` classes):

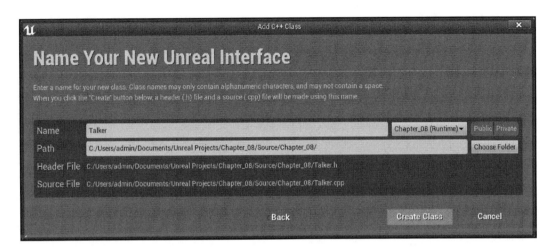

2. Add the following `UFUNCTION` implementation:

```
#pragma once

#include "CoreMinimal.h"
#include "UObject/Interface.h"
#include "Talker.generated.h"

// This class does not need to be modified.
UINTERFACE(MinimalAPI)
class UTalker : public UInterface
{
    GENERATED_BODY()
};

/**
 *
 */
class CHAPTER_08_API ITalker
{
    GENERATED_BODY()

    // Add interface functions to this class. This is the
    // class that will be inherited to implement
    // this interface.
```

```
public:
    UFUNCTION(BlueprintNativeEvent, BlueprintCallable,
Category = Talk)
    void StartTalking();

};
```

3. Create a new C++ class based on `StaticMeshActor`. Remember to check **Show All Classes** and find the class that way:

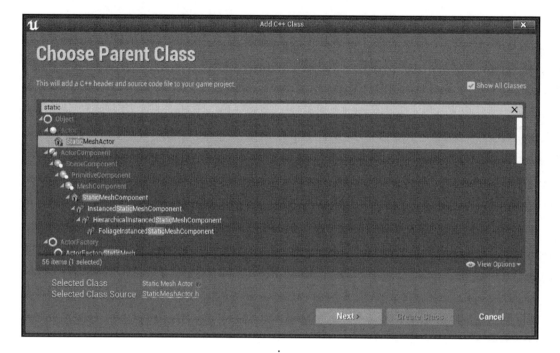

4. After clicking **Next**, name this new class `TalkingMesh`:

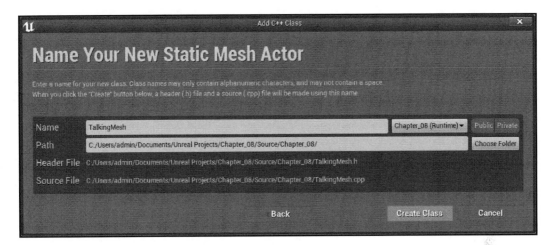

5. Add `#include` and modify the class declaration to include the talker interface:

```
#pragma once

#include "CoreMinimal.h"
#include "Engine/StaticMeshActor.h"
#include "Talker.h"
#include "TalkingMesh.generated.h"

/**
 *
 */
UCLASS()
class CHAPTER_08_API ATalkingMesh : public AStaticMeshActor,
public ITalker
```

6. Also, add the following functions to the class declaration:

```
UCLASS()
class CHAPTER_08_API ATalkingMesh : public AStaticMeshActor,
public ITalker
{
    GENERATED_BODY()
public:
    ATalkingMesh();
    void StartTalking_Implementation();
};
```

7. Within the implementation, add the following to TalkingMesh.cpp:

```
#include "TalkingMesh.h"
#include "ConstructorHelpers.h"

ATalkingMesh::ATalkingMesh() : Super()
{
    auto MeshAsset =
ConstructorHelpers::FObjectFinder<UStaticMesh>(TEXT("StaticMes
h'/Engine/BasicShapes/Cube.Cube'"));

    UStaticMeshComponent * SM = GetStaticMeshComponent();

    if(SM != nullptr)
    {
        if (MeshAsset.Object != nullptr)
        {
            SM->SetStaticMesh(MeshAsset.Object);
            SM->SetGenerateOverlapEvents(true);
        }

        SM->SetMobility(EComponentMobility::Movable);

    }
    SetActorEnableCollision(true);
}

void ATalkingMesh::StartTalking_Implementation()
{
    GEngine->AddOnScreenDebugMessage(-1, 1, FColor::Red,
                        TEXT("Hello there. What is your
name?"));
}
```

8. Create a new class based on `DefaultPawn` to function as our player character:

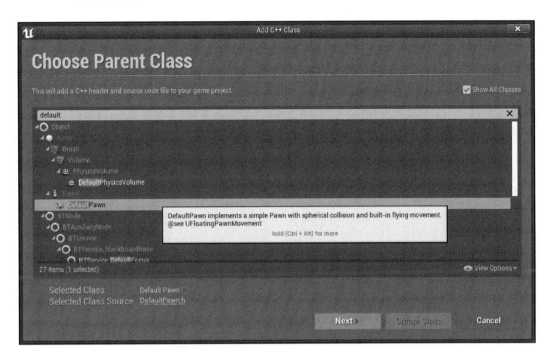

9. Once you select **Next**, give the class a **Name** of `TalkingPawn` and select **Create Class**:

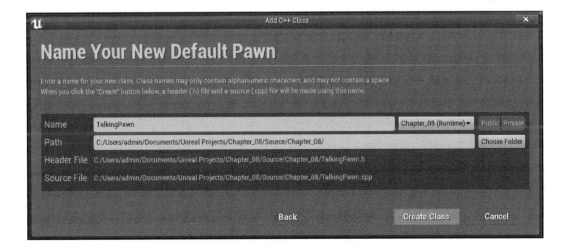

10. Add the following to our class header:

```
#pragma once

#include "CoreMinimal.h"
#include "GameFramework/DefaultPawn.h"
#include "Components/BoxComponent.h" // UBoxComponent
#include "TalkingPawn.generated.h"

/**
 *
 */
UCLASS()
class CHAPTER_08_API ATalkingPawn : public ADefaultPawn
{
    GENERATED_BODY()
public:
    // Sets default values for this character's properties
    ATalkingPawn();

    UPROPERTY()
    UBoxComponent* TalkCollider;

    UFUNCTION()
    void OnTalkOverlap(UPrimitiveComponent*
OverlappedComponent,
                       AActor* OtherActor,
                       UPrimitiveComponent* OtherComp,
                       int32 OtherBodyIndex, bool bFromSweep,
                       const FHitResult & SweepResult);


};
```

11. From the `TalkingPawn.cpp` file, make sure to include the following so that we have access to the `ITalker` and `UTalker` classes:

```
#include "TalkingPawn.h"
#include "Talker.h"
```

12. **Afterwards implement the constructor:**

```
ATalkingPawn::ATalkingPawn() : Super()
{
    // Set this character to call Tick() every frame. You can
    // turn this off to improve performance if you
    // don't need it.
    PrimaryActorTick.bCanEverTick = true;

    TalkCollider =
CreateDefaultSubobject<UBoxComponent>("TalkCollider");

    TalkCollider->SetBoxExtent(FVector(200, 200, 100));

    TalkCollider->OnComponentBeginOverlap.AddDynamic(this,
&ATalkingPawn::OnTalkOverlap);

    TalkCollider->AttachTo(RootComponent);
}
```

13. **Implement** `OnTalkOverlap`:

```
// Called to bind functionality to input
void ATalkingPawn::OnTalkOverlap(UPrimitiveComponent*
OverlappedComponent,
                                 AActor* OtherActor,
                                 UPrimitiveComponent*
OtherComp,
                                 int32 OtherBodyIndex, bool
bFromSweep,
                                 const FHitResult &
SweepResult)
{
    auto Class = OtherActor->GetClass();
    if (Class->ImplementsInterface(UTalker::StaticClass()))
    {
        ITalker::Execute_StartTalking(OtherActor);
    }
}
```

14. Compile your scripts. Create a new `GameMode` and set `TalkingPawn` as the default pawn class for the player. The quickest way to do this is to go to **Settings | World Settings** and then, under **GameMode Override**, click on the + button. From there, expand the **Selected GameMode** option and under **Default Pawn Class**, select `TalkingPawn`. Refer to the following screenshot:

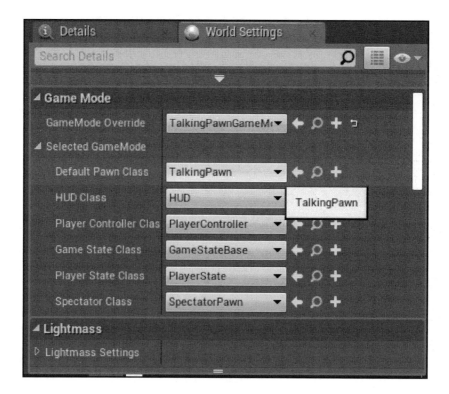

15. Drag an instance of your `ATalkingMesh` class into the level. If you play the game now, you should be able to walk close to the mesh and see it display a message:

16. Create a new Blueprint class based on `ATalkingMesh` by right-clicking on it from the **Content Browser** and selecting the appropriate option from the context menu:

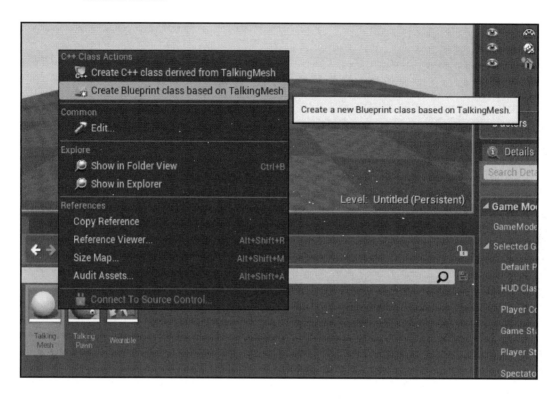

17. Name it `MyTalkingMesh` and select **Create Blueprint Class**:

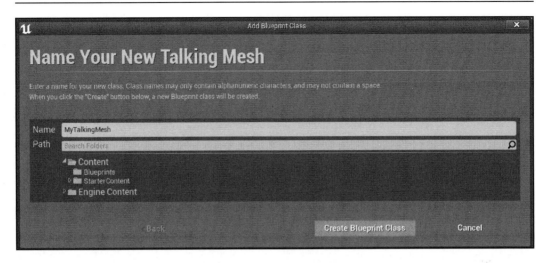

18. Inside the Blueprint Editor, create an implementation for `StartTalking`. We can do this by going to the **Event Graph** and right-clicking within the graph. Then, in the search bar, we can type in `start talking`. Under **Add Event**, select the **Event Start Talking** option.

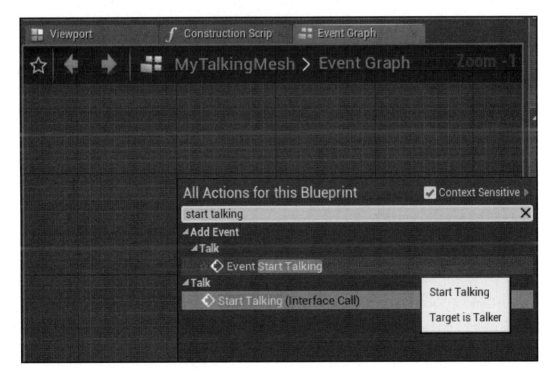

19. If you would like to call the parent version of the event, you can right-click on the event node and select the **Add call to parent function** option:

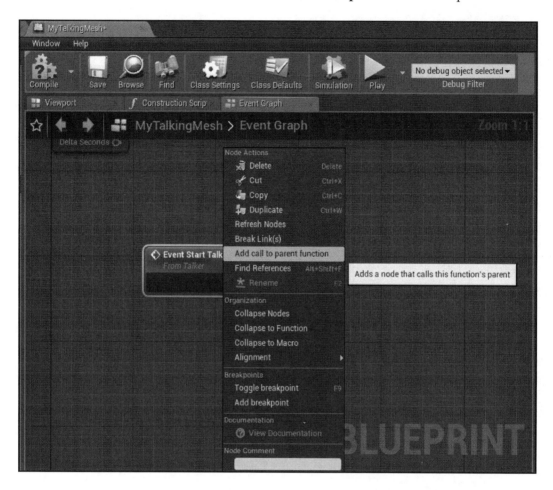

20. Afterward, you can connect the events together. To do something different from the original, create a **Print String** node and display a new **In String** message, such as I'm the overridden implementation in Blueprint. The final version of the example will look as follows:

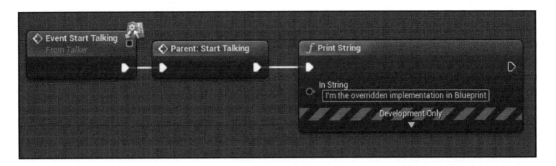

21. Compile your Blueprint. Afterwards, drag a copy of your new Blueprint into the level beside your `ATalkingMesh` instance.

22. Walk up to the two actors and verify that your custom `Pawn` is correctly invoking either the default C++ implementation or the Blueprint implementation, as appropriate:

How it works...

As always, we create a new interface, and then add some function definitions to the `IInterface` class. We use the `BlueprintNativeEvent` specifier to indicate that we want to declare a default implementation in C++ that can then be overridden in Blueprint. We create a new class (inheriting from `StaticMeshActor` for convenience) and implement the interface on it.

In the implementation of the new class constructor, we load a static mesh and set our collision as usual. We then add an implementation for our interface function, which simply prints a message to the screen.

If you were using this in a full-blown project, you could play animations, play audio, alter the user interface, and whatever else was necessary to start a conversation with your `Talker`.

At this point, though, we don't have anything to actually call `StartTalking` on our `Talker`. The simplest way to implement this is to create a new `Pawn` subclass (again, inheriting from `DefaultPawn` for convenience) that can start talking to any `Talker` actors that it collides with.

For this to work, we create a new `BoxComponent` to establish the radius at which we will trigger a conversation. As always, it is a `UPROPERTY`, so it won't get garbage collected. We also create the definition for a function that will get triggered when the new `BoxComponent` overlaps another `Actor` in the scene.

The constructor for our `TalkingPawn` initializes the new `BoxComponent`, and sets its extents appropriately. The constructor also binds the `OnTalkOverlap` function as an event handler to handle collisions with our `BoxComponent`. It also attaches the box component to our `RootComponent` so that it moves with the rest of the player character as the player moves around the level.

Inside `OnTalkOverlap`, we need to check if the other actor, which is overlapping our box, implements the `Talker` interface. The most reliable way to do this is with the `ImplementsInterface` function in `UClass`. This function uses the class information that's generated by the Unreal Header Tool during compilation, and correctly handles both C++ and Blueprint-implemented interfaces.

If the function returns `true`, we can use a special autogenerated function contained in our `IInterface` to invoke the interface method of our choice on our instance. This is a static method of the form `<IInterface>::Execute_<FunctionName>`. In our instance, our `IInterface` is `ITalker`, and the function is `StartTalking`, so the function we want to invoke is `ITalker::Execute_StartTalking()`.

The reason we need this function is that, when an interface is implemented in Blueprint, the relationship isn't actually established at compile time. C++ is, therefore, not aware of the fact that the interface is implemented, and so we can't cast the Blueprint class to `IInterface` to call functions directly.

The `Execute_` functions take a pointer to the object that implements the interface and call a number of internal methods to invoke the desired function's Blueprint implementation.

When you play the level and walk around, the custom `Pawn` is constantly receiving notifications when its `BoxComponent` overlaps other objects. If they implement the `UTalker`/`ITalker` interface, the pawn then tries to invoke `StartTalking` on the `Actor` instance in question, which then prints the appropriate message on screen.

9
Integrating C++ and the Unreal Editor: Part I

In this chapter, we will cover following recipes:

- Using a class or struct as a Blueprint variable
- Creating classes or structs that can be subclassed in Blueprint
- Creating functions that can be called in Blueprint
- Creating events that can be implemented in Blueprint
- Exposing multi-cast delegates to Blueprint
- Creating C++ enums that can be used in Blueprint
- Editing class properties in different places in the editor
- Making properties accessible in the Blueprint editor graph
- Responding to property changed events from the editor
- Implementing a native code Construction Script

Introduction

One of Unreal's primary strengths is that it provides programmers with the ability to create Actors and other objects that can be customized or used by designers in the editor. This chapter shows you how to do this. Following that, we will try to customize the editor by creating custom Blueprint and Animation nodes from scratch. We will also implement custom editor windows and custom **Details** panels to inspect the Types that are created by users.

Technical requirements

This chapter requires the use of Unreal Engine 4 and uses Visual Studio 2017 as the IDE. Instructions on how to install both pieces of software and their requirements can be found in `Chapter 1`, *UE4 Development Tools*.

Using a class or struct as a blueprint variable

Types that you declare in C++ do not automatically get incorporated into Blueprint for use as variables. This recipe shows you how to make them accessible so that you can use custom native code types as Blueprint function parameters.

How to do it...

1. Create a new class using the editor. Unlike previous chapters, we are going to create an `Object`-based class. `Object` isn't visible in the default list of common classes, so we need to tick the **Show All Classes** button in the editor UI, then select **Object**. Afterward, click on the **Next** button:

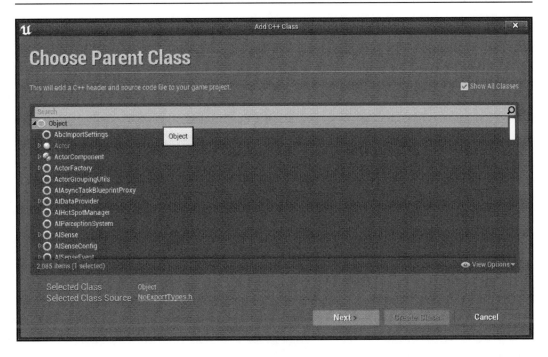

2. Name your new **Object** subclass `TileType` and then click on the **Create Class** button:

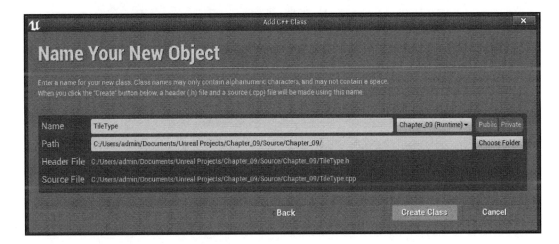

3. Add the following properties to the `TileType` definition:

```
UCLASS()
class CHAPTER_09_API UTileType : public UObject
```

```
    {
        GENERATED_BODY()
public:
        UPROPERTY()
        int32 MovementCost;

        UPROPERTY()
        bool CanBeBuiltOn;

        UPROPERTY()
        FString TileName;
    };
```

4. Compile your code.

5. Inside the editor, create a new Blueprint class based on `Actor`. Call it `Tile`:

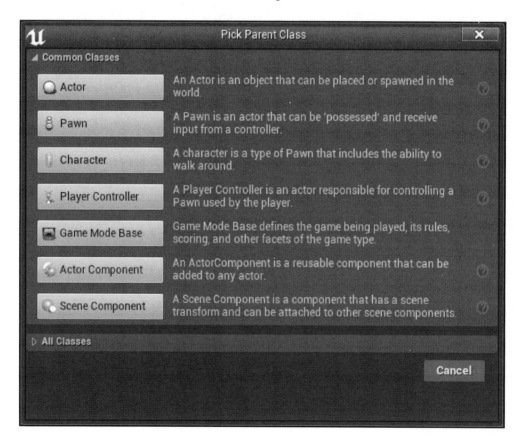

6. Within the blueprint editor for `Tile`, add a new variable to Blueprint by going to the **My Blueprint** section and moving down to the **Variables** section and then hitting the **+** button. The **Details** panel on the right-hand side of the screen will then fill up with information about this new variable, including what type it is. Check the list of types that you can create as variables under the **Variable Type** property, and verify that `TileType` is not there:

7. Return to Visual Studio and open up the `TileType.h` file. Add `BlueprintType` to the `UCLASS` macro, as follows:

```
UCLASS(BlueprintType)
class CHAPTER_09_API UTileType : public UObject
```

8. Save your script, return to the editor and recompile the project, then return to the `Tile` blueprint editor.

9. Now, when you add a new variable to your actor, you can select `TileType` as the type for your new variable:

10. You can now change the **Variable Name** to something better, such as `MyTileType`.

We've now established a *has-a* relationship between `Tile` and `TileType`. Now, `TileType` is a Blueprint type that can be used as a function parameter.

11. To do this, go to the **My Blueprint** section and scroll down to the
    Functions section. From there, you can click on the + button to create a new
    function. Name this new function `SetTileType`:

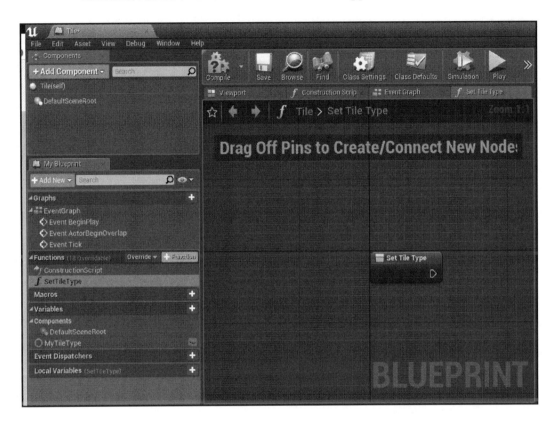

12. Once the function has been created, the **Details** tab will display information about the function itself. Under the **Inputs** section, click on the + button to add a new input:

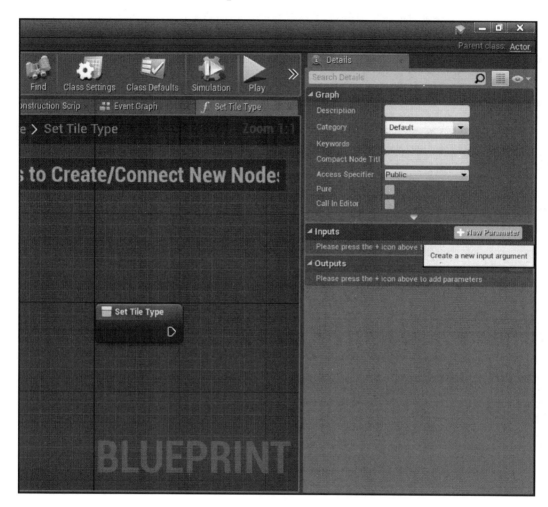

13. Once selected, you'll be able to give the variable a name and select the type from the dropdown that, by default, says `Boolean`. Set the input parameter's type to `TileType`:

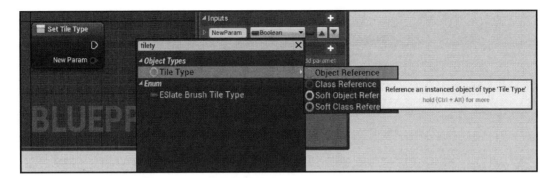

Once you do this, you'll see that the parameter has been added as an input to the **Set Tile Type** function in Blueprints:

14. Go back to the **My Blueprint** section and drag and drop the `MyTileType` variable onto the **Set Tile Type** graph, next to the first node. You can drag your `Type` variable into the viewport and select **Set MyTileType**:

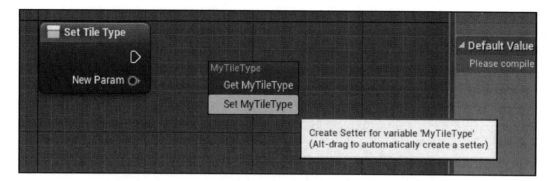

15. Now that we have the two nodes we need, connect the **Exec** output pin to the input of the **Set MyTileType** node and then connect the parameter from `SetTileType` to the **Set** node:

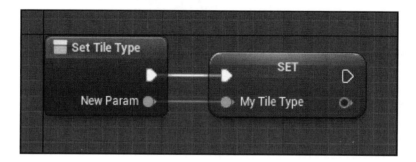

How it works...

For performance reasons, Unreal assumes that classes do not require the extra reflection code that is needed to make the type available to Blueprint.

We can override this default by specifying `BlueprintType` in our `UCLASS` macro.

With the specifier included, the type is now made available as a parameter or variable in Blueprint and can be used in all the same ways that default types can.

There's more...

This recipe shows that you can use a type as a function parameter in Blueprint if its native code declaration includes `BlueprintType`.

However, at the moment, none of the properties that we defined in C++ are accessible to Blueprint.

Other recipes in this chapter deal with making those properties accessible so that we can actually do something meaningful with our custom objects.

Creating classes or structs that can be subclassed in Blueprint

While this book focuses on C++, when developing with Unreal a more standard workflow is to implement core gameplay functionality as well as performance-critical code in C++, and expose those features to Blueprint to allow designers to prototype gameplay, which can then be refactored by programmers with additional Blueprint features, or pushed back down to the C++ layer. One of the most common tasks, then, is to **mark up** our classes and structs in such a way that they are visible to the Blueprint system.

How to do it...

1. Create a new C++ class derived from the `Actor` class using the editor wizard; name it `BaseEnemy`:

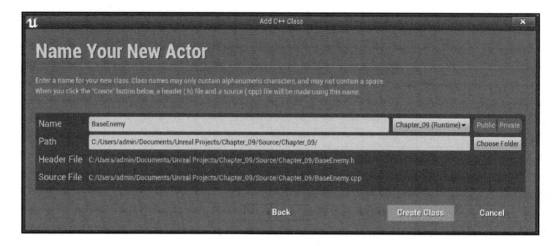

2. Add the following UPROPERTY to the class:

```
UPROPERTY()
FString WeaponName;
UPROPERTY()
int32 MaximumHealth;
```

3. Add the following class specifier to the UCLASS macro:

```
UCLASS(Blueprintable)
class CHAPTER_09_API ABaseEnemy : public AActor
```

4. Save and then compile the script.
5. Open the editor and create a new blueprint class. Expand the **All Classes** list to show all of the classes and select our `BaseEnemy` class as the parent. Afterward, click on the **Select** button:

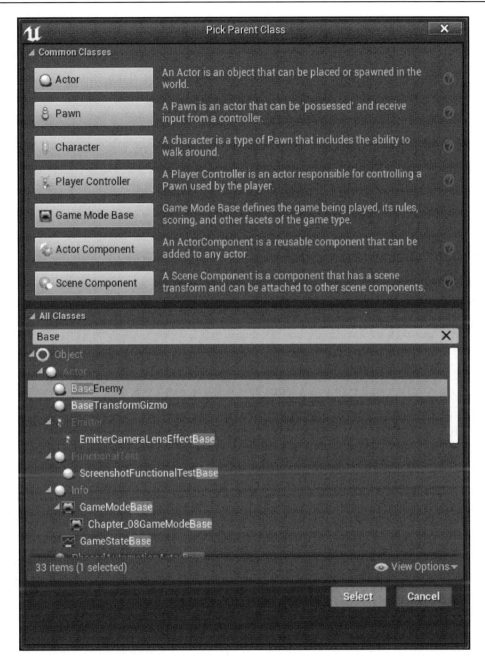

6. Name the new Blueprint EnemyGoblin and open it in the Blueprint editor.

Note that the UPROPERTY macros we created earlier still aren't there because we haven't included the appropriate markup to make them visible to Blueprint.

How it works...

The previous recipe demonstrated the use of BlueprintType as a class specifier. BlueprintType allows the type to be used as a type within the Blueprint editor (that is, it can be a variable or a function input/return value).

However, we may want to create blueprints based on our type (using inheritance) rather than composition (placing an instance of our type inside an Actor, for example).

This is why Epic provided Blueprintable as a class specifier. Blueprintable means a developer can mark a class as inheritable by Blueprint classes.

We have both BlueprintType and Blueprintable instead of a single combined specifier because sometimes you may only want to expose a partial functionality. For example, certain classes should be usable as variables, but performance reasons forbid creating them in Blueprint. In that instance, you would use BlueprintType rather than both specifiers.

On the other hand, perhaps we want to use the Blueprint editor to create new subclasses, but we don't want to pass object instances around inside the Actor blueprints. It is recommended you use Blueprintable, but omit BlueprintType in this case.

Like before, neither Blueprintable nor BlueprintType specify anything about the member functions or member variables contained inside our class. We'll make those available in later recipes.

Creating functions that can be called in Blueprint

While marking classes as BlueprintType or Blueprintable allows us to pass instances of the class around in Blueprint, or to subclass the type with a Blueprint class, those specifiers don't actually say anything about member functions or variables, and whether they should be exposed to Blueprint. This recipe shows you how to mark a function so that it can be called within Blueprint graphs.

How to do it...

1. Create a new C++ class derived from the StaticMeshActor class using the editor wizard; call it SlidingDoor.

2. Add the following text that's in bold to the new class:

```
class CHAPTER_09_API ASlidingDoor : public AStaticMeshActor
{
    GENERATED_BODY()
public:
    // Sets default values for this actor's properties
    ASlidingDoor();

protected:
    // Called when the game starts or when spawned
    virtual void BeginPlay() override;

public:
    // Called every frame
    virtual void Tick(float DeltaTime) override;

    UFUNCTION(BlueprintCallable, Category = Door)
    void Open();

    UPROPERTY()
    bool IsOpen;

    UPROPERTY()
    FVector TargetLocation;
};
```

3. Create the class implementation by adding the following text in bold to the .cpp file:

```
#include "SlidingDoor.h"
#include "ConstructorHelpers.h"

// Sets default values
ASlidingDoor::ASlidingDoor()
{
    // Set this actor to call Tick() every frame. You can turn
    // this off to improve performance if you don't need it.
    PrimaryActorTick.bCanEverTick = true;

    auto MeshAsset =
ConstructorHelpers::FObjectFinder<UStaticMesh>
        (TEXT("StaticMesh'/Engine/BasicShapes/Cube.Cube'"));
```

```cpp
    UStaticMeshComponent * SM = GetStaticMeshComponent();

    if (SM != nullptr)
    {
        if (MeshAsset.Object != nullptr)
        {
            SM->SetStaticMesh(MeshAsset.Object);
            SM->SetGenerateOverlapEvents(true);
        }

        SM->SetMobility(EComponentMobility::Movable);
        SM->SetWorldScale3D(FVector(0.3, 2, 3));
    }

    SetActorEnableCollision(true);

    IsOpen = false;
    PrimaryActorTick.bStartWithTickEnabled = true;
}

// Called when the game starts or when spawned
void ASlidingDoor::BeginPlay()
{
    Super::BeginPlay();
}

// Called every frame
void ASlidingDoor::Tick(float DeltaTime)
{
    Super::Tick(DeltaTime);

    if (IsOpen)
    {
        SetActorLocation(FMath::Lerp(GetActorLocation(),
                                     TargetLocation, 0.05));
    }
}

void ASlidingDoor::Open()
{
    TargetLocation = ActorToWorld().TransformPositionNoScale(
                                                    FVector(0,
0, 200));
    IsOpen = true;
}
```

4. Compile your code and launch the editor.

5. Drag a copy of your door out into the level:

TIP

An easy way to have objects *fall* to the ground is by using the End key with the object you want to drop selected.

6. Make sure you have your `SlidingDoor` instance selected, then open the Level blueprint by going to **Blueprints | Open Level Blueprint**. Right-click on the empty canvas and expand **Call function on Sliding Door 1**:

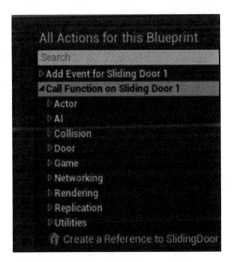

7. Expand the **Door** section and then select the Open function:

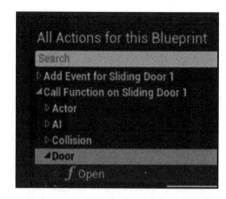

8. Link the execution pin (white arrow) from **Event BeginPlay** to the white arrow on the Open node, as shown in the following screenshot:

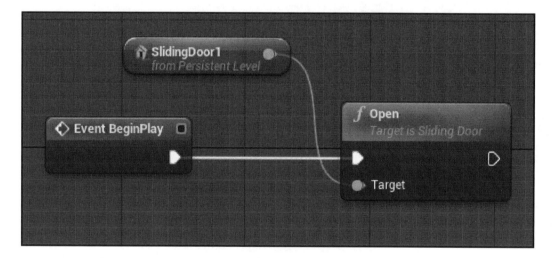

9. Play your level and verify that the door moves up as expected when Open is invoked on your door instance:

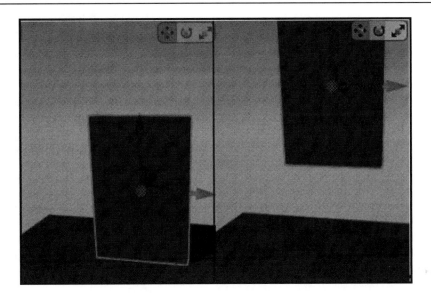

How it works...

Within the declaration of the door, we create a new function for opening the door, a Boolean to track whether the door has been told to open, and a vector allowing us to precompute the target location of the door.

We also override the `Tick` actor function so that we can perform some behavior on every frame.

Within the constructor, we load in the cube mesh and scale it to represent our door.

We also set `IsOpen` to a known good value of `false` and enable actor ticking by using `bCanEverTick` and `bStartWithTickEnabled`.

These two Booleans control whether ticking can be enabled for this actor and if ticking starts in an enabled state, respectively.

Inside the `Open` function, we calculate the target location that's relative to the door's starting position.

We also change the `IsOpen` Boolean from `false` to `true`.

Now that the `IsOpen` Boolean is `true`, inside the `Tick` function, the door tries to move itself toward the target location using `SetActorLocation` and `Lerp` to interpolate between the current location and the destination.

See also

- Chapter 5, *Handling Events and Delegates,* has a number of recipes relating to the spawning of actors

Creating events that can be implemented in Blueprints

Another way that C++ can be more tightly integrated with Blueprint is through the creation of functions that can have Blueprint implementations in native code. This allows a programmer to specify an event and invoke it, without needing to know anything about the implementation. The class can then be subclassed in Blueprint, and another member of the production team can implement a handler for the event without ever having to go near a line of C++.

How to do it...

1. Create a new `StaticMeshActor` class called `Spotter`. Remember to use the **Show All Classes** button to select `StaticMeshActor` as the parent class.

2. Make sure that the following functions are defined and overridden in the class header:

```
#pragma once

#include "CoreMinimal.h"
#include "Engine/StaticMeshActor.h"
#include "Spotter.generated.h"

UCLASS()
class CHAPTER_09_API ASpotter : public AStaticMeshActor
{
  GENERATED_BODY()
public:
    // Sets default values for this actor's properties
    ASpotter();

    // Called every frame
    virtual void Tick(float DeltaSeconds) override;
```

```
UFUNCTION(BlueprintImplementableEvent)
void OnPlayerSpotted(APawn* Player);
```

```
};
```

3. In the implementation file (Spotter.cpp), update the code to the following:

```
#include "Spotter.h"
#include "ConstructorHelpers.h"
#include "DrawDebugHelpers.h"

// Sets default values
ASpotter::ASpotter()
{
    // Set this actor to call Tick() every frame. You can
    // turn this off to improve performance if
    // you don't need it.
    PrimaryActorTick.bCanEverTick = true;

    // Set up visual aspect of the spotter
    auto MeshAsset =
    ConstructorHelpers::FObjectFinder<UStaticMesh>
    (TEXT("StaticMesh'/Engine/BasicShapes/Cone.Cone'"));
    UStaticMeshComponent * SM = GetStaticMeshComponent();

    if (SM != nullptr)
    {
        if (MeshAsset.Object != nullptr)
        {
            SM->SetStaticMesh(MeshAsset.Object);
            SM->SetGenerateOverlapEvents(true);
        }

        SM->SetMobility(EComponentMobility::Movable);
        SM->SetRelativeRotation(FRotator(90, 0, 0));
    }

}

// Called every frame
void ASpotter::Tick(float DeltaTime)
{
    Super::Tick(DeltaTime);

    auto EndLocation = GetActorLocation() +
    ActorToWorld().TransformVector(FVector(0, 0, -200));
```

```
    // Check if there is an object in front of us
    FHitResult HitResult;
    GetWorld()->SweepSingleByChannel(HitResult,
    GetActorLocation(), EndLocation, FQuat::Identity,
    ECC_Camera, FCollisionShape::MakeSphere(25),
    FCollisionQueryParams("Spot", true, this));

    APawn* SpottedPlayer = Cast<APawn>(HitResult.Actor.Get());

    // If there is call the OnPlayerSpotted function
    if (SpottedPlayer != nullptr)
    {
        OnPlayerSpotted(SpottedPlayer);
    }

    // Displays where we are checking for collision
    DrawDebugLine(GetWorld(), GetActorLocation(), EndLocation,
FColor::Red);

}
```

5. Compile and start the editor. Find your `Spotter` class in **Content Browser**, then left-click and drag a copy out into the game world.

6. When you play the level, you'll see the red line showing the trace that the `Actor` is performing:

7. However, nothing will happen if the player walks in front of it because we haven't implemented our `OnPlayerSpotted` event.

8. To implement this event, we need to create a blueprint subclass of our `Spotter`.

9. Right-click on `Spotter` in the **Content Browser** and select **Create Blueprint class based on Spotter**. Name the class `BPSpotter`:

Creating a Blueprint class based on Spotter

10. Inside the Blueprint editor, click on the **Override** button in the **Functions** section of the **My Blueprint** panel:

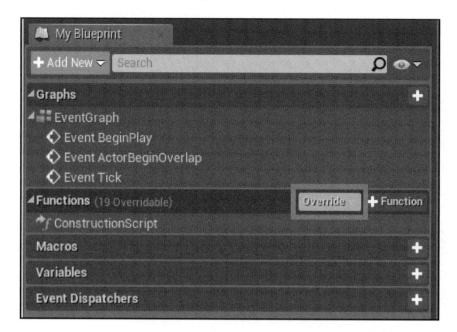

11. Select **On Player Spotted**:

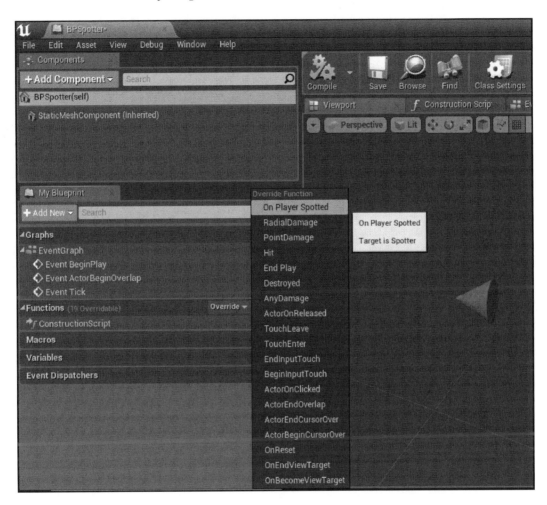

12. To see the event, click on the **Event Graph** tab. Left-click it and drag it away from the white execution pin on our event. In the context menu that appears, select and add a `Print String` node so that it is linked to the event:

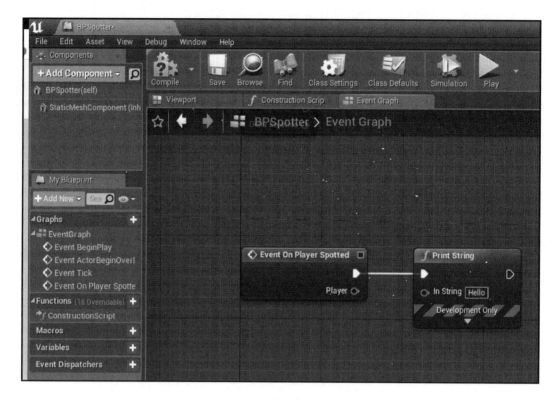

13. Delete your previous Spotter object in the level and then drag and drop a `BPSpotter` in. Play the level again and verify that walking in front of the trace that the `BPSpotter` is using now prints a string to the screen:

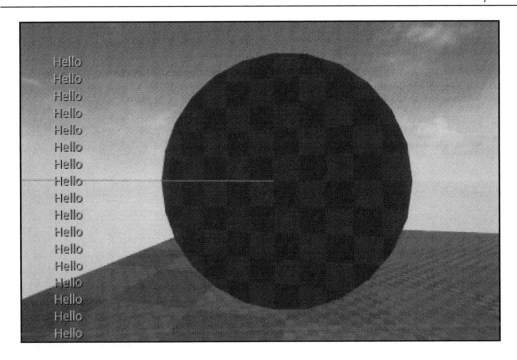

How it works...

In the constructor for our Spotter object, we load one of the basic primitives, a cone, into our Static Mesh Component as a visual representation.

We then rotate the cone so that it resembles a spotlight pointing to the X axis of the actor.

During the Tick function, we get the actor's location and then find a point 200 units away from the actor along its local X axis. We call the parent class implementation of Tick using Super:: to ensure that any other tick functionality is preserved, despite our override.

We convert a local position into a world space position by first acquiring the Actor-to-World transform for the `Actor`, then using that to transform a vector specifying the position.

The transform is based on the orientation of the root component, which is the static mesh component that we rotated during the constructor.

As a result of that existing rotation, we need to rotate the vector we want to transform. Given that we want the vector to point out of what was the bottom of the cone, we want a distance along the negative up axis; that is, we want a vector of the form (0,0,-d), where *d* is the actual distance away.

Having calculated our end location for our trace, we actually perform the trace with the `SweepSingleByChannel` function.

Once the sweep is performed, we try to cast the resulting hit `Actor` into a pawn.

If the cast was successful, we invoke our Implementable Event of `OnPlayerSpotted`, and the user-defined Blueprint code executes.

Exposing multi-cast delegates to Blueprint

Multi-cast delegates are a great way to broadcast an event to multiple objects that **listen** or **subscribe** to the event in question. They are particularly invaluable if you have a C++ module that generates events that potentially arbitrary Actors might want to be notified about. This recipe shows you how to create a multi-cast delegate in C++ that can notify a group of other Actors during runtime.

How to do it...

1. Create a new `StaticMeshActor` class called `King`. Add the following to the class header:

```
#pragma once

#include "CoreMinimal.h"
#include "Engine/StaticMeshActor.h"
#include "King.generated.h"
```

```
DECLARE_DYNAMIC_MULTICAST_DELEGATE_OneParam(FOnKingDeathSignat
ure, AKing*, DeadKing);
UCLASS()
class CHAPTER_09_API AKing : public AStaticMeshActor
{
    GENERATED_BODY()
```

2. We also want to display something on the screen, so add a definition for a constructor:

```
DECLARE_DYNAMIC_MULTICAST_DELEGATE_OneParam(FOnKingDeathSignat
ure, AKing*, DeadKing);
UCLASS()
class CHAPTER_09_API AKing : public AStaticMeshActor
{
    GENERATED_BODY()

    // Sets default values for this actor's properties
    AKing();
};
```

3. Add a new UFUNCTION to the class:

```
UFUNCTION(BlueprintCallable, Category = King)
void Die();
```

4. Add an instance of our multicast delegate to the class as well:

```
UPROPERTY(BlueprintAssignable)
FOnKingDeathSignature OnKingDeath;
```

5. Open the King.cpp file and then add in the implementation for the constructor to perform our mesh initialization (remembering to add an #include for the ConstructionHelpers.h file):

```
#include "King.h"
#include "ConstructorHelpers.h"

// Sets default values
AKing::AKing()
{
    // Set this actor to call Tick() every frame. You can turn
    // this off to improve performance if you don't need it.
    PrimaryActorTick.bCanEverTick = true;

    auto MeshAsset =
ConstructorHelpers::FObjectFinder<UStaticMesh>
        (TEXT("StaticMesh'/Engine/BasicShapes/Cone.Cone'"));
```

```
UStaticMeshComponent * SM = GetStaticMeshComponent();

if (SM != nullptr)
{
    if (MeshAsset.Object != nullptr)
    {
        SM->SetStaticMesh(MeshAsset.Object);
        SM->SetGenerateOverlapEvents(true);
    }
    SM->SetMobility(EComponentMobility::Movable);
}
}
```

6. Implement the `Die` function:

```
void AKing :: Die ()
{
  OnKingDeath.Broadcast(this);
}
```

7. Create a new class called `Peasant`, also based on `StaticMeshActor`.

8. Declare a default constructor in the class:

```
APeasant ();
```

9. Declare the following function:

```
UFUNCTION(BlueprintCallable, category = Peasant)
void Flee (AKing * DeadKing);
```

10. Implement the constructor:

```
#include "Peasant.h"
#include "ConstructorHelpers.h"

APeasant::APeasant()
{
  // Set this actor to call Tick() every frame. You can
  // turn this off to improve performance if
  // you don't need it.
  PrimaryActorTick.bCanEverTick = true;

  auto MeshAsset =
ConstructorHelpers::FObjectFinder<UStaticMesh>
  (TEXT("StaticMesh'/Engine/BasicShapes/Cube.Cube'"));

  UStaticMeshComponent * SM = GetStaticMeshComponent();
```

```
if (SM != nullptr)
{
  if (MeshAsset.Object != nullptr)
  {
    SM->SetStaticMesh(MeshAsset.Object);
    SM->SetGenerateOverlapEvents(true);
  }
  SM->SetMobility(EComponentMobility::Movable);
}
}
```

11. Implement the `Flee` function in the `.cpp` file:

```
void APeasant::Flee(AKing* DeadKing)
{
    // Display message on the screen
    GEngine->AddOnScreenDebugMessage(-1, 2, FColor::Red,
        TEXT("Waily Waily!"));

    // Get the direction away from the dead king
    FVector FleeVector = GetActorLocation() -
        DeadKing->GetActorLocation();

    // Set the magnitude (length) of the vector to 1
    FleeVector.Normalize();

    // Make the vector 500 times longer
    FleeVector *= 500;

    // Set the Actor's new location
    SetActorLocation(GetActorLocation() + FleeVector);
}
```

12. Return to the Unreal Editor and compile your scripts.

13. Afterward, create a Blueprint class based on `APeasant`. You can do this by right-clicking on the `Peasant` object in the **Content Browser** and then selecting **Create Blueprint class based on Peasant**. Call the new `BPPeasant` class. Afterward, click on the **Create Blueprint Class** button:

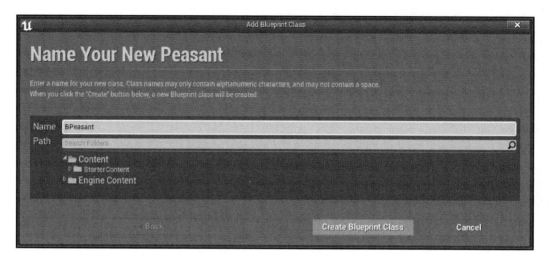

14. Within the Blueprint, click on the **Event Graph** tab and move upward to the `Event BeingPlay` node. Click and drag it away from the white (execution) pin of your `BeginPlay` node. Type `get all`, and you should see **Get All Actors Of Class**. Select the node to place it in your graph:

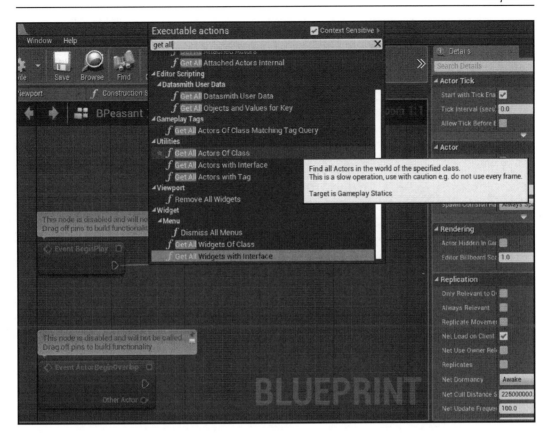

15. Set the value of the purple (class) node to King. You can type king in the search bar to make locating the class in the list easier:

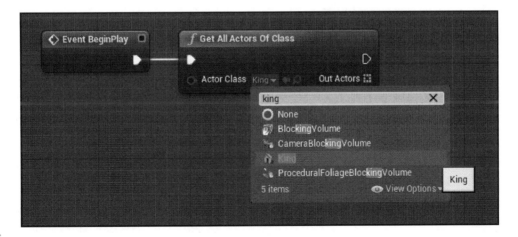

16. Drag the blue grid (object array) node out into an empty space and, from the **Actions** menu that pops up, type in the word `get`. From the options that are available, select the **Get (a copy)** option:

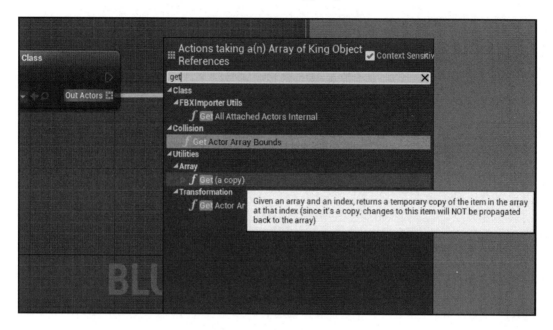

17. Drag away from the blue output pin of the get node and place a Not Equal (object) node:

18. Connect the red (bool) pin of the Not Equal node to a `Branch` node, and wire the execution pin of `Branch` to our `Get All Actors Of Class` node:

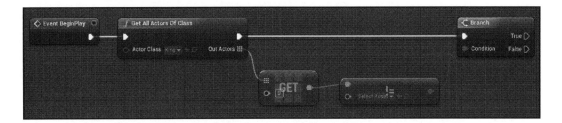

19. Connect the **True** pin of the branch to the **Bind Event to OnKing Death** node:

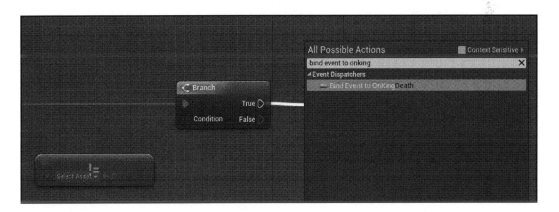

 Note that you will probably have to untick **Context Sensitive** in the context menu for the **Bind Event** node to be visible.

20. Then, connect the output of the **Get** node into the **Target** property of the **Bind Event to OnKingDeath** node:

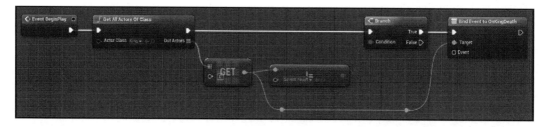

Connecting the **Get** node into the **Target** property of the **Bind Event to OnKingDeath** node

If you double-click on a connection, you can create a reroute node that you can drag to make it easier to see the connections between nodes.

21. Drag out the red pin of the **Bind Event to OnKingDeath** node and select **Add Custom Event....** Give your event the desired name:

You may need to uncheck the **Context Sensitive** option to see the **Add Custom Event...** option.

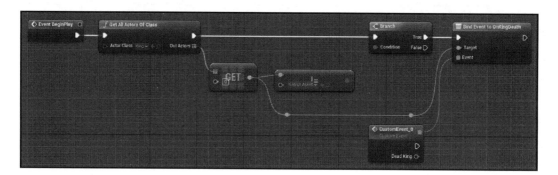

Connecting the Custom Event and the Event Binding.

22. Connect the white execution pin for the **Custom Event** to a new node named `Flee`, which we created back in Step 10:

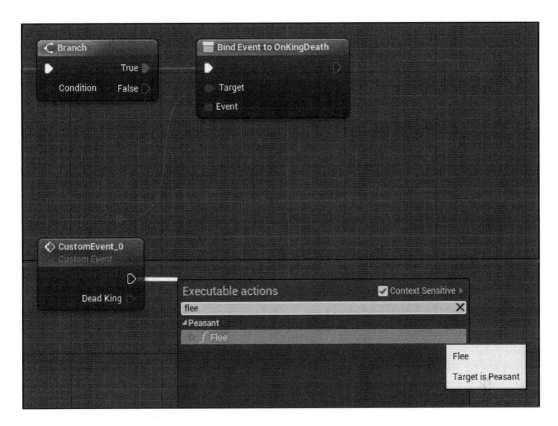

23. Lastly, drag the **Dead King** property from the **Custom Event** into the `Dead King` property of the **Flee** node.

24. Verify that your Blueprint looks like what's shown in the following screenshot:

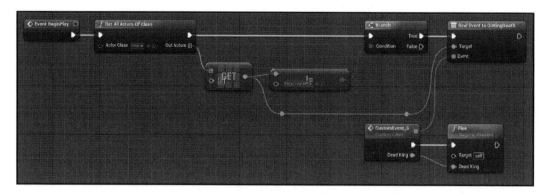

The completed Blueprint

25. Drag a copy of your `King` class into the level, and then add a few `BPPeasant` instances around it in a circle:

26. Open the level Blueprint. Inside it, drag away from `BeginPlay,` and add a `Delay` node. Set the delay to **5** seconds:

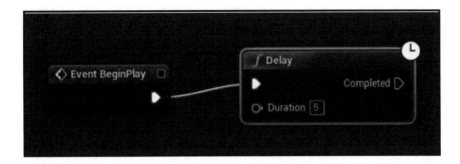

27. With your `King` instance that's selected in the level, right-click in the graph editor for the Level Blueprint.
28. Select **Call function on King 1** and look in the `King` category for a function called `Die`:

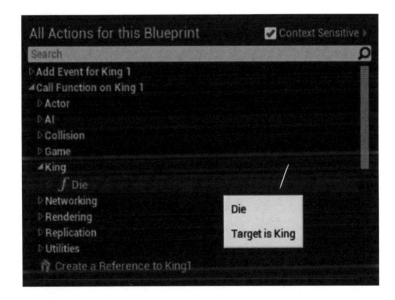

29. Select `Die`, then connect its execution pin to the output execution pin from the delay:

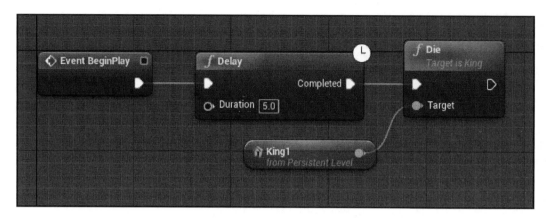

30. When you play your level, you should see that the king dies after 5 seconds:

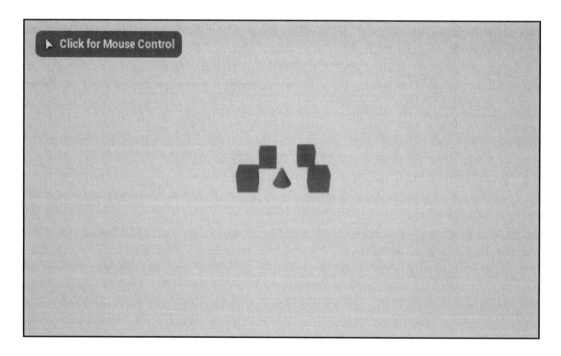

Afterward, you should see the peasants all wail and flee directly away from the king:

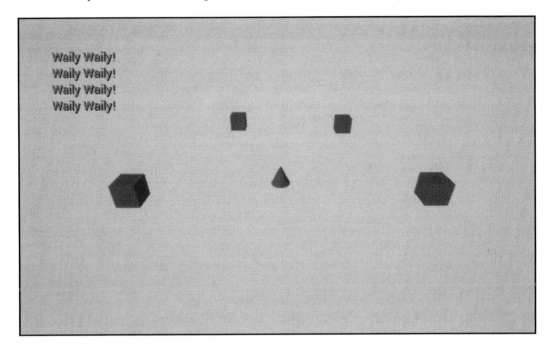

How it works...

We create a new actor (based on `StaticMeshActor` for convenience, as it saves us having to declare or create a Static Mesh component for the `Actor` visual representation).

We declare a dynamic multicast delegate using the `DECLARE_DYNAMIC_MULTICAST_DELEGATE_OneParam` macro. Dynamic multicast delegates allow an arbitrary number of objects to subscribe (listen) and unsubscribe (stop listening) so that they will be notified when the delegate is broadcast.

The macro takes a number of arguments – the type name of the new delegate signature being created, the type of the signature's parameter, then the name of the signature's parameter.

We also add a function to `King` that will allow us to tell it to die. Because we want to expose the function to Blueprints for prototyping, we mark it as `BlueprintCallable`.

The DECLARE_DYNAMIC_MULTICAST_DELEGATE macro that we used earlier only declared a type; it didn't declare an instance of the delegate, so we do that now, referencing the type name that we provided earlier when invoking the macro.

Dynamic multicast delegates can be marked as BlueprintAssignable in their UPROPERTY declaration. This indicates to Unreal that the Blueprint system can dynamically assign events to the delegate that will be called when the delegate's Broadcast function is called.

As always, we assign a simple mesh to our King so that it has a visual representation in the game scene.

Within the Die function, we call Broadcast on our own delegate. We specified that the delegate would have a parameter that is a pointer to the king which died, so we pass this pointer as a parameter to the broadcast function.

If you want the king to be destroyed, rather than playing an animation or other effect when it dies, you need to change the delegate's declaration and pass in a different type. For example, you could use FVector, and simply pass in the location of the dead king directly so that the peasants could still flee appropriately.

Without this, you potentially could have a situation where the King pointer is valid when Broadcast is called, but the call to Actor::Destroy() invalidates it before your bound functions are executed.

Within our next StaticMeshActor subclass, called Peasant, we initialize the static mesh component as usual using a different shape from the one that we used for the King.

Inside the implementation of the peasant's Flee function, we simulate the peasants playing sound by printing a message on the screen.

We then calculate a vector to make the peasants flee by first finding a vector from the dead king to this peasant's location.

We normalize the vector to retrieve a unit vector (with a length of 1) pointing in the same direction.

Scaling the normalized vector and adding it to our current location calculates a position at a fixed distance, in the exact direction for the peasant to be fleeing directly away from the dead king.

SetActorLocation is then used to actually teleport the peasants to that location.

 If you used a Character with an AI controller, you could have the Peasant pathfind to the target location rather than teleporting. Alternatively, you could use a Lerp function that's invoked during the peasant's Tick to make them slide smoothly rather than jump directly to the location.

See also

- See Chapter 4, *Actors and Components*, for more extended discussions about Actors and Components. Chapter 5, *Handling Events and Delegates*, discusses events such as Notify and ActorOverlap.

Creating C++ enums that can be used in Blueprint

Enums are commonly used in C++ as flags or inputs to switch statements. However, what if you want to pass an enum value to or from C++ from a Blueprint? Alternatively, if you want to use a switch statement in Blueprint that uses an enum from C++, how do you let the Blueprint editor know that your enum should be accessible within the editor? This recipe shows you how to make enums visible in Blueprint.

How to do it...

1. Create a new StaticMeshActor class called Tree using the editor.
2. Insert the following code above the class declaration:

```
#pragma once

#include "CoreMinimal.h"
#include "Engine/StaticMeshActor.h"
#include "Tree.generated.h"

UENUM(BlueprintType)
enum TreeType
```

```
{
    Tree_Poplar,
    Tree_Spruce,
    Tree_Eucalyptus,
    Tree_Redwood
};

UCLASS()
class CHAPTER_09_API ATree : public AStaticMeshActor
{
```

3. Add the following to the `Tree` class:

```
UCLASS()
class CHAPTER_09_API ATree : public AStaticMeshActor
{
    GENERATED_BODY()
public:
    // Sets default values for this actor's properties
    ATree();

    UPROPERTY(BlueprintReadWrite)
    TEnumAsByte<TreeType> Type;
};
```

4. Add the following to the `Tree` constructor:

```
#include "Tree.h"

#include "ConstructorHelpers.h"

// Sets default values
ATree::ATree()
{
    // Set this actor to call Tick() every frame. You can turn
    // this off to improve performance if you don't need it.
    PrimaryActorTick.bCanEverTick = true;

    auto MeshAsset =
ConstructorHelpers::FObjectFinder<UStaticMesh>
(TEXT("StaticMesh'/Engine/BasicShapes/Cylinder.Cylinder'"));

    UStaticMeshComponent * SM = GetStaticMeshComponent();

    if (SM != nullptr)
    {
        if (MeshAsset.Object != nullptr)
        {
```

```
            SM->SetStaticMesh(MeshAsset.Object);
            SM->SetGenerateOverlapEvents(true);
        }
        SM->SetMobility(EComponentMobility::Movable);
    }
}
```

5. Return to the Unreal Editor and compile your code.

6. Create a new Blueprint class called `MyTree`, based on `Tree`, by right-clicking on the Tree object and selecting **Create Blueprint class based on Tree**. Once the menu comes up, click on the **Create Blueprint Class** button.

7. Inside the blueprint editor for `MyTree`, click on the **Construction Script** tab.

8. Right-click in the empty window and type `treetype`. There is a **Get number of entries in TreeType** node:

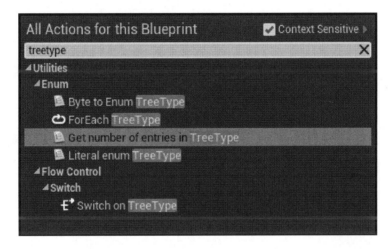

9. Where and then connect its **Return value** output pin to the **Max** property of a new **Random Integer** node:

10. Connect the **Return Value** output of the random integer to a **ToByte (Integer)** node:

11. In the **Variables** section of the **My Blueprint** panel, click on the + button. From there, go to the **Details** tab and set the **Variable Type** to Tree Type. Afterward, set the **Variable Name** to RandomTree:

12. Drag the **RandomTree** variable into the graph and select **Set Random Tree** when you see a small context menu appear.
13. Connect the **Return Value** output of the ToByte node to the input of the **SET Type** node. You'll see an extra conversion node automatically appear.
14. Lastly, connect the execution pin of **Construction Script** to the **SET Type** node's execution pin. Your Blueprint should look as follows:

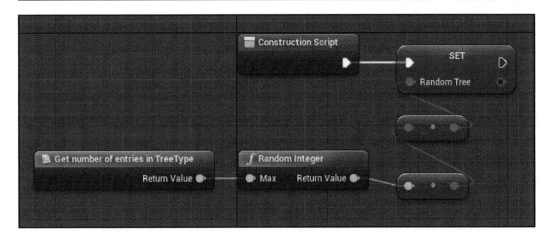

15. To verify that the blueprint is correctly functioning and randomly assigning a type to our tree, we are going to add some nodes to the Event Graph.

16. Place a `Print String` node after the **Event BeginPlay** event node:

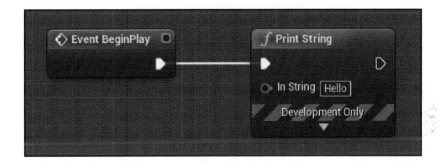

17. Place a `Format Text` node and connect its output to the input of the `Print String` node. A conversion node will be added for you:

18. Inside the `Format Text` node, add `My Type is {0}!` to the **Format** text box:

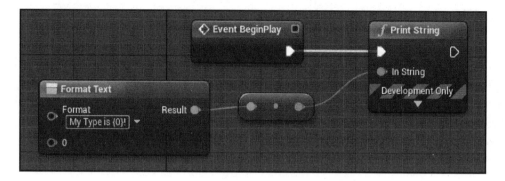

You should see that it adds a new parameter, **0**, which we can now set.

19. Drag the **RandomTree** variable from the **Variables** section of the **My Blueprint** window into the graph and select **Get** from the menu:

20. Add an **Enum to Name** node to the `Type` output pin:

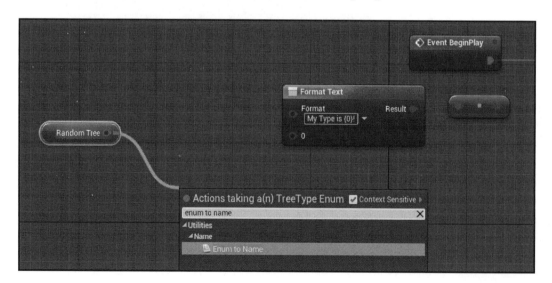

21. The **Format Text** node will not use a Name, so we will need to convert it into Text. Add a **ToText (name)** node to the **Enum to Name** output pin.

22. Connect the **Return Value** output of the ToText (name) node to the **0** input pin on the **Format Text** node. Your Event Graph should now look as follows:

The completed Blueprint graph

23. Compile your Blueprint and then return to the Unreal Editor.

24. Drag a few copies of your Blueprint into the level and hit **Play**. You should see a number of trees printing information regarding their type, verifying that types are being randomly assigned by the Blueprint code that we created:

How it works...

As usual, we use `StaticMeshActor` as the base class for our `Actor` so that we can easily give it a visual representation in the level.

Enumerated types are exposed to the reflection system using the UENUM macro.

We mark the `enum` as Blueprint-available using the `BlueprintType` specifier.

The `enum` declaration is just the same as we would use in any other context.

Our `Tree` requires a `TreeType`. Because *tree has tree-type* is the relationship we want to embody, we include an instance of `TreeType` in our `Tree` class.

As usual, we need to use UPROPERTY() to make the member variable accessible to the reflection system.

We use the `BlueprintReadWrite` specifier to mark the property as having both get and set support within Blueprint.

Enumerated types require being wrapped in the `TEnumAsByte` template when used in UPROPERTY, so we declare an instance of `TEnumAsByte<TreeType>` as the Tree's `Type` variable.

The constructor changes for `Tree` are simply the standard load and initialize our static mesh component preamble that's used in other recipes.

We create a Blueprint that inherits from our `Tree` class so that we can demonstrate the Blueprint-accessibility of the `TreeType` enum.

To have the Blueprint assign a type to the tree at random when we create an instance, we need to use the **Construction Script** Blueprint.

Within the **Construction Script**, we calculate the number of entries in the `TreeType` enum.

We generate a random number and use that as an index in the `TreeType` enum type to retrieve a value to store as our `Type`.

The Random number node, however, returns integers. Enumerated types are treated as bytes in Blueprint, so we need to use a `ToByte` node, which can then be implicitly converted by Blueprint into an `enum` value.

Now that we have **Construction Script** assigning a type to our tree instances as they are created, we need to display the tree's type at runtime.

We do so with the graph attached to the `BeginPlay` event within the Event Graph tab.

To display text on screen, we use a `Print String` node.

To perform string substitution and print our type out as a human-readable string, we use the `Format Text` node.

The `Format Text` node takes terms enclosed in curly braces and allows you to substitute other values for those terms by returning the final string.

To substitute our `Type` into the `Format Text` node, we need to convert our variable stores from the `enum` value into the actual name of the value.

We can do so by accessing our `Type` variable and then using the `Enum to Name` node.

`Names`, or `FNames` in native code, are a type of variable that can be converted into strings by Blueprint so that we can connect our `Name` to the input on the `Format Text` node.

When we hit Play, the graph executes, retrieving the type of tree instances that have been placed in the level and printing the names to the screen.

Editing class properties in different places in the editor

When developing with Unreal, it is common for programmers to implement properties on Actors or other objects in C++, and make them visible in the editor for designer use. However, sometimes, it makes sense to view a property, or make it editable, but only on the object's default state. Sometimes, the property should only be modifiable at runtime with the default specified in C++. Fortunately, there are some specifiers that can help us restrict when a property is available.

How to do it...

1. Create a new `Actor` class in the editor called `PropertySpecifierActor`:

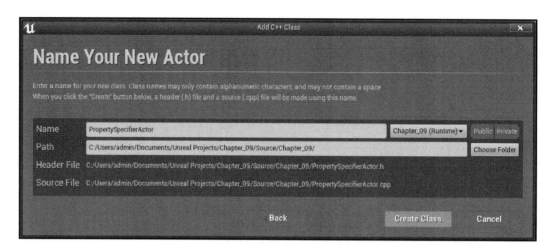

2. Add the following property definitions to the class:

```cpp
#pragma once

#include "CoreMinimal.h"
#include "GameFramework/Actor.h"
#include "PropertySpecifierActor.generated.h"

UCLASS()
class CHAPTER_09_API APropertySpecifierActor : public AActor
{
    GENERATED_BODY()
public:
    // Sets default values for this actor's properties
    APropertySpecifierActor();

protected:
    // Called when the game starts or when spawned
    virtual void BeginPlay() override;

public:
    // Called every frame
    virtual void Tick(float DeltaTime) override;

    // Property Specifiers
    UPROPERTY(EditDefaultsOnly)
```

```
    bool EditDefaultsOnly;

    UPROPERTY(EditInstanceOnly)
    bool EditInstanceOnly;

    UPROPERTY(EditAnywhere)
    bool EditAnywhere;

    UPROPERTY(VisibleDefaultsOnly)
    bool VisibleDefaultsOnly;

    UPROPERTY(VisibleInstanceOnly)
    bool VisibleInstanceOnly;

    UPROPERTY(VisibleAnywhere)
    bool VisibleAnywhere;
};
```

3. Perform a **Save, Compile** your code, and launch the editor.
4. Create a new blueprint based on the class.
5. Open the blueprint and look at the **Class Defaults** section:

6. Note which properties are editable and visible under the **Property Specifier Actor** section:

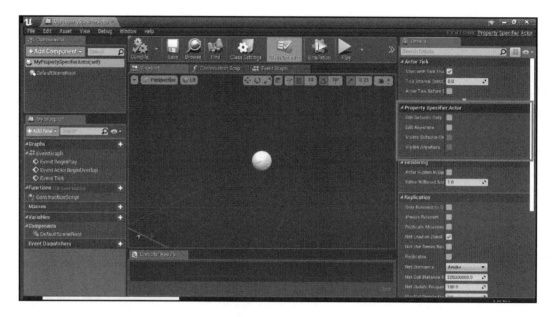

Location of the Property Specifier Actor

7. Place instances in the level and view their **Details** panels:

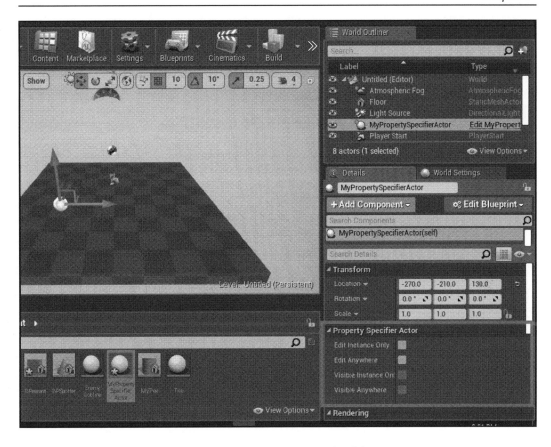

8. Note that a different set of properties is editable.

How it works...

When specifying UPROPERTY, we can indicate where we want that value to be available inside the Unreal editor.

Visible* prefixes indicate that the value is viewable in the **Details** panel for the indicated object. The value won't be editable, however.

This doesn't mean that the variable is a `const` qualifier; however, native code can change the value, for instance.

`Edit*` prefixes indicate that the property can be altered within the **Details** panels inside the editor.

`InstanceOnly` as a suffix indicates that the property will only be displayed in the **Details** panels for instances of your class that have been placed into the game. They won't be visible in the **Class Defaults** section of the Blueprint editor, for example.

`DefaultsOnly` is the inverse of `InstanceOnly` – UPROPERTY will only display in the **Class Defaults section**, and can't be viewed on individual instances within the level.

The suffix `Anywhere` is the combination of the two previous suffixes – the UPROPERTY will be visible in all the **Details** panels that inspect either the object's defaults or a particular instance in the level.

 As we mentioned previously, if you are interested in learning more about Property Specifiers, check out the following link: `https://docs.unrealengine.com/en-us/Programming/UnrealArchitecture/Reference/Properties/Specifiers`.

See also

- This recipe makes the property in question visible in the inspector, but doesn't allow the property to be referenced in the actual Blueprint Event Graph. See the following recipe for a description of how to make that possible.

Making properties accessible in the Blueprint editor graph

The specifiers we mentioned in the previous recipe are all well and good, but they only control the visibility of UPROPERTY in the **Details** panel. By default, even with those specifiers used appropriately, UPROPERTY won't be viewable or accessible in the actual editor graph for use at `runtime`. `Other` specifiers, which can optionally be used in conjunction with the ones in the previous recipe so that you can interact with properties in the Event Graph.

How to do it...

1. Create a new `Actor` class called `BlueprintPropertyActor` using the editor wizard:

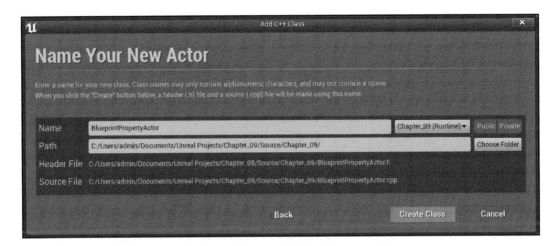

2. Add the following UPROPERTY to the class using Visual Studio:

```
#pragma once

#include "CoreMinimal.h"
#include "GameFramework/Actor.h"
#include "BlueprintPropertyActor.generated.h"

UCLASS()
class CHAPTER_09_API ABlueprintPropertyActor : public AActor
{
    GENERATED_BODY()
public:
    // Sets default values for this actor's properties
    ABlueprintPropertyActor();

protected:
    // Called when the game starts or when spawned
    virtual void BeginPlay() override;

public:
    // Called every frame
    virtual void Tick(float DeltaTime) override;

    UPROPERTY(BlueprintReadWrite, Category = Cookbook)
```

```
bool ReadWriteProperty;

UPROPERTY(BlueprintReadOnly, Category = Cookbook)
bool ReadOnlyProperty;

};
```

3. Perform a **Save**, **Compile** your project, and start the editor.
4. Create a Blueprint class based on your `BlueprintPropertyActor` and open its graph.
5. From the **My Blueprint** panel, click on the eye icon to the right of the **Search** bar. From there, select **Show Inherited Variables**:

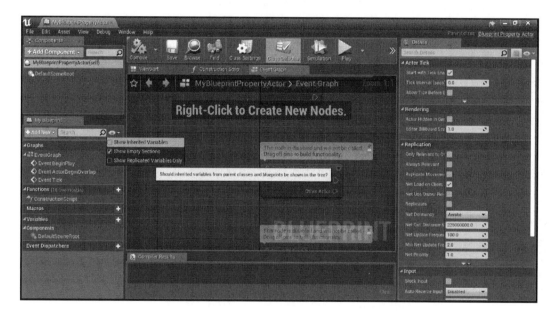

6. Verify that the properties are visible under the **Cookbook** category in the **Variables** section of the **My Blueprint** panel:

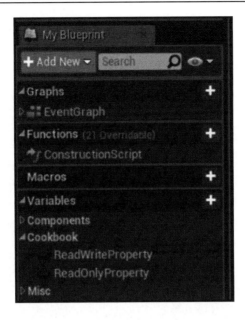

7. Left-click and drag the `ReadWriteProperty` variable into the **Event Graph**. Then select **Get ReadWriteProperty**:

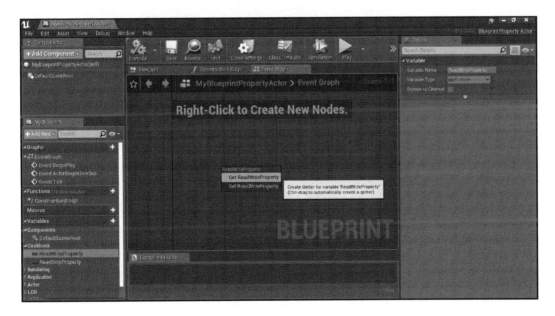

8. Repeat the previous step, but instead select **Set ReadWriteProperty**.
9. Drag the **ReadOnly** property into the graph and note that the **SET** node is disabled:

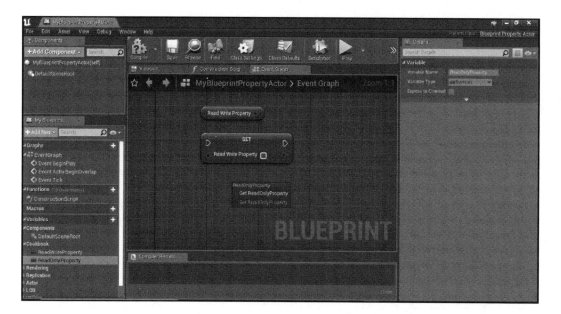

How it works...

BlueprintReadWrite as a UPROPERTY specifier indicates to the Unreal Header Tool that the property should have both Get and Set operations exposed for use in Blueprints.

BlueprintReadOnly is, as the name implies, a specifier that only allows Blueprint to retrieve the value of the property; never set it.

BlueprintReadOnly can be useful when a property is set by native code, but should be accessible within Blueprint.

It should be noted that BlueprintReadWrite and BlueprintReadOnly don't specify anything about the property being accessible in the **Details** panels or the **My Blueprint** section of the editor: these specifiers only control the generation of the getter/setter nodes for use in Blueprint graphs.

Responding to property changed events from the editor

When a designer changes the properties of an `Actor` placed in the level, it is often important to show any visual results of that change immediately rather than just when the level is simulated or played. When changes are made using the **Details** panels, there's a special event that the editor emits called `PostEditChangeProperty`, which gives the class instance a chance to respond to the property being edited. This recipe shows you how to handle `PostEditChangeProperty` for immediate in-editor feedback.

How to do it...

1. Create a new `Actor` called `PostEditChangePropertyActor` based on `StaticMeshActor`:

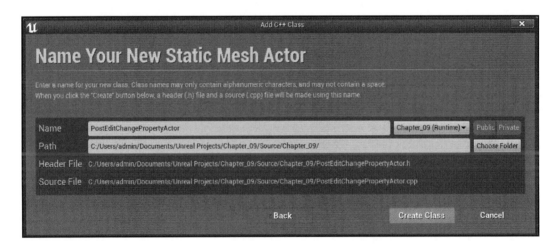

2. Add the following UPROPERTY and function definition to the class:

```
UCLASS()
class CHAPTER_09_API APostEditChangePropertyActor : public
AStaticMeshActor
{
    GENERATED_BODY()

    // Sets default values for this actor's properties
```

```
APostEditChangePropertyActor();

UPROPERTY(EditAnywhere)
bool ShowStaticMesh = true;

virtual void PostEditChangeProperty(FPropertyChangedEvent&
                                    PropertyChangedEvent)
override;
};
```

3. Create the class constructor by adding the following code to the PostEditChangePropertyActor.cpp file:

```
#include "PostEditChangePropertyActor.h"
#include "ConstructorHelpers.h"

APostEditChangePropertyActor::APostEditChangePropertyActor()
{
    // Set this actor to call Tick() every frame. You can turn
    // this off to improve performance if you don't need it.
    PrimaryActorTick.bCanEverTick = true;

    auto MeshAsset =
ConstructorHelpers::FObjectFinder<UStaticMesh>
        (TEXT("StaticMesh'/Engine/BasicShapes/Cone.Cone'"));

    UStaticMeshComponent * SM = GetStaticMeshComponent();

    if (SM != nullptr)
    {
        if (MeshAsset.Object != nullptr)
        {
            SM->SetStaticMesh(MeshAsset.Object);
            SM->SetGenerateOverlapEvents(true);
        }
        SM->SetMobility(EComponentMobility::Movable);
    }
}
```

4. Implement PostEditChangeProperty:

```
void APostEditChangePropertyActor::PostEditChangeProperty(
FPropertyChangedEvent& PropertyChangedEvent)
{
    // Check if property is valid
    if (PropertyChangedEvent.Property != nullptr)
    {
        // Get the name of the changed property
```

```
        const FName PropertyName(
PropertyChangedEvent.Property->GetFName());

        // If the changed property is ShowStaticMesh then we
        // will set the visibility of the actor
        if (PropertyName == GET_MEMBER_NAME_CHECKED(
                        APostEditChangePropertyActor,
ShowStaticMesh))
        {
            UStaticMeshComponent * SM =
GetStaticMeshComponent();

            if (SM != nullptr)
            {
                SM->SetVisibility(ShowStaticMesh);
            }
        }
    }

        // Then call the parent version of this function
        Super::PostEditChangeProperty(PropertyChangedEvent);
}
```

5. Compile your code and launch the editor.
6. Drag an instance of your class into the game world and verify that toggling the Boolean value for ShowStaticMesh toggles the visibility of the mesh in the editor viewport:

The location of the **Show Static Mesh** property

Then, if you ever toggle it off, you'll see the object disappear, as follows:

How it works...

We create a new `Actor` based on `StaticMeshActor` for easy access to a visual representation via the Static Mesh.

`UPROPERTY` is added to give us a property to change, which causes `PostEditChangeProperty` events to be triggered.

`PostEditChangeProperty` is a virtual function that's defined in `Actor`.

As a result, we override the function in our class.

Within our class constructor, we initialize our mesh as usual, and set the default state of our `bool` property to match the visibility of the component it controls.

Inside `PostEditChangeProperty`, we first check that the property is valid.

Assuming it is, we retrieve the name of the property using `GetFName()`.

`FNames` are stored internally by the engine as a table of unique values.

Next, we need to use the `GET_MEMBER_NAME_CHECKED` macro. The macro takes a number of parameters.

The first one is the name of the class to check, while the second parameter is the property to check the class for.

The macro will, at compile-time, verify that the class contains the member specified by name.

We compare the class member name that the macro returns against the name that our property contains.

If they are the same, then we verify that our `StaticMeshComponent` is initialized correctly.

If it is, we set its visibility to match the value of our `ShowStaticMesh` Boolean.

Implementing a native code Construction Script

Within Blueprint, a **Construction Script** is an **Event Graph** that runs any time a property is changed on the object it is attached to – whether it's being dragged in the editor viewport or changed via a direct entry in a **Details** panel. Construction Scripts allow the object in question to *rebuild* itself based on its new location, for instance, or to change the components it contains based on user-selected options. When coding in C++ with Unreal Engine, the equivalent concept is the `OnConstruction` function.

How to do it...

1. Create a new `Actor` called `OnConstructionActor` based on `StaticMeshActor`:

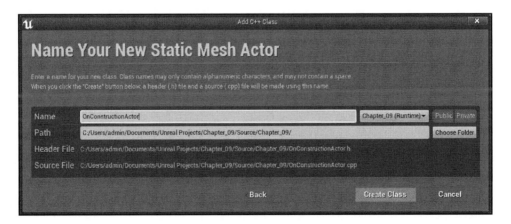

2. Update the header file to the following:

```
#pragma once

#include "CoreMinimal.h"
#include "Engine/StaticMeshActor.h"
#include "OnConstructionActor.generated.h"

UCLASS()
class CHAPTER_09_API AOnConstructionActor : public
AStaticMeshActor
{
  GENERATED_BODY()

public:
    AOnConstructionActor();

    virtual void OnConstruction(const FTransform& Transform)
override;

    UPROPERTY(EditAnywhere)
        bool ShowStaticMesh;
};
```

3. Go to the implementation file (OnConstructionActor.cpp) and implement the class constructor:

```
#include "OnConstructionActor.h"
#include "ConstructorHelpers.h"

AOnConstructionActor::AOnConstructionActor()
{
    // Set this actor to call Tick() every frame. You can turn
    // this off to improve performance if you don't need it.
    PrimaryActorTick.bCanEverTick = true;

    auto MeshAsset =
ConstructorHelpers::FObjectFinder<UStaticMesh>(
TEXT("StaticMesh'/Engine/BasicShapes/Cone.Cone'"));

    UStaticMeshComponent * SM = GetStaticMeshComponent();

    if (SM != nullptr)
    {
        if (MeshAsset.Object != nullptr)
        {
            SM->SetStaticMesh(MeshAsset.Object);
            SM->SetGenerateOverlapEvents(true);
```

```
        }
        SM->SetMobility(EComponentMobility::Movable);
    }

    // Default value of property
    ShowStaticMesh = true;
}
```

4. Implement OnConstruction:

```
void AOnConstructionActor::OnConstruction(const FTransform&
Transform)
{
    GetStaticMeshComponent()->SetVisibility(ShowStaticMesh);
}
```

5. Compile your code and launch the editor.
6. Drag an instance of your class into the game world, and verify that toggling the Boolean value for ShowStaticMesh toggles the visibility of the mesh in the editor viewport:

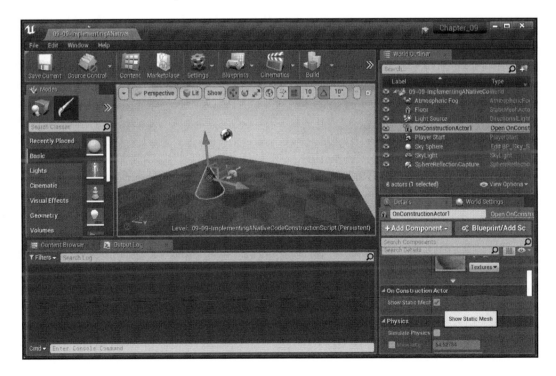

7. OnConstruction does not currently run for C++ actors that are placed in a level if they are moved.

8. To test this, place a breakpoint in your OnConstruction function, and then move your actor around the level.

To place a breakpoint, place your cursor on the desired line and hit *F9* in Visual Studio.

9. You'll notice that the function doesn't get called, but if you toggle the ShowStaticMesh Boolean, it does, causing your breakpoint to trigger.

To see why, take a look at the beginning of the AActor::PostEditMove function:

```
void AActor::PostEditMove(bool bFinished)
{
    if ( ReregisterComponentsWhenModified() &&
!FLevelUtils::IsMovingLevel())
    {
        UBlueprint* Blueprint =
Cast<UBlueprint>(GetClass()->ClassGeneratedBy);
        if (bFinished || bRunConstructionScriptOnDrag ||
(Blueprint && Blueprint->bRunConstructionScriptOnDrag))
        {
            FNavigationLockContext NavLock(GetWorld(),
ENavigationLockReason::AllowUnregister);
            RerunConstructionScripts();
        }
    }

    // ....
```

The top line here casts UClass for the current object to UBlueprint, and will only run the construction scripts and OnConstruction again if the class is a Blueprint.

How it works...

We create a new Actor based on StaticMeshActor for easy access to a visual representation via the Static Mesh.

UPROPERTY is added to give us a property to change, which causes PostEditChangeProperty events to be triggered.

OnConstruction is a virtual function that's defined in Actor.

As a result, we override the function in our class.

Within our class constructor, we initialize our mesh as usual, and set the default state of our bool property to match the visibility of the component that it controls.

Inside OnConstruction, the actor rebuilds itself using any properties that are required to do so.

For this simple example, we set the visibility of the mesh to match the value of our ShowStaticMesh property.

This could also be extended to changing other values based on the value of the ShowStaticMesh variable.

You'll note that we don't explicitly filter on a particular property being changed, like the previous recipe does with PostEditChangeProperty.

The OnConstruction script runs in its entirety for every property that gets changed on the object.

It has no way of testing which property was just edited, so you need to be judicious about placing computationally intensive code within it.

10
Integrating C++ and the Unreal Editor: Part II

In this chapter, we will cover the following recipes:

- Creating a new editor module
- Creating new toolbar buttons
- Creating new menu entries
- Creating a new editor window
- Creating a new Asset type
- Creating custom context menu entries for Assets
- Creating new console commands
- Creating a new graph pin visualizer for Blueprint
- Inspecting types with custom **Details** panels

Introduction

In game development, in addition to creating games, you'll often need to create tools for other developers to use that have been customized to fit the project that you're working on. In fact, this is often one of the more common entry-level game developer positions in the AAA game industry. In this chapter, we will learn how to implement custom editor windows and custom detail panels to inspect types that have been created by users.

Creating a new editor module

The following recipes all interact with editor mode-specific code and engine modules. As a result, it is considered good practice to create a new module that will only be loaded when the engine is running in editor mode, so that we can place all our editor-only code inside it.

How to do it...

1. Open your project's `.uproject` file in a text editor such as Notepad or Notepad++. You can find the file inside your project folder, and it should look similar to what's shown in the following screenshot:

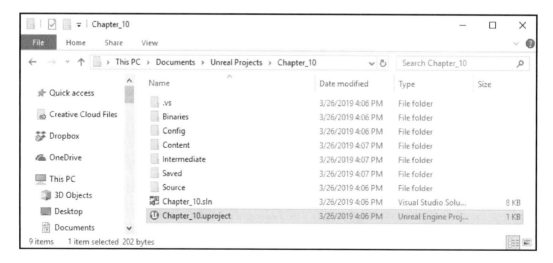

2. Add the bold section of text in the following snippet to the file:

```
{
  "FileVersion": 3,
  "EngineAssociation": "4.21",
  "Category": "",
  "Description": "",
  "Modules": [
    {
      "Name": "Chapter_10",
      "Type": "Runtime",
      "LoadingPhase": "Default"
    },
    {
      "Name": "Chapter_10Editor",
      "Type": "Editor",
      "LoadingPhase": "PostEngineInit",
      "AdditionalDependencies": [
        "Engine",
        "CoreUObject"
      ]
    }
  ]
}
```

Note the comma after the first module before the second set of curly braces.

3. In your `Source` folder, create a new folder using the same name as you specified in your `uproject` file (in this instance, `"Chapter_10Editor"`):

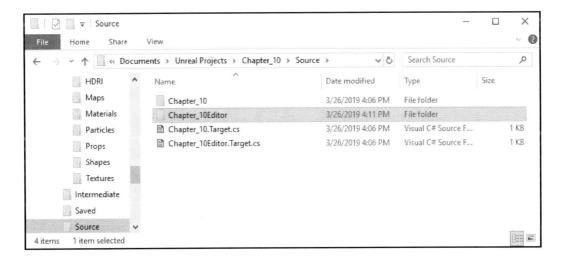

4. Open up the `Chapter_10Editor.Target.cs` file and update it to the following:

```
using UnrealBuildTool;
using System.Collections.Generic;

public class Chapter_10EditorTarget : TargetRules
{
  public Chapter_10EditorTarget(TargetInfo Target) :
base(Target)
   {
     Type = TargetType.Editor;

     ExtraModuleNames.AddRange( new string[] {
"Chapter_10Editor" } );
   }
}
```

5. Inside this new folder, create a blank `.txt` file and rename it to `Chapter_10Editor.Build.cs`:

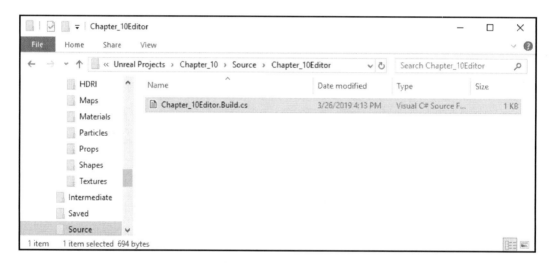

6. Insert the following into the file:

```
using UnrealBuildTool;

public class Chapter_10Editor : ModuleRules
{
    public Chapter_10Editor(ReadOnlyTargetRules Target) :
    base(Target)
```

```
        {
            PCHUsage = PCHUsageMode.UseExplicitOrSharedPCHs;

            PublicDependencyModuleNames.AddRange(new string[] {
"Core",
            "CoreUObject", "Engine", "InputCore", "RHI",
"RenderCore",
            "ShaderCore", "MainFrame", "AssetTools",
"AppFramework",
            "PropertyEditor"});
            PublicDependencyModuleNames.Add("Chapter_10");

            PrivateDependencyModuleNames.AddRange(new string[] {
            "UnrealEd", "Slate", "SlateCore", "EditorStyle",
            "GraphEditor", "BlueprintGraph" });

        }
    }
```

7. Still inside of the `Chapter10_Editor` folder, create a new file called `Chapter_10Editor.h` and add the following:

```
#pragma once

#include "Engine.h"
#include "Modules/ModuleInterface.h"
#include "Modules/ModuleManager.h"
#include "UnrealEd.h"


class FChapter_10EditorModule: public IModuleInterface
{
};
```

8. Lastly, create a new source file called `Chapter_10Editor.cpp`.

9. Add the following code:

```
#include "Chapter_10Editor.h"
#include "Modules/ModuleManager.h"
#include "Modules/ModuleInterface.h"

IMPLEMENT_GAME_MODULE(FChapter_10EditorModule,
Chapter_10Editor)
```

10. Finally, close Visual Studio if you have it open. Then, right-click on the `.uproject` file and select **Generate Visual Studio Project files**:

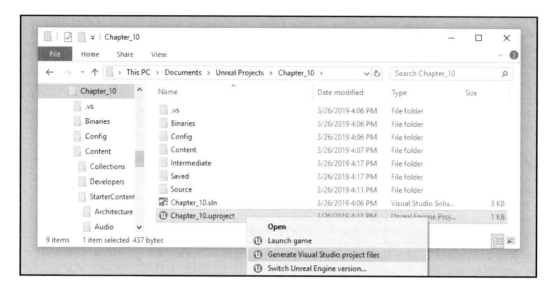

11. You should see a small window launch, display a progress bar, and then close:

12. You can now launch Visual Studio, verify that your new module is visible in the IDE, and compile your project successfully:

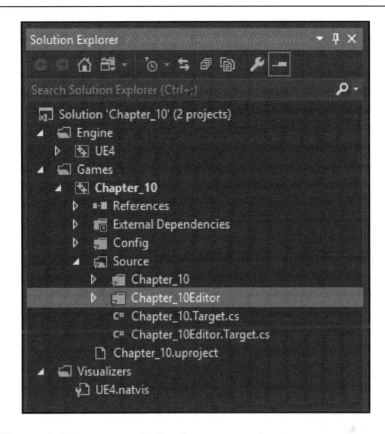

13. The module is now ready for the next set of recipes.

 Code changes made in this editor module won't support hot-reloading in the same way that code in runtime modules does. If you get a compilation error that mentions changes to generated header files, simply close the editor and rebuild it from within your IDE instead.

How it works...

Unreal projects use the .uproject file format to specify a number of different pieces of information about the project.

This information is used to inform the Header and Build tools about the modules that comprise this project, and is used for code generation and makefile creation.

The file uses JSON-style formatting.

These include the following:

- The engine version that the project should be opened in
- A list of modules that are used in the project
- A list of module declarations

Each of these module declarations contain the following:

- The name of the module.
- The type of module—is it an editor module (only runs in editor builds, has access to editor-only classes) or a runtime module (runs in both editor and Shipping builds)?
- The loading phase of the module—modules can be loaded at different points during program startup. This value specifies the point at which the module should be loaded, for example, if there are dependencies in other modules that should be loaded first.
- A list of dependencies for the module. These are essential modules that contain exported functions or classes that the module relies on.

We added a new module to the `uproject file`. The module's name is `Chapter_10Editor` (Conventionally, `Editor` should be appended to the main game module for an editor module).

This module is marked as an editor module, and is set to load after the baseline engine so that it can use the classes that have been declared in Engine code.

Our module's dependencies are left at the default values for now.

With the `uproject` file altered to contain our new module, we need a build script for it.

Build scripts are written in C#, and take the name `<ModuleName>.Build.cs`.

C#, unlike C++, doesn't use a separate header file and implementation – it's all there in the one `.cs` file.

We want to access the classes that have been declared in the `UnrealBuildTool` module, so we include a `using` statement to indicate that we want to access that namespace.

We create a `public` class with the same name as our module, which inherits from `ModuleRules`.

Inside our constructor, we add a number of modules to the dependencies of this module. There are both private dependencies and public dependencies.

According to the code of the `ModuleRules` class, public dependencies are modules that your module's public header files depend on. Private dependencies are modules that the private code depends on. Anything used in both public headers and private code should go into the `PublicDependencyModuleNames` array.

You'll note that our `PublicDependencyModuleNames` array contains our main game module. This is because some recipes in this chapter will extend the editor to better support the classes that are defined within our main game module.

Now that we've told the build system that we have a new module to build through the project file, and we've specified how to build the module with the build script, we need to create the C++ class that is our actual module.

We create a header file that includes the Engine header, the `ModuleManager` header, and the `UnrealEd` header.

We include `ModuleManager` because it defines `IModuleInterface`, the class that our module will inherit from.

We also include `UnrealEd` because we're writing an editor module that will need to access the editor functionality.

The class we declare inherits from `IModuleInterface`, and takes its name from the usual prefix, `F`, followed by the module name.

Inside the `.cpp` file, we include our module's header, and then use the `IMPLEMENT_GAME_MODULE` macro.

`IMPLEMENT_GAME_MODULE` declares an exported C function, `InitializeModule()`, which returns an instance of our new module class.

This means that Unreal can simply call `InitializeModule()` on any library that exports it to retrieve a reference to the actual module implementation without needing to know what class it is.

Having added our new module, we now need to rebuild our Visual Studio solution, so we close Visual Studio and then regenerate the project files using the context menu.

With the project rebuilt, the new module will be visible in Visual Studio, and we can add code to it as usual.

Creating new toolbar buttons

If you have created a custom tool or window for display within the editor, you probably need some way to let the user make it appear. The easiest way to do this is to create a toolbar customization that adds a new toolbar button, and have it display your window when clicked. Create a new engine module by following the previous recipe, as we'll need it to initialize our toolbar customization.

How to do it...

1. Inside of the `Chapter_10Editor` folder, create a new header file, `CookbookCommands.h`, and insert the following class declaration:

```
#pragma once
#include "Commands.h"
#include "EditorStyleSet.h"


class FCookbookCommands : public TCommands<FCookbookCommands>
{
public:
  FCookbookCommands()
    : TCommands<FCookbookCommands>(
      FName(TEXT("UE4_Cookbook")),
      FText::FromString("Cookbook Commands"),
      NAME_None,
      FEditorStyle::GetStyleSetName())
  {
  };

  virtual void RegisterCommands() override;

  TSharedPtr<FUICommandInfo> MyButton;
  TSharedPtr<FUICommandInfo> MyMenuButton;
};
```

2. Implement the new class by placing the following in the `.cpp` file:

```
#include "CookbookCommands.h"
#include "Chapter_10Editor.h"
```

```
#include "Commands.h"


void FCookbookCommands::RegisterCommands()
{
#define LOCTEXT_NAMESPACE ""
  UI_COMMAND(MyButton, "Cookbook", "Demo Cookbook Toolbar
Command", EUserInterfaceActionType::Button, FInputGesture());
  UI_COMMAND(MyMenuButton, "Cookbook", "Demo Cookbook Toolbar
Command", EUserInterfaceActionType::Button, FInputGesture());
#undef LOCTEXT_NAMESPACE
}
```

3. Next, we will need to update our module class (`Chapter_10Editor.h`) to the following:

```
#pragma once

#include "Engine.h"
#include "Modules/ModuleInterface.h"
#include "Modules/ModuleManager.h"
#include "UnrealEd.h"
#include "CookbookCommands.h"
#include
"Editor/MainFrame/Public/Interfaces/IMainFrameModule.h"


class FChapter_10EditorModule: public IModuleInterface
{
    virtual void StartupModule() override;
    virtual void ShutdownModule() override;

    TSharedPtr<FExtender> ToolbarExtender;
    TSharedPtr<const FExtensionBase> Extension;

    void MyButton_Clicked()
    {
        TSharedRef<SWindow> CookbookWindow = SNew(SWindow)
            .Title(FText::FromString(TEXT("Cookbook Window")))
            .ClientSize(FVector2D(800, 400))
            .SupportsMaximize(false)
            .SupportsMinimize(false);

        IMainFrameModule& MainFrameModule =
FModuleManager::LoadModuleChecked<IMainFrameModule>
            (TEXT("MainFrame"));

        if (MainFrameModule.GetParentWindow().IsValid())
```

```
            {
                FSlateApplication::Get().AddWindowAsNativeChild
                (CookbookWindow, MainFrameModule.GetParentWindow()
                    .ToSharedRef());
            }
            else
            {
FSlateApplication::Get().AddWindow(CookbookWindow);
            }
        };

        void AddToolbarExtension(FToolBarBuilder &builder)
        {
            FSlateIcon IconBrush =
                FSlateIcon(FEditorStyle::GetStyleSetName(),
                    "LevelEditor.ViewOptions",
                    "LevelEditor.ViewOptions.Small");
builder.AddToolBarButton(FCookbookCommands::Get()
                        .MyButton, NAME_None,
FText::FromString("My Button"),
                        FText::FromString("Click me to display a
message"),
                        IconBrush, NAME_None);
        };
};
```

Be sure to #include the header file for your command class as well.

4. We now need to implement StartupModule and ShutdownModule:

```
#include "Chapter_10Editor.h"
#include "Modules/ModuleManager.h"
#include "Modules/ModuleInterface.h"
#include "LevelEditor.h"
#include "SlateBasics.h"
#include "MultiBoxExtender.h"
#include "CookbookCommands.h"

IMPLEMENT_GAME_MODULE(FChapter_10EditorModule,
Chapter_10Editor)

void FChapter_10EditorModule::StartupModule()
{
    FCookbookCommands::Register();
    TSharedPtr<FUICommandList> CommandList = MakeShareable(new
FUICommandList());
    CommandList->MapAction(FCookbookCommands::Get().MyButton,
FExecuteAction::CreateRaw(this,
```

```
    &FChapter_10EditorModule::MyButton_Clicked),
FCanExecuteAction());
    ToolbarExtender = MakeShareable(new FExtender());

    FLevelEditorModule& LevelEditorModule =
FModuleManager::LoadModuleChecked<FLevelEditorModule>(
"LevelEditor" );

    Extension =
ToolbarExtender->AddToolBarExtension("Compile",
EExtensionHook::Before, CommandList,
FToolBarExtensionDelegate::CreateRaw(this,
&FChapter_10EditorModule::AddToolbarExtension));
LevelEditorModule.GetToolBarExtensibilityManager()->AddExtende
r(ToolbarExtender);
}

void FChapter_10EditorModule::ShutdownModule()
{
    ToolbarExtender->RemoveExtension(Extension.ToSharedRef());
    Extension.Reset();
    ToolbarExtender.Reset();
}
```

5. Regenerate your project piles if needed, compile your project from Visual Studio and start the editor.
6. Verify that there's a new button on the toolbar in the main level editor, which can be clicked on to open a new window:

How it works...

Unreal's editor UI is based on the concept of commands. Commands are a design pattern that allows looser coupling between the UI and the actions that it needs to perform.

To create a class that contains a set of commands, it is necessary to inherit from TCommands.

TCommands is a template class that leverages the **Curiously Recurring Template Pattern (CRTP)**. The CRTP is used commonly throughout Slate UI code as a means of creating compile-time polymorphism.

In the initializer list for FCookbookCommands constructor, we invoke the parent class constructor, passing in a number of parameters:

- The first parameter is the name of the command set, and is a simple FName.
- The second parameter is a tooltip/human readable string, and, as such, uses FText so that it can support localization if necessary.
- If there's a parent group of commands, the third parameter contains the name of the group. Otherwise, it contains NAME_None.
- The final parameter for the constructor is the Slate Style set that contains any command icons that the command set will be using.

The RegisterCommands() function allows TCommands-derived classes to create any command objects that they require. The resulting FUICommandInfo instances that are returned from that function are stored inside the Commands class as members so that UI elements or functions can be bound to the commands.

This is why we have the member variable TSharedPtr<FUICommandInfo> MyButton.

In the implementation for the class, we simply need to create our commands in RegisterCommands.

The UI_COMMAND macro that was used to create an instance of FUICommandInfo expects a localization namespace to be defined, even if it is just an empty default namespace. As a result, we need to enclose our UI_COMMAND calls with #defines to set a valid value for LOCTEXT_NAMESPACE, even if we don't intend to use localization.

The actual UI_COMMAND macro takes a number of parameters:

- The first parameter is the variable to store the FUICommandInfo in
- The second parameter is a human-readable name for the command
- The third parameter is a description for the command
- The fourth parameter is EUserInterfaceActionType

This enumeration essentially specifies what sort of button is being created. It supports `Button`, `ToggleButton`, `RadioButton`, and `Check` as valid types.

Buttons are simple generic buttons. A toggle button stores on and off states. The radio button is similar to a toggle, but is grouped with other radio buttons, and only one can be enabled at a time. Lastly, the checkbox displays a read-only checkbox that's adjacent to the button.

The last parameter for `UI_COMMAND` is the input chord, or the combination of keys that are required to activate the command.

This parameter is primarily useful for defining key combinations for hotkeys linked to the command in question, rather than buttons. As a result, we use an empty `InputGesture`.

So, we now have a set of commands, but we haven't told the engine we want to add the set to the commands that show on the toolbar. We also haven't set up what actually happens when the button is clicked. To do this, we need to perform some initialization when our module begins, so we place some code into the `StartupModule`/`ShutdownModule` functions.

Inside `StartupModule`, we call the static `Register` function on the commands class that we defined earlier.

We then create a shared pointer to a list of commands using the `MakeShareable` function.

In the command list, we use `MapAction` to create a mapping, or association, between the `UICommandInfo` object, which we set as a member of the `FCookbookCommands`, and the actual function we want to execute when the command is invoked.

You'll note that we don't explicitly set anything regarding what could be used to invoke the command here.

To perform this mapping, we call the `MapAction` function. The first parameter to `MapAction` is a `FUICommandInfo` object, which we can retrieve from `FCookbookCommands` by using its static `Get()` method to retrieve the instance.

`FCookbookCommands` is implemented as a singleton – a class with a single instance that exists throughout the application. You'll see the pattern in most places – there's a static `Get()` method available in the engine.

The second parameter of the `MapAction` function is a delegate bound to the function to be invoked when the command is executed.

Because `Chapter_10EditorModule` is a raw C++ class rather than a `UObject`, and we want to invoke a member function rather than a `static` function, we use `CreateRaw` to create a new delegate that's bound to a raw C++ member function.

`CreateRaw` expects a pointer to the object instance, and a function reference to the function to invoke on that pointer.

The third parameter for `MapAction` is a delegate to call to test if the action can be executed. Because we want the command to be executable all the time, we can use a simple predefined delegate that always returns `true`.

With an association created between our command and the action it should call, we now need to actually tell the extension system that we want to add new commands to the toolbar.

We can do this via the `FExtender` class, which can be used to extend menus, context menus, or toolbars.

We initially create an instance of `FExtender` as a shared pointer so that our extensions are uninitialized when the module is shut down.

We then call `AddToolBarExtension` on our new extender, storing the results in a shared pointer so that we can remove it on module uninitialization.

First argument of `AddToolBarExtension` is the name of the extension point where we want to add our extension.

To find where we want to place our extension, we first need to turn on the display of extension points within the editor UI.

To do so, open **Editor Preferences** in the **Edit** menu within the editor:

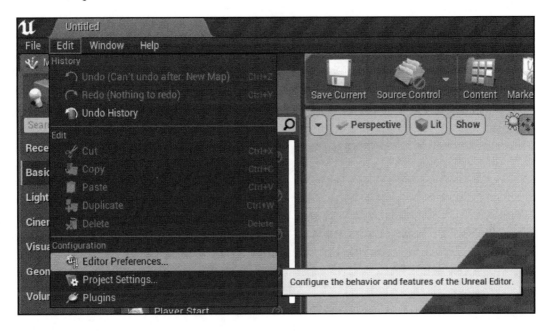

Open **General** | **Miscellaneous** and select **Display UIExtension Points**:

Restart the editor, and you should see green text overlaid on the Editor UI, as shown in the following screenshot:

Green text overlaying the Editor UI

The green text indicates `UIExtensionPoint`, and the text's value is the string we should provide to the `AddToolBarExtension` function.

We're going to add our extension to the **Compile** extension point in this recipe, but of course, you could use any other extension point you wish.

It's important to note that adding a toolbar extension to a menu extension point will fail silently, and vice versa.

The second parameter to `AddToolBarExtension` is a location anchor relative to the extension point that's specified. We've selected `FExtensionHook::Before`, so our icon will be displayed before the compile point.

The next parameter is our command list that contains mapped actions.

Finally, the last parameter is a delegate that is responsible for actually adding UI controls to the toolbar at the extension point and the anchor that we specified earlier.

The delegate is bound to a function that has the form void (*func) (FToolBarBuilder and builder). In this instance, it is a function called AddToolbarExtension, which is defined in our module class.

When the function is invoked, calling commands on the builder that adds UI elements will apply those elements to the location in the UI we specified.

Lastly, we need to load the level editor module within this function so that we can add our extender to the main toolbar within the level editor.

As usual, we can use ModuleManager to load a module and return a reference to it.

With that reference in hand, we can get the Toolbar Extensibility Manager for the module, and tell it to add our Extender.

While this may seem cumbersome at first, the intention is to allow you to apply the same toolbar extension to multiple toolbars in different modules, if you would like to create a consistent UI layout between different editor windows.

The counterpart to initializing our extension, of course, is removing it when our module is unloaded. To do that, we remove our extension from the extender, then null the shared pointers for both Extender and extension, thus reclaiming their memory allocation.

The AddToolBarExtension function within the editor module is the one that is responsible for actually adding UI elements to the toolbar that can invoke our commands.

It does this by calling functions on the FToolBarBuilder instance that's passed in as a function parameter.

First, we retrieve an appropriate icon for our new toolbar button using the FSlateIcon constructor. Then, with the icon loaded, we invoke AddToolBarButton on the builder instance.

AddToolbarButton has a number of parameters. The first parameter is the command to bind to – you'll notice it's the same MyButton member that we accessed earlier when binding the action to the command. The second parameter is an override for the extension hook we specified earlier, but we don't want to override that, so we can use NAME_None. The third parameter is a label override for the new button that we create. Parameter four is a tooltip for the new button. The second to last parameter is the button's icon, and the last parameter is a name that's used to refer to this button element for highlighting support if you wish to use the in-editor tutorial framework.

Creating new menu entries

The workflow for creating new menu entries is almost identical to that for creating new toolbar buttons, so this recipe will build on the previous one and show you how to add the command created therein to a menu rather than a toolbar.

How to do it...

1. Create a new function inside of the `FChapter_10EditorModule` class, which is in `Chapter10_Editor.h`:

```
void AddMenuExtension (FMenuBuilder &builder)
{
  FSlateIcon IconBrush =
  FSlateIcon (FEditorStyle::GetStyleSetName(),
  "LevelEditor.ViewOptions",
  "LevelEditor.ViewOptions.Small");

  builder.AddMenuEntry (FCookbookCommands::Get().MyButton);
};
```

2. In the implementation file (`Chapter_10Editor.cpp`), find the following code within the `StartupModule` function:

```
EExtension = ToolbarExtender->AddToolBarExtension ("Compile",
EExtensionHook::Before, CommandList,
FToolBarExtensionDelegate::CreateRaw(this,
&FChapter_10EditorModule::AddToolbarExtension));
LevelEditorModule.GetToolBarExtensibilityManager()->AddExtende
r(ToolbarExtender);
```

3. Replace the preceding code with the following:

```
Extension = ToolbarExtender->AddMenuExtension ("LevelEditor",
EExtensionHook::Before, CommandList,
FMenuExtensionDelegate::CreateRaw(this,&FChapter_10EditorModul
e::AddMenuExtension));
LevelEditorModule.GetMenuExtensibilityManager()->AddExtender(T
oolbarExtender);
```

4. Compile your code and launch the editor.

5. Verify that you now have a menu entry under the **Window** menu that
displays the **Cookbook** window when clicked. If you followed the
preceding recipe, you'll also see the green text listing the UI extension
points, including the one we used in this recipe (**LevelEditor**):

How it works...

You'll note that `ToolbarExtender` is of type `FExtender` rather than `FToolbarExtender` or `FMenuExtender`.

By using a generic `FExtender` class rather than a specific subclass, the framework allows you to create a series of command-function mappings that can be used on either menus or toolbars. The delegate that actually adds the UI controls (in this instance, `AddMenuExtension`) can link those controls to a subset of commands from your `FExtender`.

This way, you don't need to have different `TCommands` classes for different types of extensions, and you can place the commands into a single central class regardless of where those commands are invoked from the UI.

As a result, the only changes that are required are as follows:

- Swapping calls to `AddToolBarExtension` with `AddMenuExtension`
- Creating a function that can be bound to `FMenuExtensionDelegate` rather than `FToolbarExtensionDelegate`
- Adding the extender to a Menu Extensibility Manager rather than a Toolbar Extensibility Manager

Creating a new editor window

Custom editor windows are useful when you have a new tool with user-configurable settings, or want to display some information to people using your customized editor. Ensure that you have have an editor module by following the recipe earlier in this chapter before you start. Read through either the *Creating new menu entries* or *Creating new toolbar buttons* recipes so that you can create a button within the editor that will launch our new window.

How to do it...

1. Inside your command's bound function (in our case,
   the `MyButton_Clicked` function in the `FChapter_10EditorModule` class
   that's found in `Chapter_10Editor.h`), add the following code:

```
void MyButton_Clicked()
{
    TSharedRef<SWindow> CookbookWindow = SNew(SWindow)
        .Title(FText::FromString(TEXT("Cookbook Window")))
        .ClientSize(FVector2D(800, 400))
        .SupportsMaximize(false)
        .SupportsMinimize(false)
        [
            SNew(SVerticalBox)
            + SVerticalBox::Slot()
        .HAlign(HAlign_Center)
        .VAlign(VAlign_Center)
        [
            SNew(STextBlock)
            .Text(FText::FromString(TEXT("Hello from Slate")))
        ]
        ];

    IMainFrameModule& MainFrameModule =
        FModuleManager::LoadModuleChecked<IMainFrameModule>
        (TEXT("MainFrame"));

    if (MainFrameModule.GetParentWindow().IsValid())
    {
        FSlateApplication::Get().AddWindowAsNativeChild
        (CookbookWindow, MainFrameModule.GetParentWindow()
            .ToSharedRef());
    }
    else
    {
        FSlateApplication::Get().AddWindow(CookbookWindow);
    }
};
```

   Note that we removed the ; at the end of the line
   stating `.SupportsMinimize(false)`.

2. Compile your code and launch the editor.

3. When you activate the command you created, either by selecting the custom menu option or the toolbar option that you added, you should see that the window has been displayed with some centered text in the middle:

How it works...

Your new editor window won't display itself, and so, at the start of this recipe, it is mentioned that you should have implemented a custom menu or toolbar button or a console command that we can use to trigger the display of our new window.

All of Slate's widgets are usually interacted with in the form of TSharedRef< > or TSharedPtr< >.

The SNew() function returns a TSharedRef that's been templated on the requested widget class.

As we mentioned previously, Slate widgets have a number of functions that they implement, which all return the object that the function was invoked on. This allows for method chaining to be used to configure the object at creation time.

This is what allows for the Slate syntax of <Widget>.Property(Value).Property(Value).

The properties that are set on the widget in this recipe are the window title, the window size, and whether the window can be maximized and minimized.

Once all the requisite properties on a widget have been set, the bracket operators ([ ]) can be used to specify the content to be placed inside the widget, for example, a picture or label inside a button.

SWindow is a top-level widget with only one slot for child widgets, so we don't need to add a slot for it ourselves. We place content into that slot by creating it inside the pair of brackets.

The content we create is SVerticalBox, which is a widget that can have an arbitrary number of slots for child widgets that are displayed in a vertical list.

For each widget we want to place into the vertical list, we need to create a **slot**.

The easiest way to do this is to use the overloaded + operator and the SVerticalBox::Slot() function.

Slot() returns a widget like any other, so we can set properties on it like we did on our SWindow.

This recipe centers the Slot's content on both horizontal and vertical axes using HAlign and VAlign.

A Slot has a single child widget, and it's created inside the [] operators, just like they are for SWindow.

Inside the Slot content, we create a text block with some custom text.

Our new SWindow now has its child widgets added, but it isn't being displayed yet because it hasn't been added to the window hierarchy.

The main frame module is used to check if we have a top-level editor window, and if it exists, our new window is added as a child.

If there's no top-level window to be added as a child to, then we use the Slate Application singleton to add our window without a parent.

If you would like to see the hierarchy of the window we've created, you can use the Slate Widget Reflector, which can be accessed via **Window | Developer Tools | Widget Reflector**.

If you select **Pick Painted Widget** and hover your cursor over the text in the center of our custom window, you will be able to see the **SWindow** with our custom widgets added to its hierarchy:

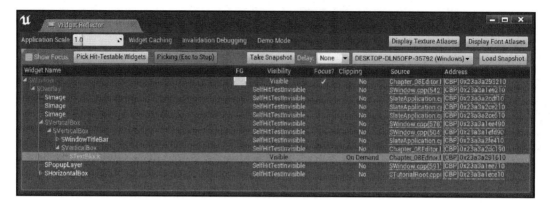

See also

- Chapter 11, *Working with UE4 APIs*, is all about UI, and will show you how to add additional elements to your new custom window

Creating a new Asset type

At some point in your project, you might need to create a new custom Asset class, for example, an Asset to store conversation data in an RPG. To properly integrate these with **Content Browser**, you'll need to create a new Asset type.

How to do it...

1. Create a new C++ class based on UObject called MyCustomAsset:

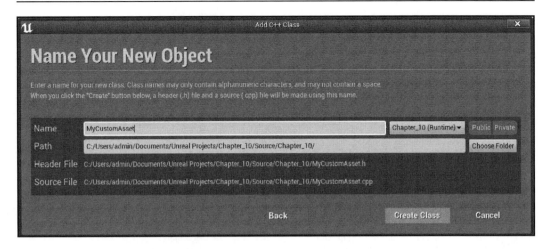

2. Open up the script and update the code of the .h file to the following:

```
#pragma once

#include "CoreMinimal.h"
#include "UObject/NoExportTypes.h"
#include "MyCustomAsset.generated.h"

/**
 *
 */
UCLASS()
class CHAPTER_10_API UMyCustomAsset : public UObject
{
    GENERATED_BODY()

public:
    UPROPERTY(EditAnywhere, Category = "Custom Asset")
    FString Name;
};
```

3. Next, create a class based on `UFactory`:

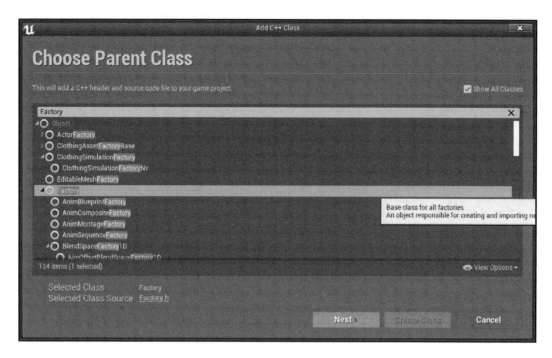

4. Give the script a name of `CustomAssetFactory` and press the **Create Class** button.

5. Open the script in Visual Studio and update the `CustomAssetFactory.h` file to the following:

```cpp
#pragma once

#include "CoreMinimal.h"
#include "Factories/Factory.h"
#include "CustomAssetFactory.generated.h"

UCLASS()
class CHAPTER_10_API UCustomAssetFactory : public UFactory
{
    GENERATED_BODY()
public:
    UCustomAssetFactory();

    virtual UObject* FactoryCreateNew(UClass* InClass,
        UObject* InParent, FName InName, EObjectFlags Flags,
        UObject* Context, FFeedbackContext* Warn, FName
```

```
                    CallingContext) override;
    };
```

6. Then, switch over to the CustomAssetFactory.cpp file and implement the class:

```cpp
#include "CustomAssetFactory.h"
#include "Chapter_10.h"
#include "MyCustomAsset.h"


UCustomAssetFactory::UCustomAssetFactory()
    :Super()
{
    bCreateNew = true;
    bEditAfterNew = true;
    SupportedClass = UMyCustomAsset::StaticClass();
}

UObject* UCustomAssetFactory::FactoryCreateNew(UClass*
    InClass, UObject* InParent, FName InName, EObjectFlags
    Flags, UObject* Context, FFeedbackContext* Warn, FName
    CallingContext)
{
    auto NewObjectAsset = NewObject<UMyCustomAsset>(InParent,
        InClass, InName, Flags);
    return NewObjectAsset;
}
```

7. Compile your code and open the editor.

8. Right-click in **Content Browser**, from the **Content** folder and, under the **Miscellaneous** tab of the **Create Advanced Asset** section, you should see your new class and be able to create instances of your new custom type:

How it works...

The first class is the actual object that can exist in the game at runtime. It's your texture, data file, or curve data – whatever you require.

For the purpose of this recipe, the simplest example is an asset that has an FString property to contain a name.

The property is marked as UPROPERTY so that it remains in memory, and additionally marked as EditAnywhere so that it is editable on both the default object and on instances of it.

The second class is Factory. Unreal uses the Factory design pattern to create instances of assets.

This means that there is a generic base Factory that uses virtual methods to declare the interface of object creation, and then Factory subclasses are responsible for creating the actual object in question.

The advantage of this approach is that the user-created subclass can potentially instantiate one of its own subclasses if required; it hides the implementation details regarding deciding which object to create away from the object requesting the creation.

With UFactory as our base class, we include the appropriate header.

The constructor is overridden, because there are a number of properties that we want to set for our new factory after the default constructor has run.

bCreateNew signifies that the factory is currently able to create a new instance of the object in question from scratch.

bEditAfterNew indicates that we would like to edit the newly created object immediately after creation.

The SupportedClass variable is an instance of UClass containing reflection information about the type of object the factory will create.

The most significant function of our UFactory subclass is the actual factory method – FactoryCreateNew.

FactoryCreateNew is responsible for determining the type of object that should be created, and using NewObject to construct an instance of that type. It passes a number of parameters through to the NewObject call.

`InClass` is the class of object that will be constructed. `InParent` is the object that should be containing the new object that will be created. If this isn't specified, the object is assumed to go into the transient package, which means that it won't be automatically saved. `Name` is the name of the object to be created. `Flags` is a bitmask of creation flags that control things such as making the object visible outside of the package it is contained in.

Within `FactoryCreateNew`, decisions can be made regarding which subclass should be instantiated. Other initialization can also be performed; for example, if there are sub-objects that require manual instantiation or initialization, they can be added here.

An example from the engine code for this function is as follows:

```
UObject* UCameraAnimFactory::FactoryCreateNew(UClass*
 Class,UObject* InParent,FName Name,EObjectFlags
 Flags,UObject* Context,FFeedbackContext* Warn)
{
  UCameraAnim* NewCamAnim =
    NewObject<UCameraAnim>(InParent, Class, Name, Flags);
NewCamAnim->CameraInterpGroup =
    NewObject<UInterpGroupCamera>(NewCamAnim);
  NewCamAnim->CameraInterpGroup->GroupName = Name;
  return NewCamAnim;
}
```

As we can see, there's a second call to `NewObject` to populate the `CameraInterpGroup` member of the `NewCamAnim` instance.

See also

- The *Editing class properties in different places in the editor* recipe earlier in this chapter gives more context to the `EditAnywhere` property specifier

Creating custom context menu entries for Assets

Custom Asset types commonly have special functions you wish to be able to perform on them. For example, converting images into sprites is an option you wouldn't want to add to any other Asset type. You can create custom context menu entries for specific Asset types to make those functions accessible to users.

How to do it...

1. From the `Chapter_10Editor` folder, create two new files called `MyCustomAssetActions.h` and `MyCustomAssetActions.cpp`.

2. Return to your project file and update your Visual Studio project. Once finished, open up the project in Visual Studio.

3. Open `MyCustomAssetActions.h` and use the following code:

```
#pragma once
#include "AssetTypeActions_Base.h"
#include
"Editor/MainFrame/Public/Interfaces/IMainFrameModule.h"

class CHAPTER_10EDITOR_API FMyCustomAssetActions : public
FAssetTypeActions_Base
{
public:
    virtual bool HasActions(const TArray<UObject*>& InObjects)
    const override;

    virtual void GetActions(const TArray<UObject*>& InObjects,
    FMenuBuilder& MenuBuilder) override;

    virtual FText GetName() const override;

    virtual UClass* GetSupportedClass() const override;

    virtual FColor GetTypeColor() const override;

    virtual uint32 GetCategories() override;

    void MyCustomAssetContext_Clicked()
    {
        TSharedRef<SWindow> CookbookWindow = SNew(SWindow)
            .Title(FText::FromString(TEXT("Cookbook Window")))
            .ClientSize(FVector2D(800, 400))
            .SupportsMaximize(false)
            .SupportsMinimize(false);

        IMainFrameModule& MainFrameModule =
        FModuleManager::LoadModuleChecked<IMainFrameModule>
        (TEXT("MainFrame"));

        if (MainFrameModule.GetParentWindow().IsValid())
        {
FSlateApplication::Get().AddWindowAsNativeChild(CookbookWindow
```

```
                    MainFrameModule.GetParentWindow().ToSharedRef());
        }
        else
        {
FSlateApplication::Get().AddWindow(CookbookWindow);
        }

    };
};
```

4. Open `MyCustomAssetActions.cpp` and add the following code:

```cpp
#include "MyCustomAssetActions.h"
#include "Chapter_10Editor.h"
#include "MyCustomAsset.h"

bool FMyCustomAssetActions::HasActions(const TArray<UObject*>&
InObjects) const
{
  return true;
}

void FMyCustomAssetActions::GetActions(const TArray<UObject*>&
InObjects, FMenuBuilder& MenuBuilder)
{
  MenuBuilder.AddMenuEntry(
    FText::FromString("CustomAssetAction"),
    FText::FromString("Action from Cookbook Recipe"),
    FSlateIcon(FEditorStyle::GetStyleSetName(),
    "LevelEditor.ViewOptions"),
    FUIAction(
      FExecuteAction::CreateRaw(this,
      &FMyCustomAssetActions::MyCustomAssetContext_Clicked),
      FCanExecuteAction()
      ));
}

uint32 FMyCustomAssetActions::GetCategories()
{
  return EAssetTypeCategories::Misc;
}

FText FMyCustomAssetActions::GetName() const
{
  return FText::FromString(TEXT("My Custom Asset"));
}
```

```
UClass* FMyCustomAssetActions::GetSupportedClass() const
{
  return UMyCustomAsset::StaticClass();
}

FColor FMyCustomAssetActions::GetTypeColor() const
{
  return FColor::Emerald;
}
```

5. Open up the `Chapter_10Editor.h` file and add the following property to the class:

```
#pragma once

#include "Engine.h"
#include "Modules/ModuleInterface.h"
#include "Modules/ModuleManager.h"
#include "UnrealEd.h"
#include "CookbookCommands.h"
#include "Editor/MainFrame/Public/Interfaces/IMainFrameModule.h"
#include "Developer/AssetTools/Public/IAssetTypeActions.h"

 class FChapter_10EditorModule: public IModuleInterface
{
    virtual void StartupModule() override;
    virtual void ShutdownModule() override;

    TArray< TSharedPtr<IAssetTypeActions> > CreatedAssetTypeActions;

    TSharedPtr<FExtender> ToolbarExtender;
    TSharedPtr<const FExtensionBase> Extension;
```

 Don't forget to add the `#include` for `IAssetTypeActions.h`.

6. Within your editor module (`Chapter_10Editor.cpp`), add the following code to the `StartupModule()` function:

```
#include "Developer/AssetTools/Public/IAssetTools.h"
#include "Developer/AssetTools/Public/AssetToolsModule.h"
#include "MyCustomAssetActions.h"
// ...

void FChapter_10EditorModule::StartupModule()
```

```
    {
        FCookbookCommands::Register();
        TSharedPtr<FUICommandList> CommandList = MakeShareable(new
    FUICommandList());
        CommandList->MapAction(FCookbookCommands::Get().MyButton,
    FExecuteAction::CreateRaw(this,
    &FChapter_10EditorModule::MyButton_Clicked),
    FCanExecuteAction());
        ToolbarExtender = MakeShareable(new FExtender());

        FLevelEditorModule& LevelEditorModule =
    FModuleManager::LoadModuleChecked<FLevelEditorModule>("LevelEd
    itor");

        IAssetTools& AssetTools =
        FModuleManager::LoadModuleChecked<FAssetToolsModule>
        ("AssetTools").Get();

        auto Actions = MakeShareable(new FMyCustomAssetActions);
        AssetTools.RegisterAssetTypeActions(Actions);
        CreatedAssetTypeActions.Add(Actions);
    }
```

7. Add the following code inside the module's `ShutdownModule()` function:

```
    void FChapter_10EditorModule::ShutdownModule()
    {
        ToolbarExtender->RemoveExtension(Extension.ToSharedRef());
        Extension.Reset();
        ToolbarExtender.Reset();

        IAssetTools& AssetTools =
    FModuleManager::LoadModuleChecked<FAssetToolsModule>("Asset
    Tools").Get();

      for (auto Action : CreatedAssetTypeActions)
      {
      AssetTools.UnregisterAssetTypeActions(Action.ToSharedRef());
      }
    }
```

8. Compile your project and launch the editor.
9. Create an instance of your custom Asset inside the **Content Browser** by right-clicking and selecting **Miscellaneous | My Custom Asset**.

10. Right-click on your new asset to see our custom command in the context menu:

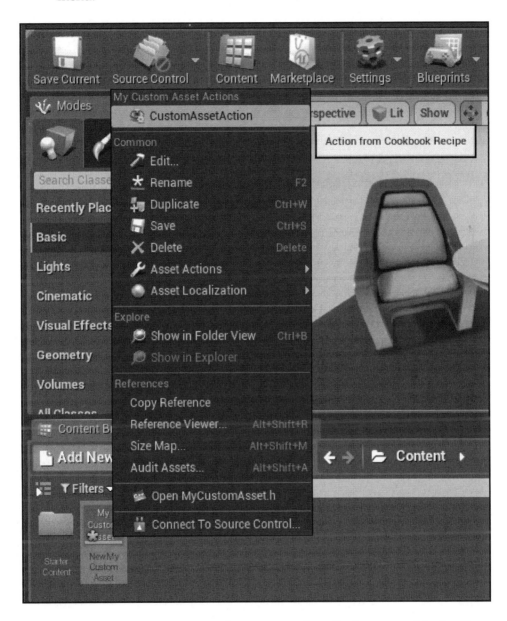

11. Select the **CustomAssetAction** command to display a new blank editor window.

How it works...

The base class for all asset type-specific context menu commands is `FAssetTypeActions_Base`, so we need to inherit from that class.

`FAssetTypeActions_Base` is an abstract class that defines a number of virtual functions that allow us to extend the context menu. The interface that contains the original information for these virtual functions can be found in `IAssetTypeActions.h`.

We also declare a function that we bind to our custom context menu entry.

`IAssetTypeActions::HasActions ( const TArray<UObject*>& InObjects )` is the function that's called by the engine code to see if our `AssetTypeActions` class contains any actions that can be applied to the selected objects.

`IAssetTypeActions::GetActions(const TArray<UObject*>& InObjects, class FMenuBuilder& MenuBuilder)` is called if the `HasActions` function returns `true`. It calls functions on `MenuBuilder` to create the menu options for the actions that we provide.

`IAssetTypeActions::GetName()` returns the name of this class.

`IAssetTypeActions::GetSupportedClass()` returns an instance of `UClass` that our actions class supports.

`IAssetTypeActions::GetTypeColor()` returns the color associated with this class and actions.

`IAssetTypeActions::GetCategories()` returns a category that's appropriate for the asset. This is used to change the category under which the actions show up in the context menu.

Our overridden implementation of `HasActions` simply returns `true` under all circumstances, and relies on filtering based on the results of `GetSupportedClass`.

Inside the implementation of `GetActions`, we can call some functions on the `MenuBuilder` object that we are given as a function parameter. The `MenuBuilder` is passed as a reference, so any changes that are made by our function will persist after it returns.

`AddMenuEntry` has a number of parameters. The first parameter is the name of the action itself. This is the name that will be visible within the context menu. The name is an `FText` so that it can be localized should you wish. For the sake of simplicity, we construct `FText` from a string literal and don't concern ourselves with multiple language support.

The second parameter is also `FText`, which we construct by calling `FText::FromString`. This parameter is the text that's displayed in a tooltip if the user hovers over our command for more than a small period of time.

The next parameter is `FSlateIcon` for the command, which is constructed from the `LevelEditor.ViewOptions` icon within the editor style set.

The last parameter to this function is an `FUIAction` instance. The `FUIAction` is a wrapper around a delegate binding, so we use `FExecuteAction::CreateRaw` to bind the command to the `MyCustomAsset_Clicked` function on this very instance of `FMyCustomAssetActions`.

This means that when the menu entry is clicked, our `MyCustomAssetContext_Clicked` function will be run.

Our implementation of `GetName` returns the name of our Asset type. This string will be used on the thumbnail for our Asset if we don't set one ourselves, apart from being used in the title of the menu section that our custom Assets will be placed in.

As you'd expect, the implementation of `GetSupportedClass` returns `UMyCustomAsset::StaticClass()`, as this is the Asset type we want our actions to operate on.

`GetTypeColor()` returns the color that will be used for color coding in **Content Browser** – the color is used in the bar at the bottom of the asset thumbnail. I've used Emerald here, but any arbitrary color will work.

The real workhorse of this recipe is the `MyCustomAssetContext_Clicked()` function.

The first thing that this function does is create a new instance of `SWindow`.

`SWindow` is the Slate Window – a class from the Slate UI framework.

Slate Widgets are created using the `SNew` function, which returns an instance of the widget requested.

Slate uses the `builder` design pattern, which means that all of the functions that are **chained** after `SNew`, return a reference to the object that was being operated on.

In this function, we create our new `SWindow`, then set the window title, its client size or area, and whether it can be maximized or minimized.

With our new Window ready, we need to get a reference to the root window for the editor so that we can add our window to the hierarchy and get it displayed.

We do this using the `IMainFrameModule` class. It's a module, so we use the **Module Manager** to load it.

`LoadModuleChecked` will assert if we can't load the module, so we don't need to check it.

If the module was loaded, we check that we have a valid parent window. If that window is valid, then we use `FSlateApplication::AddWindowAsNativeChild` to add our window as a child of the top-level parent window.

If we don't have a top-level parent, the function uses `AddWindow` to add the new window without parenting it to another window within the hierarchy.

So, now we have a class that will display custom actions on our custom Asset type, but what we actually need to do is tell the engine that it should ask our class to handle custom actions for the type. To do that, we need to register our class with the Asset Tools module.

The best way to do this is to register our class when our editor module is loaded, and unregister it when it is shut down.

As a result, we place our code into the `StartupModule` and `ShutdownModule` functions.

Inside `StartupModule`, we load the Asset Tools module using **Module Manager**.

With the module loaded, we create a new shared pointer that references an instance of our custom Asset actions class.

All we need to do then is call `AssetModule.RegisterAssetTypeActions` and pass in an instance of our actions class.

We then need to store a reference to that `Actions` instance so that we can unregister it later.

The sample code for this recipe uses an array of all the created asset actions in case we want to add custom actions for other classes as well.

Within ShutdownModule, we again retrieve an instance of the Asset Tools module.

Using a range-based for loop, we iterate over the array of Actions instances that we populated earlier and call UnregisterAssetTypeActions, passing in our Actions class so it can be unregistered.

With our class registered, the editor has been instructed to ask our registered class if it can handle assets that are right-clicked on.

If the asset is of the Custom Asset class, then its StaticClass will match the one returned by GetSupportedClass. The editor will then call GetActions, and display the menu with the alterations made by our implementation of that function.

When the CustomAssetAction button is clicked, our custom MyCustomAssetContext_Clicked function will be called via the delegate that we created.

Creating new console commands

During development, console commands can be very helpful by allowing a developer or tester to easily bypass content or disable the mechanics that are irrelevant to the current test being run. The most common way to implement this is via console commands, which can invoke functions during runtime. The console can be accessed using the tilde key (~) or the equivalent in the upper-left area of the alphanumeric zone of your keyboard:

Getting ready

If you haven't already followed the *Creating a new editor module* recipe, do so, as this recipe will need a place to initialize and register the console command.

How to do it...

1. Open your editor module's header file (`Chapter_10Editor.h`) and add the following code:

```
class FChapter_10EditorModule: public IModuleInterface
{
    virtual void StartupModule() override;
    virtual void ShutdownModule() override;

    TArray< TSharedPtr<IAssetTypeActions> >
CreatedAssetTypeActions;

    TSharedPtr<FExtender> ToolbarExtender;
    TSharedPtr<const FExtensionBase> Extension;

    IConsoleCommand* DisplayTestCommand;
    IConsoleCommand* DisplayUserSpecifiedWindow;
```

2. Add the following code within the implementation of `StartupModule`:

```
DisplayTestCommand =
IConsoleManager::Get().RegisterConsoleCommand(TEXT("DisplayTes
tCommandWindow"), TEXT("test"),
FConsoleCommandDelegate::CreateRaw(this,
&FChapter_10EditorModule::DisplayWindow, FString(TEXT("Test
Command Window"))), ECVF_Default);

    DisplayUserSpecifiedWindow =
IConsoleManager::Get().RegisterConsoleCommand(TEXT("DisplayWin
dow"), TEXT("test"),
FConsoleCommandWithArgsDelegate::CreateLambda(
        [&](const TArray< FString >& Args)
    {
        FString WindowTitle;
        for (FString Arg : Args)
        {
            WindowTitle += Arg;
            WindowTitle.AppendChar(' ');
        }
```

```
            this->DisplayWindow(WindowTitle);
    }

    ), ECVF_Default);
```

3. Inside ShutdownModule, **add the following code:**

```
if(DisplayTestCommand)
{
IConsoleManager::Get().UnregisterConsoleObject(DisplayTestComm
and);
    DisplayTestCommand = nullptr;
}

if(DisplayUserSpecifiedWindow)
{
IConsoleManager::Get().UnregisterConsoleObject(DisplayUserSpec
ifiedWindow);
    DisplayUserSpecifiedWindow = nullptr;
}
```

4. Implement the following function in the editor module
   (Chapter_10Editor.h):

```
void DisplayWindow(FString WindowTitle)
{
  TSharedRef<SWindow> CookbookWindow = SNew(SWindow)
  .Title(FText::FromString(WindowTitle))
  .ClientSize(FVector2D(800, 400))
  .SupportsMaximize(false)
  .SupportsMinimize(false);
  IMainFrameModule& MainFrameModule =
   FModuleManager::LoadModuleChecked<IMainFrameModule>
   (TEXT("MainFrame"));
  if (MainFrameModule.GetParentWindow().IsValid())
  {
    FSlateApplication::Get().AddWindowAsNativeChild
     (CookbookWindow, MainFrameModule.GetParentWindow()
     .ToSharedRef());
  }
  else
  {
    FSlateApplication::Get().AddWindow(CookbookWindow);
  }
}
```

5. Compile your code and launch the editor.
6. Play the level, and then hit the tilde key to bring up the console.
7. Type `DisplayTestCommandWindow` and hit *Enter*:

8. You should see our tutorial window open up:

How it works...

Console commands are usually provided by a module. The best way to get the module to create the command when it is loaded is to place the code in the `StartupModule` method.

`IConsoleManager` is the module that contains the console functionality for the engine.

As it is a sub-module of the core module, we don't need to add any additional information to the build scripts to link in additional modules.

To call functions within the console manager, we need to get a reference to the current instance of `IConsoleManager` that is being used by the engine. To do so, we invoke the static `Get` function, which returns a reference to the module in a similar way to a singleton.

`RegisterConsoleCommand` is the function that we can use to add a new console command and make it available in the console:

```
virtual IConsoleCommand* RegisterConsoleCommand(const
  TCHAR* Name, const TCHAR* Help, const
  FConsoleCommandDelegate& Command, uint32 Flags);
```

The parameters for the function are as follows:

- `Name`: The actual console command that will be typed by users. It should not include spaces.
- `Help`: The tooltip that appears when users are looking at the command in the console. If your console command takes arguments, this is a good place to display usage information to users.
- `Command`: This is the actual function delegate that will be executed when the user types in the command.
- `Flags`: These flags control the visibility of the command in a shipping build, and are also used for console variables. `ECVF_Default` specifies the default behavior wherein the command is visible, and has no restrictions on availability in a release build.

To create an instance of the appropriate delegate, we use the `CreateRaw` static function on the `FConsoleCommand` delegate type. This lets us bind a raw C++ function to the delegate. The extra argument that is supplied after the function reference, the `FString`"Test Command Window", is a compile-time defined parameter that is passed to the delegate so that the end user doesn't have to specify the window name.

The second console command, `DisplayUserSpecifiedWindow`, is one that demonstrates the use of arguments with console commands.

The primary difference with this console command, aside from the different name for users to invoke it, is the use of `FConsoleCommandWithArgsDelegate` and the `CreateLambda` function on it in particular.

This function allows us to bind an anonymous function to a delegate. It's particularly handy when you want to wrap or adapt a function so that its signature matches that of a particular delegate.

In our particular use case, the type of `FConsoleCommandWithArgsDelegate` specifies that the function should take a `const  TArray` of `FStrings`. Our `DisplayWindow` function takes a single `FString` to specify the window title, so we need to somehow concatenate all the arguments of the console command into a single `FString` to use as our window title.

The lambda function allows us to do that before passing the `FString` onto the actual `DisplayWindow` function.

The first line of the function, `[&](const  TArray<FString>& Args)`, specifies that this lambda or anonymous function wants to capture the context of the declaring function by reference by including the ampersand in the capture options, `[&]`.

The second part is the same as a normal function declaration, specifying that our lambda takes in `const  Tarray`, which contains an FString as a parameter called `Args`.

Within the lambda body, we create a new `FString` and concatenate the strings that make up our arguments together, adding a space between them to separate them so that we don't get a title without spaces.

It uses a range-based `for` loop for brevity to loop over them all and perform the concatenation.

Once they're all concatenated, we use the this pointer (captured by the & operator we mentioned earlier) to invoke DisplayWindow with our new title.

For our module to remove the console command when it is unloaded, we need to maintain a reference to the console command object.

To achieve this, we create a member variable in the module of type IConsoleCommand*, called DisplayTestCommand. When we execute the RegisterConsoleCommand function, it returns a pointer to the console command object that we can use as a handle later.

This allows us to enable or disable console commands at runtime based on gameplay or other factors.

Within ShutdownModule, we check to see if DisplayTestCommand refers to a valid console command object. If it does, we get a reference to the IConsoleManager object and call UnregisterConsoleCommand, passing in the pointer that we stored earlier in our call to RegisterConsoleCommand.

The call to UnregisterConsoleCommand deletes the IConsoleCommand instance via the passed-in pointer, so we don't need to deallocate the memory ourselves – we just reset DisplayTestCommand to nullptr so that we can be sure that the old pointer doesn't dangle.

The DisplayWindow function takes in the window title as an FString parameter. This allows us to either use a console command that takes arguments to specify the title, or a console command that uses payload parameters to hard-code the title for other commands.

The function itself uses a function called SNew() to allocate and create an SWindow object.

SWindow is a Slate Window, a top-level window that uses the Slate UI framework.

Slate uses the Builder design pattern to allow for easy configuration of the new window.

The Title, ClientSize, SupportsMaximize, and SupportsMinimize functions that are used here are all member functions of SWindow, and they return a reference to an SWindow (usually, the same object that the method was invoked on, but sometimes, a new object is constructed with the new configuration).

The fact that all these member methods return a reference to the configured object allows us to chain these method invocations together to create the desired object in the right configuration.

The functions used in `DisplayWindow` create a new top-level Window that has a title based on the function parameter. It is 800 x 400 pixels wide, and cannot be maximized or minimized.

With our new Window created, we retrieve a reference to the main application frame module. If the top-level window for the editor exists and is valid, we add our new window instance as a child of that top-level window.

To do this, we retrieve a reference to the Slate interface and call `AddWindowAsNativeChild` to insert our window in the hierarchy.

If there isn't a valid top-level window, we don't need to add our new window as a child of anything, so we can simply call `AddWindow` and pass in our new window instance.

See also

- Refer to `Chapter 5`, *Handling Events and Delegates*, to learn more about delegates. It explains payload variables in greater detail.
- For more information on Slate, refer to `Chapter 11`, *Working with UE4 APIs*.

Creating a new graph pin visualizer for Blueprint

Within the Blueprint system, we can use instances of our `MyCustomAsset` class as variables, provided we mark that class as a `BlueprintType` in its `UCLASS` macro. However, by default, our new asset is simply treated as a `UObject`, and we can't access any of its members:

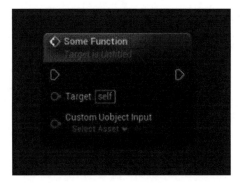

For some types of assets, we might wish to enable in-line editing of literal values in the same way that classes such as FVector support the following:

To enable this, we need to use a **Graph Pin** visualizer. This recipe will show you how to enable in-line editing of an arbitrary type using a custom widget defined by you.

How to do it...

1. First, we will update the MyCustomAsset class to be editable in Blueprints and reflect what we'll be doing in this recipe. Go to MyCustomAsset.h and update it to the following code:

```
#pragma once

#include "CoreMinimal.h"
#include "UObject/NoExportTypes.h"
#include "MyCustomAsset.generated.h"


UCLASS(BlueprintType, EditInlineNew)
```

```
class CHAPTER_10_API UMyCustomAsset : public UObject
{
  GENERATED_BODY()

public:
    UPROPERTY(BlueprintReadWrite, EditAnywhere, Category =
"Custom Asset")
    FString ColorName;
};
```

2. From the `Chapter_10Editor` folder, create a new file called `MyCustomAssetPinFactory.h`.

3. Inside the header, add the following code:

```
#pragma once
#include "EdGraphUtilities.h"
#include "MyCustomAsset.h"
#include "SGraphPinCustomAsset.h"


struct CHAPTER_10EDITOR_API FMyCustomAssetPinFactory : public
FGraphPanelPinFactory
{
public:
  virtual TSharedPtr<class SGraphPin> CreatePin(class
UEdGraphPin* Pin) const override
  {
    if (Pin->PinType.PinSubCategoryObject ==
UMyCustomAsset::StaticClass())
    {
      return SNew(SGraphPinCustomAsset, Pin);
    }
    else
    {
      return nullptr;
    }
  };
};
```

4. Create another header file called `SGraphPinCustomAsset.h`:

```
#pragma once
#include "SGraphPin.h"


class CHAPTER_10EDITOR_API SGraphPinCustomAsset : public
SGraphPin
```

```
{
  SLATE_BEGIN_ARGS(SGraphPinCustomAsset) {}
  SLATE_END_ARGS()

  void Construct(const FArguments& InArgs, UEdGraphPin*
InPin);
protected:
  virtual FSlateColor GetPinColor() const override { return
FSlateColor(FColor::Black); };

  virtual TSharedRef<SWidget> GetDefaultValueWidget()
override;
  void ColorPicked(FLinearColor SelectedColor);
};
```

5. Implement SGraphPinCustomAsset **by creating the** .cpp **file:**

```
#include "SGraphPinCustomAsset.h"
#include "Chapter_10Editor.h"
#include "SColorPicker.h"
#include "MyCustomAsset.h"

void SGraphPinCustomAsset::Construct(const FArguments& InArgs,
UEdGraphPin* InPin)
{
  SGraphPin::Construct(SGraphPin::FArguments(), InPin);
}

TSharedRef<SWidget>
SGraphPinCustomAsset::GetDefaultValueWidget()
{
  return SNew(SColorPicker)
    .OnColorCommitted(this,
&SGraphPinCustomAsset::ColorPicked);

}

void SGraphPinCustomAsset::ColorPicked(FLinearColor
SelectedColor)
{
  UMyCustomAsset* NewValue = NewObject<UMyCustomAsset>();
  NewValue->ColorName = SelectedColor.ToFColor(false).ToHex();
  GraphPinObj->GetSchema()->TrySetDefaultObject(*GraphPinObj,
NewValue);
}
```

6. Regenerate your Visual Studio project.

7. Add `#include "MyCustomAssetPinFactory.h"` to the `Chapter_10Editor.h` module implementation file.

8. Add the following member to the editor module class (`FChapter_10EditorModule`):

```
TSharedPtr<FMyCustomAssetPinFactory> PinFactory;
```

9. Open `Chapter_10Editor.cpp` and then add the following to `StartupModule()`:

```
PinFactory = MakeShareable(new FMyCustomAssetPinFactory());
FEdGraphUtilities::RegisterVisualPinFactory(PinFactory);
```

10. Also add the following code to `ShutdownModule()`:

```
FEdGraphUtilities::UnregisterVisualPinFactory(PinFactory);
PinFactory.Reset();
```

11. Compile your code and launch the editor.

12. Create a new **Function** inside of the **Level Blueprint** by clicking on the plus symbol beside **Functions** within the **My Blueprint** panel:

13. Add an input parameter:

14. Set its type to `MyCustomAsset` (**Object Reference**):

15. In the Level Blueprint's **Event Graph**, place an instance of your new function and verify that the input pin now has a custom visualizer in the form of a color picker:

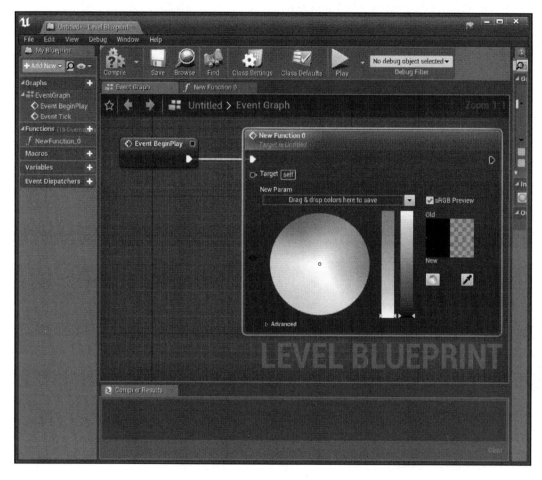

Newly added color picker visualizer

How it works...

Customizing how objects appear as literal values on Blueprint pins is done using the FGraphPanelPinFactory class.

This class defines a single virtual function:

```
virtual TSharedPtr<class SGraphPin> CreatePin(class
  UEdGraphPin* Pin) const
```

The function of `CreatePin`, as the name implies, is to create a new visual representation of the graph pin.

It receives a `UEdGraphPin` instance. `UEdGraphPin` contains information about the object that the pin represents so that our factory class can make an informed decision regarding which visual representation we should be displaying.

Within our implementation of the function, we check that the pin's type is our custom class.

We do this by looking at the `PinSubCategoryObject` property, which contains a `UClass`, and comparing it to the `UClass` associated with our custom asset class.

If the pin's type meets our conditions, we return a new shared pointer to a Slate Widget, which is the visual representation of our object.

If the pin is of the wrong type, we return a null pointer to indicate a failed state.

The next class, `SGraphPinCustomAsset`, is the Slate Widget class, which is a visual representation of our object as a literal.

It inherits from `SGraphPin`, the base class for all graph pins.

The `SGraphPinCustomAsset` class has a `Construct` function, which is called when the widget is created.

It also implements some functions from the parent class: `GetPinColor()` and `GetDefaultValueWidget()`.

The last function that is defined is `ColorPicked`, a handler for when a user selects a color in our custom pin.

In the implementation of our custom class, we initialize our custom pin by calling the default implementation of `Construct`.

The role of `GetDefaultValueWidget` is to actually create the widget that is the custom representation of our class, and return it to the engine code.

In our implementation, it creates a new SColorPicker instance – we want the user to be able to select a color and store the hex-based representation of that color inside the FString property in our custom class.

This SColorPicker instance has a property called OnColorCommitted – this is a slate event that can be assigned to a function on an object instance.

Before returning our new SColorPicker, we link OnColorCommitted to the ColorPicked function on this current object so that it will be called if the user selects a new color.

The ColorPicked function receives the selected color as an input parameter.

Because this widget is used when there's no object connected to the pin we are associated with, we can't simply set the property on the associated object to the desired color string.

We need to create a new instance of our custom asset class, and we do that by using the NewObject template function.

This function behaves similarly to the SpawnActor function we discussed in other chapters, and initializes a new instance of the specified class before returning a pointer to it.

With a new instance in hand, we can set its ColorName property. FLinearColors can be converted into FColor objects, which define a ToHex() function that returns an FString with the hexadecimal representation of the color that was selected on the new widget.

Finally, we need to actually place our new object instance into the graph so that it will be referenced when the graph is executed.

To achieve this, we need to access the graph pin object that we represent, and use the GetSchema function. This function returns the Schema for the graph that owns the node that contains our pin.

The Schema contains the actual values that correspond to graph pins, and is a key element during graph evaluation.

Now that we have access to the Schema, we can set the default value for the pin that our widget represents. This value will be used during graph evaluation if the pin isn't connected to another pin, and acts like a default value that's provided during a function definition in C++.

As with all the extensions we've made in this chapter, there has to be some sort of initialization or registration to tell the engine to defer to our custom implementation before using its default inbuilt representation.

To do this, we need to add a new member to our editor module to store our `PinFactory` class instance.

During `StartupModule`, we create a new shared pointer that references an instance of our `PinFactory` class.

We store it inside the editor module's member so that it can be unregistered later. Then, we call `FEdGraphUtilities::RegisterVisualPinFactory(PinFactory)` to tell the engine to use our `PinFactory` to create the visual representation.

During `ShutdownModule`, we unregister the pin factory using `UnregisterVisualPinFactory`.

Finally, we delete our old `PinFactory` instance by calling `Reset()` on the shared pointer that contains it.

Inspecting types with custom Details panels

By default, `UObject`-derived UAssets open in the generic property editor. It looks as follows:

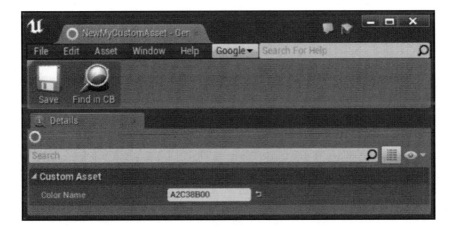

However, at times, you may wish for custom widgets so that you can edit the properties on your class. To facilitate this, Unreal supports **Details Customization**, which is the focus of this recipe.

How to do it...

1. From the `Chapter_10Editor` folder, create two new files called `MyCustomAssetDetailsCustomization.h` and `MyCustomAssetDetailsCustomization.cpp`.

2. Return to your project file and update your Visual Studio project. Once finished, open up the project in Visual Studio.

3. Add the following `#pragma` and `#includes` to the header (`MyCustomAssetDetailsCustomization.h`):

```
#pragma once

#include "MyCustomAsset.h"
#include "DetailLayoutBuilder.h"
#include "IDetailCustomization.h"
#include "IPropertyTypeCustomization.h"
```

4. Define our customization class, as follows:

```
class FMyCustomAssetDetailsCustomization : public
IDetailCustomization
{

public:
    virtual void CustomizeDetails(IDetailLayoutBuilder&
DetailBuilder) override;

    void ColorPicked(FLinearColor SelectedColor);
    static TSharedRef<IDetailCustomization> MakeInstance()
    {
        return MakeShareable(new
FMyCustomAssetDetailsCustomization);
    }
    TWeakObjectPtr<class UMyCustomAsset> MyAsset;
};
```

5. Below that, define the following additional class:

```
class FMyCustomAssetPropertyDetails : public
IPropertyTypeCustomization
```

```
{
public:
  void ColorPicked(FLinearColor SelectedColor);
  static TSharedRef<IPropertyTypeCustomization> MakeInstance()
  {
    return MakeShareable(new FMyCustomAssetPropertyDetails);
  }

  UMyCustomAsset* MyAsset;
  virtual void CustomizeChildren(TSharedRef<IPropertyHandle>
PropertyHandle, IDetailChildrenBuilder& ChildBuilder,
IPropertyTypeCustomizationUtils& CustomizationUtils) override;

  virtual void CustomizeHeader(TSharedRef<IPropertyHandle>
PropertyHandle, FDetailWidgetRow& HeaderRow,
IPropertyTypeCustomizationUtils& CustomizationUtils) override;

};
```

6. In the implementation file, add the following includes at the top of the file:

```
#include "MyCustomAssetDetailsCustomization.h"
#include "Chapter_10Editor.h"
#include "IDetailsView.h"
#include "DetailLayoutBuilder.h"
#include "DetailCategoryBuilder.h"
#include "SColorPicker.h"
#include "SBoxPanel.h"
#include "DetailWidgetRow.h"
```

7. Afterwards, create an implementation for CustomizeDetails:

```
void
FMyCustomAssetDetailsCustomization::CustomizeDetails(IDetailLa
youtBuilder& DetailBuilder)
{
    const TArray< TWeakObjectPtr<UObject> >& SelectedObjects =
DetailBuilder.GetDetailsView()->GetSelectedObjects();

    for (int32 ObjectIndex = 0; !MyAsset.IsValid() &&
ObjectIndex < SelectedObjects.Num(); ++ObjectIndex)
    {
        const TWeakObjectPtr<UObject>& CurrentObject =
SelectedObjects[ObjectIndex];
        if (CurrentObject.IsValid())
        {
            MyAsset =
Cast<UMyCustomAsset>(CurrentObject.Get());
```

```
            }
        }

        DetailBuilder.EditCategory("CustomCategory",
    FText::GetEmpty(), ECategoryPriority::Important)
    .AddCustomRow(FText::GetEmpty())
        [
        SNew(SVerticalBox)
        + SVerticalBox::Slot()
        .VAlign(VAlign_Center)
            [
                SNew(SColorPicker)
                .OnColorCommitted(this,
    &FMyCustomAssetDetailsCustomization::ColorPicked)
            ]
        ];
    }
```

8. Also, create a definition for `ColorPicked`:

```
    void
    FMyCustomAssetDetailsCustomization::ColorPicked(FLinearColor
    SelectedColor)
    {
        if (MyAsset.IsValid())
        {
            MyAsset.Get()->ColorName =
    SelectedColor.ToFColor(false).ToHex();
        }
    }
```

9. Beneath all of the scripts in
   `MyCustomAssetDetailsCustomization.cpp`, add the following code:

```
    void
    FMyCustomAssetPropertyDetails::CustomizeChildren(TSharedRef<IP
    ropertyHandle> PropertyHandle, IDetailChildrenBuilder&
    ChildBuilder, IPropertyTypeCustomizationUtils&
    CustomizationUtils)
    {
    }

    void
    FMyCustomAssetPropertyDetails::CustomizeHeader(TSharedRef<IPro
    pertyHandle> PropertyHandle, FDetailWidgetRow& HeaderRow,
    IPropertyTypeCustomizationUtils& CustomizationUtils)
    {
        UObject* PropertyValue = nullptr;
```

```
    auto GetValueResult =
PropertyHandle->GetValue(PropertyValue);

    HeaderRow.NameContent()
        [
            PropertyHandle->CreatePropertyNameWidget()
        ];
    HeaderRow.ValueContent()
        [
            SNew(SVerticalBox)
            + SVerticalBox::Slot()
        .VAlign(VAlign_Center)
        [
            SNew(SColorPicker)
            .OnColorCommitted(this,
&FMyCustomAssetPropertyDetails::ColorPicked)
        ]
        ];
}

void FMyCustomAssetPropertyDetails::ColorPicked(FLinearColor
SelectedColor)
{
    if (MyAsset)
    {
        MyAsset->ColorName =
SelectedColor.ToFColor(false).ToHex();
    }
}
```

10. In our editor module source file (`Chapter_10Editor.cpp`), add the
    following to your `#includes` in the `Chapter_10Editor.cpp` file:

    ```
    #include "PropertyEditorModule.h"
    #include "MyCustomAssetDetailsCustomization.h"
    #include "MyCustomAssetPinFactory.h"
    ```

11. Add the following to the implementation of `StartupModule`:

    ```
    FPropertyEditorModule& PropertyModule =
    FModuleManager::LoadModuleChecked<FPropertyEditorModule>("Prop
    ertyEditor");
    PropertyModule.RegisterCustomClassLayout(UMyCustomAsset::Stati
    cClass()->GetFName(),
    FOnGetDetailCustomizationInstance::CreateStatic(&FMyCustomAsse
    tDetailsCustomization::MakeInstance));
    PropertyModule.RegisterCustomPropertyTypeLayout(UMyCustomAsset
    ::StaticClass()->GetFName(),
    ```

```
FOnGetPropertyTypeCustomizationInstance::CreateStatic(&FMyCust
omAssetPropertyDetails::MakeInstance));
```

12. Add the following to `ShutdownModule`:

```
FPropertyEditorModule& PropertyModule =
FModuleManager::LoadModuleChecked<FPropertyEditorModule>("Prop
ertyEditor");
PropertyModule.UnregisterCustomClassLayout(UMyCustomAsset::Sta
ticClass()->GetFName());
```

13. Compile your code and launch the editor. Create a new instance of `MyCustomAsset` via the **Content Browser**.

14. Double-click on it to verify that the default editor that comes up now shows your custom layout:

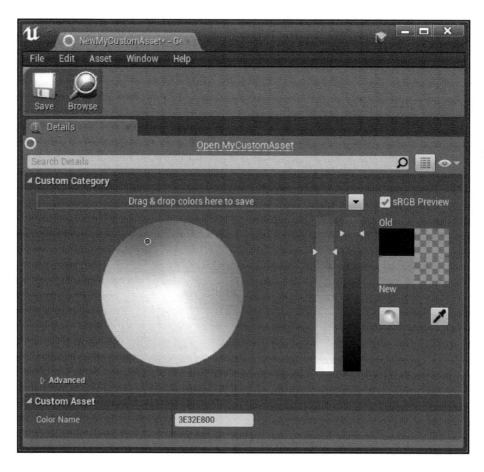

How it works...

Details Customization is performed through the `IDetailCustomization` interface, which developers can inherit when defining a class that customizes the way assets of a certain class are displayed.

The main function that `IDetailCustomization` uses to allow for this process to occur is as follows:

```
virtual void CustomizeDetails(IDetailLayoutBuilder& DetailBuilder)
override;
```

Within our implementation of this function, we use methods on `DetailBuilder` that are passed in as parameters to get an array of all selected objects. The loop then scans those to ensure that at least one selected object is of the correct type.

Customizing the representation of a class is done by calling methods on the `DetailBuilder` object. We create a new category for our details view by using the `EditCategory` function.

The first parameter of the `EditCategory` function is the name of the category we are going to manipulate.

The second parameter is optional, and contains a potentially localized display name for the category.

The third parameter is the priority of the category. A higher priority means it is displayed further up the list.

`EditCategory` returns a reference to the category itself as `CategoryBuilder`, allowing us to chain additional method calls onto an invocation of `EditCategory`.

As a result, we call `AddCustomRow()` on `CategoryBuilder`, which adds a new key-value pair to be displayed in the category.

Using the Slate syntax, we then specify that the row will contain a Vertical Box with a single center-aligned slot.

Inside the slot, we create a color picker control and bind its `OnColorCommitted` delegate to our local `ColorPicked` event handler.

Of course, this requires us to define and implement `ColourPicked`. It has the following signature:

```
void FMyCustomAssetDetailsCustomization::ColorPicked(FLinearColor
SelectedColor)
```

Inside the implementation of `ColorPicked`, we check to see if one of our selected assets was of the correct type, because, if at least one selected asset was correct, then `MyAsset` will be populated with a valid value.

Assuming we have a valid asset, we set the `ColorName` property to the hex string value corresponding to the color that was selected by the user.

11
Working with UE4 APIs

The **application programming interface (API)** is the way in which you, as the programmer, instruct the engine, and therefore the PC, what to do. Some of the interesting APIs that we'll explore in the recipes in this chapter are as follows:

- Core/Logging API – defining a custom log category
- Core/Logging API – FMessageLog to write messages to the Message Log
- Core/Math API – rotation using FRotator
- Core/Math API – rotation using FQuat
- Core/Math API – rotation using FRotationMatrix to have one object face another
- Landscape API – landscape generation with Perlin noise
- Foliage API – adding trees procedurally to your level
- Landscape and Foliage APIs – map generation using Landscape and Foliage APIs
- GameplayAbilities API – triggering an actor's gameplay abilities with game controls
- GameplayAbilities API – implementing stats with AttributeSet
- GameplayAbilities API – implementing buffs with GameplayEffect
- GameplayTags API – attaching GameplayTags to an actor
- GameplayTasks API – making things happen with GameplayTasks
- HTTP API – downloading web pages using web requests
- HTTP API – displaying downloaded progress

Introduction

All of UE4's functionality is encapsulated in modules, including very basic and core functionality. Each module has an API for it. To use an API, there is a very important linkage step, where you must list all APIs that you will be using in your build in a `ProjectName.Build.cs` file, which is located in your **Solution Explorer** window.

 Do not name any of your UE4 projects with the exact same name as one of the UE4 API names!

There are a variety of APIs inside the UE4 engine that expose functionality to various essential parts of it.

The UE4 engine's base functionality, which is available in the editor, is quite broad. The functionality from C++ code is actually grouped into little sections called APIs. There is a separate API module for each important functionality in the UE4 codebase. This is done to keep the codebase highly organized and modular.

 Using different APIs may require special linkage in your `Build.cs` file! If you are getting build errors, be sure to check that the linkage with the correct APIs is there!

The complete API listing is located in the following documentation: `https://docs. unrealengine.com/latest/INT/API/`.

Technical requirements

This chapter requires the use of Unreal Engine 4 and uses Visual Studio 2017 as the IDE. Instructions on how to install both pieces of software and the requirements for them can be found in `Chapter 1`, *UE4 Development Tools*, of this book.

Core/Logging API – defining a custom log category

UE4 itself defines several logging categories, including categories such as `LogActor`, which has any log messages to do with the `Actor` class, and `LogAnimation`, which logs messages about animations. In general, UE4 defines a separate logging category for each module. This allows developers to output their log messages to different logging streams. Each log stream's name is prefixed to the outputted message, as shown in the following example log messages from the engine:

```
LogContentBrowser: Native class hierarchy updated for
 'HierarchicalLODOutliner' in 0.0011 seconds. Added 1 classes and 2
 folders.
LogLoad: Full Startup: 8.88 seconds (BP compile: 0.07 seconds)
LogStreaming:Warning: Failed to read file
 '../../../Engine/Content/Editor/Slate/Common/Selection_16x.png'
 error.
LogExternalProfiler: Found external profiler: VSPerf
```

These log messages are samples from the engine, each prefixed with their log category. Warning messages appear in yellow and have **Warning** added to the front as well.

The example code you will find on the internet tends to use `LogTemp` for a UE4 project's own messages, as follows:

```
UE_LOG( LogTemp, Warning, TEXT( "Message %d" ), 1 );
```

We can actually improve upon this formula by defining our own custom `LogCategory`.

Getting ready

Have a UE4 project ready in which you'd like to define a custom log. Open a header file that will be included in almost all files using this log.

How to do it...

1. Open the main header file for your project; for example, if your project's name is `Chapter_11`, you'll open `Chapter_11.h`. Add the following line of code:

```
#pragma once

#include "CoreMinimal.h"

DECLARE_LOG_CATEGORY_EXTERN(LogCh11, Log, All);
```

As defined in `AssertionMacros.h`, there are three arguments to this declaration, which are as follows:

   - `CategoryName`: This is the log category name being defined (`LogCh11` here)
   - `DefaultVerbosity`: This is the default verbosity to use on log messages
   - `CompileTimeVerbosity`: This is the verbosity to bake into compiled code

2. Inside the main `.cpp` file for your project (`Chapter_11.cpp` in our case), include the following line of code:

```
#include "Chapter_11.h"
#include "Modules/ModuleManager.h"

IMPLEMENT_PRIMARY_GAME_MODULE( FDefaultGameModuleImpl,
Chapter_11, "Chapter_11" );

DEFINE_LOG_CATEGORY(LogCh11);
```

3. Now, we can use this log category in our own scripts. As an example, open up your project's `GameModeBase` file (in this case, `Chapter_11GameModeBase.h`) and add the following function declaration:

```
UCLASS()
class CHAPTER_11_API AChapter_11GameModeBase : public
AGameModeBase
{
    GENERATED_BODY()
    void BeginPlay();
```

```
};
```

4. Then, go to the implementation (`Chapter_11GameModeBase.cpp`) and use
the following code as an example of the various display categories:

```cpp
#include "Chapter_11GameModeBase.h"
#include "Chapter_11.h"

void AChapter_11GameModeBase::BeginPlay()
{
    // Traditional Logging
    UE_LOG(LogTemp, Warning, TEXT("Message %d"), 1);

    // Our custom log type
    UE_LOG(LogCh11, Display, TEXT("A display message, log is
working" ) ); // shows in gray
    UE_LOG(LogCh11, Warning, TEXT("A warning message"));
    UE_LOG(LogCh11, Error, TEXT("An error message "));
}
```

5. Compile your scripts. Afterwards, open the **World Settings** menu and set
the **GameMode Override** property to `Chapter_11GameModeBase` and
then run the game:

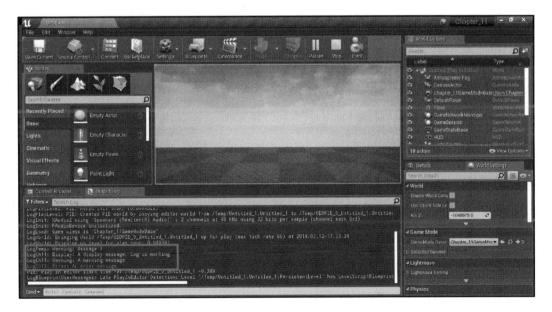

The location of the logged messages from the Output Log window

As you can see, we can see our custom log messages being displayed!

How it works...

Logging works by outputting messages to the **Output Log** (**Window** | **Developer Tools** | **Output Log**) as well as a file. All information outputted to the **Output Log** is also mirrored to a simple text file that is located in your project's /Saved/Logs folder. The extension of the log files is .log, with the most recent one being named YourProjectName.log.

There's more...

You can enable or suppress log messages for a particular log channel from within the editor using the following console commands:

```
Log LogName off // Stop LogName from displaying at the output
Log LogName Log // Turn LogName's output on again
```

If you'd like to edit the initial values of the output levels of some of the built-in log types, you can use a C++ class to create changes for the engine.ini config file. You can change the initial values in the engine.ini configuration file.

See https://wiki.unrealengine.com/Logs,_Printing_Messages_To_Yourself_During_Runtime for more details.

UE_LOG sends its output to **Output Window**. If you'd like to use the more specialized **Message Log** window in addition to this, you can use the FMessageLog object to write your output messages. FMessageLog writes to both the **Message Log** and the **Output Window**. See the next recipe for details.

Core/Logging API – FMessageLog to write messages to the Message Log

FMessageLog is an object that allows you to write output messages to the **Message Log (Window | Developer Tools | Message Log)** and **Output Log (Window | Developer Tools | Output Log)** simultaneously.

Getting ready

Have your project ready and some information to log to **Message Log**. Display the **Message Log (Window | Developer Tools | Message Log)** in your UE4 Editor.

How to do it...

1. Add #define to your main header file (ProjectName.h), defining LOCTEXT_NAMESPACE as something unique to your codebase:

   ```
   #define LOCTEXT_NAMESPACE "Chapter11Namespace"
   ```

   This #define is used by the LOCTEXT() macro, which we use to generate FText objects, but is not seen in output messages.

2. Declare your FMessageLog by constructing it somewhere very global. You can use extern in your ProjectName.h file. Consider the following piece of code as an example:

   ```
   #define LOCTEXT_NAMESPACE "Chapter11Namespace"
   #define FTEXT(x) LOCTEXT(x, x)

   extern FName LoggerName;

   void CreateLog(FName logName);
   ```

3. Then, create your FMessageLog by defining it in a .cpp file and registering it with MessageLogModule. Be sure to give your logger a clear and unique name on construction. It's the category of your log that will appear to the left of your log messages in **Output Log**. For example, ProjectName.cpp:

   ```
   #include "Chapter_11.h"
   #include "Modules/ModuleManager.h"
   ```

```
#include "MessageLog/Public/MessageLogModule.h"
#include "MessageLog.h"

// ...

FName LoggerName("MessageLogChapter11");

void CreateLog(FName logName)
{
    FMessageLogModule& MessageLogModule =
FModuleManager::LoadModuleChecked<FMessageLogModule>("MessageL
og");
    FMessageLogInitializationOptions InitOptions;
    InitOptions.bShowPages = true;
    InitOptions.bShowFilters = true;
    FText LogListingName = FTEXT("Chapter 11's Log Listing");
    MessageLogModule.RegisterLogListing(logName,
LogListingName, InitOptions);
}
```

4. Then, head back to somewhere in your code to actually create the log and use it. For example, we can add the following GameModeBase class's BeginPlay method:

```
void AChapter_11GameModeBase::BeginPlay()
{
    // 11-01 - Core/Logging API - Defining a custom log
    // category
    // Traditional Logging
    UE_LOG(LogTemp, Warning, TEXT("Message %d"), 1);

    // Our custom log type
    UE_LOG(LogCh11, Display, TEXT("A display message, log is
working" ) ); // shows in gray
    UE_LOG(LogCh11, Warning, TEXT("A warning message"));
    UE_LOG(LogCh11, Error, TEXT("An error message "));

    // 11-02 - Core/Logging API - FMessageLog to write
    // messages to the Message Log
    CreateLog(LoggerName);
    // Retrieve the Log by using the LoggerName.
    FMessageLog logger(LoggerName);
    logger.Warning(FTEXT("A warning message from gamemode"));
}
```

The KEY to LOCTEXT (first argument) must be unique or you will get a previously hashed string back. If you'd like, you can include a `#define` that repeats the argument to LOCTEXT twice, as we did earlier:

```
#define FTEXT(x) LOCTEXT(x, x)
```

5. Log your messages using the following code:

```
logger.Info( FTEXT( "Info to log" ) );
logger.Warning( FTEXT( "Warning text to log" ) );
logger.Error( FTEXT( "Error text to log" ) );
```

This code utilizes the `FTEXT()` macro we defined earlier. Ensure it is in your codebase.

How it works...

This recipe displays a message to the Message Log. As we discussed previously, you can see logged information at the **Message Log (Window | Developer Tools | Message Log)** and **Output Log (Window | Developer Tools | Output Log)** .

Constructing your message log again after initialization retrieves a copy of the original message log. For example, at any place in the code, you can write the following code:

```
FMessageLog( LoggerName ).Info(FTEXT( "An info
message"));
```

Core/Math API – rotation using FRotator

Rotation in UE4 has such a complete implementation that it can be hard to choose how to rotate your objects. There are three main methods: `FRotator`, `FQuat`, and `FRotationMatrix`. This recipe outlines the construction and use of the first of the three different methods for the rotation of objects—the `FRotator`. Using this, and the following two recipes, you can select a method to use to rotate your objects.

Getting ready

Open a UE4 project that has an object you can get a C++ interface with. For example, you can construct a C++ class Coin that derives from `Actor` to test out rotations. Override the `Coin::Tick()` method to apply your rotations from the C++ code. Alternatively, you can call these rotation functions in the `Tick` event from Blueprints.

In this example, we will rotate an object at a rate of one degree per second by making use of an Actor component. The actual rotation will be the accumulated time since the object was created. To get this value, we'll just call `GetWorld()->TimeSeconds`.

How to do it...

1. From the **Modes** tab, under the **Place** section and under **Basic**, drag and drop a **Cube** object into your scene.
2. From the **Details** tab, go to the **Transform** component and change the **Mobility** property to **Movable**.
3. Afterwards, click on the **Add Component** button and select **New C++ Component**.
4. From the menu that pops up, select **Actor Component** and select **Next**:

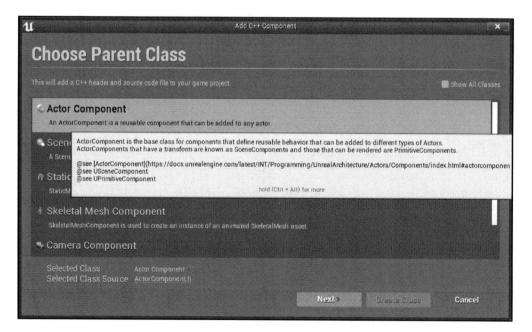

5. From there, give your component a name, for example, `RotateActorComponent`, and then press the **Create Class** button.

6. Construct your `FRotator`. `FRotators` can be constructed using a stock pitch, yaw, and roll constructor, as shown in the following example:

```
FRotator( float InPitch, float InYaw, float InRoll );
```

7. Your `FRotator` will be constructed as follows:

```
FRotator rotator( 0, GetWorld()->TimeSeconds, 0 );
```

8. The standard orientation for an object in UE4 is with Forward facing down the +X-axis. Right is the +Y-axis, and Up is +Z.

9. Pitch is rotation about the Y-axis (across), yaw is rotation about the Z-axis (up), and roll is rotation about the X-axis. This is best understood in the following three points:

- **Pitch**: If you think of an airplane in UE4 standard coordinates, the Y-axis goes along the wingspan (pitching tilts it forward and backward)
- **Yaw**: The Z-axis goes straight up and down (yawing turns it left and right)
- **Roll**: The X-axis goes straight along the fuselage of the plane (rolling does barrel rolls)

You should note that in other conventions, the X-axis is pitch, the Y-axis is yaw, and the Z-axis is roll.

10. Apply your `FRotator` to your actor using the `SetActorRotation` member function, as follows:

```
// Called every frame
void URotateActorComponent::TickComponent(float DeltaTime,
ELevelTick TickType, FActorComponentTickFunction*
ThisTickFunction)
{
    Super::TickComponent(DeltaTime, TickType,
ThisTickFunction);

    FRotator rotator(0, GetWorld()->TimeSeconds, 0);
    GetOwner()->SetActorRotation(rotator);
}
```

Core/Math API – rotation using FQuat

Quaternions sound intimidating, but they are extremely easy to use. You may want to review the theoretical math behind them by viewing the following videos:

- *Fantastic Quaternions* by Numberphile: https://www.youtube.com/watch?v=3BR8tK-LuB0
- *Understanding Quaternions* by Jim Van Verth: http://gdcvault.com/play/1017653/Math-for-Game-Programmers-Understanding

However, we won't cover the math background here! In fact, you don't need to understand much about the math background of quaternions to use them effectively.

Getting ready

Have a project ready and an `Actor` with an override `::Tick()` function that we can enter the C++ code into.

How to do it...

1. To construct a quaternion, the best constructor to use is as follows:

```
FQuat( FVector Axis, float AngleRad );
```

Quaternions have quaternion addition, quaternion subtraction, multiplication by a scalar, and division by a scalar defined for them, among other functions. They are extremely useful to rotate things at arbitrary angles, and point objects at one another.

2. For example, if you wanted to use an FQuat inside of the `RotateActorComponent.cpp` file, it would look similar to this:

```
void URotateActorComponent::TickComponent(float DeltaTime,
ELevelTick TickType, FActorComponentTickFunction*
ThisTickFunction)
{
    Super::TickComponent(DeltaTime, TickType,
ThisTickFunction);

    // 11-04 - Rotation using FQuat
    FQuat quat = FQuat(FVector(0, 1, 0),
GetWorld()->TimeSeconds * PI / 4.f);
```

```
    GetOwner()->SetActorRotation(quat);

}
```

Upon compiling your code and returning to the game, you should notice the cube moving at a constant rate:

How it works...

Quaternions are a bit strange, but using them is quite simple. If v is the axis around which to rotate, and θ is the magnitude of the angle of rotation, then we get the following equations for the components of a quaternion:

$$
\begin{vmatrix}
x = v_x \sin\left(\dfrac{\theta}{2}\right) \\[2mm]
y = v_y \sin\left(\dfrac{\theta}{2}\right) \\[2mm]
z = v_z \sin\left(\dfrac{\theta}{2}\right) \\[2mm]
w = \cos\left(\dfrac{\theta}{2}\right)
\end{vmatrix}
$$

So, for example, rotation about $v=(1,2,1)=\left(\dfrac{1}{\sqrt{5}},\dfrac{2}{\sqrt{5}},\dfrac{1}{\sqrt{5}}\right)$ by an angle of $\dfrac{\pi}{2}$ will have the following quaternion components:

$$(x,y,z,w)=\left(\dfrac{1}{\sqrt{10}},\dfrac{2}{\sqrt{10}},\dfrac{1}{\sqrt{10}},\dfrac{1}{\sqrt{2}}\right)$$

Three of the four components of the quaternion (x, y, and z) define the axis around which to rotate (scaled by the sine of half the angle of rotation), while the fourth component (w) has only the cosine of half the angle to rotate with.

There's more...

Quaternions, being vectors themselves, can be rotated. Simply extract the (x, y, z) components of the quaternion, normalize, and then rotate that vector. Construct a new quaternion from that new unit vector with the desired angle of rotation.

Multiplying quaternions together represents a series of rotations that happen subsequently. For example, a rotation of 45º about the X-axis, followed by a rotation of 45º about the Y-axis will be composed by the following:

```
FQuat( FVector( 1, 0, 0 ), PI/4.f ) *
FQuat( FVector( 0, 1, 0 ), PI/4.f );
```

This would give you a result that would look similar to this:

API – rotation using FRotationMatrix to have one object face another

`FRotationMatrix` offers matrix construction using a series of `::Make*` routines. They are easy to use and useful to get one object to face another. Say you have two objects, one of which is following the other. We want the rotation of the follower to always be facing what it is following. The construction methods of `FRotationMatrix` make this easy to do.

Getting ready

Have two actors in a scene, one of which should face the other.

How to do it...

1. Add a new **C++ Actor Component** for the follower called `FollowActorComponent` (see the *Core/Math API – rotation using FRotator* recipe if you need help with this).

2. From the `FollowActorComponent.h` file, we need to have a reference to the object we want to follow, so add the following:

```
UCLASS( ClassGroup=(Custom),
meta=(BlueprintSpawnableComponent) )
class CHAPTER_11_API UFollowActorComponent : public
UActorComponent
{
    GENERATED_BODY()

public:
    // Sets default values for this component's properties
    UFollowActorComponent();

protected:
    // Called when the game starts
    virtual void BeginPlay() override;

public:
    // Called every frame
    virtual void TickComponent(float DeltaTime, ELevelTick
TickType, FActorComponentTickFunction* ThisTickFunction)
override;
```

```
UPROPERTY(EditAnywhere)
AActor * target;
};
```

3. Then, in the `FollowActorComponent.cpp` file, in the `TickComponent` function, look into the available constructors under the `FRotationMatrix` class. A bunch of constructors are available that will let you specify a rotation for an object (from stock position) by reorienting one or more of the *X-*, *Y-*, or *Z*-axes, named with the `FRotationMatrix::Make*()` pattern.

4. Assuming you have a default stock orientation for your actor (with Forward facing down the +*X*-axis, and up facing up the +*Z*-axis), find the vector from the follower to the object they want to follow, as shown in this piece of code:

```
// Called every frame
void UFollowActorComponent::TickComponent(float DeltaTime,
ELevelTick TickType, FActorComponentTickFunction*
ThisTickFunction)
{
    Super::TickComponent(DeltaTime, TickType,
ThisTickFunction);

    FVector toFollow = target->GetActorLocation() -
GetOwner()->GetActorLocation();

    FMatrix rotationMatrix =
FRotationMatrix::MakeFromXZ(toFollow,
GetOwner()->GetActorUpVector());

    GetOwner()->SetActorRotation(rotationMatrix.Rotator());

}
```

5. Compile your script and assign the **Target** property inside of the **Follow Actor Component** from the **Details** tab. This can be done using the eyedropper button to the right of the property or by using the drop-down list:

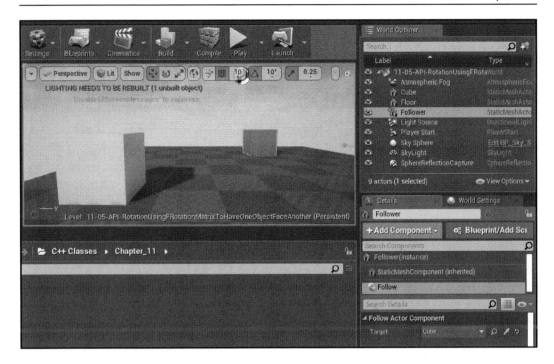

If all went well, you should see the actor rotate correctly to face the target:

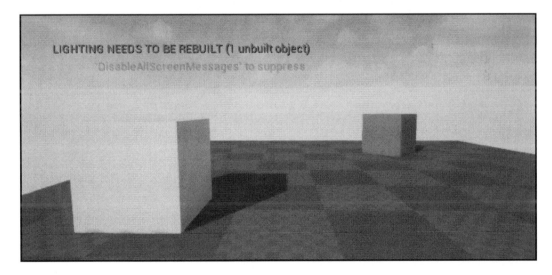

How it works...

Getting one object to look at another, with a desired up vector, can be done by calling the correct function, depending on your object's stock orientation. Usually, you want to reorient the *X*-axis (Forward), while specifying either the *Y*-axis (Right) or *Z*-axis (Up) vectors (`FRotationMatrix::MakeFromXY()`). For example, to make an actor look along a `lookAlong` vector, with its right side facing right, we'd construct and set `FRotationMatrix` for it, as follows:

```
FRotationMatrix rotationMatrix = FRotationMatrix::MakeFromXY(
  lookAlong, right );
actor->SetActorRotation( rotationMatrix.Rotator() );
```

GameplayAbilities API – triggering an actor's gameplay abilities with game controls

The **GameplayAbilities** API can be used to attach C++ functions to invoke on certain button pushes, triggering the game unit to exhibit its abilities during play in response to keystroke events. In this recipe, we will show you how to do that.

Getting ready

Enumerate and describe your game character's abilities. You will need to know what your character does in response to key events to code in this recipe.

There are several objects that we need to use here; they are as follows:

- The `UGameplayAbility` class—this is needed to derive the C++ class instances of the `UGameplayAbility` class, with one derivative class for each ability:
  - Define what each ability does in `.h` and `.cpp` by overriding the available functions, such as
    `UGameplayAbility::ActivateAbility`,
    `UGameplayAbility::InputPressed`,
    `UGameplayAbility::CheckCost`,
    `UGameplayAbility::ApplyCost`,
    `UGameplayAbility::ApplyCooldown`, and so on

- `GameplayAbilitiesSet` is a `DataAsset` derivative object that contains a series of enum'd command values, and blueprints of the corresponding `UGameplayAbility` derivative classes that define the behavior for that particular input command. Each GameplayAbility is kicked off by a keystroke or mouse-click, which is set in `DefaultInput.ini`.

How to do it...

In the following code, we'll implement a `UGameplayAbility` derivative called `UGameplayAbility_Attack` for a `Warrior` class object. We'll attach this gameplay functionality to the input command string `Ability1`, which we'll activate on the left-mouse button-click:

1. Open up your `.Build.cs` file (in our case, `Chapter_11.Build.cs`) and add the following dependencies:

```
using UnrealBuildTool;

public class Chapter_11 : ModuleRules
{
    public Chapter_11(ReadOnlyTargetRules Target) :
    base(Target)
    {
        PCHUsage = PCHUsageMode.UseExplicitOrSharedPCHs;
        PublicDependencyModuleNames.AddRange(new string[] {
        "Core", "CoreUObject", "Engine", "InputCore" });
        PublicDependencyModuleNames.AddRange(new string[] {
        "GameplayAbilities", "GameplayTags", "GameplayTasks"
});

        PrivateDependencyModuleNames.AddRange(new string[] {
});
    }
}
```

2. Compile your code.
3. From the Unreal Editor, go to **Settings** | **Plugins**.

4. From the menu that pops up, search for `GameplayAbilities` and check it. You'll get a message asking if you are sure. Click on the **Yes** button:

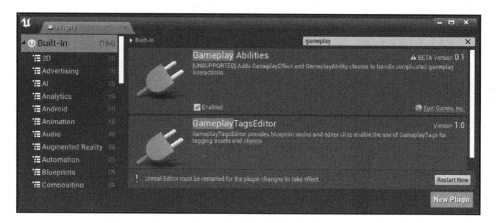

5. Afterwards, click on the **Restart Now** button. The classes should be added to your project correctly.

6. Now, access the **Add C++ Class** wizard by selecting from the Content Browser **Add New | New C++ Class...** and check the **Show All Classes** option. From there, type in `gameplayability` and select the base **GameplayAbility** class to base our new class on:

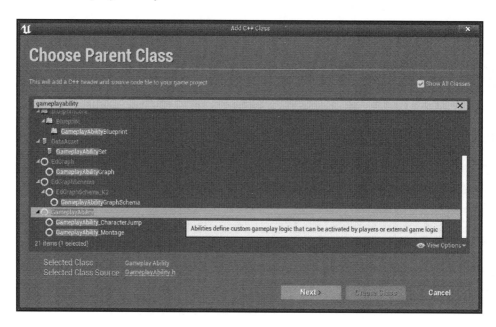

7. Give the new gameplay ability a name of `GameplayAbility_Attack` and press **Create Class**.

8. At the very least, you want to override the following:

   - The `UGameplayAbility_Attack::CanActivateAbility` member function to indicate when the actor is allowed to invoke the ability.
   - The `UGameplayAbility_Attack::CheckCost` function to indicate whether the player can afford to use an ability or not. This is extremely important because if this returns false, ability invocation should fail.
   - The `UGameplayAbility_Attack::ActivateAbility` member function to write the code that the `Warrior` is to execute when their `Attack` ability is activated.
   - The `UGameplayAbility_Attack::InputPressed` member function and to respond to the key input event assigned to the ability:

```
#pragma once

#include "CoreMinimal.h"
#include "Abilities/GameplayAbility.h"
#include "GameplayAbility_Attack.generated.h"

UCLASS()
class CHAPTER_11_API UGameplayAbility_Attack : public
UGameplayAbility
{
  GENERATED_BODY()

        /** Returns true if this ability can be activated
        right now. Has no side effects */
        virtual bool CanActivateAbility(const
FGameplayAbilitySpecHandle Handle, const
FGameplayAbilityActorInfo* ActorInfo, const
FGameplayTagContainer* SourceTags = nullptr, const
FGameplayTagContainer* TargetTags = nullptr, OUT
FGameplayTagContainer* OptionalRelevantTags = nullptr) const {
        UE_LOG(LogTemp, Warning, TEXT("ability_attack
        CanActivateAbility!"));
        return true;
    }

        /** Checks cost. returns true if we can pay for the
        ability. False if not */
        virtual bool CheckCost(const FGameplayAbilitySpecHandle
Handle,
        const FGameplayAbilityActorInfo* ActorInfo, OUT
```

```
        FGameplayTagContainer* OptionalRelevantTags = nullptr)
const {
        UE_LOG(LogTemp, Warning, TEXT("ability_attack
CheckCost!"));
        return true;
        //return Super::CheckCost( Handle, ActorInfo,
        //OptionalRelevantTags );
    }

    virtual void ActivateAbility(const
FGameplayAbilitySpecHandle
    Handle,
        const FGameplayAbilityActorInfo* ActorInfo, const
        FGameplayAbilityActivationInfo ActivationInfo,
        const FGameplayEventData* TriggerEventData)
    {
        UE_LOG(LogTemp, Warning, TEXT("Activating
        ugameplayability_attack().. swings weapon!"));
        Super::ActivateAbility(Handle, ActorInfo,
ActivationInfo,
        TriggerEventData);
    }

    /** Input binding stub. */
    virtual void InputPressed(const FGameplayAbilitySpecHandle
    Handle, const FGameplayAbilityActorInfo* ActorInfo, const
    FGameplayAbilityActivationInfo ActivationInfo) {
        UE_LOG(LogTemp, Warning, TEXT("ability_attack
        inputpressed!"));
        Super::InputPressed(Handle, ActorInfo,
ActivationInfo);
    }
};
```

9. Derive a Blueprint class from your `UGameplayAbility_Attack` object inside the UE4 Editor.

10. Inside the Editor, navigate to **Content Browser** and create a
    `GameplayAbilitiesSet` object by doing the following:

    - Right-clicking on **Content Browser** and selecting **Miscellaneous |
      Data Asset**:

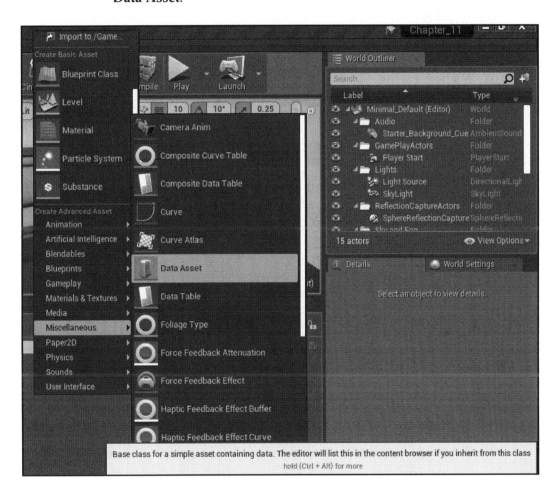

- In the dialog box that follows, select `GameplayAbilitySet` for
the **Data Asset Class**:

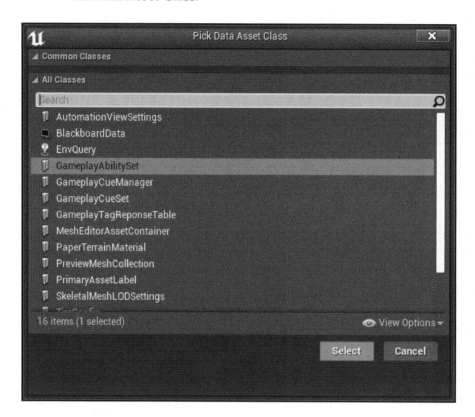

In fact, the `GameplayAbilitySet` object is
a `UDataAsset` derivative. It is located
in `GameplayAbilitySet.h` and contains a single member
function, `GameplayAbilitySet::GiveAbilities()`, which I
strongly recommend you not to use for reasons listed in a later step.

11. Name your `GameplayAbilitySet` data asset something related to
the `WarriorAbilitySet` object so that we know to put it into the `Warrior`
class (for example, `WarriorAbilitySet`).

12. Double-click to open and edit the new `WarriorAbilitySet` Data Asset.
Stack in a list of `GameplayAbility` class derivative Blueprints by clicking
+ on the `TArray` object inside of it. Your `UGameplayAbility_Attack`
object must appear in the dropdown:

13. We now need to create a `Character` class-derived object so that we can contain this ability set. In this example, we will call this class `Warrior`.

14. Add a `UPROPERTY UGameplayAbilitySet* gameplayAbilitySet` member to your `Warrior` class:

```
#pragma once

#include "CoreMinimal.h"
#include "GameFramework/Character.h"
#include "GameplayAbilitySet.h"
#include "AbilitySystemInterface.h"
#include "Warrior.generated.h"

#define FS(x,...) FString::Printf( TEXT( x ), __VA_ARGS__ )

UCLASS()
class CHAPTER_11_API AWarrior : public ACharacter, public
IAbilitySystemInterface
{
    GENERATED_BODY()
```

```
public:
    // Sets default values for this character's properties
    AWarrior();

protected:
    // Called when the game starts or when spawned
    virtual void BeginPlay() override;

public:
    // Called every frame
    virtual void Tick(float DeltaTime) override;

    // Called to bind functionality to input
    virtual void SetupPlayerInputComponent(class
UInputComponent* PlayerInputComponent) override;

    // Lists key triggers for various abilities for the
    // player.
    // Selects an instance of UGameplayAbilitySet (which is a
//      \
    UDataAsset derivative
    // that you construct in the Content Browser).
    UPROPERTY(EditAnywhere, BlueprintReadWrite, Category =
    Stats)
    UGameplayAbilitySet* gameplayAbilitySet;

    // The AbilitySystemComponent itself
    UPROPERTY(EditAnywhere, BlueprintReadWrite, Category =
    Stats)
    UAbilitySystemComponent* AbilitySystemComponent;

    // IAbilitySystemInterface implementation:
    virtual UAbilitySystemComponent*
GetAbilitySystemComponent() const { return
AbilitySystemComponent; }

};
```

Ensure that your Actor class derivative also derives from the UAbilitySystemInterface interface. This is extremely important so that calls to (Cast<IAbilitySystemInterface>(yourActor))->GetAbilitySystemComponent() succeed.

15. Create a Blueprint of the Warrior class and set the **Gameplay Ability Set** to the **Warrior Ability Set** we created earlier, and set the **Ability System Component** to the **Ability System Component**:

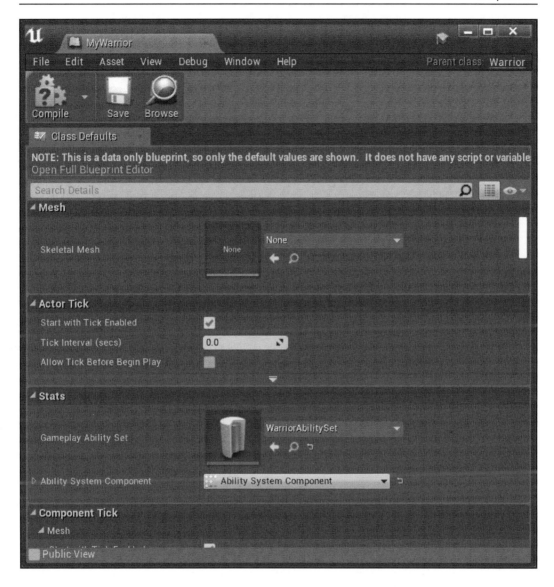

If you are unable to see the **Ability System Component**, close and reopen the Blueprint.

16. Once finished, assign `MyWarrior` as the **Default Pawn Class** of your Game Mode.

17. Compile, run, and select-in `WarriorAbilitySet` as it sits in **Content Browser** (created in Steps 5 to 7) of the abilities of which this `Warrior` is capable.

18. Some time after the construction of your actor, call `gameplayAbilitySet->GiveAbilities( abilitySystemComponent )`; or enter a loop, as shown in the following step where you invoke `abilitySystemComponent->GiveAbility()` for each ability listed in your `gameplayAbilitySet`.

19. Write an override for `AWarrior::SetupPlayerInputComponent( UInputComponent* Input )` to connect the input controller to the Warrior's `GameplayAbility` activations. After doing so, iterate over each `GameplayAbility` listed in your `GameplayAbilitySet`'s **Abilities** group:

```cpp
#include "AbilitySystemComponent.h"

// ...

// Called to bind functionality to input
void AWarrior::SetupPlayerInputComponent(UInputComponent*
Input)
{
    Super::SetupPlayerInputComponent(Input);

    // Connect the class's AbilitySystemComponent
    // to the actor's input component
    AbilitySystemComponent->BindToInputComponent(Input);

    // Go thru each BindInfo in the gameplayAbilitySet.
    // Give & try and activate each on the
    // AbilitySystemComponent.
    for (const FGameplayAbilityBindInfo& BindInfo :
       gameplayAbilitySet->Abilities)
    {

        FGameplayAbilitySpec spec(
            // Gets you an instance of the UClass
            BindInfo.GameplayAbilityClass->
            GetDefaultObject<UGameplayAbility>(),
            1, (int32)BindInfo.Command);

        // STORE THE ABILITY HANDLE FOR LATER INVOKATION
        // OF THE ABILITY
        FGameplayAbilitySpecHandle abilityHandle =
```

```
        AbilitySystemComponent->GiveAbility(spec);

    // The integer id that invokes the ability
    // (ith value in enum listing)
    int32 AbilityID = (int32)BindInfo.Command;

    // CONSTRUCT the inputBinds object, which will
    // allow us to wire-up an input event to the
    // InputPressed() / InputReleased() events of
    // the GameplayAbility.
    FGameplayAbilityInputBinds inputBinds(
        // These are supposed to be unique strings that
        // define what kicks off the ability for the actor
        // instance.
        // Using strings of the format
        // "ConfirmTargetting_Player0_AbilityClass"
        FS("ConfirmTargetting_%s_%s", *GetName(),
            *BindInfo.GameplayAbilityClass->GetName()),
        FS("CancelTargetting_%s_%s", *GetName(),
            *BindInfo.GameplayAbilityClass->GetName()),
        "EGameplayAbilityInputBinds", // The name of the
        // ENUM that has the abilities listing
        // (GameplayAbilitySet.h).
        AbilityID, AbilityID
    );
    // MUST BIND EACH ABILITY TO THE INPUTCOMPONENT,
    // OTHERWISE THE ABILITY CANNOT "HEAR" INPUT EVENTS.
    // Enables triggering of InputPressed() /
    // InputReleased() events, which you can in-turn use
    // to call
    // TryActivateAbility() if you so choose.
    AbilitySystemComponent->BindAbilityActivationToInputComponent(
        Input, inputBinds
    );

    // Test-kicks the ability to active state.
    // You can try invoking this manually via your
    // own hookups to keypresses in this Warrior class
    // TryActivateAbility() calls ActivateAbility() if
    // the ability is indeed invokable at this time
    // according to rules internal to the Ability's class
    // (such as cooldown is ready and cost is met)
    AbilitySystemComponent->TryActivateAbility(
        abilityHandle, 1);
  }
}
```

20. Compile your code and then play the game:

How it works...

You must subclass and link in a set of `UGameplayAbility` objects to your actor's `UAbilitySystemComponent` object through a series of calls to `UAbilitySystemComponent::GiveAbility( spec )` with appropriately constructed `FGameplayAbilitySpec` objects. What this does is deck out your actor with this bunch of `GameplayAbilities`. The functionality of each `UGameplayAbility`, as well as its cost, cooldown, and activation, is all neatly contained within the `UGameplayAbility` class derivative that you will construct.

Do not use the `GameplayAbilitySet::GiveAbilities()` member function because it doesn't give you access to the set of `FGameplayAbilitySpecHandle` objects that you actually need later to bind and invoke the ability to an input component.

There's more...

You'll want to carefully code in a bunch of the other functions that are available in the GameplayAbility.h header file, including implementations for the following:

- SendGameplayEvent: This is a function to notify GameplayAbility that some general gameplay event has happened.
- CancelAbility: This is a function to stop an ability's usage midway through, and to give the ability an interrupted state.
- Keep in mind that there are a bunch of existing UPROPERTY specifiers near the bottom of the UGameplayAbility class declaration that either activate or cancel the ability upon addition or removal of certain GameplayTags. See the following *GameplayTags API – attaching GameplayTags to an actor* recipe for more details.
- There are a bunch more! Explore the API and implement those functions you find to be useful in your code.

See also

- The GameplayAbilities API is a rich and nicely interwoven series of objects and functions. Explore GameplayEffects, GameplayTags, and GameplayTasks and how they integrate with the UGameplayAbility class to fully explore the functionality the library has to offer. You can read more about the API here: https://api.unrealengine.com/INT/API/Plugins/GameplayAbilities/index.html

GameplayAbilities API - Implementing stats with UAttributeSet

The GameplayAbilities API allows you to associate a set of attributes, that is, UAttributeSet, to an Actor. UAttributeSet describes properties appropriate for that Actor's in-game attributes, such as Hp, Mana, Speed, Armor, AttackDamage, and so on. You can either define a single game-wide set of attributes common to all Actors, or several different sets of attributes appropriate for the different classes of actors.

Getting ready

`AbilitySystemComponent` is the first thing you will need to add to your actors to equip them to use the `GameplayAbilities` API and `UAttributeSet` classes. To define your custom `UAttributeSet`, you will simply derive from the `UAttributeSet` base class and extend the base class with your own series of `UPROPERTY` members. After that, you must register your custom `AttributeSet` with your `Actor` class's `AbilitySystemComponent`.

How to do it...

1. If you have not done so already, complete Steps 1-4 of the *Gameplay Abilities API – triggering an actor's gameplay abilities with game controls* recipe to link to the `GameplayAbilities` API in your `ProjectName.Build.cs` file and enable its functionality.

2. Create a new C++ class by going to the **Content Browser** and selecting **Add New | Add C++ Class**. From the **Add C++ Class** menu, check the **Show All Classes** option. From there, type in `attr` and select `AttributeSet` as your parent class. From there, click the **Next** button:

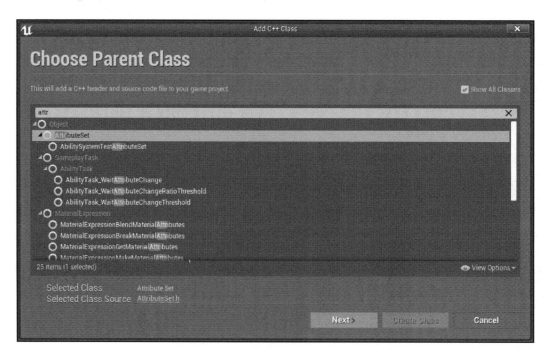

3. Give the class a **Name** of `GameUnitAttributeSet` and click on **Create Class**:

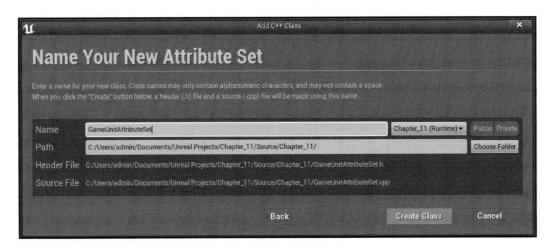

Once created, deck the class out with a set of UPROPERTY specifiers that you want each Actor to have in their property set.

4. For example, you might want to declare your UAttributeSet derivate class similar to what's given in the following piece of code:

```
#pragma once

#include "CoreMinimal.h"
#include "AttributeSet.h"
#include "GameUnitAttributeSet.generated.h"

/**
 *
 */
UCLASS(Blueprintable, BlueprintType)
class CHAPTER_11_API UGameUnitAttributeSet : public
UAttributeSet
{
    GENERATED_BODY()
public:
    UPROPERTY(EditAnywhere, BlueprintReadWrite, Category =
GameUnitAttributes)
    float Hp;

    UPROPERTY(EditAnywhere, BlueprintReadWrite, Category =
GameUnitAttributes)
```

```
    float Mana;

    UPROPERTY(EditAnywhere, BlueprintReadWrite, Category =
GameUnitAttributes)
    float Speed;
};
```

If your code is networked, you might want to enable replication on each of the UPROPERTY specifiers with the replicated declaration in the UPROPERTY macro.

5. Connect GameUnitAttributeSet with your AbilitySystemComponent inside your Actor class. We can do this with the Warrior class we created previously by opening the Warrior.h file and adding the following function declaration:

```
virtual void PostInitializeComponents() override;
```

6. Then, open Warrior.cpp and add the following #include:

```
#include "GameUnitAttributeSet.h"
```

7. Afterwards, implement that function:

```
void AWarrior::PostInitializeComponents()
{
    Super::PostInitializeComponents();

    if(AbilitySystemComponent)
    {
AbilitySystemComponent->InitStats(UGameUnitAttributeSet::Stati
cClass(), NULL);
    }
}
```

You can put this call somewhere in PostInitializeComponents(), or in code that is called later than that.

8. Once you have registered UAttributeSet, you can move on with the next recipe and apply GameplayEffect to some of the elements in the attribute set.

9. Be sure your `Actor` class object implements `IAbilitySystemInterface` by deriving from it. This is extremely important as the `UAbilitySet` object will attempt a cast to `IAbilitySystemInterface` to call `GetAbilitySystemComponent()` on it at various places in the code.

How it works...

`UAttributeSets` simply allow you to enumerate and define attributes of different actors. `GameplayEffects` will be your means to make changes to the attributes of a specific actor.

There's more...

You can code in definitions of `GameplayEffects`, which will be things that act on the `AbilitySystemComponent`'s `AttributeSet` collections. You can also write `GameplayTasks` for generic functions that run at specific times or follow particular events, or even in response to a tag addition (`GameplayTagResponseTable.cpp`). You can define `GameplayTags` to modify `GameplayAbility` behavior, as well as select and match gameplay units during play.

GameplayAbilities API – implementing buffs with GameplayEffect

A buff is just an effect that introduces a temporary, permanent, or recurring change to a game unit's attributes from its `AttributeSet`. Buffs can either be good or bad, supplying either bonuses or penalties. For example, you might have a hex buff that slows a unit to half speed, an angel wing buff that increases unit speed by 2x, or a cherub buff that recovers 5 hp every 5 seconds for 3 minutes. A `GameplayEffect` affects an individual gameplay attribute in the `UAttributeSet` that's attached to an `AbilitySystemComponent` of an Actor.

Getting ready

Brainstorm your game units' effects that happen during the game. Be sure that you've created an `AttributeSet`, as shown in the previous recipe, with gameplay attributes that you'd like to affect. Select an effect to implement and follow the succeeding steps with your example.

 You may want to turn `LogAbilitySystem` into a `VeryVerbose` setting by going to the **Output Log** and typing `` ` ``, and then `Log LogAbilitySystem All`. This will display much more information from `AbilitySystem` in the **Output Log,** making it easier to see what's going on within the system.

How to do it...

In the following steps, we'll construct a quick `GameplayEffect` that heals `50 hp` to the selected unit's `AttributeSet`:

1. Open up the `Warrior.h` file we created previously. In there, add the following function definition:

   ```
   void TestGameplayEffect();
   ```

2. Afterwards, open up `Warrior.cpp` and add the following methods:

   ```
   inline UGameplayEffect* ConstructGameplayEffect(FString name)
   {
       return NewObject<UGameplayEffect>(GetTransientPackage(),
   FName(*name));
   }

   inline FGameplayModifierInfo& AddModifier(
       UGameplayEffect* Effect, UProperty* Property,
       EGameplayModOp::Type Op,
       const FGameplayEffectModifierMagnitude& Magnitude)
   {
       int32 index = Effect->Modifiers.Num();
       Effect->Modifiers.SetNum(index + 1);
       FGameplayModifierInfo& Info = Effect->Modifiers[index];
       Info.ModifierMagnitude = Magnitude;
       Info.ModifierOp = Op;
       Info.Attribute.SetUProperty(Property);
       return Info;
   }
   ```

3. Then, add the following code to implement:

```
void AWarrior::TestGameplayEffect()
{
    // Construct & retrieve UProperty to affect
    UGameplayEffect* RecoverHP =
ConstructGameplayEffect("RecoverHP");

    // Compile-time checked retrieval of Hp UPROPERTY()
    // from our UGameUnitAttributeSet class (listed in
    // UGameUnitAttributeSet.h)
    UProperty* hpProperty = FindFieldChecked<UProperty>(
        UGameUnitAttributeSet::StaticClass(),
        GET_MEMBER_NAME_CHECKED(UGameUnitAttributeSet, Hp));

}
```

4. Use the `AddModifier` function to change the `Hp` field of `GameUnitAttributeSet`, as follows:

```
// Command the addition of +5 HP to the hpProperty
  AddModifier(RecoverHP, hpProperty, EGameplayModOp::Additive,
FScalableFloat(50.f));
```

5. Fill in the other properties of `GameplayEffect`, including fields such as `DurationPolicy` and `ChanceToApplyToTarget`, or any other fields that you'd like to modify, as follows:

```
// .. for a fixed-duration of 10 seconds ..
RecoverHP->DurationPolicy =
EGameplayEffectDurationType::HasDuration;
RecoverHP->DurationMagnitude = FScalableFloat(10.f);

// .. with 100% chance of success ..
RecoverHP->ChanceToApplyToTarget = 1.f;

// .. with recurrency (Period) of 0.5 seconds
RecoverHP->Period = 0.5f;
```

6. Apply the effect to an `AbilitySystemComponent` of your choice. The underlying `UAttributeSet` will be affected and modified by your call, as shown in the following piece of code:

```
FActiveGameplayEffectHandle recoverHpEffectHandle =
    AbilitySystemComponent->ApplyGameplayEffectToTarget(
        RecoverHP, AbilitySystemComponent, 1.f);
```

How it works...

GamePlayEffects are simply little objects that effect changes to an actor's
AttributeSet. GameplayEffects can occur once, or repeatedly, in intervals over a
Period. You can program-in effects pretty quickly, and the GameplayEffect class
creation is intended to be inline.

There's more...

Once the GameplayEffect is active, you will receive an
FActiveGameplayEffectHandle. You can use this handle to attach a function
delegate to run when the effect is over using the OnRemovedDelegate member of the
FActiveGameplayEffectHandle. For example, you might call the following code:

```
FOnActiveGameplayEffectRemoved* ep = AbilitySystemComponent->
    OnGameplayEffectRemovedDelegate(recoverHpEffectHandle);

if (ep)
{
    ep->AddLambda([]()
    {
        UE_LOG(LogTemp, Warning, TEXT("Recover effect has been
removed."), 1);
    });
}
```

GameplayTasks API – making things
happen with GameplayTasks

GameplayTasks are used to wrap up some gameplay functionality in a reusable
object. All you have to do to use them is derive from the UGameplayTask base class
and override some of the member functions that you prefer to implement.

Getting ready

If you have not done so already, complete Steps 1-4 of the *GameplayAbilities API – triggering an actor's gameplay abilities with game controls* recipe to link to the `GameplayTasks` API in your `ProjectName.Build.cs` file and enable its functionality.

Afterwards, go in the UE4 Editor and navigate to **Class Viewer** by going to **Window | Developer Tools | Class Viewer**. Under **Filters**, uncheck the **Actors Only** and **Placeable Only** options.

Ensure that the `GameplayTask` object type exists:

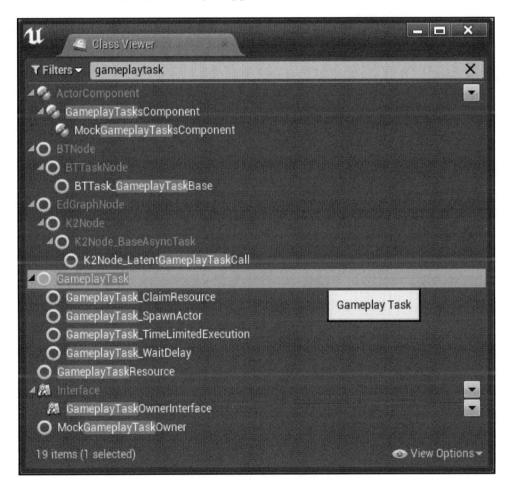

How to do it...

1. Click on **File** | **Add C++ Class....** Choose to derive from GameplayTask. To do so, you must first tick **Show All Classes**, and then type gameplaytask into the filter box. Click on **Next**:

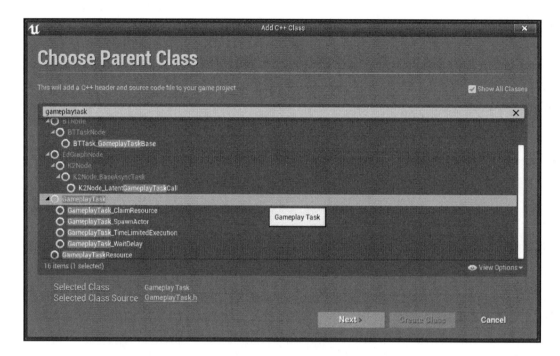

2. Name your C++ class (something like GameplayTask_TaskName is the convention), then add the class to your project. The example spawns a particle emitter and is called GameplayTask_CreateParticles:

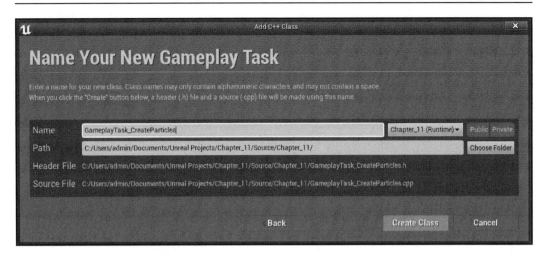

3. Once your `GameplayTask_CreateParticles.h` and `.cpp` pair are created, navigate to the `.h` file and update the class to the following:

```
#pragma once

#include "CoreMinimal.h"
#include "GameplayTask.h"
#include "Particles/ParticleSystem.h"
#include "GameplayTask_CreateParticles.generated.h"

/**
 *
 */
UCLASS()
class CHAPTER_11_API UGameplayTask_CreateParticles : public
UGameplayTask
{
    GENERATED_BODY()
public:
    virtual void Activate();

    // A static constructor for an instance of a
    // UGameplayTask_CreateEmitter instance,
    // including args of (what class of emitter, where to
    // create it).
    UFUNCTION(BlueprintCallable, Category = "GameplayTasks",
meta = (AdvancedDisplay = "TaskOwner", DefaultToSelf =
"TaskOwner", BlueprintInternalUseOnly = "TRUE"))
        static UGameplayTask_CreateParticles* ConstructTask(
            TScriptInterface<IGameplayTaskOwnerInterface>
TaskOwner,
```

```
                UParticleSystem* particleSystem,
                FVector location);

        UParticleSystem* ParticleSystem;
        FVector Location;

    };
```

4. Then, implement the `GameplayTask_CreateParticles.cpp` file, as follows:

```
#include "GameplayTask_CreateParticles.h"
#include "Kismet/GameplayStatics.h"

// Like a constructor.
UGameplayTask_CreateParticles*
UGameplayTask_CreateParticles::ConstructTask(
    TScriptInterface<IGameplayTaskOwnerInterface> TaskOwner,
    UParticleSystem* particleSystem,
    FVector location)
{
    UGameplayTask_CreateParticles* task =
    NewTask<UGameplayTask_CreateParticles>(TaskOwner);
    // Fill fields
    if (task)
    {
        task->ParticleSystem = particleSystem;
        task->Location = location;
    }
    return task;
}

void UGameplayTask_CreateParticles::Activate()
{
    Super::Activate();

    UGameplayStatics::SpawnEmitterAtLocation(GetWorld(),
    ParticleSystem, Location);
}
```

5. Open up your `Warrior.h` file and add the following interface to the class definition:

```
UCLASS()
class CHAPTER_11_API AWarrior : public ACharacter, public
IAbilitySystemInterface, public IGameplayTaskOwnerInterface
{
    GENERATED_BODY()
```

6. Afterwards, add the following new properties to it:

```
UPROPERTY(EditAnywhere, BlueprintReadWrite, Category = Stats)
UGameplayTasksComponent* GameplayTasksComponent;

// This is the particleSystem that we create with the
// GameplayTask_CreateParticles object.
UPROPERTY(EditAnywhere, BlueprintReadWrite, Category = Stats)
UParticleSystem* particleSystem;
```

7. Below that, add the following function definitions for the `GameplayTaskOwnerInterface`:

```
// <GameplayTaskOwnerInterface>

virtual UGameplayTasksComponent* GetGameplayTasksComponent(const
UGameplayTask& Task) const { return GameplayTasksComponent; }

// This gets called both when task starts and when task gets
// resumed.
// Check Task.GetStatus() if you want to differentiate.
virtual void OnTaskActivated(UGameplayTask& Task) { }
virtual void OnTaskDeactivated(UGameplayTask& Task) { }

virtual AActor* GetOwnerActor(const UGameplayTask* Task) const {
    return Task->GetOwnerActor(); // This will give us the
// accurate answer for the Task..
}
// </End GameplayTaskOwnerInterface>
```

8. Afterwards, go to the `Warrior.cpp` file and update the class constructor to the following:

```
AWarrior::AWarrior()
{
    // Set this character to call Tick() every frame. You can
    // turn this off to improve performance if you don't need
    // it.
    PrimaryActorTick.bCanEverTick = true;
```

```
    AbilitySystemComponent =
CreateDefaultSubobject<UAbilitySystemComponent>
    ("UAbilitySystemComponent");
    GameplayTasksComponent =
CreateDefaultSubobject<UGameplayTasksComponent>
    ("UGameplayTasksComponent");
}
```

9. Save your scripts, return to the Unreal Editor, and compile your code. Once compiled, open your `Actor` class derivative (`MyWarrior`) and then scroll down to the **Stats** section and set the **Particle System** property to something you'd like to see, for instance, the `P_Fire` option if you included the sample content when you created your project:

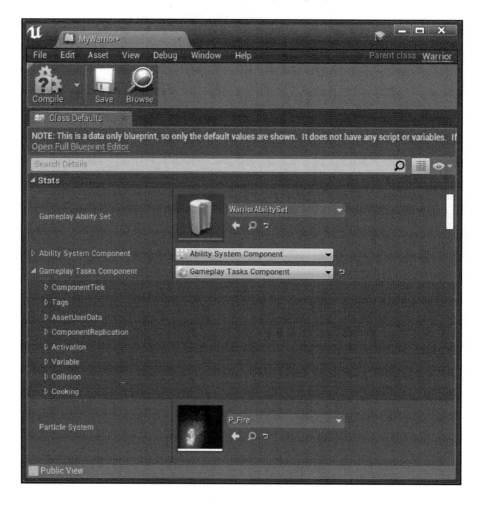

10. Which is available in the **Full Blueprint Editor** in the **Components** drop-down of the **Components** tab in the Blueprint editor. Add `GameplayTasksComponent` to

11. Create and add an instance of your `GameplayTask` inside your `Actor` derivative (`MyWarrior`) instance using the following code:

```
UGameplayTask_CreateParticles* task =
    UGameplayTask_CreateParticles::ConstructTask(this,
    particleSystem, FVector(200.f, 0.f, 200.f));

if (GameplayTasksComponent && task)
{
    GameplayTasksComponent->AddTaskReadyForActivation(*task);
}
```

This code runs anywhere in your `Actor` class derivative, any time after `GameplayTasksComponent` is initialized (any time after `PostInitializeComponents()`).

12. Compile your code. Set your level to use `MyWarrior` as the **Default Pawn Type** and when the game starts, you should notice that the particle plays:

How it works...

GamePlayTasks simply register with the GameplayTasksComponent situated inside an Actor class derivative of your choice. You can activate any number of GameplayTasks at any time during gameplay to trigger their effects.

GameplayTasks can also kick off GameplayEffects to change attributes of AbilitySystemsComponents if you wish.

There's more...

You can derive GameplayTasks for any number of events in your game. What's more is that you can override a few more virtual functions to hook into additional functionality.

HTTP API – downloading webpages using web requests

When you're maintaining scoreboards or other such things that require regular HTTP request access to servers, you can use the HTTP API to perform such web request tasks.

Getting ready

Have a server that you're allowed to request data via HTTP from. You can use a public server of any type to try out HTTP requests, if you'd like.

How to do it...

1. Link to the HTTP API in your ProjectName.Build.cs file:

```
using UnrealBuildTool;

public class Chapter_11 : ModuleRules
{
    public Chapter_11(ReadOnlyTargetRules Target) :
base(Target)
```

```
        {
                PCHUsage = PCHUsageMode.UseExplicitOrSharedPCHs;
                PublicDependencyModuleNames.AddRange(new string[] {
                "Core", "CoreUObject", "Engine", "InputCore" });
                PublicDependencyModuleNames.AddRange(new string[] {
                "GameplayAbilities", "GameplayTags", "GameplayTasks"
        });

                PublicDependencyModuleNames.AddRange(new string[] {
                "HTTP" });

                PrivateDependencyModuleNames.AddRange(new string[] {
        });

                // Uncomment if you are using Slate UI
                // PrivateDependencyModuleNames.AddRange(new string[]
                // { "Slate", "SlateCore" });
                // Uncomment if you are using online features
                //
        PrivateDependencyModuleNames.Add("OnlineSubsystem");

                // To include OnlineSubsystemSteam, add it to the
        plugins section in your uproject file with the Enabled
        attribute set to true
            }
        }
```

2. In the file that you will send your web request from (in my case, I'll be using the `Chapter_11GameModeBase` class), include the new additions to the following code snippet:

```
#pragma once

#include "CoreMinimal.h"
#include "GameFramework/GameModeBase.h"
#include "Runtime/Online/HTTP/Public/HttpManager.h"
#include "Runtime/Online/HTTP/Public/HttpModule.h"
#include "Runtime/Online/HTTP/Public/HttpRetrySystem.h"
#include
"Runtime/Online/HTTP/Public/Interfaces/IHttpResponse.h"
using namespace FHttpRetrySystem;
#include "Chapter_11GameModeBase.generated.h"
```

3. Construct an `IHttpRequest` object from `FHttpModule` using the following code:

```
TSharedRef<IHttpRequest>
 http=FHttpModule::Get().CreateRequest();
```

FHttpModule is a singleton object. One copy of it exists for the entire program that you are meant to use for all interactions with the FHttpModule class.

4. Attach your function to run to the IHttpRequest object's FHttpRequestCompleteDelegate, which has the following signature:

```
void HttpRequestComplete( FHttpRequestPtr request,
    FHttpResponsePtr response, bool success );
```

5. The delegate is found inside of the IHttpRequest object as http->OnProcessRequestComplete():

```
FHttpRequestCompleteDelegate& delegate = http-
    >OnProcessRequestComplete();
```

There are a few ways to attach a callback function to the delegate. You can use the following methods:

- A lambda using delegate.BindLambda():

```
delegate.BindLambda(
    // Anonymous, inlined code function (aka lambda)
    []( FHttpRequestPtr request, FHttpResponsePtr response, bool
    success ) -> void
{
    UE_LOG( LogTemp, Warning, TEXT( "Http Response: %d, %s" ),
    request->GetResponse()->GetResponseCode(),
    *request->GetResponse()->GetContentAsString() );
});
```

6. Specify the URL of the site you'd like to hit:

```
http->SetURL( TEXT( "http://unrealengine.com" ) );
```

7. Process the request by calling ProcessRequest:

```
http->ProcessRequest();
```

Then, when you run this code, you should notice the contents of the URL you pointed to being displayed:

HTML content of unrealengine.com displayed

Of course, in this instance, it's a web page, but you can easily point this to a CSV file, text document, or anything to obtain information for your project!

How it works...

The HTTP object is all you need to send off HTTP requests to a server and get HTTP responses. You can use the HTTP request/response for anything that you wish; for example, submitting scores to a high scores table or to retrieve text to display in-game from a server.

They are decked out with a URL to visit and a function callback to run when the request is complete. Finally, they are sent off via `FManager`. When the web server responds, your callback is called and the results of your HTTP response can be shown.

There's more...

There are also other ways in which you can attach a callback function to the delegate:

- Using any UObject's member function:

```
delegate.BindUObject(this,
&AChapter_11GameModeBase::HttpRequestComplete);
```

You cannot attach to UFunction directly here as the .BindUFunction() command requests arguments that are all UCLASS, USTRUCT, or UENUM.

- With any plain old C++ object's member function, using .BindRaw:

```
PlainObject* plainObject = new PlainObject();
delegate.BindRaw( plainObject, &PlainObject::httpHandler );
  // plainObject cannot be DELETED Until httpHandler gets
  // called..
```

You have to ensure that your plainObject refers to a valid object in memory at the time that the HTTP request completes. This means that you cannot use TAutoPtr on plainObject, because that will deallocate plainObject at the end of the block in which it is declared, but that may be before the HTTP request completes.

- Using a global C-style static function:

```
// C-style function for handling the HTTP response:
void httpHandler( FHttpRequestPtr request,
FHttpResponsePtr response, bool success )
{
   Info( "static: Http req handled" );
}
delegate.BindStatic( &httpHandler );
```

When using a delegate callback with an object, be sure that the object instance that you're calling back on lives on at least until the point at which the HttpResponse arrives back from the server. Processing the HttpRequest takes real time to run. It is a web request after all—think of waiting for a web page to load.

You have to be sure that the object instance on which you're calling the callback function has not deallocated on you between the time of the initial call and the invocation of your `HttpHandler` function. The object must still be in memory when the callback returns after the HTTP request completes.

You cannot simply expect that the `HttpResponse` function happens immediately after you attach the callback function and call `ProcessRequest()`! Using a reference counted `UObject` instance to attach the `HttpHandler` member function is a good idea to ensure that the object stays in memory until the HTTP request completes.

You can see an example of all seven possible ways it can be used inside of the `Chapter_11GameModeBase.cpp` file in the Example Code for this chapter.

You can set additional HTTP request parameters via the following member functions:

- `SetVerb()`, to change whether you are using the GET or POST method in your HTTP request
- `SetHeaders()`, to modify any general header settings you would like

HTTP API – displaying downloaded progress

The `IHttpRequest` object from the HTTP API will report HTTP download progress via a callback on a `FHttpRequestProgressDelegate`, which is accessible via `OnRequestProgress()`. The signature of the function we can attach to the `OnRequestProgress()` delegate is as follows:

```
HandleRequestProgress( FHttpRequestPtr request, int32
  sentBytes, int32 receivedBytes )
```

The three parameters of the function you may write include the original `IHttpRequest` object, the bytes sent, and the bytes received so far. This function gets called back periodically until the `IHttpRequest` object completes, which is when the function you attach to `OnProcessRequestComplete()` when it gets called. You can use the values passed to your `HandleRequestProgress` function to find out your progress.

Getting ready

You will need an internet connection to use this recipe. We will be requesting a file from a public server. You can use a public server or your own private server for your HTTP request, if you'd like.

In this recipe, we will bind a callback function to just the `OnRequestProgress()` delegate to display the download progress of a file from a server. Have a project ready where we can write a piece of code that will perform `IHttpRequest`, and a nice interface on which to display percentage progress.

How to do it...

1. Link to the `HTTP` API in your `ProjectName.Build.cs` file.
2. Construct an `IHttpRequest` object using the following code:

```
TSharedRef<IHttpRequest> http =
  HttpModule::Get().CreateRequest();
```

3. Provide a callback function to call when the request progresses, which updates our user:

```
http->OnRequestProgress().BindLambda(
    [this](FHttpRequestPtr request, int32 sentBytes, int32
    receivedBytes)
    -> void
    {
        int32 contentLen =
        request->GetResponse()->GetContentLength();
        float percentComplete = 100.f * receivedBytes /
        contentLen;

        UE_LOG(LogTemp, Warning, TEXT("Progress sent=%d bytes
/
        received=%d/%d bytes [%.0f%%]"), sentBytes,
receivedBytes,
        contentLen, percentComplete);

    });
```

4. Process your request with `http->ProcessRequest()`.

How it works...

The `OnRequestProgress()` callback gets fired every so often with the bytes sent and bytes received HTTP progress. We will compute the total percentage of the download that is completed by calculating `(float) receivedBytes/totalLen`, where `totalLen` is the HTTP response's total length in bytes. Using the lambda function we attached to the `OnRequestProgress()` delegate callback, we can display the information through text.

 With the code in the previous *How to do it...* section as a base, it would be possible to create a UMG widget for a progress bar and call the `.SetPercent()` member function to reflect the download's progress.

12
Multiplayer Networking in UE4

In this chapter, we are going to cover the following topics:

- Testing your game as a client and a server simultaneously
- Replicating properties over the network
- Replicating functions over the network
- Handling UI network events

Introduction

Networking is one of the more complex things you can do as a programmer. Thankfully, Unreal Engine has been designed with networking in mind since the original Unreal Engine released in 1998. Unreal uses a client-server model for communication between multiple computers. In this case, the **server** is the person who started the game and the **clients** are those who are playing the game with the first person. For things that are happening in everyone's game to work correctly, we need to call certain code at certain times for certain people.

For example, when a client wants to shoot his/her gun, they send a message to the server, which will then determine whether they hit anything and then tells all the clients what happened using replication. This can be important because some things, such as the game mode, only exist on the server.

 For more information on the client-server model, check out `https:/`
`/en.wikipedia.org/wiki/Client%E2%80%93server_model`.

Since we are going to want to see multiple characters on the screen, in this chapter, we will be using a base project based on the **Third Person** C++ template:

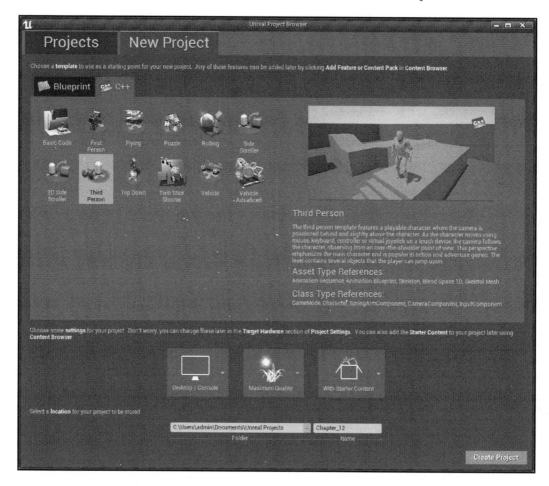

Technical requirements

This chapter requires the use of Unreal Engine 4 and uses Visual Studio 2017 as the IDE. Instructions on how to install both pieces of software and the requirements for them can be found in Chapter 1, *UE4 Development Tools*, of this book.

Testing your game as a client and a server simultaneously

When working on networked games, it's always a good idea to test your project often. Instead of having to use two separate computers, Unreal comes with an easy way to play a game with multiple players at the same time built in.

How to do it...

Generally, when we play the game, we only have one player on the screen. We can modify this with the **Play** settings:

1. From the Unreal Editor, with the `ThirdPersonExampleMap` open, click on the arrow drop-down next to the **Play** button. Under there, set the **Number of Players** property to 2:

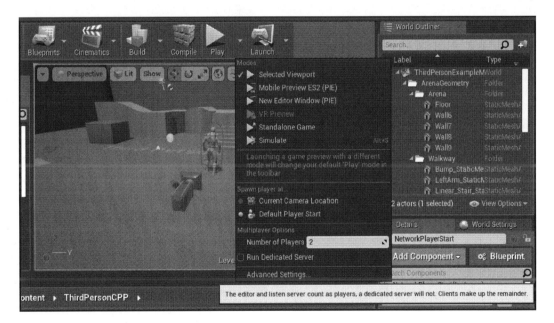

2. Afterwards, click on the **Play** button:

As you can see, you now have two windows added to the screen!

 Remember that you can return mouse control from a window by pressing *Shift + F1*.

How it works...

In addition to the character that is also placed in the scene, there is another object within the world called `NetworkPlayerStart`, which is where networked players will be spawned:

> **TIP**
>
> If you add more **Player Start** objects into the scene, by default, objects will pick a **Player Start** randomly from the ones available. You can quickly create new ones by holding the *Alt* key down and dragging an object in the new direction.

Replicating properties over the network

To ensure that the values are the same on both clients and servers, we use the process of replication. In this recipe, we will see just how easy it is to do so.

How to do it...

For this simple example, let's create a variable to store how many times each player jumps within the game:

1. Open up Visual Studio and open the definition for your character for your project (in my case, it is `Chapter_12Character.h`). Add the following property and function declaration to the file:

   ```
   UPROPERTY(Replicated, EditAnywhere)
   uint32 JumpCount;

   void Jump() override;
   ```

2. Then, go to the implementation file and add the following `#include`:

   ```
   #include "UnrealNetwork.h" // DOREPLIFETIME
   ```

3. Afterwards, we need to tell the `SetupPlayerInputComponent` method to use our version of `Jump` instead of the parent class's:

   ```
   void AChapter_12Character::SetupPlayerInputComponent(class
   UInputComponent* PlayerInputComponent)
   {
     // Set up gameplay key bindings
     check(PlayerInputComponent);
     PlayerInputComponent->BindAction("Jump", IE_Pressed, this,
   &AChapter_12Character::Jump);
     PlayerInputComponent->BindAction("Jump", IE_Released, this,
   &ACharacter::StopJumping);

     . . .
   ```

4. Then, we need to add the following functions:

```cpp
void AChapter_12Character::Jump()
{
    Super::Jump();

    JumpCount++;

    if (Role == ROLE_Authority)
    {
        // Only print function once
        GEngine->AddOnScreenDebugMessage(-1, 5.0f,
            FColor::Green,
            FString::Printf(TEXT("%s called Jump %d times!"),
            *GetName(), JumpCount)
        );
    }


}

void
AChapter_12Character::GetLifetimeReplicatedProps(TArray<FLifet
imeProperty>&
    OutLifetimeProps) const
{
    Super::GetLifetimeReplicatedProps(OutLifetimeProps);

    // Replicate to every client
    //DOREPLIFETIME(AChapter_12Character, JumpCount);
}
```

5. Save your script and return to the Unreal Editor. Compile your script and play your game:

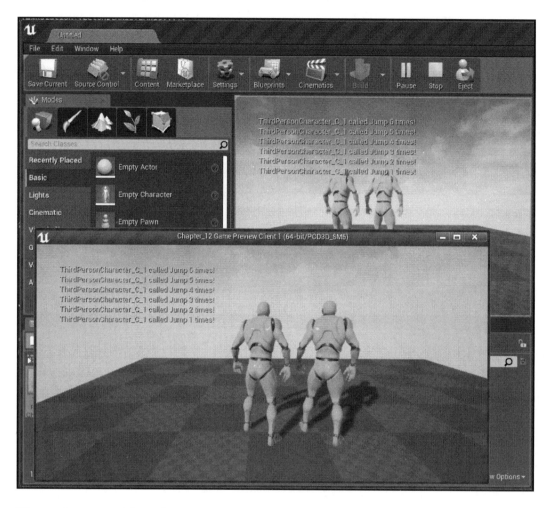

Now, whenever either player presses the *spacebar*, you'll see a message displaying their name and the value that it will have.

How it works...

Property replication is simple in theory. Whenever a variable changes its value, the network should notify all clients of the change and then update the variable. This is often used for things like health, where the value is extremely important to know.

When you register a variable like this, this variable should only be modified by the server and then replicated to the other clients. To mark something to be replicated, we use the `Replicated` specifier inside of the UPROPERTY.

After marking something as replicated, we have to define a new function called `GetLifetimeReplicatedProps`, which does not need to be declared in the header file. Inside of this function, we use the DOREPLIFETIME macro to state that whenever the `JumpCount` variable changes on the server, all clients need to modify the value as well.

Inside of the `Jump` function, we added in some new functionality, but we first check the `Role` variable to determine if something should happen or not. `ROLE_Authority` is the highest level, which means that you're the server. This ensures that our functionality will only happen once rather than multiple times.

For replication to work, make sure that the `bReplicates` variable is set to `true`. This should be done in the constructor of the class.

There's more...

For those that want to add a bit of optimization to their code, instead of our current DOREPLIFETIME macro, you could use the following instead:

```
void
AChapter_12Character::GetLifetimeReplicatedProps(TArray<FLifetimeProperty>&
    OutLifetimeProps) const
{
    Super::GetLifetimeReplicatedProps(OutLifetimeProps);

    // Replicate to every client
    //DOREPLIFETIME(AChapter_12Character, JumpCount);

    // Value is already updated locally, so we can skip replicating
    // the value for the owner
    DOREPLIFETIME_CONDITION(AChapter_12Character, JumpCount,
COND_SkipOwner);
}
```

This makes it so that the value is only replicated on other clients and not the original value.

For more information on DOREPLIFETIME_CONDITION and some other tips and tricks for networking, check out https://www.unrealengine.com/en-US/blog/network-tips-and-tricks.

Replicating functions over the network

In this recipe, we will see a nontrivial example of replication in use with a simple pickup object that we may want a player to keep track of.

How to do it...

The first step in creating our collectible would be to actually create the class we are going to use:

1. Navigate to **File | New C++ Class** and from there, in the **Choose Parent Class** window, select **Actor** and then click on **Next**:

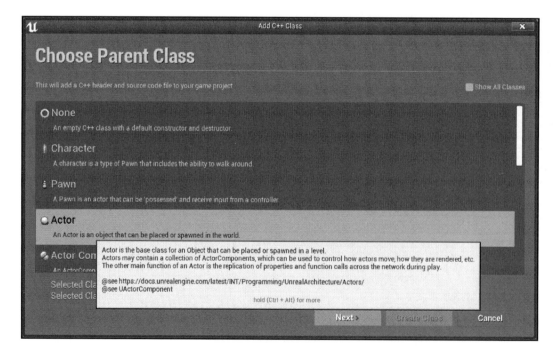

2. From the next window, set the **Name** property to `CollectibleObject` and click on the **Create Class** button to add it to the project and compile the base code:

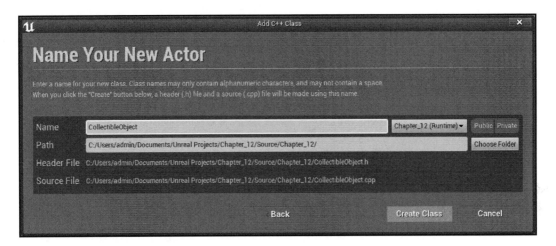

3. Once Visual Studio opens up, update `CollectibleObject.h` to the following:

```
#pragma once

#include "CoreMinimal.h"
#include "GameFramework/Actor.h"
#include "CollectibleObject.generated.h"

UCLASS()
class CHAPTER_12_API ACollectibleObject : public AActor
{
    GENERATED_BODY()
public:
    // Sets default values for this actor's properties
    ACollectibleObject();

    // Event called when something starts to overlaps the
    // sphere collider
    // Note: UFUNCTION required for replication callbacks
    UFUNCTION()
    void OnBeginOverlap(class UPrimitiveComponent*
        HitComp,
        class AActor* OtherActor,
        class UPrimitiveComponent*
        OtherComp,
```

```
        int32 OtherBodyIndex, bool
        bFromSweep,
        const FHitResult& SweepResult);

    // Our server function to update the score.
    UFUNCTION(Reliable, Server, WithValidation)
    void UpdateScore(int32 Amount);

    void UpdateScore_Implementation(int32 Amount);
    bool UpdateScore_Validate(int32 Amount);

protected:
    // Called when the game starts or when spawned
    virtual void BeginPlay() override;

public:
    // Called every frame
    virtual void Tick(float DeltaTime) override;

};
```

4. Then, inside of `CollectibleObject.cpp`, update the constructor of the class to the following:

```
#include "ConstructorHelpers.h"
#include "Components/SphereComponent.h"

// ...

// Sets default values
ACollectibleObject::ACollectibleObject()
{
    // Set this actor to call Tick() every frame. You can turn
this off to improve performance if you don't need it.
    PrimaryActorTick.bCanEverTick = true;

    // Must be true for an Actor to replicate anything
    bReplicates = true;

    // Create a sphere collider for players to hit
    USphereComponent * SphereCollider =
CreateDefaultSubobject<USphereComponent>(TEXT("SphereComponent
"));

    // Sets the root of our object to be the sphere collider
    RootComponent = SphereCollider;

    // Sets the size of our collider to have a radius of
```

```
    // 64 units
    SphereCollider->InitSphereRadius(64.0f);

    // Makes it so that OnBeginOverlap will be called
    // whenever something hits this.
    SphereCollider->OnComponentBeginOverlap.AddDynamic(this,
&ACollectibleObject::OnBeginOverlap);

    // Create a visual to make it easier to see
    UStaticMeshComponent * SphereVisual =
CreateDefaultSubobject<UStaticMeshComponent>(TEXT("Static
Mesh"));

    // Attach the static mesh to the root
    SphereVisual->SetupAttachment(RootComponent);

    // Get a reference to a sphere mesh
    auto MeshAsset =
ConstructorHelpers::FObjectFinder<UStaticMesh>(TEXT("StaticMes
h'/Engine/BasicShapes/Sphere.Sphere'"));

    // Assign the mesh if valid
    if (MeshAsset.Object != nullptr)
    {
        SphereVisual->SetStaticMesh(MeshAsset.Object);
    }

    // Resize to be smaller than the larger sphere collider
    SphereVisual->SetWorldScale3D(FVector(0.5f));


}
```

5. Afterwards, implement the `OnBeginOverlap` function:

```
// Event called when something starts to overlaps the
// sphere collider
void ACollectibleObject::OnBeginOverlap(
    class UPrimitiveComponent* HitComp,
    class AActor* OtherActor,
    class UPrimitiveComponent* OtherComp,
    int32 OtherBodyIndex,
    bool bFromSweep,
    const FHitResult& SweepResult)
{
    // If I am the server
    if (Role == ROLE_Authority)
    {
```

```
        // Then a coin will be gained!
        UpdateScore(1);
        Destroy();
    }
}
```

6. Then, implement the `UpdateScore_Implementation` and `UpdateScore_Validate` methods:

```
// Do something here that modifies game state.
void ACollectibleObject::UpdateScore_Implementation(int32
    Amount)
{
    if (GEngine)
    {
        GEngine->AddOnScreenDebugMessage(-1, 5.0f,
            FColor::Green,
            "Collected!");
    }
}

// Optionally validate the request and return false if the
// function should not be run.
bool ACollectibleObject::UpdateScore_Validate(int32 Amount)
{
    return true;
}
```

7. Save the scripts and then return to the Unity Editor. Compile your scripts and then drag an instance of the `Collectible Object` class into a scene. Save your level and play the game using two players, as shown in the previous recipe.
8. Upon collecting the object, you should see a message displayed on the screen:

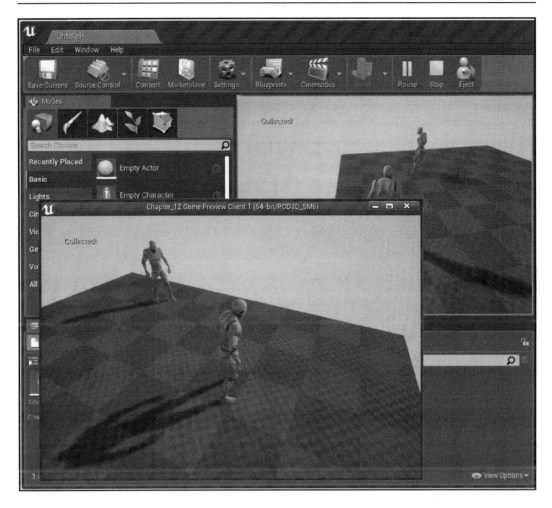

With this, you can see how we can have a message replicated from a server to the client!

How it works...

In the `CollectibleObject` class's constructor, we make sure that our object is going to be replicated. After that, we create a sphere collider that we tell (via a listener) to call the `OnBeginOverlap` function when it collides with another object. To do that, we use the `OnComponentBeginOverlap` function.

For more information on the `OnComponentBeginOverlap` function and the function that needs to be given to it, refer to `https://docs.unrealengine.com/latest/INT/API/ Runtime/Engine/Components/ UPrimitiveComponent/ OnComponentBeginOverlap/index.html`.

After this, inside our `OnBeginOverlap` function, we first check if we are currently on the server. We don't want things to get called multiple times, and we want the server to be the one that tells the other clients that we've increased our score.

We also call the `UpdateScore` function. This function has had the following function specifiers added to it:

- `Reliable`: The function will be replicated over the network and make it so that it is guaranteed to arrive, regardless of network errors or bandwidth issues. It requires us to select either `Client` or `Server` as an additional specifier.
- `Server`: Specifies that the function should only be called on the server. Adds an additional function that has `_Implementation` at the end of it, which is where the implementation should happen. The automatically generated code will use this function as needed.
- `WithValidation`: Adds an additional function that needs to be implemented with `_Validate` at the end. This function will take in the same parameters as the function given, but will return a bool that indicates whether the call to the main function should happen or not.

For more information on the other function specifiers, such as `Unreliable`, check out `https://docs.unrealengine.com/en-US/ Programming/UnrealArchitecture/Reference/ Functions#functionspecifiers`.

Calling `UpdateScore` will, in turn, call the `UpdateScore_Implementation` function that we created and it will display a message, saying that we've collected the object by printing out some text like we used earlier.

Finally, the `UpdateScore_Validate` function is required and just tells the game that we should always run the implementation for the `UpdateScore` function.

For some recommendations on performance and bandwidth settings that may be useful for working with levels with a lot of replication, check out the following link: `https://docs.unrealengine.com/en-US/Gameplay/Networking/Actors/ReplicationPerformance`.

See also...

If you're interested in seeing another example of using networking and replication, refer to `https://wiki.unrealengine.com/ Networking/Replication`.

In addition, you can also check out the Shooter Game example project included with Unreal Engine 4 and read the files to get a feeling for how it's used in a complete example. To read more about that, check out `https://docs.unrealengine.com/en-us/Resources/SampleGames/ShooterGame`.

Handling UI network events

Since each player has their own screen, it makes sense that their UI will only display information that is relevant to them. In this recipe, we will see how to handle UI network events.

Getting ready...

You should complete the *Replication properties over the network* recipe in this chapter, as well as be familiar with creating HUDs, which you can learn more about in `Chapter 14`, *User Interfaces – UI and UMG*.

How to do it...

1. From your Visual Studio project (**File | Open Visual Studio**), open the `Source\<Module>` folder and from there, open the `<Module>.build.cs` file (in my case, it would be `Source\Chapter_12\Chapter_12.build.cs`) and uncomment/add the following line of code:

```
using UnrealBuildTool;

public class Chapter_12 : ModuleRules
{
  public Chapter_12(ReadOnlyTargetRules Target) : base(Target)
  {
    PCHUsage = PCHUsageMode.UseExplicitOrSharedPCHs;

    PublicDependencyModuleNames.AddRange(new string[] {
```

```
"Core", "CoreUObject", "Engine", "InputCore",
"HeadMountedDisplay" });

        PrivateDependencyModuleNames.AddRange(new string[] {
"Slate", "SlateCore" });
    }
}
```

2. Create a new HUD subclass using the **Add C++ Class** wizard:

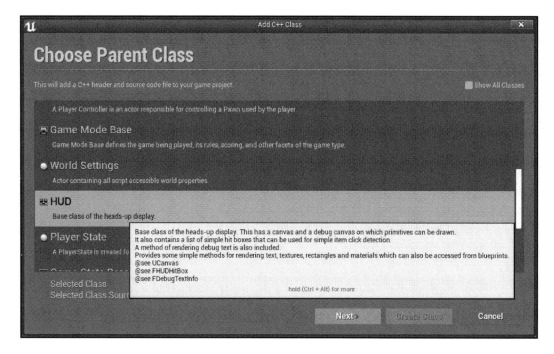

3. When asked for the name, put in NetworkHUD, and click on the **Create Class** button:

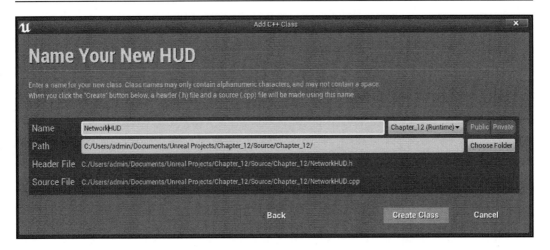

4. Once created, open up a GameMode that you are planning on using (I'm using the Chapter_12GameMode.cpp file) and add the following to the constructor implementation:

```cpp
#include "Chapter_12GameMode.h"
#include "Chapter_12Character.h"
#include "NetworkHUD.h"
#include "UObject/ConstructorHelpers.h"

AChapter_12GameMode::AChapter_12GameMode()
{
  // set default pawn class to our Blueprinted character
  static ConstructorHelpers::FClassFinder<APawn>
PlayerPawnBPClass(TEXT("/Game/ThirdPersonCPP/Blueprints/ThirdP
ersonCharacter"));
  if (PlayerPawnBPClass.Class != NULL)
  {
    DefaultPawnClass = PlayerPawnBPClass.Class;
  }

  HUDClass = ANetworkHUD::StaticClass();
}
```

5. Inside NetworkHUD.h, add the following function with the override keyword to the class:

```cpp
#pragma once

#include "CoreMinimal.h"
#include "GameFramework/HUD.h"
#include "NetworkHUD.generated.h"
```

```
/**
 *
 */
UCLASS()
class CHAPTER_12_API ANetworkHUD : public AHUD
{
    GENERATED_BODY()

public:
    virtual void DrawHUD() override;
};
```

6. Now, implement the function:

```
#include "NetworkHUD.h"
#include "Engine/Canvas.h"
#include "Chapter_12Character.h"

void ANetworkHUD::DrawHUD()
{
    Super::DrawHUD();

    AChapter_12Character* PlayerCharacter =
Cast<AChapter_12Character>(GetOwningPawn());

    if(PlayerCharacter)
    {
        Canvas->DrawText(GEngine->GetMediumFont(),
FString::Printf(TEXT("Called Jump %d times!"),
PlayerCharacter->JumpCount), 10, 10);
    }
}
```

7. Finally, we can comment out the original debug message since our HUD will handle it for us:

```
void AChapter_12Character::Jump()
{
    Super::Jump();

    JumpCount++;

    //if (Role == ROLE_Authority)
    //{
    // // Only print function once
    // GEngine->AddOnScreenDebugMessage(-1, 5.0f,
    // FColor::Green,
    // FString::Printf(TEXT("%s called Jump %d times!"),
```

```
*GetName(), JumpCount));
    //}
}
```

8. Compile your code and launch the editor.

9. Within the editor, open the **World Settings** panel from the **Settings** drop-down menu:

10. In the **World Settings** dialog, select `Chapter_12GameMode` from the list under **GameMode Override**:

11. Play and verify that your custom HUD is drawing to the screen and that each character has their own jump value:

And with that, we can take these concepts to display any property that is being replicated!

How it works...

The GetOwningPawn method will return a pointer to the Pawn class the HUD is attached to. We cast that to our custom character-derived class and then can access the properties that the class has. In our case, we are using the variable that we previously added a Replicated tag to, which allows the HUD to update properly, depending on which screen we are using.

> For more information and additional examples of replication in use, check out https://wiki.unrealengine.com/Replication.

See also...

For those that would like to learn more about networking with Unreal Engine 4, Cedric 'eXi' Neukirchen has created a great guide that I recommend reading. You can find that at http://cedric-neukirchen.net/Downloads/Compendium/UE4_Network_Compendium_by_Cedric_eXi_Neukirchen.pdf.

AI for Controlling NPCs

13

In this chapter, we will cover the following recipes:

- Implementing a simple following behavior
- Laying down a Navigation Mesh
- Creating a Blackboard
- Creating a Behavior Tree
- Connecting a Behavior Tree to a Character
- Creating a BTService
- Creating a BTTask

Introduction

AI includes many aspects of a game's NPC, as well as player behavior. The general topic of AI includes pathfinding and NPC behavior. Generally, we term the selection of what the NPC does for a period of time within the game as behavior.

AI in UE4 is well supported. A number of constructs exist to allow basic AI programming from within the editor, but we will be focusing on using C++ to program elements while touching on engine aspects when needed.

To make it easier to visualize our AI character and the interactions with the player, in this chapter, I will be using the **C++ Third Person** template:

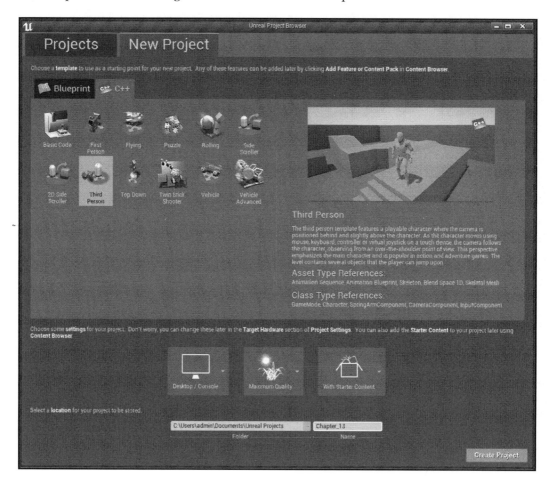

While I would love to cover all aspects of working with AI in Unreal Engine 4, that could take a whole book of its own. If you are interested in exploring AI even more after reading this chapter, I suggest that you check out *Unreal Engine 4 AI Programming Essentials*, also available from Packt Publishing.

Technical requirements

This chapter requires the use of Unreal Engine 4 and uses Visual Studio 2017 as the IDE. Instructions on how to install both pieces of software and the requirements for them can be found in `Chapter 1`, *UE4 Development Tools*.

Implementing a simple following behavior

The most simple way to implement any kind of AI is to just write it out by hand. This allows you to get something up-and-running quickly, but lacks the elegance and finesse that using Unreal's built-in systems gives us. This recipe gives us a super-simple implementation of making an object follow another one.

Getting ready

Have a UE4 project ready with a simple landscape or set of geometry on the ground, ideally with a *cul-de-sac* somewhere in the geometry to test AI movement functions. The `ThirdPersonExampleMap` that comes with the **C++ Third Person** template should work just fine.

How to do it...

1. Create a new C++ class that derives from `Character` by going to **Add New | New C++ Class**. Under the **Add C++ Class** menu, select **Character** and hit the **Next** button:

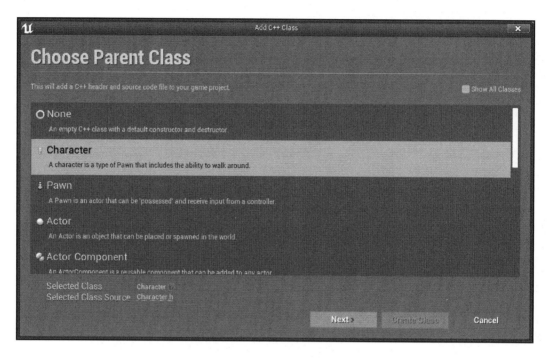

2. From the next screen, **Name** the class `FollowingCharacter` and click on the **Create Class** button:

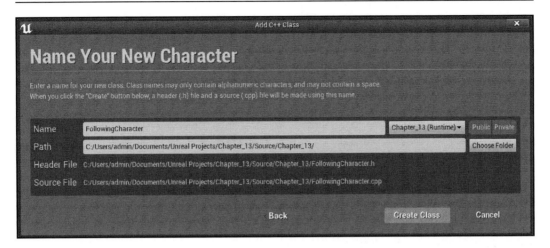

3. From the `FollowingCharacter.cpp` file, update the `Tick` function to the following:

```
void AFollowingCharacter::Tick(float DeltaTime)
{
    Super::Tick(DeltaTime);

    // Get current location
    auto startPos = GetActorLocation();

    // Get player's location
    FVector playerPos =
GetWorld()->GetFirstPlayerController()->GetPawn()->GetActorLoc
ation();

    // Get the direction to move in
    FVector direction = playerPos - startPos;
    direction.Normalize();

    // Move the player in that direction
    SetActorLocation(startPos + direction);
}
```

The `auto` keyword can be used for variable declarations if the compiler can deduce what the type of an object is from the assignment given to it.

4. Save your script and compile your code.

5. Drag and drop the **Following Character** into your scene. There is currently no visualization of the character, so go ahead and select the object. Then, from the **Details** tab, click the **Add Component** button. From there, select the **Cylinder** shape:

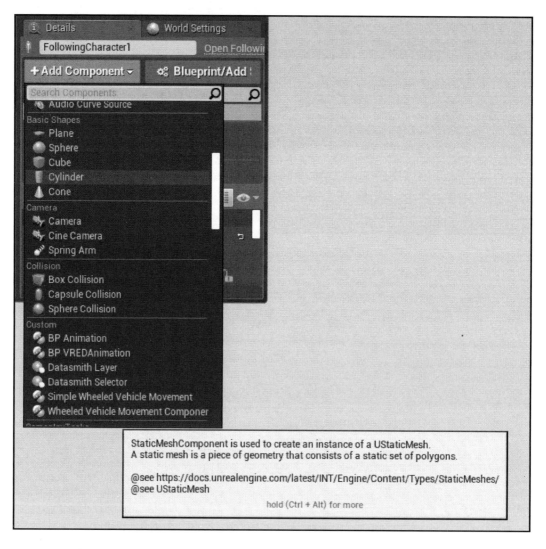

If all goes well, you should see the object on the screen.

The Following Character with a Cylinder shape added

6. Run the game and move around. You should notice that the cylinder will follow the player, no matter where they go!

How it works...

In this example, we are effectively *hard-coding* this enemy to follow the player character by doing simple vector math ourselves. While this technically works, it doesn't make use of Unreal's built-in AI functionality. It will also stop the AI at walls since there is no actual path-finding going on, and it will break the player character if you let the AI catch up. The player won't be able to move anymore due to collisions.

The rest of this chapter will be working with Unreal's actual built-in systems, which create a much more robust implementation.

Laying down a Navigation Mesh

A Navigation Mesh (also known as a **Nav Mesh**) is basically a definition of areas that an AI-controlled unit considers passable (that is, areas that the "AI-controlled" unit is allowed to move into or across). A Nav Mesh does not include geometry that would block the player if the player tried to move through it.

Getting ready

Constructing a Nav Mesh based on your scene's geometry is fairly easy in UE4. Start with a project that has some obstacles around it, or one that uses terrain. The `ThirdPersonExampleMap` included with the **C++ Third Person** template works well for this purpose.

How to do it...

To construct your Nav Mesh, simply perform the following steps:

1. Go to **Modes | Volumes**.
2. Drag the **Nav Mesh Bounds Volume** option onto your viewport.
3. Use the **Scale** tool to increase the size of the Nav Mesh so that it covers the area the actors that use the Nav Mesh should be allowed to navigate and pathfind in. To toggle the visibility of the completed Nav Mesh, press the *P* key:

A Nav Mesh drawn within the bounds of the Nav Mesh Bounds Volume

How it works...

A Nav Mesh doesn't block the player pawn (or other entities) from stepping on a certain geometry, but it serves to guide AI-controlled entities as to where they can and cannot go.

For more information on scaling objects in UE4, check out the following link: https://docs.unrealengine.com/en-us/Engine/Actors/Transform.

Creating a Blackboard

A **Blackboard** is a container for variables that are often used with Behavior Trees. This data is used for decision-making purposes, either by a single AI or a whole group of others. We will be creating a Blackboard here that we will then use in future recipes.

How to do it...

1. From the **Content Browser** under the Content folder, select **Add New** |
   Artificial Intelligence | **Blackboard**:

2. When asked for a name, provide `EnemyBlackboard`. Double-click on the file to open the Blackboard Editor.

3. From the Blackboard tab, click **New Key | Object**:

4. When asked for the name of the object, insert `Target`. Then, open the **Key Type** property by clicking the arrow to the left of the name and set the **Base Class** property to `Actor`:

5. Add any other properties you wish to have access to and then click on the **Save** button.

How it works...

In this recipe, we created a blackboard that we will later use in code to set and get the value of the player that we will use in our behavior tree.

Creating a Behavior Tree

If a Blackboard is the shared memory of an AI, the Behavior Tree is the AI's processor, which will contain the logic of the AI. It makes decisions, and then acts on those decisions to enable an AI to actually do something when the game is running. In this recipe, we will create a Behavior Tree and then assign its Blackboard.

How to do it...

1. From the **Content Browser** under the Content folder, select **Add New |
Artificial Intelligence | Behavior Tree**:

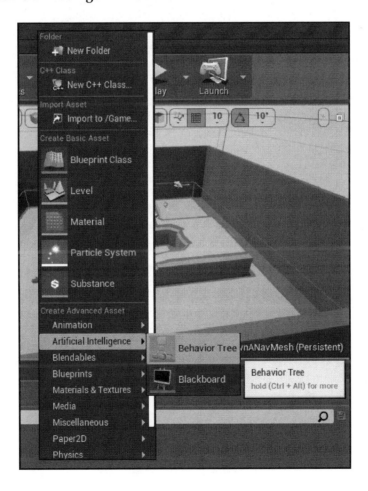

2. When asked for a name, provide `EnemyBehaviorTree`. Double-click on the file to open the Behavior Tree Editor.

3. Once opened, under the **Details** tab, open the **AI | Behavior Tree** section and verify that the **Blackboard Asset** property is set to `EnemyBlackboard`. You should notice the **Target** property we created listed under **Keys**. If not, close the editor and open it again:

A view of the Behavior Tree Editor

4. Once finished, click on the **Save** button.

How it works...

In this recipe, we created a Behavior Tree, which is required by the AI system so that it can fulfill tasks and other assorted features. In future recipes, we will use this to create our own custom Character classes.

Connecting a Behavior Tree to a Character

A `BehaviorTree` chooses a behavior to be exhibited by an AI-controlled unit at any given moment. Behavior Trees are relatively simple to construct, but there is a lot of setting up to do to get one running. You also have to be familiar with the components that are available for constructing your **Behavior Tree** to do so effectively.

A Behavior Tree is extremely useful for defining NPC behavior that is more varied than simply moving toward an opponent (as shown in the previous recipe with `AIMoveTo`).

Getting ready

Before starting this recipe, verify that you have completed the following recipes:

- *Laying down a Navigation Mesh*
- *Creating a Blackboard*
- *Creating a Behavior Tree*

How to do it...

1. Open up your `.Build.cs` file (in our case, `Chapter_13.Build.cs`) and add the following dependencies:

```
using UnrealBuildTool;

public class Chapter_13 : ModuleRules
{
  public Chapter_13(ReadOnlyTargetRules Target) : base(Target)
  {
    PCHUsage = PCHUsageMode.UseExplicitOrSharedPCHs;
```

```
        PublicDependencyModuleNames.AddRange(new string[] {
"Core", "CoreUObject", "Engine", "InputCore",
"HeadMountedDisplay" });
        PublicDependencyModuleNames.AddRange(new string[] {
"AIModule", "GameplayTasks" });


    }
}
```

2. Compile your code.

3. From the **Content Browser**, select **Add New | New C++ Class**. At the **Add C++ Class** menu, check the **Show All Classes** option type in AIController, and then select the AIController class. Then, click on **Next**:

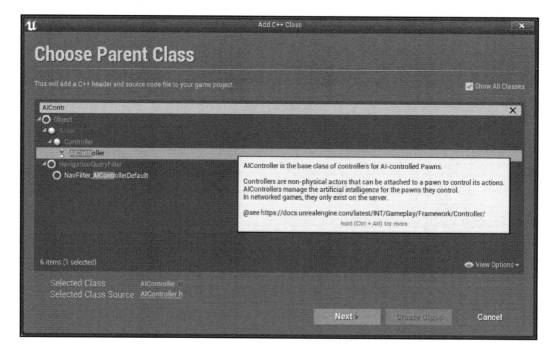

4. When asked for a name for the class, name it EnemyAIController and click on the **Create Class** button.

5. Open up Visual Studio and update the `EnemyAIController.h` file to the following:

```
#pragma once

#include "CoreMinimal.h"
#include "AIController.h"
#include "BehaviorTree/BehaviorTreeComponent.h"
#include "BehaviorTree/BlackboardComponent.h"
#include "EnemyAIController.generated.h"

/**
 *
 */
UCLASS()
class CHAPTER_13_API AEnemyAIController : public AAIController
{
    GENERATED_BODY()
private:
    // AI Component references
    UBehaviorTreeComponent* BehaviorComp;
    UBlackboardComponent* BlackboardComp;

public:
    AEnemyAIController();

    // Called when the controller possesses a Pawn/Character
    virtual void Possess(APawn* InPawn) override;

    FBlackboard::FKey TargetKeyID;

};
```

6. After creating the function declarations, we need to define them in the `EnemyAIController.cpp` file:

```
#include "EnemyAIController.h"

AEnemyAIController::AEnemyAIController()
{
    //Initialize components
    BehaviorComp =
CreateDefaultSubobject<UBehaviorTreeComponent>(TEXT("BehaviorC
omp"));
    BlackboardComp =
CreateDefaultSubobject<UBlackboardComponent>(TEXT("BlackboardC
omp"));
}
```

```
// Called when the controller possesses a Pawn/Character
void AEnemyAIController::Possess(APawn* InPawn)
{
    Super::Possess(InPawn);
}
```

In addition to an AI Controller, we also need to have a Character.

7. Create a new C++ class that derives from `Character` by going to **Add New | New C++ Class**. Under the **Add C++ Class** menu, select **Character** and hit the **Next** button:

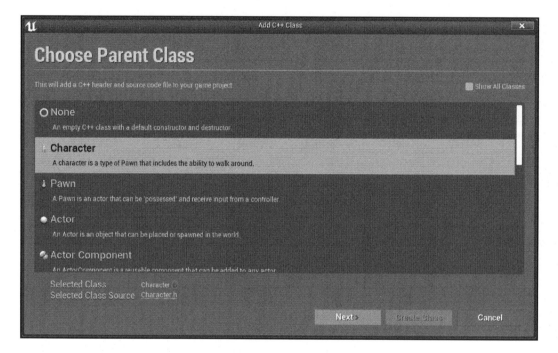

8. From the next screen, `Name` the class `EnemyCharacter` and click on the **Create Class** button.

9. Open Visual Studio. Under the `EnemyCharacter.h` file, add the following property:

```
#pragma once

#include "CoreMinimal.h"
#include "GameFramework/Character.h"
#include "EnemyCharacter.generated.h"

UCLASS()
class CHAPTER_13_API AEnemyCharacter : public ACharacter
{
    GENERATED_BODY()

public:
    // Sets default values for this character's properties
    AEnemyCharacter();

    UPROPERTY(EditAnywhere, Category = Behavior)
    class UBehaviorTree *EnemyBehaviorTree;

protected:
    // Called when the game starts or when spawned
    virtual void BeginPlay() override;

public:
    // Called every frame
    virtual void Tick(float DeltaTime) override;

    // Called to bind functionality to input
    virtual void SetupPlayerInputComponent(class
UInputComponent* PlayerInputComponent) override;

};
```

10. Then, we can go back into the `EnemyAIController.cpp` file and update the `Possess` function since our Character class exists:

```
#include "EnemyAIController.h"
#include "EnemyCharacter.h"
#include "BehaviorTree/BehaviorTree.h"


AEnemyAIController::AEnemyAIController()
{
    // Initialize components
    BehaviorComp =
CreateDefaultSubobject<UBehaviorTreeComponent>(TEXT("BehaviorC
```

```
omp"));
    BlackboardComp =
CreateDefaultSubobject<UBlackboardComponent>(TEXT("BlackboardC
omp"));
}

// Called when the controller possesses a Pawn/Character
void AEnemyAIController::Possess(APawn* InPawn)
{
    Super::Possess(InPawn);

    // Convert InPawn to EnemyCharacter
    auto Character = Cast<AEnemyCharacter>(InPawn);

    // Check if pointers are valid
    if(Character && Character->EnemyBehaviorTree)
    {
BlackboardComp->InitializeBlackboard(*Character->EnemyBehavior
Tree->BlackboardAsset);

        TargetKeyID = BlackboardComp->GetKeyID("Target");

BehaviorComp->StartTree(*Character->EnemyBehaviorTree);
    }
}
```

11. Save your scripts and compile your code.

    Now, we will create a Blueprint version of the two classes we just created and assign our variables.

12. From the **Content Browser** under the C++ Classes/Chapter_13 folder, right-click on the EnemyAIController object and select the **Create Blueprint class based on EnemyAIController** option. Give it a name and click on the **Create Blueprint Class** button.

13. Likewise, do the same thing for the EnemyCharacter object.

14. Double-click on your `MyEnemyCharacter` Blueprint and, under the **Details** tab, set the **Enemy Behavior Tree** property to **EnemyBehaviorTree**. Then, set the **AI Controller Class** property to `MyEnemyAIController`:

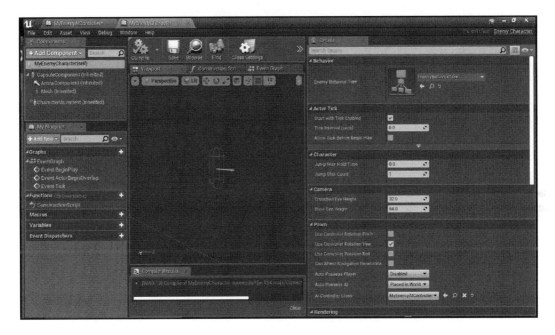

Assigning the Enemy Behavior Tree and AI Controller Class properties

15. You'll likely want a visual component for the character as well, so from the **Components** tab, click on the **Add Component** button and select **Cube**. Afterward, modify the **Scale** to (`0.5, 0.5, 1.5`).

    As we discussed previously, you may need to click on the **Open Full Blueprint Editor** text to see all of the available options.

16. Then, hit **Compile** and save all of your assets:

The completed enemy character

And with that, we've set up a connection between an AI Character, an AI Controller, and a Behavior Tree!

How it works...

The AI Controller class we created will add both the Behavior Tree and the Blackboard that we created in the previous two recipes.

A Behavior Tree is connected to an AI Controller, which in turn is connected to a Character. We will control the behavior of `Character` through the Behavior Tree by entering Task and Service nodes in the diagram.

A Behavior Tree hosts six different types of node, as follows:

1. **Task**: Task nodes are the purple nodes in the Behavior Tree that contain Blueprint code to run. It's something that the AI-controlled unit has to do (code-wise). Tasks must return either `true` or `false`, depending on whether the task succeeded or not (by providing a `FinishExecution()` node at the end).

2. **Decorator**: A decorator is just a Boolean condition for the execution of a node. It checks a condition, and is typically used within a Selector or Sequence block.

3. **Service**: This runs some Blueprint code when it ticks. The tick interval for these nodes is adjustable (it can run slower than a per-frame tick, for example, every 10 seconds). You can use these to query the scene for updates, a new opponent to chase, and so on. The Blackboard can be used to store queried information. Service nodes do not have a `FinishExecute()` call at the end of them.

4. **Selector**: This runs all subtrees from left to right until it encounters a success. When it encounters a success, the execution goes back up the tree.

5. **Sequence**: This runs all subtrees from left to right until it encounters a failure. When a failure is encountered, the execution goes back up the tree.

6. **Simple Parallel**: This runs a single task (purple) in parallel with a subtree (gray).

Creating a BTService

Services attach to nodes in Behavior Trees and will execute at their defined frequency; that is, as long as their branch is being executed. Similar to Parallel nodes in other Behavior Tree systems, these are often used to make checks and to update the Blackboard, which we will use in this recipe to find our player object and assign it to our Blackboard.

Getting ready...

Finish the previous recipe, *Connecting a Behavior Tree to a Character*.

How to do it...

1. From the Content Browser, select **Add New | New C++ Class**. From the **Choose Parent Class** menu, check the **Show All Classes** option and look for the BTService class. Select it and then hit the **Next** button:

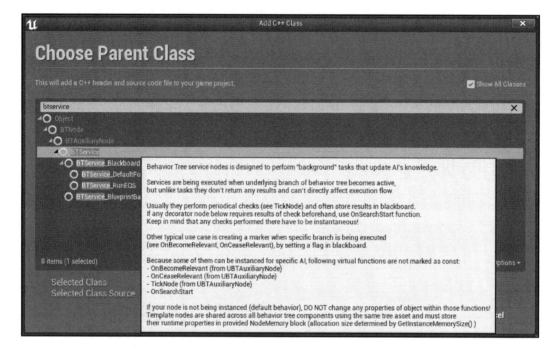

2. At the next menu, set its name to BTService_FindPlayer and then click on the **Create Class** option.

3. From the BTService_FindPlayer.h file, use the following code:

```
#pragma once

#include "CoreMinimal.h"
#include "BehaviorTree/BTService.h"
#include "BehaviorTree/BehaviorTreeComponent.h"
#include "BTService_FindPlayer.generated.h"

/**
 *
 */
UCLASS()
class CHAPTER_13_API UBTService_FindPlayer : public UBTService
```

```
{
    GENERATED_BODY()

public:
    UBTService_FindPlayer();
    /** update next tick interval
    * this function should be considered as const (don't
modify state of object) if node is not instanced! */
    virtual void TickNode(UBehaviorTreeComponent& OwnerComp,
uint8* NodeMemory, float DeltaSeconds) override;

};
```

4. From the `BTService_FindPlayer.cpp` file, use the following code:

```cpp
#include "BTService_FindPlayer.h"
#include "EnemyAIController.h"
#include "BehaviorTree/Blackboard/BlackboardKeyType_Object.h"

UBTService_FindPlayer::UBTService_FindPlayer()
{
    bCreateNodeInstance = true;
}

void UBTService_FindPlayer::TickNode(UBehaviorTreeComponent&
OwnerComp, uint8* NodeMemory, float DeltaSeconds)
{
    Super::TickNode(OwnerComp, NodeMemory, DeltaSeconds);

    auto EnemyAIController =
Cast<AEnemyAIController>(OwnerComp.GetAIOwner());

    if(EnemyAIController)
    {
        auto PlayerPawn =
GetWorld()->GetFirstPlayerController()->GetPawn();
OwnerComp.GetBlackboardComponent()->SetValue<UBlackboardKeyType_Object>(EnemyAIController->TargetKeyID, PlayerPawn);
        UE_LOG(LogTemp, Warning, TEXT("Target has been
set!"));

    }

}
```

5. Save your scripts and compile them.

6. In the **Content Browser**, go to the `Content` folder where the `EnemyBehaviorTree` we created previously is located and double-click on it to open the Behavior Tree editor.

7. From there, drag a line from **ROOT** down and select **Selector**:

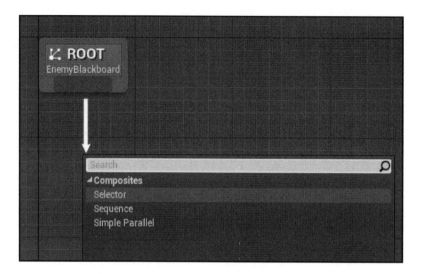

It's important to note that you need to drag from the darker gray rectangle on the bottom. If you try to drag from the middle of **ROOT**, you'll just move the node.

8. Right-click on the Selector node and select **Add Service | FindPlayer**:

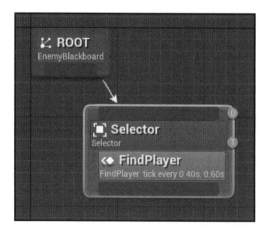

9. Now, drag and drop an instance of your `MyEnemyCharacter` object into your scene and run the game:

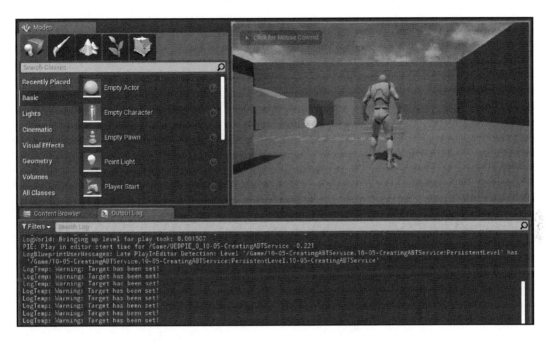

As you can see, the value has been set!

How it works...

Our Behavior Tree will continue to call the Selector as there are no other nodes for it to transition to.

Creating a BTTask

In addition to Services, we also have Tasks, which are leaf nodes of Behavior Trees. These are the things that actually perform actions. In our example, we are going to have our AI follow our target, the player.

Getting ready...

Finish the previous recipe, *Creating a BTService*.

How to do it...

1. From the Content Browser, select **Add New | New C++ Class**. From the **Choose Parent Class** menu, check the **Show All Classes** option and look for the BTTask_BlackboardBase class. Select it and then hit the **Next** button:

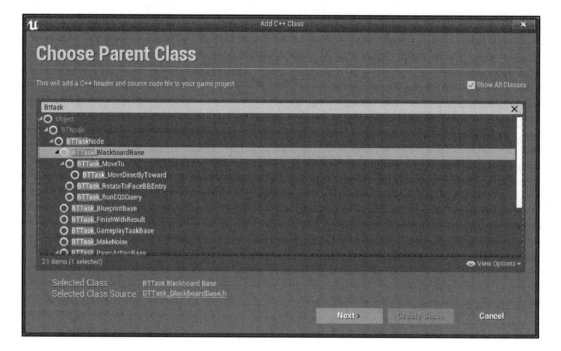

2. At the next menu, set its name to BTTask_MoveToPlayer and then click on the **Create Class** option:

3. Open Visual Studio and add the following function to
   BTTask_MoveToPlayer.h:

```
#pragma once

#include "CoreMinimal.h"
#include "BehaviorTree/Tasks/BTTask_BlackboardBase.h"
#include "BTTask_MoveToPlayer.generated.h"

/**
 *
 */
UCLASS()
class CHAPTER_13_API UBTTask_MoveToPlayer : public
UBTTask_BlackboardBase
{
    GENERATED_BODY()

public:
    /** starts this task, should return Succeeded, Failed or
InProgress
     * (use FinishLatentTask() when returning InProgress)
     * this function should be considered as const (don't
modify state of object) if node is not instanced! */
    virtual EBTNodeResult::Type
ExecuteTask(UBehaviorTreeComponent& OwnerComp, uint8*
NodeMemory) override;
};
```

4. Then, open the `BTTask_MoveToPlayer.cpp` file and update it to the following:

```
#include "BTTask_MoveToPlayer.h"
#include "EnemyAIController.h"
#include "GameFramework/Character.h"
#include "BehaviorTree/Blackboard/BlackboardKeyType_Object.h"

EBTNodeResult::Type
UBTTask_MoveToPlayer::ExecuteTask(UBehaviorTreeComponent&
OwnerComp, uint8* NodeMemory)
{
    auto EnemyController =
Cast<AEnemyAIController>(OwnerComp.GetAIOwner());
    auto Blackboard = OwnerComp.GetBlackboardComponent();

    ACharacter * Target =
Cast<ACharacter>(Blackboard->GetValue<UBlackboardKeyType_Objec
t>(EnemyController->TargetKeyID));

    if(Target)
    {
        EnemyController->MoveToActor(Target, 50.0f);
        return EBTNodeResult::Succeeded;
    }

    return EBTNodeResult::Failed;
}
```

5. Save your files and return to the Unreal Editor. Compile your code.
6. In the **Content Browser**, go to the `Content` folder where the `EnemyBehaviorTree` we created previously is located and double-click on it to open the Behavior Tree editor.

7. Drag this below the Selector node and select **Tasks | Move to Player**:

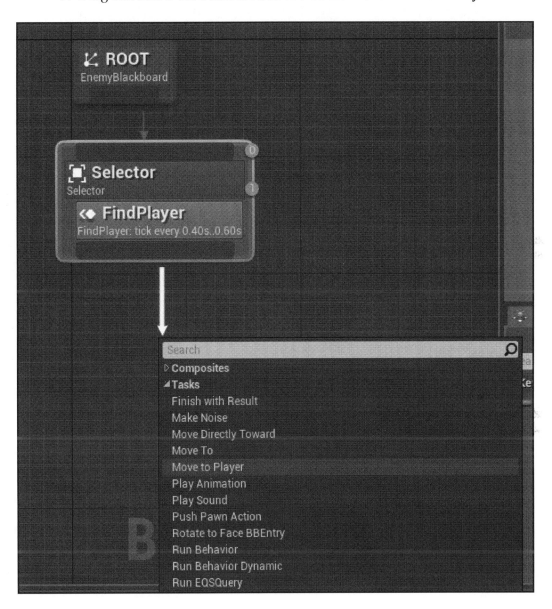

8. Save the Behavior Tree and return to the Unreal Editor. Drag and drop a `MyEnemyCharacter` object into the scene if you haven't done so already and play the game:

As you can see, our enemy is now following our player, which will happen for as long as the NavMesh covers the area!

How it works...

This recipe takes all of the materials we've covered so far and compiles them all together. The `ExecuteTask` method will be called as long as the BehaviorTree is inside this state. This function requires us to return an `EBTNodeResult`, which should return `Succeeded`, `Failed`, or `InProgress` to let the BehaviorTree know whether we can change states or not.

In our case, we first obtain the `EnemyController` and the `Target` objects so that we can figure out who we want to move and where we want to move to. As long as those properties are valid, we can call the `MoveToActor` function.

There are a lot of other properties that the `MoveToActor` function offers that may be useful so that you can customize your movement. For more information, check out the following link: `https://api.unrealengine.com/INT/API/Runtime/AIModule/AAIController/MoveToActor/index.html`.
For those of you who are interested in exploring additional AI concepts with UE4, I highly suggest checking out Orfeas Eleftheriou's UE4 AI
Tutorials: `https://orfeasel.com/category/ue_tuts/ai-programming/`.

User Interfaces - UI and UMG
14

In this chapter, we will cover the following recipes:

- Drawing using Canvas
- Adding Slate Widgets to the screen
- Creating screen size-aware scaling for the UI
- Displaying and hiding a sheet of UMG elements in-game
- Attaching function calls to Slate events
- Using Data Binding with Unreal Motion Graphics
- Controlling widget appearance with Styles
- Creating a custom SWidget/UWidget

Introduction

Displaying feedback to the player is one of the most important elements within game design, and this will usually involve some sort of HUD, or at least menus, within your game.

In previous versions of Unreal, there was simple HUD support, which allowed you to draw simple shapes and text to the screen. However, it was somewhat limited in terms of aesthetics, and so solutions such as **Scaleform** became common to work around these limitations. Scaleform leveraged Adobe's Flash file format to store vector images and UI scripts. It was not without its own cons for developers, though, not least the cost – it was a third-party product requiring a (sometimes, expensive) license.

As a result, Epic developed Slate for the Unreal 4 editor and the in-game UI framework. Slate is a collection of widgets (UI elements) and a framework that allows for a cross-platform interface for the Editor. It is also usable in-game to draw widgets, such as sliders and buttons, for menus and HUDs.

Slate uses declarative syntax to allow for an XML-style representation of user interface elements in their hierarchy in native C++. It accomplishes this by making heavy use of macros and operator overloading.

That said, not everybody wants to ask their programmers to design the game's HUD. One of the significant advantages of using Scaleform within Unreal 3 was the ability to develop the visual appearance of game UIs using the Flash visual editor so that visual designers didn't need to learn a programming language. Programmers could then insert the logic and data separately. This is the same paradigm that's espoused by the **Windows Presentation Framework (WPF)**, for example.

In a similar fashion, Unreal provides **Unreal Motion Graphics (UMG)**. UMG is a visual editor for Slate widgets that allows you to visually style, lay out, and animate user interfaces. UI widgets (or controls, if you've come from a Win32 background) can have their properties controlled by either Blueprint code (written in the Graph view of the UMG window) or from C++. This chapter primarily deals with displaying UI elements, creating widget hierarchies, and creating base `SWidget` classes that can be styled and used within UMG.

Technical requirements

This chapter requires the use of Unreal Engine 4 and uses Visual Studio 2017 as the IDE. Instructions on how to install both pieces of software and the requirements for them can be found in `Chapter 1`, *UE4 Development Tools*.

Drawing using Canvas

Canvas is a continuation of the simple HUD that's implemented within Unreal 3. While it isn't so commonly used within shipping games, mostly being replaced by Slate/UMG, it's simple to use, especially when you want to draw text or shapes to the screen. Canvas drawing is still used extensively by console commands that are used for debugging and performance analysis, such as `stat game` and the other `stat` commands.

Getting ready...

Refer to `Chapter 4`, *Actors and Components*, if you need a refresher on using the C++ Code Wizard.

How to do it...

1. From your Visual Studio project (**File** | **Open Visual Studio**), open the
   `Source\<Module>` folder and, from there, open the `<Module>.build.cs`
   file (in my case, it would be
   `Source\Chapter_14\Chapter_14.build.cs`). Uncomment/add the
   following line of code:

```
using UnrealBuildTool;

public class Chapter_14 : ModuleRules
{
  public Chapter_14(ReadOnlyTargetRules Target) : base(Target)
  {
    PCHUsage = PCHUsageMode.UseExplicitOrSharedPCHs;
    PublicDependencyModuleNames.AddRange(new string[] {
"Core",
    "CoreUObject", "Engine", "InputCore" });

    PrivateDependencyModuleNames.AddRange(new string[] { });

    // Uncomment if you are using Slate UI
    PrivateDependencyModuleNames.AddRange(new string[] {
"Slate",
    "SlateCore" });
    // Uncomment if you are using online features
    // PrivateDependencyModuleNames.Add("OnlineSubsystem");

    // To include OnlineSubsystemSteam, add it to the plugins
section in your uproject file with the Enabled attribute set
to true
  }
}
```

2. Create a new `GameModeBase` called `CustomHUDGameMode` using the editor
   class wizard.

3. Add a constructor to the class:

```
#pragma once

#include "CoreMinimal.h"
#include "GameFramework/GameModeBase.h"
#include "CustomHUDGameMode.generated.h"

/**
 *
```

```
    */
UCLASS()
class CHAPTER_14_API ACustomHUDGameMode : public AGameModeBase
{
    GENERATED_BODY()

    ACustomHUDGameMode();
};
```

4. Add the following to the constructor implementation:

```
#include "CustomHUDGameMode.h"
#include "CustomHUD.h"

ACustomHUDGameMode::ACustomHUDGameMode() : AGameModeBase()
{
    HUDClass = ACustomHUD::StaticClass();
}
```

At this point, you will get compile errors, because the CustomHUD class does not exist. That is what we will be creating next.

5. Create a new HUD subclass using the **Add C++ Class** wizard:

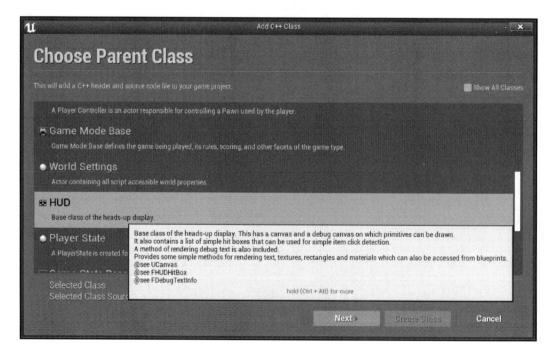

6. When asked for the name, put in `CustomHUD`, and click on the **Create Class** button:

7. Inside `CustomHUD.h`, add the following function with the `override` keyword to the class:

```
#pragma once

#include "CoreMinimal.h"
#include "GameFramework/HUD.h"
#include "CustomHUD.generated.h"

/**
 *
 */
UCLASS()
class CHAPTER_14_API ACustomHUD : public AHUD
{
    GENERATED_BODY()
public:
    virtual void DrawHUD() override;

};
```

8. Now, implement the function:

```
#include "CustomHUD.h"
#include "Engine/Canvas.h"

void ACustomHUD::DrawHUD()
{
    Super::DrawHUD();
    Canvas->DrawText(GEngine->GetSmallFont(), TEXT("Test
string to be printed to screen"), 10, 10);
    FCanvasBoxItem ProgressBar(FVector2D(5, 25),
FVector2D(100, 5));
    Canvas->DrawItem(ProgressBar);
    DrawRect(FLinearColor::Blue, 5, 25, 100, 5);
}
```

9. Compile your code and launch the editor.

10. Within the editor, open the **World Settings** panel from the **Settings** drop-down menu:

11. In the **World Settings** dialog, select CustomHUDGameMode from the list under **GameMode Override**:

12. Play and verify that your custom HUD is drawing to the screen:

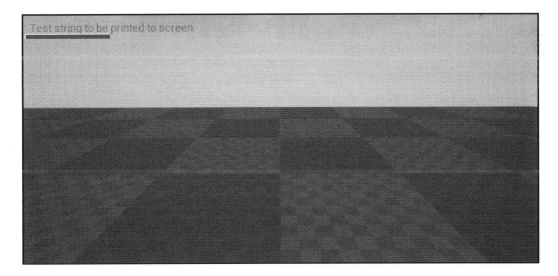

How it works...

All the UI recipes here will be using Slate for drawing, so we need to add a dependency between our module and the Slate framework so that we can access the classes that have been declared in that module. The best place to put custom Canvas draw calls for a game HUD is inside a subclass of AHUD.

To tell the engine to use our custom subclass, though, we need to create a new GameMode and specify the type of our custom class.

Within the constructor of our custom Game Mode, we assign the UClass for our new HUD type to the HUDClass variable. This UClass is passed on to each player's controller as they spawn in, and the controller is then responsible for the AHUD instance that it creates.

With our custom GameMode loading our custom HUD, we need to actually create said custom HUD class. AHUD defines a virtual function called DrawHUD(), which is invoked in every frame to allow us to draw elements to the screen. As a result, we override that function and perform our drawing inside the implementation.

The first method that's used is as follows:

```
float DrawText(constUFont* InFont, constFString&InText,
  float X, float Y, float XScale = 1.f, float YScale = 1.f,
  constFFontRenderInfo&RenderInfo = FFontRenderInfo());
```

DrawText requires a font to draw with. The default font used by stat and other HUD drawing commands in the engine code is actually stored in the GEngine class, and can be accessed by using the GetSmallFont function, which returns an instance of the UFont as a pointer.

The remaining arguments that we are using are the actual text that should be rendered, and the offset, in pixels, at which the text should be drawn.

DrawText is a function that allows you to directly pass in the data that is to be displayed. The general DrawItem function is a Visitor implementation that allows you to create an object that encapsulates the information about the object to be drawn and reuse that object on multiple draw calls.

In this recipe, we create an element that can be used to represent a progress bar. We encapsulate the required information regarding the width and height of our box into an `FCanvasBoxItem`, which we then pass to the `DrawItem` function on our Canvas.

The third item that we draw is a filled rectangle. This function uses convenience methods that are defined in the HUD class rather than on the Canvas itself. The filled rectangle is placed at the same location as our `FCanvasBox` so that it can represent the current value inside the progress bar.

See also...

- Refer to `Chapter 10`, *Integrating C++ and the Unreal Editor – Part II*, and the *Creating new console commands* recipe within, to learn how to create your own console commands

Adding Slate Widgets to the screen

The previous recipe used the `FCanvas` API to draw to the screen. However, `FCanvas` suffers from a number of limitations, for example, animations are difficult to implement, and drawing graphics on the screen involves creating textures or materials. `FCanvas` also doesn't implement anything in the way of widgets or window controls, making data entry or other forms of user input more complex than necessary. This recipe will show you how to begin creating HUD elements on-screen using Slate, which provides a number of built-in controls.

Getting ready

Add `Slate` and `SlateCore` to your module's dependencies if you haven't done so already (see the *Drawing using Canvas* recipe to learn how to do this).

How to do it...

1. Create a new `PlayerController` subclass using the **Add C++ Class** wizard:

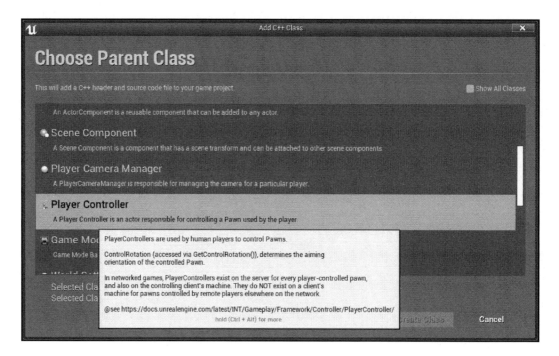

2. When asked for the name of the class, type
in `CustomHUDPlayerController` and press the **Create Class** button:

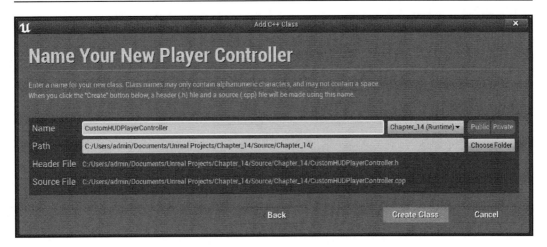

3. Override the `BeginPlay` virtual method within your new subclass:

```
#pragma once

#include "CoreMinimal.h"
#include "GameFramework/PlayerController.h"
#include "CustomHUDPlayerController.generated.h"

/**
 *
 */
UCLASS()
class CHAPTER_14_API ACustomHUDPlayerController : public
APlayerController
{
    GENERATED_BODY()
public:
    virtual void BeginPlay() override;

};
```

4. Add the following code for your overridden `BeginPlay()` virtual method inside the subclass' implementation:

```
#include "CustomHUDPlayerController.h"
#include "SlateBasics.h"


void ACustomHUDPlayerController::BeginPlay()
{
    Super::BeginPlay();
```

```
                TSharedRef<SVerticalBox> widget = SNew(SVerticalBox)
                    + SVerticalBox::Slot()
                    .HAlign(HAlign_Center)
                    .VAlign(VAlign_Center)
                    [
                        SNew(SButton)
                        .Content()
                    [
                        SNew(STextBlock)
                        .Text(FText::FromString(TEXT("Test button")))
                    ]
                    ];
        GEngine->GameViewport->AddViewportWidgetForPlayer(GetLocalPlay
        er(), widget, 1);
        }
```

5. Create a new class based on GameModeBase called SlateHUDGameMode.

6. Add a constructor inside the Game Mode:

```
#pragma once

#include "CoreMinimal.h"
#include "GameFramework/GameModeBase.h"
#include "SlateHUDGameMode.generated.h"

/**
 *
 */
UCLASS()
class CHAPTER_14_API ASlateHUDGameMode : public AGameModeBase
{
    GENERATED_BODY()
    ASlateHUDGameMode();
};
```

7. Implement the constructor with the following code:

```
#include "SlateHUDGameMode.h"
#include "CustomHUDPlayerController.h"

ASlateHUDGameMode::ASlateHUDGameMode() : Super()
{
 PlayerControllerClass =
ACustomHUDPlayerController::StaticClass();
}
```

8. Within the Editor, open the **World Settings** menu from the toolbar by going to **Settings | World Settings**:

9. Inside **World Settings**, override the level's **Game Mode** to be our `SlateHUDGameMode`:

10. Play the level. You will see your new UI displayed on the screen:

Button located on the game screen

How it works...

For us to reference Slate classes or functions in our code, our module must link with the `Slate` and `SlateCore` modules, so we add those to the module dependencies.

We need to instantiate our UI in one of the classes that loads when the game runs, so for this recipe, we use our custom `PlayerController` in the `BeginPlay` function as the place to create our UI.

Inside the `BeginPlay` implementation, we create a new `SVerticalBox` using the `SNew` function. We add a slot for a widget to our box, and set that slot to both horizontal and vertical centering.

Inside the slot, which we access using square brackets, we create a button that has `Textblock` inside it. In `Textblock`, we set the `Text` property to a string literal value.

With the UI now created, we call `AddViewportWidgetForPlayer` to display this widget on the local player's screen.

With our custom `PlayerController` ready, we now need to create a custom `GameMode` to specify that it should use our new `PlayerController`. With the custom `PlayerController` being loaded at the start of the game, when `BeginPlay` is called, our UI will be shown.

The UI is very small at this screen size. Refer to the following recipe for information on how to scale it appropriately for the resolution of the game window.

Creating screen size-aware scaling for the UI

If you have followed the previous recipe, you will notice that when you use **Play In Editor**, the button that loads is unusually small.

The reason for this is UI Scaling, a system that allows you to scale the user interface based on the screen size. User interface elements are represented in terms of pixels, usually in absolute terms (the button should be 10 pixels tall).

The problem with this is that if you use a higher-resolution panel, 10 pixels might be much smaller, because each pixel is smaller in size.

Getting ready

The UI scaling system in Unreal allows you to control a global scale modifier, which will scale all the controls on the screen based on the screen resolution. Given the previous example, you might wish to adjust the size of the button so that its apparent size is unchanged when you view your UI on a smaller screen. This recipe shows two different methods for altering the scaling rates.

How to do it...

1. Create a custom `PlayerController` subclass. Call it `ScalingUIPlayerController`.

2. Inside the class, override `BeginPlay`:

   ```
   #pragma once

   #include "CoreMinimal.h"
   ```

```
#include "GameFramework/PlayerController.h"
#include "ScalingUIPlayerController.generated.h"

/**
 *
 */
UCLASS()
class CHAPTER_14_API AScalingUIPlayerController : public
APlayerController
{
    GENERATED_BODY()
public:
    virtual void BeginPlay() override;
};
```

3. Add the following code in the implementation of that function inside of
   ScalingUIPlayerController.cpp:

```
#include "ScalingUIPlayerController.h"
#include "SlateBasics.h"

void AScalingUIPlayerController::BeginPlay()
{
    Super::BeginPlay();
    TSharedRef<SVerticalBox> widget = SNew(SVerticalBox)
        + SVerticalBox::Slot()

        .HAlign(HAlign_Center)
        .VAlign(VAlign_Center)
        [
            SNew(SButton)
            .Content()
        [
            SNew(STextBlock)
            .Text(FText::FromString(TEXT("Test button")))
        ]
        ];
GEngine->GameViewport->AddViewportWidgetForPlayer(GetLocalPlay
er(), widget, 1);
}
```

4. Create a new GameModeBase subclass called ScalingUIGameMode and
   give it a default constructor:

```
#pragma once

#include "CoreMinimal.h"
#include "GameFramework/GameModeBase.h"
```

```
#include "ScalingUIGameMode.generated.h"

/**
 *
 */
UCLASS()
class CHAPTER_14_API AScalingUIGameMode : public AGameModeBase
{
    GENERATED_BODY()
    AScalingUIGameMode();
};
```

5. Within the default constructor, set the default player controller class to
   `ScalingUIPlayerController`:

```
#include "ScalingUIGameMode.h"
#include "CustomHUDPlayerController.h"

AScalingUIGameMode::AScalingUIGameMode() : AGameModeBase()
{
    PlayerControllerClass =
ACustomHUDPlayerController::StaticClass();
}
```

6. Save and compile your new classes.
7. Within the Editor, open the **World Settings** menu from the toolbar by
   going to **Settings | World Settings**.
8. Inside **World Settings**, override the level's Game Mode to be
   our `ScalingUIGameMode`.

This should give you a user interface like the one from the previous recipe. Note that the UI is very tiny if you use **Play In Editor**:

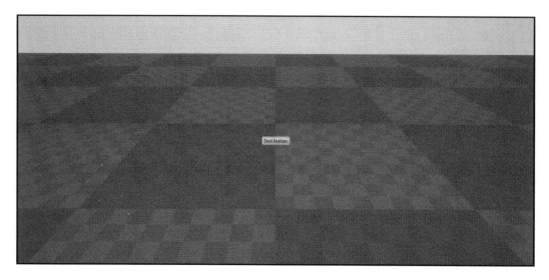

Tiny button on the game screen

To alter the rate at which the UI scales down or up, we need to change the scaling curve. We can do that through two different methods.

Using the In-Editor method

1. Launch Unreal, then open the **Project Settings** dialog through the **Edit** menu:

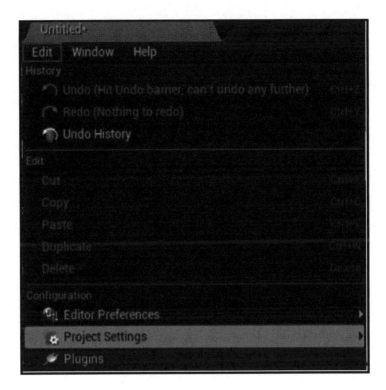

2. Under the **Engine - User Interface** section, there is a curve called the **DPI Curve**, which can be used to alter the UI scaling factor based on the short dimension of your screen:

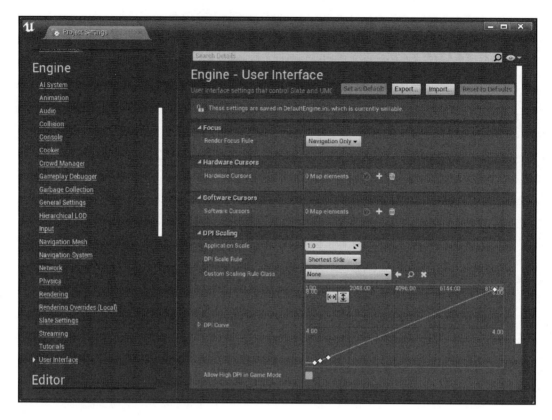

3. Click on the second dot, or keypoint, on the graph.
4. Change its **Scale** value to 1. Then, do the same for the first dot and set its **Scale** value to 1 as well:

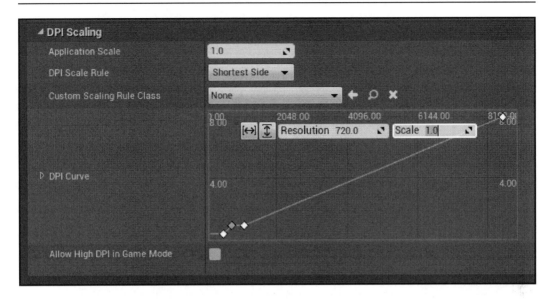

5. Return to the main editor and run the game again. You should notice that the button is larger than it was before:

Easier to see button on the game screen

Using the Config file method

1. Browse to your project directory and look inside the `Config` folder:

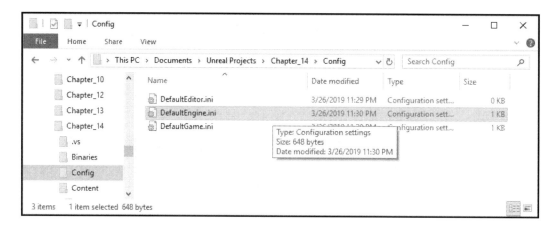

2. Open `DefaultEngine.ini`, which is located in the `Config` folder of your project, inside your text editor of choice.

3. Find the `[/Script/Engine.UserInterfaceSettings]` section:

```
[/Script/Engine.UserInterfaceSettings]
UIScaleCurve=(EditorCurveData=(PreInfinityExtrap=RCCE_Constant
,PostInfinityExtrap=RCCE_Constant,DefaultValue=340282346638528
85981170418348451692544.000000,Keys=((Time=480.000000,Value=1
.000000),(Time=720.000000,Value=1.000000),(Time=1080.000000,Va
lue=1.000000),(Time=8640.000000,Value=8.000000))),ExternalCurv
e=None)
```

4. Look for a key called `UIScaleCurve` in that section.

5. In the value for that key, you'll notice a number of `(Time=x,Value=y)` pairs. Edit the second pair so that its `Time` value is `720.000000` and the `Value` is `1.000000` if it isn't already.

6. Restart the editor if you have it open.

7. Start the **Play In Editor** preview to confirm that your UI now remains readable at the **PIE** screen's resolution (assuming you are using a 1080p monitor so that the PIE window is running at 720p or thereabouts):

8. You can also see how the scaling works if you use a **New Editor Window** to preview your game.

9. To do so, click on the arrow to the right of **Play** on the toolbar.

10. Select **New Editor Window**.

11. Inside this window, you can use the console command `r.SetRes widthxheight` to change the resolution (for example, `r.SetRes 200x200`), and observe the changes that result from doing so.

How it works...

As usual, when we want to use a custom `PlayerController`, we need a custom `GameMode` to specify which `PlayerController` to use.

We create both a custom `PlayerController` and `GameMode`, and then place some `Slate` code in the `BeginPlay` method of `PlayerController` so that some UI elements are drawn.

Because the main game viewport is usually quite small within the Unreal editor, the UI initially shows in a scaled-down fashion. This is intended to allow for the game UI to take up less room on smaller resolution displays, but this can have the side effect of making the text very difficult to read if the window isn't being stretched to fit the full screen.

Unreal stores the configuration data that should persist between sessions but not necessarily be hard coded into the executable inside config files. Config files use an extended version of the `.ini` file format, which has been commonly used with Windows software.

Config files store data using the following syntax:

```
[Section Name]
Key=Value
```

Unreal has a `UserInterfaceSettings` class, with a property called `UIScaleCurve` on it. That `UPROPERTY` is marked as config, so Unreal serializes the value to the `.ini` file.

As a result, it stores the `UIScale` data in the `DefaultEngine.ini` file, in the `Engine.UserInterfaceSettings` section.

The data is stored using a text format, which contains a list of key points. Editing the `Time`, `Value` pairs alters or adds new key points to the curve.

The **Project Settings** dialog is a simple frontend for directly editing the `.ini` files yourself, and for designers, it is an intuitive way to edit the curve. However, having the data stored textually allows for programmers to potentially develop build tools that modify properties such as `UIScale` without having to recompile their game.

`Time` refers to the input value. In this case, the input value is the narrower dimension of the screen (usually, the height).

`Value` is the universal scaling factor that's applied to the UI when the screen's narrow dimension is approximately the height of the value in the `Time` field.

So, to set the UI to remain normal-sized at a 1280 x 720 resolution, set the time/input factor to 720 and the scale factor to 1.

See also

- You can refer to the UE4 documentation for more information regarding config files: `https://docs.unrealengine.com/en-US/Programming/Basics/ConfigurationFiles`.

Displaying and hiding a sheet of UMG elements in-game

We have already discussed how to add a widget to the viewport, which means that it will be rendered on the player's screen.

However, what if we want to have UI elements that are toggled based on other factors, such as proximity to certain Actors, or a player holding a key down, or if we want a UI that disappears after a specified time?

How to do it...

1. Create a new `GameModeBase` class called `ToggleHUDGameMode`:

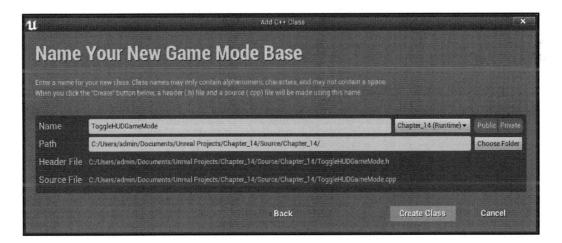

2. Add the following UPROPERTY and function definitions to the ToggleHUDGameMode.h file:

```
#pragma once

#include "CoreMinimal.h"
#include "GameFramework/GameModeBase.h"
#include "SlateBasics.h"
#include "ToggleHUDGameMode.generated.h"

UCLASS()
class CHAPTER_14_API AToggleHUDGameMode : public AGameModeBase
{
  GENERATED_BODY()

public:
  UPROPERTY()
  FTimerHandle HUDToggleTimer;

  TSharedPtr<SVerticalBox> widget;

  virtual void BeginPlay() override;
  virtual void EndPlay(const EEndPlayReason::Type
EndPlayReason) override;
};
```

3. Implement BeginPlay with the following code in the method body:

```
void AToggleHUDGameMode::BeginPlay()
{
    Super::BeginPlay();
    widget = SNew(SVerticalBox)
        + SVerticalBox::Slot()
        .HAlign(HAlign_Center)
        .VAlign(VAlign_Center)
        [
            SNew(SButton)
            .Content()
        [
            SNew(STextBlock)
            .Text(FText::FromString(TEXT("Test button")))
        ]
        ];

    auto player =
GetWorld()->GetFirstLocalPlayerFromController();

    GEngine->GameViewport->AddViewportWidgetForPlayer(player,
```

```
widget.ToSharedRef(), 1);

    auto lambda = FTimerDelegate::CreateLambda
    ([this]
    {
        if (this->widget->GetVisibility().IsVisible())
        {
            this->widget->SetVisibility(EVisibility::Hidden);

        }
        else
        {
            this->widget->SetVisibility(EVisibility::Visible);
        }
    });

    GetWorld()->GetTimerManager().SetTimer(HUDToggleTimer,
lambda, 5, true);
    }
```

4. Implement `EndPlay`:

```
void AToggleHUDGameMode::EndPlay(const EEndPlayReason::Type
EndPlayReason)
{
    Super::EndPlay(EndPlayReason);
    GetWorld()->GetTimerManager().ClearTimer(HUDToggleTimer);
}
```

5. Compile your code and start the editor.

6. Within the Editor, open **World Settings** from the toolbar:

7. Inside **World Settings**, override the level's **Game Mode** to be our
   `AToggleHUDGameMode`:

8. Play the level and verify that the UI toggles its visibility every five seconds.

How it works...

As with most of the other recipes in this chapter, we are using a custom `GameMode` class to display our single-player UI on the player's viewport for convenience.

We override `BeginPlay` and `EndPlay` so that we can correctly handle the timer that will be toggling our UI on and off for us. To make that possible, we need to store a reference to the timer as a `UPROPERTY` to ensure it won't be garbage collected.

Within `BeginPlay`, we create a new `VerticalBox` using the `SNew` macro, and place a button in its first slot. Buttons have `Content`, which can be some other widget to host inside them, such as `SImage` or `STextBlock`.

In this instance, we place an STextBlock into the Content slot. The contents of the text block are irrelevant, that is, as long as they are long enough for us to be able to see our button properly.

Having initialized our widget hierarchy, we add the root widget to the player's viewport so that it can be seen by them.

Now, we set up a timer to toggle the visibility of our widget. We are using a timer to simplify this recipe rather than having to implement user input and input bindings, but the principle is the same. To do this, we get a reference to the game world and its associated timer manager.

With the timer manager in hand, we can create a new timer. However, we need to actually specify the code to run when the timer expires. One simple way to do this is to use a lambda function for our toggle the hud function.

Lambdas are anonymous functions. Think of them as literal functions. To link a lambda function to the timer, we need to create a timer delegate.

The FTimerDelegate::CreateLambda function is designed to convert a lambda function into a delegate, which the timer can call at the specified interval.

The lambda needs to access the this pointer from its containing object, our GameMode, so that it can change properties on the widget instance that we have created. To give it the access it needs, we begin our lambda declaration with the [] operators, which enclose variables that should be captured into the lambda, and are accessible inside it. The curly braces then enclose the function body in the same way they would with a normal function declaration.

Inside the function, we check if our widget is visible. If it is visible, then we hide it using SWidget::SetVisibility. If the widget isn't visible, then we turn it on using the same function call.

In the rest of the call to SetTimer, we specify the interval (in seconds) to call the timer, and set the timer to loop.

One thing we need to be careful of, though, is the possibility of our object being destroyed between two timer invocations, potentially leading to a crash if a reference to our object is left dangling. To fix this, we need to remove the timer.

Given that we set the timer during BeginPlay, it makes sense to clear the timer during EndPlay. EndPlay will be called whenever GameMode either ends play or is destroyed, so we can safely cancel the timer during its implementation.

With `GameMode` set as the default game mode, the UI is created when the game begins to play, and the timer delegate executes every five seconds to switch the visibility of the widgets between `true` and `false`.

When you close the game, `EndPlay` clears the timer reference, avoiding any problems.

Attaching function calls to Slate events

While creating buttons is all well and good, at the moment, any UI element you add to the player's screen just sits there without anything happening, even if a user clicks on it. We don't have any event handlers attached to the Slate elements at the moment, so events such as mouse clicks don't actually cause anything to happen.

Getting ready

This recipe shows you how to attach functions to these events so that we can run custom code when they occur.

How to do it...

1. Create a new `GameModeBase` subclass called `ClickEventGameMode`:

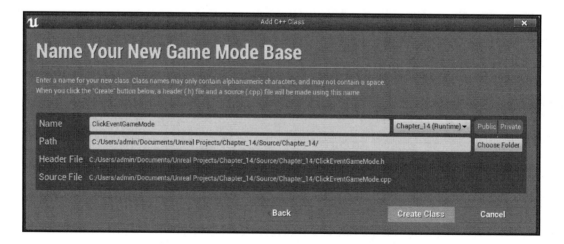

2. From the `ClickEventGameMode.h` file, add the following functions and `private` members to the class:

```
#pragma once

#include "CoreMinimal.h"
#include "GameFramework/GameModeBase.h"
#include "SlateBasics.h"
#include "ClickEventGameMode.generated.h"

UCLASS()
class CHAPTER_14_API AClickEventGameMode : public
AGameModeBase
{
    GENERATED_BODY()
private:
    TSharedPtr<SVerticalBox> Widget;
    TSharedPtr<STextBlock> ButtonLabel;

public:
    virtual void BeginPlay() override;
    FReply ButtonClicked();
};
```

3. Within the `.cpp` file, add the implementation for `BeginPlay`:

```
void AClickEventGameMode::BeginPlay()
{
    Super::BeginPlay();

    Widget = SNew(SVerticalBox)
        + SVerticalBox::Slot()
        .HAlign(HAlign_Center)
        .VAlign(VAlign_Center)
        [
            SNew(SButton)
            .OnClicked(FOnClicked::CreateUObject(this,
&AClickEventGameMode::ButtonClicked))
            .Content()
            [
                SAssignNew(ButtonLabel, STextBlock)
                .Text(FText::FromString(TEXT("Click me!")))
            ]
        ];

    auto player =
GetWorld()->GetFirstLocalPlayerFromController();
```

```
        GEngine->GameViewport->AddViewportWidgetForPlayer(player,
    Widget.ToSharedRef(), 1);

        GetWorld()->GetFirstPlayerController()->bShowMouseCursor =
    true;

        auto pc =
    GEngine->GetFirstLocalPlayerController(GetWorld());

        EMouseLockMode lockMode = EMouseLockMode::DoNotLock;

        auto inputMode =
    FInputModeUIOnly().SetLockMouseToViewportBehavior(lockMode).Se
    tWidgetToFocus(Widget);

        pc->SetInputMode(inputMode);

    }
```

4. Also, add an implementation for `ButtonClicked()`:

```
FReply AClickEventGameMode::ButtonClicked()
{
    ButtonLabel->SetText(FString(TEXT("Clicked!")));
    return FReply::Handled();
}
```

5. **Compile** your code and launch the editor.
6. Override the game mode in **World Settings** to be `ClickEventGameMode`.
7. Preview this in the editor and verify that the UI shows a button that changes from **Click Me!** to **Clicked!** when you use the mouse cursor to click on it:

Button displays Clicked! after being clicked

How it works...

As with most of the recipes in this chapter, we use GameMode to create and display our UI to minimize the number of classes that are extraneous to the point of the recipe that you need to create.

Within our new game mode, we need to retain references to the Slate Widgets that we create so that we can interact with them after their creation.

As a result, we create two shared pointers as member data within our GameMode – one to the overall parent or root widget of our UI, and the other to the label on our button, because we're going to be changing the label text at runtime later.

We override BeginPlay, as it is a convenient place to create our UI after the game has started, and we will be able to get valid references to our player controller.

We also create a function called ButtonClicked. It returns FReply, a struct indicating if an event was handled. The function signature for ButtonClicked is determined by the signature of FOnClicked, a delegate that we will be using in a moment.

Inside our implementation of `BeginPlay`, the first thing we do is call the implementation we are overriding to ensure that the class is initialized appropriately.

Then, as usual, we use our `SNew` function to create `VerticalBox`, and we add a slot to it, which is centered.

We create a new `Button` inside that slot, and we add a value to the `OnClicked` attribute that the button contains.

`OnClicked` is a delegate property. This means that the `Button` will broadcast the `OnClicked` delegate any time a certain event happens (as the name implies in this instance, when the button is clicked).

To subscribe or listen to the delegate, and be notified of the event that it refers to, we need to assign a delegate instance to the property.

We do that using the standard delegate functions such as `CreateUObject`, `CreateStatic`, or `CreateLambda`. Any of those will work – we can bind `UObject` member functions, static functions, lambdas, and other functions.

 Check out Chapter 5, *Handling Events and Delegates,* to learn more about delegates and look at the other types of functions that we can bind to delegates.

`CreateUObject` expects a pointer to a class instance, and a pointer to the member function that's defined in that class to call. The function has to have a signature that can be converted into the signature of the delegate:

```
/** The delegate to execute when the button is clicked */
FOnClickedOnClicked;
```

As we can see, the `OnClicked` delegate type is `FOnClicked` – this is why the `ButtonClicked` function that we declared has the same signature as `FOnClicked`.

By passing in a pointer to this, and the pointer to the function to invoke, the engine will call that function on this specific object instance when the button is clicked.

After setting up the delegate, we use the `Content()` function, which returns a reference to the single slot that the button has for any content that it should contain.

We then use `SAssignNew` to create our button's label by using the `TextBlock` widget. `SAssignNew` is important because it allows us to use Slate's declarative syntax, and yet assigns variables to point to specific child widgets in the hierarchy. `SAssignNew`'s first argument is the variable that we want to store the widget in, and the second argument is the type of that widget.

With `ButtonLabel` now pointing at our button's `TextBlock`, we can set its `Text` attribute to a static string.

Finally, we add the widget to the player's viewport using `AddViewportWidgetForPlayer`, which expects, as parameters, `LocalPlayer` to add the widget to, the widget itself, and a depth value (higher values to the front).

To get the `LocalPlayer` instance, we assume we are running without split screen, and so the first player controller will be the only one, that is, the player's controller. The `GetFirstLocalPlayerFromController` function is a convenience function that simply fetches the first player's controller and returns its local player object.

We also need to focus the widget so that the player can click on it and display a cursor so that the player knows where their mouse is on the screen.

We know from the previous step that we can assume the first local player controller is the one we're interested in, so we can access it and change its `ShowMouseCursor` variable to `true`. This will cause the cursor to be rendered on screen.

`SetInputMode` allows us to focus on a widget so that the player can interact with it among other UI-related functionality, such as locking the mouse to the game's viewport. It uses an `FInputMode` object as its only parameter, which we can construct with the specific elements that we wish to include by using the `builder` pattern.

The `FInputModeUIOnly` class is an `FInputMode` subclass that specifies that we want all input events to be redirected to the UI layer rather than the player controller and other input handling.

The `builder` pattern allows us to chain the method calls to customize our object instance before it is sent into the function as the parameter.

We chain `SetLockMouseToViewport(false)` to specify that the player's mouse can leave the boundary of the game screen with `SetWidgetToFocus(Widget)`, which specifies our top-level widget as the one that the game should direct player input to.

Finally, we have our actual implementation for `ButtonClicked`, which is our event handler. When the function is run due to our button being clicked, we change our button's label to indicate it has been clicked. We then need to return an instance of `FReply` to the caller to let the UI framework know that the event has been handled, and to not continue propagating the event back up the widget hierarchy.

`FReply::Handled()` returns `FReply` set up to indicate this to the framework. We could have used `FReply::Unhandled()`, but this would have told the framework that the click event wasn't actually the one we were interested in, and it should look for other objects that might be interested in the event instead.

Using Data Binding with Unreal Motion Graphics

So far, we've been assigning static values to the attributes of our UI widgets. However, what if we want to be more dynamic with widget content, or parameters such as border color? We can use a principle called data binding to dynamically link properties of our UI with variables in the broader program.

Unreal uses the Attribute system to allow us to bind the value of an attribute to the return value from a function, for example. This means that changing those variables will automatically cause the UI to change in response, according to our wishes.

How to do it...

1. Create a new `GameModeBase` subclass called `AttributeGameMode`.
2. Update the `AttributeGameMode.h` file to the following:

```
#pragma once

#include "CoreMinimal.h"
#include "GameFramework/GameStateBase.h"
#include "SlateBasics.h"
#include "AttributeGameMode.generated.h"

/**
 *
 */
UCLASS()
class CHAPTER_14_API AAttributeGameMode : public AGameModeBase
```

```
{
    GENERATED_BODY()

    TSharedPtr<SVerticalBox> Widget;
    FText GetButtonLabel() const;

public:
    virtual void BeginPlay() override;

};
```

3. Add the implementation for `BeginPlay` within the `.cpp` file:

```
void AAttributeGameMode::BeginPlay()
{
    Super::BeginPlay();

    Widget = SNew(SVerticalBox)
        + SVerticalBox::Slot()
        .HAlign(HAlign_Center)
        .VAlign(VAlign_Center)
        [
            SNew(SButton)
            .Content()
        [
            SNew(STextBlock)
.Text(TAttribute<FText>::Create(TAttribute<FText>::FGetter::Cr
eateUObject(this, &AAttributeGameMode::GetButtonLabel)))
        ]
        ];
GEngine->GameViewport->AddViewportWidgetForPlayer(GetWorld()->
GetFirstLocalPlayerFromController(), Widget.ToSharedRef(), 1);

}
```

4. Also, add an implementation for `GetButtonLabel()`:

```
FText AAttributeGameMode::GetButtonLabel() const
{
    FVector ActorLocation =
GetWorld()->GetFirstPlayerController()->GetPawn()->GetActorLoc
ation();
    return FText::FromString(FString::Printf(TEXT("%f, %f,
%f"), ActorLocation.X, ActorLocation.Y, ActorLocation.Z));
}
```

5. Compile your code and launch the editor.

6. Override the game mode in **World Settings** to be `AAttributeGameMode`.

7. Note that, in a **Play In Editor** session, the value on the UI's button changes as the player moves around the scene:

How it works...

Just like almost all the other recipes in this chapter, the first thing we need to do is create a game mode as a convenient host for our UI. We create the UI in the same fashion as in the other recipes, that is, by placing `Slate` code inside the `BeginPlay()` method of our game mode.

The interesting feature of this recipe concerns how we set the value of our button's label text:

```
.Text(
TAttribute<FText>::Create(TAttribute<FText>::FGetter::Creat
eUObject(this, &AAttributeGameMode::GetButtonLabel)))
```

The preceding syntax is unusually verbose, but what it is actually doing is comparatively simple. We assign something to the `Text` property, which is of the type `FText`. We can assign `TAttribute<FText>` to this property, and the `TAttribute Get()` method will be called whenever the UI wants to ensure that the value of `Text` is up to date.

To create `TAttribute`, we need to call the static `TAttribute<VariableType>::Create()` method. This function expects a delegate of some description. Depending on the type of delegate that's passed to `TAttribute::Create`, `TAttribute::Get()` invokes a different type of function to retrieve the actual value.

In the code for this recipe, we invoke a member function of `UObject`. This means that we know we will be calling the `CreateUObject` function on some delegate type.

We can use `CreateLambda`, `CreateStatic`, or `CreateRaw` to invoke a `lambda`, a `static`, or a `member` function on a raw C++ class, respectively. This will give us the current value for the attribute.

But what delegate type do we want to create an instance of? Because we're templating the `TAttribute` class on the actual variable type that the attribute will be associated with, we need a delegate that is also templated on the variable type as its return value.

That is to say, if we have `TAttribute<FText>`, the delegate that's connected to it needs to return an `FText`.

We have the following code within `TAttribute`:

```
template<typenameObjectType>
 classTAttribute
 {
 public:
 /**
 * Attribute 'getter' delegate
 *
 * ObjectTypeGetValue() const
 *
 * @return The attribute's value
 */
 DECLARE_DELEGATE_RetVal(ObjectType, FGetter);
 (...)
 }
```

The `FGetter` delegate type is declared inside the `TAttribute` class, so its return value can be templated on the `ObjectType` parameter of the `TAttribute` template. This means that `TAttribute<Typename>::FGetter` automatically defines a delegate with the correct return type of `Typename`. So, we need to create a UObject-bound delegate of type and signature for `TAttribute<FText>::FGetter`.

Once we have that delegate, we can call `TAttribute::Create` on the delegate to link the delegate's return value to our `TextBlock` member variable `Text`. With our UI defined and a binding between the `Text` property, a `TAttribute<FText>`, and a delegate returning `FText`, we can now add the UI to the player's screen so that it's visible.

Every frame, the game engine checks all of the properties to see if they are linked to `TAttributes`. If there's a connection, then the `TAttributeGet()` function is called, invoking the delegate and returning the delegate's return value so that Slate can store it inside the widget's corresponding member variable.

For our demonstration of this process, `GetButtonLabel` retrieves the location of the first player pawn in the game world. We then use `FString::Printf` to format the location data into a human readable string, and wrap that in an `FText` so that it can be stored as the `TextBlock` text value.

Controlling widget appearance with Styles

So far in this chapter, we've been creating UI elements that use the default visual representation. This recipe shows you how to create a Style in C++ that can be used as a common look and feel across your whole project.

How to do it...

1. Create a new class for your project by using the **Add C++ Class** wizard and selecting None as your parent class:

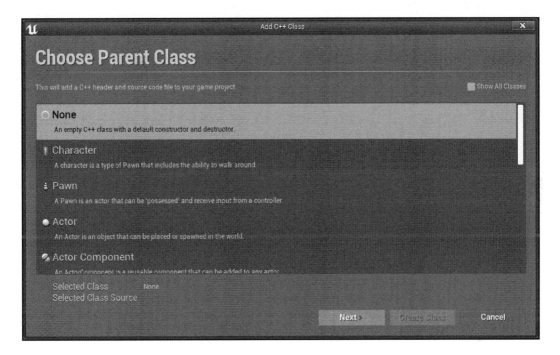

2. Under the name option, use `CookbookStyle` and click on the **Create Class** button:

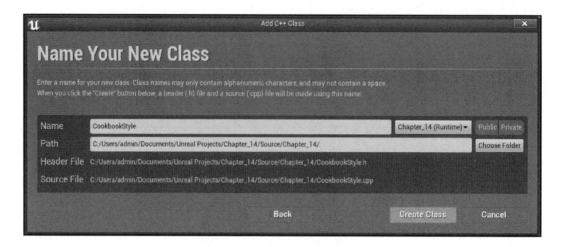

3. Replace the code in the `CookbookStyle.h` file with the following code:

```cpp
#pragma once
#include "SlateBasics.h"
#include "SlateExtras.h"

class FCookbookStyle
{
public:
    static void Initialize();
    static void Shutdown();
    static void ReloadTextures();
    static const ISlateStyle& Get();
    static FName GetStyleSetName();

private:
    static TSharedRef< class FSlateStyleSet > Create();
private:
    static TSharedPtr< class FSlateStyleSet >
CookbookStyleInstance;
};
```

4. Open the `CookbookStyle.cpp` file and use the following code for it:

```
#include "CookbookStyle.h"
#include "SlateGameResources.h"

TSharedPtr< FSlateStyleSet >
FCookbookStyle::CookbookStyleInstance = NULL;

void FCookbookStyle::Initialize()
{
    if (!CookbookStyleInstance.IsValid())
    {
        CookbookStyleInstance = Create();
FSlateStyleRegistry::RegisterSlateStyle(*CookbookStyleInstance
);
    }
}

void FCookbookStyle::Shutdown()
{
FSlateStyleRegistry::UnRegisterSlateStyle(*CookbookStyleInstan
ce);
    ensure(CookbookStyleInstance.IsUnique());
    CookbookStyleInstance.Reset();
}

FName FCookbookStyle::GetStyleSetName()
{
    static FName StyleSetName(TEXT("CookbookStyle"));
    return StyleSetName;
}
```

5. Add the following content below the previously created script in the `CookbookStyle.cpp` file to describe how to draw the screen:

```
#define IMAGE_BRUSH( RelativePath, ... ) FSlateImageBrush(
FPaths::GameContentDir() / "Slate"/ RelativePath +
TEXT(".png"), __VA_ARGS__ )
#define BOX_BRUSH( RelativePath, ... ) FSlateBoxBrush(
FPaths::GameContentDir() / "Slate"/ RelativePath +
TEXT(".png"), __VA_ARGS__ )
#define BORDER_BRUSH( RelativePath, ... ) FSlateBorderBrush(
FPaths::GameContentDir() / "Slate"/ RelativePath +
TEXT(".png"), __VA_ARGS__ )
#define TTF_FONT( RelativePath, ... ) FSlateFontInfo(
FPaths::GameContentDir() / "Slate"/ RelativePath +
```

```
TEXT(".ttf"), __VA_ARGS__ )
#define OTF_FONT( RelativePath, ... ) FSlateFontInfo(
FPaths::GameContentDir() / "Slate"/ RelativePath +
TEXT(".otf"), __VA_ARGS__ )

TSharedRef< FSlateStyleSet > FCookbookStyle::Create()
{
    TSharedRef<FSlateStyleSet> StyleRef =
FSlateGameResources::New(FCookbookStyle::GetStyleSetName(),
"/Game/Slate", "/Game/Slate");
    FSlateStyleSet& Style = StyleRef.Get();

    Style.Set("NormalButtonBrush",
        FButtonStyle().
        SetNormal(BOX_BRUSH("Button", FVector2D(54, 54),
FMargin(14.0f / 54.0f))));
    Style.Set("NormalButtonText",
        FTextBlockStyle(FTextBlockStyle::GetDefault())
        .SetColorAndOpacity(FSlateColor(FLinearColor(1, 1, 1,
1))));
    return StyleRef;
}


#undef IMAGE_BRUSH
#undef BOX_BRUSH
#undef BORDER_BRUSH
#undef TTF_FONT
#undef OTF_FONT

void FCookbookStyle::ReloadTextures()
{
FSlateApplication::Get().GetRenderer()->ReloadTextureResources
();
}

const ISlateStyle& FCookbookStyle::Get()
{
    return *CookbookStyleInstance;
}
```

6. Create a new `GameModeBase` **subclass**, `StyledHUDGameMode`:

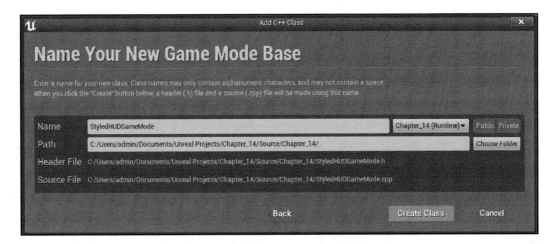

7. Once Visual Studio opens, add the following code to its declaration:

```
#pragma once

#include "CoreMinimal.h"
#include "GameFramework/GameModeBase.h"
#include "SlateBasics.h"
#include "StyledHUDGameMode.generated.h"

/**
 *
 */
UCLASS()
class CHAPTER_14_API AStyledHUDGameMode : public AGameModeBase
{
    GENERATED_BODY()
    TSharedPtr<SVerticalBox> Widget;

public:
    virtual void BeginPlay() override;
};
```

8. Likewise, implement GameMode:

```
#include "StyledHUDGameMode.h"
#include "CookbookStyle.h"

void AStyledHUDGameMode::BeginPlay()
{
    Super::BeginPlay();

    Widget = SNew(SVerticalBox)
        + SVerticalBox::Slot()
        .HAlign(HAlign_Center)
        .VAlign(VAlign_Center)
        [
            SNew(SButton)
            .ButtonStyle(FCookbookStyle::Get(),
"NormalButtonBrush")
            .ContentPadding(FMargin(16))
            .Content()
            [
                SNew(STextBlock)
                .TextStyle(FCookbookStyle::Get(),
"NormalButtonText")
                .Text(FText::FromString("Styled Button"))
            ]
        ];
GEngine->GameViewport->AddViewportWidgetForPlayer(GetWorld()->
GetFirstLocalPlayerFromController(), Widget.ToSharedRef(), 1);

}
```

9. Lastly, create a 54 x 54 pixel PNG file with a border around it for our button:

10. Save it to the Content | Slate folder with the name Button.png, creating the folder if needed:

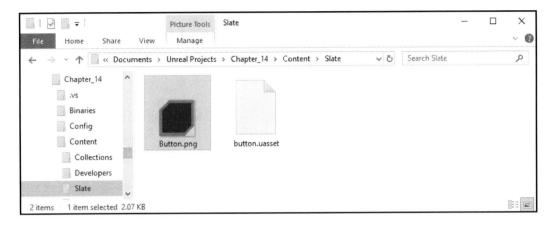

11. You may be asked if you'd like to import the image into your project. Go ahead and say yes.

12. Finally, we need to set our game's module to properly initialize the style when it is loaded. In your game module's implementation file (`Chapter_14.h`), ensure it looks like this:

```
#pragma once

#include "CoreMinimal.h"
#include "CookbookStyle.h"

class Chapter_14Module : public FDefaultGameModuleImpl
{
    virtual void StartupModule() override
    {
        FCookbookStyle::Initialize();
    };
    virtual void ShutdownModule() override
    {
        FCookbookStyle::Shutdown();
    };
};
```

13. Then, go to the `Chapter_14.cpp` file and modify the code to the following:

```
#include "Chapter_14.h"
#include "Modules/ModuleManager.h"

IMPLEMENT_PRIMARY_GAME_MODULE(Chapter_14Module, Chapter_14,
"Chapter_14" );
```

14. Compile the code and set your game mode override to the new game mode, like we did in the other recipes in this chapter.

15. When you play the game, you will see that your custom border is around the button, and that the text is white rather than black:

How it works...

For us to create styles that can be shared across multiple Slate widgets, we need to create an object to contain the styles and keep them in scope.

Epic provides the `FSlateStyleSet` class for this purpose. `FSlateStyleSet` contains a number of styles that we can access within Slate's declarative syntax to skin widgets.

However, it's inefficient to have multiple copies of our `StyleSet` object scattered through the program. We really only need one of these objects.

Because `FSlateStyleSet` itself is not a singleton, that is, an object that can only have one instance, we need to create a class that will manage our `StyleSet` object and ensure that we only have the single instance.

This is the reason we have the `FCookbookStyle` class. It contains an `Initialize()` function, which we will call in our module's startup code. In the `Initialize()` function, we check if we have an instance of our `StyleSet`. If we do not have a valid instance, we call the private `Create()` function to instantiate one.

We then register the style with the `FSlateStyleRegistry` class.

When our module is unloaded, we will need to reverse this registration process, then erase the pointer so that it doesn't dangle.

We now have an instance of our class that was created during module initialization by calling `Create()`. You'll notice that `Create` is wrapped by a number of macros that all have a similar form. These macros are defined before the function, and undefined after it.

These macros make it easier for us to simplify the code that's required within the `Create` function by eliminating the need to specify a path and extension for all the image resources that our Style might want to use.

Within the `Create` function, we create a new `FSlateStyleSet` object using the `FSlateGameResources::New()` function. `New()` needs a name for the style, and the folder paths that we want to search for in this Style Set.

This allows us to declare multiple Style Sets that are pointing to different directories, but using the same names for the images. It also allows us to skin or restyle the whole UI simply by switching to a Style Set in one of the other base directories.

`New()` returns a shared reference object, so we retrieve the actual `FStyleSet` instance using the `Get()` function.

With this reference in hand, we can create the styles we want this set to contain. To add styles to a set, we use the `Set()` method. Set expects the name of the style, and then a style object. Style objects can be customized using the `builder` pattern.

We first add a style called `"NormalButtonBrush"`. The name can be arbitrary. Because we want to use this style to change the appearance of buttons, we need to use `FButtonStyle` for the second parameter.

To customize the style to our requirements, we use the Slate builder syntax, chaining whatever method calls that we need to set properties on our style.

For the first style in this set, we just change the visual appearance of the button when it isn't being clicked or is in a non-default state. This means that we want to change the brush that's used when the button is in the normal state, and so the function we use is SetNormal().

Using the BOX_BRUSH macro, we tell Slate that we want to use Button.png, which is an image of 54 x 54 pixel size, and that we want to keep the 14 pixels in each corner unstretched for the purposes of nine-slice scaling.

 For a more visual explanation of the nine-slice scaling functionality, take a look at SlateBoxBrush.h in the engine source.

For the second style in our Style Set, we create a style called "NormalButtonText". For this style, we don't want to change everything from defaults in the style; we just want to alter one property. As a result, we access the default text style and clone it using the copy constructor.

With our fresh copy of the default style, we then change the color of the text to white, first creating a linear color of R=1 G=1 B=1 A=1, and then convert that into a Slate color object.

With our Style Set configured with our two new styles, we can then return it to the calling function, which is Initialize. Initialize stores our Style Set reference and eliminates the need for us to create further instances.

Our style container class also has a Get() function, which is used to retrieve the actual StyleSet for use in Slate. Because Initialize() has already been called at module startup, Get() simply returns the StyleSet instance that was created within that function.

Within the game module, we add the code that actually calls Initialize and Shutdown. This ensures that while our module is loaded, we will always have a valid reference to our Slate Style.

As always, we create a Game Mode as the host for our UI, and we override BeginPlay so that we can create the UI when the game starts.

The syntax for creating the UI is exactly the same as we've used in previous recipes – creating a `VerticalBox` using `SNew`, and then using Slate's declarative syntax to populate the box with other widgets.

It is important to note the two following lines:

```
.ButtonStyle(FCookbookStyle::Get(), "NormalButtonBrush")
 .TextStyle(FCookbookStyle::Get(), "NormalButtonText")
```

The preceding lines are part of the declarative syntax for our button, and the text that makes its label. When we set the style for our widgets using a `<Class>Style()` method, we pass in two parameters.

The first parameter is our actual Style Set, which is retrieved by using `FCookbookStyle::Get()`, and the second is a string parameter with the name of the style that we want to use.

With these minor changes, we override the styling of the widgets to use our custom styles so that when we add the widgets to the player's viewport, they display our customizations.

Creating a custom SWidget/UWidget

The recipes in this chapter so far have shown you how to create UIs using the existing primitive widgets.

Sometimes, it is convenient for developers to use composition to collect a number of UI elements to define a button class that automatically has a `TextBlock` as a label rather than manually specifying the hierarchy every time they are declared, for example.

Furthermore, if you are manually specifying the hierarchy in C++, rather than declaring a compound object consisting of subwidgets, you won't be able to instantiate those widgets as a group using UMG.

Getting ready

This recipe shows you how to create a compound SWidget that contains a group of widgets and exposes new properties to control elements of those subwidgets. It will also show you how to create a UWidget wrapper, which will expose the new compound SWidget class to UMG so that it can be used by designers.

How to do it...

1. We need to add the UMG module to our module's dependencies.
2. Open up <YourModule>.build.cs, which in our case is Chapter_14.Build.cs, and add UMG to the following code:

```
using UnrealBuildTool;

public class Chapter_14 : ModuleRules
{
  public Chapter_14(ReadOnlyTargetRules Target) : base(Target)
  {
    PCHUsage = PCHUsageMode.UseExplicitOrSharedPCHs;
    PublicDependencyModuleNames.AddRange(new string[] {
"Core", "CoreUObject", "Engine", "InputCore" });

    PrivateDependencyModuleNames.AddRange(new string[] { });

    // Uncomment if you are using Slate UI
    PrivateDependencyModuleNames.AddRange(new string[] {
"Slate",
    "SlateCore", "UMG" });
    // Uncomment if you are using online features
    // PrivateDependencyModuleNames.Add("OnlineSubsystem");

    // To include OnlineSubsystemSteam, add it to the plugins
    // section in your uproject file with the Enabled
attribute
    // set to true
  }
}
```

3. Create a new class based on the Slate Widget parent class
   (SCompoundWidget):

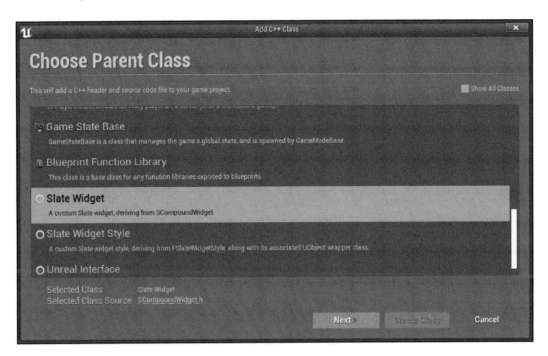

4. When asked for a name, call it CustomButton.

5. Once created, add the following code to its declaration:

```
#pragma once

#include "CoreMinimal.h"
#include "Widgets/SCompoundWidget.h"

class CHAPTER_14_API SCustomButton : public SCompoundWidget
{
    SLATE_BEGIN_ARGS(SCustomButton)
        : _Label(TEXT("Default Value"))
        , _ButtonClicked()
    {}
    SLATE_ATTRIBUTE(FString, Label)
        SLATE_EVENT(FOnClicked, ButtonClicked)
        SLATE_END_ARGS()

public:
    void Construct(const FArguments& InArgs);
    TAttribute<FString> Label;
    FOnClicked ButtonClicked;
};
```

6. Implement the class with the following in the corresponding .cpp file:

```
#include "CustomButton.h"
#include "SlateOptMacros.h"
#include "Chapter_14.h"


void SCustomButton::Construct(const FArguments& InArgs)
{
    Label = InArgs._Label;
    ButtonClicked = InArgs._ButtonClicked;
    ChildSlot.VAlign(VAlign_Center)
        .HAlign(HAlign_Center)
        [SNew(SButton)
        .OnClicked(ButtonClicked)
        .Content()
        [
            SNew(STextBlock)
            .Text_Lambda([this] {return
FText::FromString(Label.Get()); })
        ]
        ];
}
```

7. Create a second class, this time based on `Widget`:

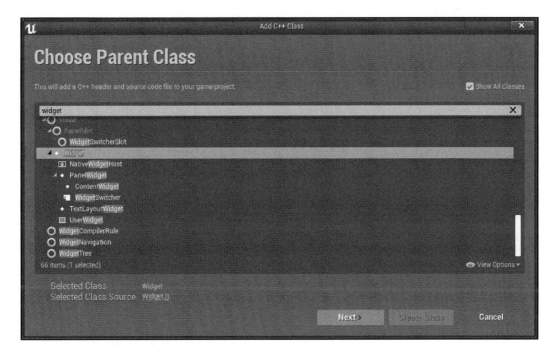

8. Call this new class `CustomButtonWidget` and press **Create Class**.

9. Add the bold code in the following snippet to the `CustomButtonWidget.h` file:

```
#pragma once

#include "CoreMinimal.h"
#include "Components/Widget.h"
#include "CustomButton.h"
#include "SlateDelegates.h"
#include "CustomButtonWidget.generated.h"

DECLARE_DYNAMIC_DELEGATE_RetVal(FString, FGetString);
DECLARE_DYNAMIC_MULTICAST_DELEGATE(FButtonClicked);

UCLASS()
class CHAPTER_14_API UCustomButtonWidget : public UWidget
{
    GENERATED_BODY()
protected:
    TSharedPtr<SCustomButton> MyButton;
```

```
        virtual TSharedRef<SWidget> RebuildWidget() override;

public:
    UCustomButtonWidget();
    //multicast
    UPROPERTY(BlueprintAssignable)
    FButtonClicked ButtonClicked;

    FReply OnButtonClicked();

    UPROPERTY(BlueprintReadWrite, EditAnywhere)
        FString Label;

    //MUST be of the form varnameDelegate
    UPROPERTY()
        FGetString LabelDelegate;

    virtual void SynchronizeProperties() override;
};
```

10. Now, create the implementation for `UCustomButtonWidget`:

```
#include "CustomButtonWidget.h"
#include "Chapter_14.h"

TSharedRef<SWidget> UCustomButtonWidget::RebuildWidget()
{
    MyButton = SNew(SCustomButton)
        .ButtonClicked(BIND_UOBJECT_DELEGATE(FOnClicked,
OnButtonClicked));
    return MyButton.ToSharedRef();
}

UCustomButtonWidget::UCustomButtonWidget()
    :Label(TEXT("Default Value"))
{

}

FReply UCustomButtonWidget::OnButtonClicked()
{
    ButtonClicked.Broadcast();
    return FReply::Handled();
}


void UCustomButtonWidget::SynchronizeProperties()
{
```

```
    Super::SynchronizeProperties();
    TAttribute<FString> LabelBinding =
OPTIONAL_BINDING(FString, Label);
    MyButton->Label = LabelBinding;
}
```

11. Save your scripts and compile your code.
12. Create a new Widget Blueprint by right-clicking on the **Content Browser** and selecting **User Interface** and then **Widget Blueprint**:

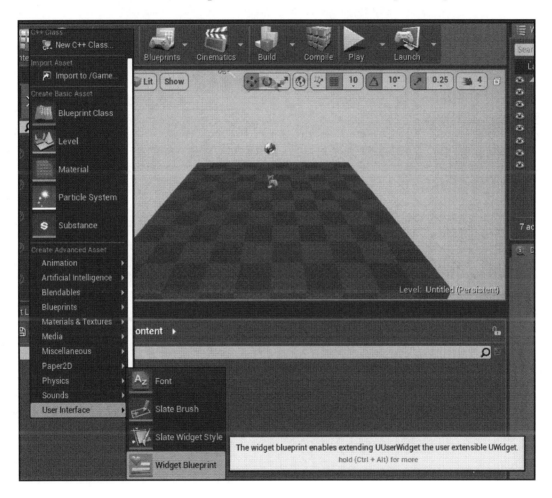

You can use the mouse wheel in the context menu to scroll to the **User Interface** section.

13. Open your new **Widget Blueprint** by double-clicking on it.
14. Find the **Custom Button Widget** in the Widget Palette:

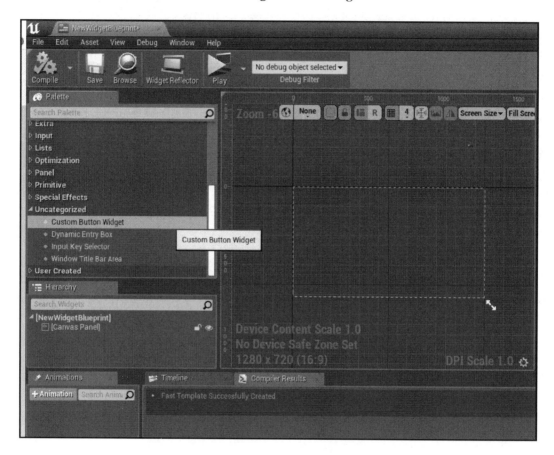

15. Drag an instance of it out into the main area.

16. With the instance selected, change the **Label** property in the **Details** panel:

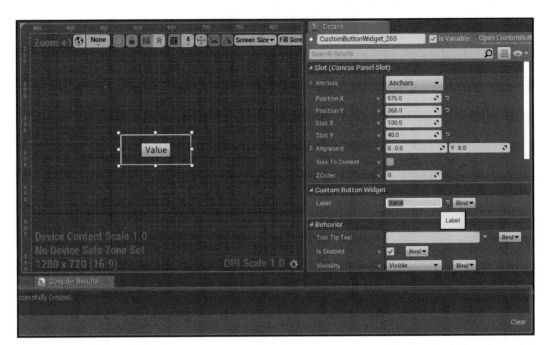

Verify that your button has changed its label.

17. Now, we will create a binding to demonstrate that we can link arbitrary blueprint functions to the label property on our widget, which, in turn, drives the Widget's textblock label.

18. Click on **Bind** to the right of the **Label** property and select **Create Binding**:

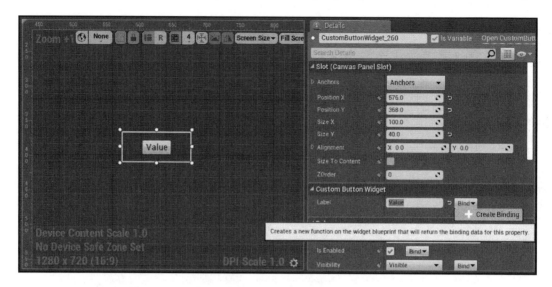

19. Within the graph that is now displayed, place a **Get Game Time in Seconds** node by right-clicking within the main area:

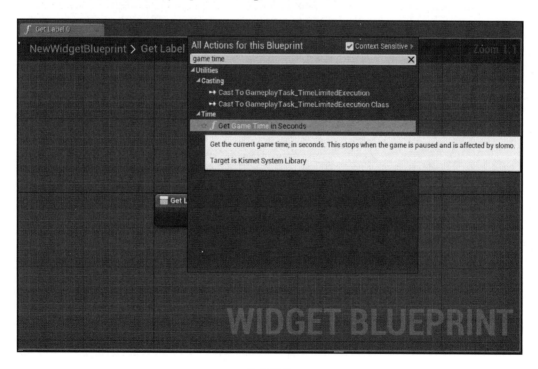

20. Link the return value from the Get Game Time node to the **Return Value** pin in the function:

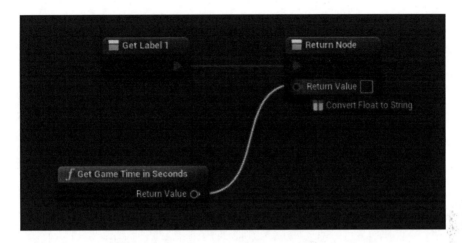

21. A **Convert Float to String** node will be automatically inserted for you:

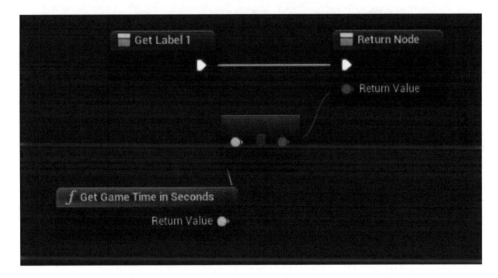

22. Compile the blueprint to ensure it is working correctly.

23. Next, open the **Level Blueprints** by clicking on the **Blueprints** button on the taskbar and then selecting **Open Level Blueprint**:

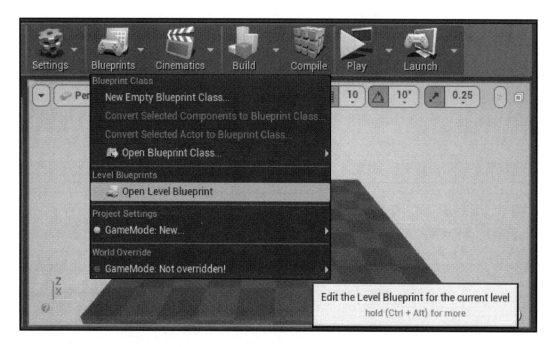

24. To the right of the **Event BeginPlay** node, place a **Create Widget** node into the graph:

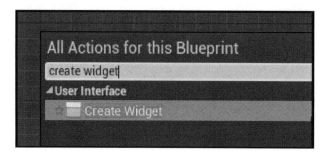

25. Select the **Class** of widget to spawn it as the new Widget Blueprint that we created a moment ago within the editor:

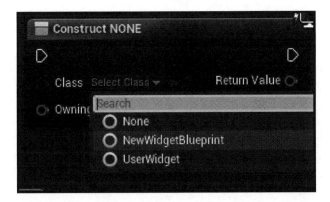

26. Click and drag away from the **Owning Player** pin on the create widget node and place a **Get Player Controller** node:

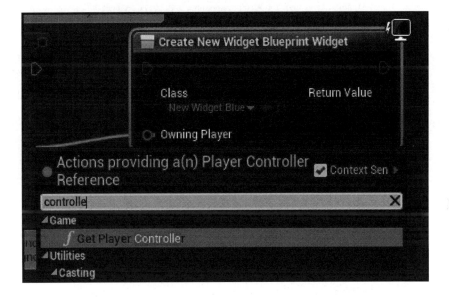

27. Likewise, drag away from the return value of the **Create Widget** node and place an **Add to Viewport** node:

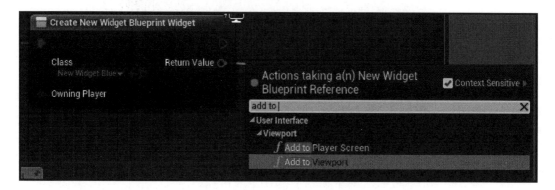

28. Lastly, link the `BeginPlay` node to the execution pin on the create widget node:

29. Preview your game and verify that the widget we've displayed onscreen is our new custom button, with its label bound to the number of seconds that have elapsed since the game started:

Button displaying the elapsed time in the level

How it works...

To use the UWidget class, our module needs to include the UMG module as one of its dependencies, because UWidget is defined inside the UMG module.

The first class that we need to create, however, is our actual SWidget class.

Because we want to aggregate two widgets together into a compound structure, we create our new widget as a CompoundWidget subclass. CompoundWidget allows you to encapsulate a widget hierarchy as a widget itself.

Inside the class, we use the SLATE_BEGIN_ARGS and SLATE_END_ARGS macros to declare an internal struct called FArguments on our new SWidget. Within SLATE_BEGIN_ARGS and SLATE_END_ARGS, the SLATE_ATTRIBUTE and SLATE_EVENT macros are used. SLATE_ATTRIBUTE creates TAttribute for the type we give it. In this class, we declare a TAttribute called _Label, which is more specifically a TAttribute<FString>.

SLATE_EVENT allows us to create member delegates that we can broadcast when something happens internally to the widget.

In `SCustomButton`, we declare a delegate with the signature `FOnClicked`, called `ButtonClicked`.

`SLATE_ARGUMENT` is another macro (which wasn't used in this recipe) that creates an internal variable with the type and name you provide, appending an underscore to the start of the variable name.

`Construct()` is the function that widgets implement to self-initialize when they are being instantiated. You'll notice we also create `TAttribute` and `FOnClicked` instances ourselves, without the underscores. These are the actual properties of our object into which the arguments that we declared earlier will be copied.

Inside the implementation of `Construct`, we retrieve the arguments that were passed to us in the `FArgumentsstruct`, and store them inside our actual member variables for this instance.

We assign `Label` and `ButtonClicked` based on what was passed in, and then we actually create our widget hierarchy. We use the same syntax as usual for this with one thing to note, namely the use of `Text_Lambda` to set the text value of our internal text block. We use a `lambda` function to retrieve the value of our `Label TAttribute` using `Get()`, convert it into `FText`, and store it as our text block's `Text` property.

Now that we have our `SWidget` declared, we need to create a wrapper `UWidget` object that will expose this widget to the UMG system so that designers can use the widget within the **WYSIWYG** editor. This class will be called `UCustomButtonWidget`, and it inherits from `UWidget` rather than `SWidget`.

The `UWidget` object needs a reference to the actual `SWidget` that it owns, so we place a protected member in the class that will store it as a shared pointer.

A constructor is declared, as well as a `ButtonClicked` delegate that can be set in Blueprint. We also mirror a `Label` property that is marked as `BlueprintReadWrite` so that it can be set in the UMG editor.

Because we want to be able to bind our button's label to a delegate, we add the last of our member variables, which is a delegate that returns a `String`.

The `SynchronizeProperties` function applies properties that have been mirrored in our `UWidget` class across to the `SWidget` that we are linked with.

RebuildWidget reconstructs the native widget that UWidget is associated with. It uses SNew to construct an instance of our SCustomButton widget, and uses the Slate declarative syntax to bind the UWidget's OnButtonClicked method to the ButtonClicked delegate inside the native widget. This means that when the native widget is clicked, the UWidget will be notified by having OnButtonClicked called.

OnButtonClicked re-broadcasts the clicked event from the native button via the UWidget's ButtonClicked delegate. This means that UObjects and the UMG system can be notified of the button being clicked without having a reference to the native button widget themselves. We can bind to UCustomButtonWidget::ButtonClicked so that we're notified about this.

OnButtonClicked then returns FReply::Handled() to indicate that the event does not need to propagate further. Inside SynchronizeProperties, we call the parent method to ensure that any properties in the parent are also synchronized properly.

We use the OPTIONAL_BINDING macro to link the LabelDelegate delegate in our UWidget class to TAttribute, and, in turn, the native button's label. It is important to note that the OPTIONAL_BINDING macro expects the delegate to be called NameDelegate based on the second parameter to the macro.

OPTIONAL_BINDING allows the value to be overridden by a binding made via UMG, but only if the UMG binding is valid.

This means that when UWidget is told to update itself, for example, because the user customizes a value in the **Details** panel within UMG, it will recreate the native SWidget if necessary, and then copy the values set in Blueprint/UMG via SynchronizeProperties so that everything continues to work as expected.

Other Books You May Enjoy

If you enjoyed this book, you may be interested in these other books by Packt:

Mastering Game Development with Unreal Engine 4 - Second Edition
Matt Edmonds

ISBN: 9781788991445

- The fundamentals of a combat-based game that will let you build and work all other systems from the core gameplay: the input, inventory, A.I. enemies, U.I., and audio
- Manage performance tools and branching shaders based on platform capabilities in the Material Editor
- Explore scene or level transitions and management strategies
- Improve visuals using UE4 systems such as Volumetric Lightmaps, Precomputed Lighting, and Cutscenes
- Implement audio-to-animation timelines and trigger them from visual FX
- Integrate Augmented Reality into a game with UE4's brand new ARKit and ARCore support
- Perform almost any game logic needed via Blueprint Visual Scripting, and know when to implement it in Blueprint as opposed to C++

Unreal Engine Blueprints Visual Scripting Projects
Lauren S. Ferro

ISBN: 9781789532425

- Set up Unreal Engine and all of its foundational components
- Add basic movement to game objects and create collision mechanism
- Design and implement interfaces to extend player interaction
- Create a dynamically filling inventory system along with a UI to interact with it
- Add audio effects based on triggered events to various parts of the game environment
- Use analytic information to tune their game values
- Create complex enemy AI that can sense the world around it in a multiplayer game
- Deploy your game to multiple platforms and share it with the world

Leave a review - let other readers know what you think

Please share your thoughts on this book with others by leaving a review on the site that you bought it from. If you purchased the book from Amazon, please leave us an honest review on this book's Amazon page. This is vital so that other potential readers can see and use your unbiased opinion to make purchasing decisions, we can understand what our customers think about our products, and our authors can see your feedback on the title that they have worked with Packt to create. It will only take a few minutes of your time, but is valuable to other potential customers, our authors, and Packt. Thank you!

Index

C

editor window
  creating 454, 456, 458
events handlers
  customization, by overriding virtual function
    186, 188, 190, 191
events
  creating, for implementation in Blueprint 382,
    385, 390

F

First Person Shooter (FPS)
  respawning pickup, creating 225, 226, 229,
    231
FMessageLog
  used, for writing messages to Message Log
    503, 505
FObjectFinder
  used, for loading assets into components
    137, 138, 140
following behavior
  implementing 577, 580, 581
FPS character
  gamepad directional input 234, 236, 238
  keyboard, setting up 234
  mouse, setting up 234
FQuat
  used, for rotation 508, 510
FRotationMatrix
  used, for object rotation 511, 514
FRotator
  used, for rotation 505
FString
  creating 53
function calls
  attaching, to Slate events 638, 640, 642,
    643
function specifiers
  reference 566
functions
  creating, for calling within Blueprint graphs
    376, 379, 381

G

game modes
  hot reloading 48

reference 46
GameplayAbilities API
  buffs, implementing with GameplayEffect 531
  reference 527
  UAttributeSet, used for implementing stats
    527, 531
  used, for triggering actor's gameplay abilities
    514, 517, 520, 526
GameplayEffect
  used, for implementing buffs 531, 534
garbage collection
  about 82
  forcing 108
graph pin visualizer
  creating, for Blueprint 480, 484, 487, 489

H

hot spots
  identifying, profiler used 112
HTTP API
  used, for displaying downloaded progress
    547, 549
  used, for downloading webpages 542, 546

I

Ignore
  used, for letting objects pass through 261,
    263
interaction system
  implementing, with UInterfaces 311, 315,
    318, 322
InventoryComponent
  creating, for RPG 159, 163, 167, 171, 173

L

level-editing tools 8

M

macro 49
malloc( )/free( ) function
  used, for allocating unmanaged memory 96
managed memory
  ConstructObject, using 100
  de-allocating 103

Made in the USA
San Bernardino, CA
09 March 2020

65470282R00395